The Philosophy of Rawls

A Collection of Essays

Series Editors

Henry S. Richardson
Georgetown University

Paul J. Weithman
University of Notre Dame

A GARLAND SERIES
READINGS IN PHILOSOPHY

ROBERT NOZICK, *ADVISOR*
HARVARD UNIVERSITY

Contents of the Series

Development and Main Outlines
of Rawls's Theory of Justice

Edited with an introduction by

Henry S. Richardson
Georgetown University

GARLAND PUBLISHING, INC.
A MEMBER OF THE TAYLOR & FRANCIS GROUP
New York & London
1999

Library of Congress Cataloging-in-Publication Data

Development and main outlines in Rawls's theory of justice / edited
with an introduction by Henry S. Richardson.
     p. cm. — (The philosophy of Rawls ; 1)
     "A Garland series, readings in philosophy."
     Includes bibliographical references.
     ISBN 0-8153-2925-3 (alk. paper)
     1. Rawls, John 1921– Theory of justice.
I. Richardson, Henry S. II. Series.

JC578.D49 1999
320'.01'1—dc21   99-048605

Printed on acid-free, 250-year-life paper
Manufactured in the United States of America

Contents

Series Introduction

John Rawls is the pre-eminent political philosopher of our time. His 1971 masterpiece, *A Theory of Justice*, permanently changed the landscape of moral and political theory, revitalizing the normative study of social issues and taking stands about justice, ethics, rationality, and philosophical method that continue to draw followers and critics today. His *Political Liberalism* (rev. ed., 1996) squarely faced the fundamental challenges posed by cultural, religious, and philosophical pluralism. It should be no surprise, then, that turn-of-the-century searches of the periodical indices in philosophy, economics, law, the humanities, and related fields turn up almost three thousand articles devoted to a critical discussion of Rawls's theory. In these Volumes we reprint a wide-ranging selection of the most influential and insightful articles on Rawls.

While it was impossible, even in a collection of this size, to reprint all of the important material, the selection here should provide the student and scholar with a route into all of the significant controversies that have surrounded Rawls's theories since he first began enunciating them in the nineteen-fifties — issues that the Introductions to each Volume of this series delineate. Eight criteria guided our selection. First, these volumes form part of a series devoted to *secondary* literature. We reprint no articles by Rawls: most of these have just appeared together for the first time in his *Collected Papers*.[1] Second, we reprint only self-contained articles published in English, rather than selections from books or articles in other languages. Third, the articles reprinted here are all *about* Rawls's view, as opposed to being original reflections inspired by Rawls's work. Fourth, we aimed for a broad coverage of controversies and of the main features of Rawls's theory that they surround. Since the Volumes are organized in terms of these controversies, we include very few overall assessments or book reviews. Some central elements of Rawls's theory, while relatively novel and well-articulated, have not been controversial enough to draw critical fire in the secondary literature. The Volume Introductions mention many of these features. Fifth, we aimed to include the most influential articles that have appeared. In identifying these, we used a systematic search of the citation indices to supplement our own judgment. Naturally, we also took special notice of pieces cited by Rawls himself. Sixth, we sought to reprint articles by a large number of authors representing the widest possible range of points of view. In some cases, this meant refraining from reprinting a certain article because its author was already well represented in the selections. Seventh, we have sought to exhibit through our selections the broadly interdisciplinary influence of Rawls's writings. We have included articles by political theorists, economists, lawyers, religious thinkers, and social scientists as well as by philosophers. Eighth, we have favored including articles that are now relatively hard to find. For this reason, with the exception of H.L.A. Hart's exceptionally influential essay, we refrained from including any of the fine articles that were reprinted in Norman Daniels's 1975 collection, *Reading Rawls*,[2] which the reader interested in the early reception of Rawls's views should consult.

Utilizing all of these selection criteria did not leave us without painful choices. The secondary literature on Rawls is so deep that another set of five volumes could cover all the main issues with a completely non-overlapping set of fine articles. Some articles unfortunately had to be cut because of their sheer length: dropping one of them allowed us to include two or three others. Others, more arbitrarily, fell victim to the high permissions costs set by their initial publishers. We particularly regret that it proved impossible to find a short enough, self-contained essay by Robert Nozick that would have represented his trenchant libertarian critique of Rawls. While we do include (in Vol. 3) some of the secondary literature that responds to and picks up on Nozick's influential arguments, one should consult Nozick's *Anarchy, State, and Utopia* (1974) to appreciate their richness, subtlety, and power.[3]

The five volumes are arranged in roughly chronological order. The first volume includes articles on Rawls's early statements of his view and on its central contractarian ideas. Volume 2 covers the two principles of justice as fairness and Rawls's most general ideas about their justification. Volume 3 focuses on the concrete implications of Rawls's view and on the debates between Rawls and his utilitarian, perfectionist, libertarian, conservative, radical, and feminist critics. Volume 4 treats of Rawls's moral psychology and his attempt to accommodate the value of community. Volume 5, on Rawls's most recent work, is entitled "Reasonable Pluralism."

The serious student of Rawls's initial impact is greatly assisted by *John Rawls and His Critics: An Annotated Bibliography*, put together by J.H. Wellbank, Denis Snook, and David T. Mason, which catalogues and provides abstracts for most of the secondary literature in English prior to 1982.[4] While this work was of great help with that earlier period, completing the onerous task of collecting and sorting through the voluminous secondary literature, which has since continued to balloon, would not have been possible without the able and thorough research assistance of Rachael Yocum. We are grateful to the Dean of Georgetown College and to the Graduate School of Georgetown University for their generosity in supporting this research assistance.

Henry S. Richardson

Paul J. Weithman

Notes

[1] John Rawls, *Collected Papers*, ed. Samuel Freeman (Cambridge, Mass.: Harvard University Press, 1999).

[2] Norman Daniels, ed., *Reading Rawls* (N.Y.: Basic Books, 1975).

[3] Robert Nozick, *Anarchy, State, and Utopia* (N.Y.: Basic Books, 1974).

[4] J.H. Wellbank, Denis Snook, and David T. Mason, *John Rawls and His Critics: An Annotated Bibliography* (New York: Garland, 1982).

Volume Introduction

This Volume presents a selection of the secondary literature most important to understanding the development and the main outlines of the view that Rawls set out in *A Theory of Justice* [*TJ*].[1] The articles reprinted in this Volume provide a window into the evolution of Rawls's views prior to *TJ* and cover the most controversial aspects of his compelling new articulation of the social-contract tradition. While the main structure of his social-contract view is covered here, Volume 2 is devoted to the principles that, he argues, an ideal social contract would support, while broader considerations about the justification of this view are addressed in Volumes 3 and 4.

When Rawls's *TJ* first appeared in 1971, it had been long awaited. Two of Rawls's articles in moral theory, "Outline of a Decision Procedure for Ethics" (1951) and "Two Concepts of Rules" (1955) had already drawn considerable attention in the literature.[2] They did not yet indicate, however, the main lines of the original direction Rawls would take. In 1957 and 1958, Rawls published two articles that would float initial versions of his theory of justice, draw considerable critical attention to it, and give his theory its name: "Justice as Fairness."[3] Prior to 1971, these articles had each been reprinted and had also been much commented upon. In the subsequent thirteen years, leading up to the publication of *TJ*, Rawls published seven more articles, each developing an important piece of his eventual view. Accordingly, any attempt to arrive at a thorough understanding of justice as fairness would do well to consider the evolution of Rawls's earlier views and the philosophical context in which they originated — a context well described by Amy Gutmann's article (this Vol.).

Isaiah Berlin wrote that, in deciding upon his career path in the 1940s, he steered into the history of ideas rather than into political philosophy, thinking, at mid-century, that little progress was to be made in the latter.[4] It is often said, in hindsight, that Rawls's theory of justice revitalized normative political philosophy which, in the English-speaking world at least, had become moribund. As a blanket judgment, of course, this claim about Rawls's impact is both gross and an exaggeration. It leaves out, for instance, H.L.A. Hart's magisterial work on the philosophy of law, which crucially shaped Rawls's thought that a theory of justice must focus on institutions. (As we learn in Thomas Pogge's insightful biographical sketch of Rawls, here printed for the first time in English, Rawls attended Hart's lectures in Oxford in 1952–53.) Other philosophers, including R.B. Brandt and R.M. Hare, were hard at work defending the utilitarian view, which embraces the political within its broader purview. In addition to exaggerating in this way, this blanket assessment is insufficiently fine-grained to prepare us for understanding the methodological innovation (or rediscovery) that enabled Rawls to make new headway. The three other philosophers just mentioned all proceeded under the influence of Anglo-American philosophy's "linguistic turn," which in turn depended for its appeal on laying stress on the distinction between analytic and synthetic truths — between those truths that hold as a matter of the meaning of words or concepts and those that rest on the facts. In so doing, they aimed to provide analyses of moral and political concepts that would be proof against counterexamples. From his earliest published work, however, Rawls had another purpose. "Outline of a Decision Procedure" (1951) declared that his theory there "in no way concerns itself with the sense of ethical expressions or with their linguistic meaning" (185). Instead, he writes, "Perhaps the principal aim of ethics is the formulation of justifiable principles which may be used in cases wherein there are conflicting interests to determine which of them should be given preference" (186f.). From the beginning, Rawls's effort has been to contribute to the practical justification of principles — *practical*, in the sense of being aimed at helping us cope with controversies or with quandaries in which people disagree or we ourselves "are of two minds" (*TJ*, 580), and *justification*, understood as argument addressed to those in such practical difficulties (ibid.). Of principles, yes: but Rawls's 1950 review of Stephen Toulmin's *Examination of the Place of Reason in Ethics* already signals us that he had come to the view — perhaps with the help of his Wittgensteinian mentors Norman Malcolm and Max Black — that all principles are open textured, and hence stand in need of interpretation or specification.[5] We can thus see in Rawls's earliest work three strands — a practical purpose, a practical conception of justification, and a view of principles as open textured — that get woven together masterfully in *TJ* and go a long way to limning his distinctive approach.

"Outline of a Decision Procedure," which developed out of Rawls's dissertation, shows him struggling to overcome the deficiencies of indeterminacy that had plagued ideal-observer theories (see *TJ*, 185n.) while relaxing, as we have seen, the attempt to provide a linguistic analysis of moral terms. It is interesting to compare this early articulation of a method for ethics with his mature method. Finding in the piece both something like what we recognize now as the notion of a "considered judgment" (*TJ*, 47–8) and the "circularity," or mutual support in many directions, that will later characterize Rawls's justificatory ideal of reflective equilibrium (on which, see Vol. 3), the piece by Anthony M. Mardiros included here helps us trace out this connection.

Rawls declares in the Preface (viii) that the principal aim of *TJ* is "to construct a workable and systematic moral conception to oppose" utilitarianism — a fact that is sometimes forgotten in the cross-fire of objections from other directions (libertarian, communitarian, feminist, and so on) that the view has subsequently drawn. From this point of view, it is important to know that Rawls's opposition to utilitarianism is informed by a deep respect for and knowledge of this moral position, in both its historical and contemporary forms. In "Two Concepts of Rules" (1955) in fact, he defended utilitarianism, trying to fend off intuitive objections to the view by shifting to an institutionally centered form of rule utilitarianism. Joseph Margolis's critical response to this article (this Vol.) argues — in a way that, though now generally familiar, is also tailored to Rawls's specific attempt — that this way of trying to save utilitarianism from the intuitive objections will not work because it collapses back into act utilitarianism. One distinctive feature of Rawls's attempt is the notion of institutions that he there develops — important, in retrospect, as justice as fairness is a theory of institutional justice. H.J. McCloskey's critical discussion (this Vol.) probes the contours of this early articulation of the idea of an "institution."

The early articles presenting justice as fairness already invoked the idea of a social contract, initially using, not the "veil of ignorance" which became a central feature of *TJ*'s contract device, but the related idea of considering how things would be if one's enemy assigned one's place in society. These articles, however, were less than ideally clear about what the function of the social contract idea or metaphor is supposed to be. This question, indeed, has continued to be a touchy one for the theory. We reprint here Norman Care's early piece on this, which argues that the social contract procedure is a way of articulating or formulating a theory rather than a method of choosing between them. While this point seems deeply critical of Rawls's approach, it is crucial to note that in *TJ* (xi) he acknowledges Care's point as "sound." In fact, Rawls often notes in *TJ* (e.g., 21) that different interpretations of the social contract and its initial choice situation correspond to different moral principles, and that this correlation provides a way of making vivid to ourselves the assumptions, and the strengths and weaknesses, of these principles. Instead of a "decision procedure," then, we have a hypothetical device that aids our imaginative and analytic attempts to arrive at reflective equilibrium. Whether the initial versions of this device well supported the early statements of justice as fairness and whether the principles could do the practical work that Rawls hoped were questions raised in the early critical literature. As these doubts have been superseded by corresponding ones about the later work, we have not included representatives of these other early reactions.[6]

While the main features of Rawls's social contract view, as presented in *TJ*, have been adumbrated, it will be useful to collect them here. A hypothetical social contract is used to help us think about the arguments for and against alternative principles that are to govern the basic institutions (Rawls now says, "the constitutional essentials") of a just society, conceived as an ongoing scheme of mutual, fair cooperation. The alternative principles are to be offered to the hypothetical "parties" to the contract in a limited menu (see *TJ*, 123, 581): it is not the task of the parties to generate principles from scratch. As we have noted, it would be possible to define the initial choice situation in various ways, producing various results. The interpretation that Rawls finds to be best supportable, both in terms of the direct arguments in its favor and in terms of the acceptability, on due reflection, of its moral implications, he calls "the original position" (OP). Now, recall that from his earliest work, Rawls aimed to find a way of generating more determinate implications than could the traditional ideal-observer theories. The point of view of impartial benevolence, he notes, is confounded by the many conflicts among all of the beloved (*TJ*, 190). To circumvent such sources of indeterminacy, therefore — and for other reasons he develops in the course of his argument — Rawls proposes supplanting the traditional idea of impartial benevolence with a potent combination of (1) an assumption that the parties are mutually disinterested (caring only about their own shares) and (2) an assumption that they are blocked, by a "Veil of Ignorance," from knowing any particular facts about themselves or their society. They know all general facts about how human societies work; but about their own society, for which they are choosing the fundamental institutional principles, they know only that it is marked by "the circumstances of justice." This last notion, which Rawls adapted from Hume, includes (simplifying somewhat) both an "objective" aspect, namely that society is marked by conditions of moderate scarcity, and a "subjective" aspect, namely that society is also marked by a plurality of competing and fundamentally irreconcilable conceptions of the good. Knowing this, the parties will be motivated to ensure that institutions are set up so as to generate a fair distribution of the benefits of cooperation without trampling upon individuals' potentially deep-seated attachments to their conceptions of the good. The assumption that the parties are mutually disinterested enables a simple conception of these hypothetical entities. They are defined as having a single specific motivation, namely, they want more so-called "primary goods" (*TJ*, sec. 15) rather than less. The primary goods include rights and liberties, opportunities and powers, income and wealth, and the social basis of self-respect. Defined in *TJ* as items that "things which it is supposed a rational man wants whatever else he wants" (92), these primary goods later got an entirely different justification (see Vol. 2, under "The Kantian Interpretation"). The final aspect of the OP to be covered in the present volume, and the one that generated the most initial controversy, is Rawls's suggestion that the parties will — in light of their knowledge that they must protect citizens' ability to adhere to and pursue the conceptions of the good to which they are attached, but which are unknown to the parties, and in light of the fact that nothing whatsoever is known about the society these citizens will enter, except that it is characterized by the circumstances of justice — choose so as to give absolute priority to the basic liberties and, that done, to protecting and improving the well-being (indexed in primary goods) of the least well off citizens. It will be rational, Rawls suggests, for the parties to the OP to use the so-called "maximin" approach to choice under uncertainty, which directs them to maximize the expectations of the least well-off representative group. (The formulation and content of the two principles of justice as fairness, which, Rawls argues, the parties to the OP would favor, will be covered in Vol. 2.)

The articles reprinted here touch on almost every feature of Rawls's view mentioned in the last paragraph. The full implications of Rawls's focus on the justice of basic institutions has taken a long time for philosophers fully to assimilate. Those in other fields have often ignored this aspect of Rawls's view altogether. For instance, a whole strain of normative economics, sometimes known as "fairness theory," proceeds to consider Rawls's principle about maximizing the chances of the least well off in complete abstraction from its intended application to institutions.[7] We reprint two articles that early focussed on Rawls's distinctive conception of the subject-matter of his theory: T.M. Scanlon's and Hugo Adam Bedau's. This issue, however, is also important to understanding the debate between Rawls and his libertarian critics (Vol. 3), as well as the ongoing controversy about whether Rawls can confine the application of his distributive principle to the institutional level (see the pieces by Van Parijs and G.A. Cohen in Vol. 2).

Turning from the subject-matter of the theory to its social-contract structure, there has been much controversy about Rawls's claim to be building upon the social-contract tradition. Jean Hampton's article in this Volume probes this matter rigorously yet sympathetically, pushing Rawls towards greater stress on the Kantian aspects of his view (see Vol. 2; it should be remembered that Kant, too, described an ideal social contract). The eminent European philosopher Paul Ricoeur, in his reprinted article, provides some insightful reflections on Rawls's place within the social-contract tradition.[8]

It would be hard to exaggerate the scope and diversity of the literature devoted to Rawls's characterization of the rationality and motivation of the parties to the OP. The essay by eminent economist Kenneth Arrow was one of the first to raise criticisms about Rawls's use of primary goods as a basis of interpersonal comparison. Questions were raised about the moral neutrality of that basis — a neutrality that Rawls had actually already disowned (see *TJ*, 12, 120, 130, 529, 584ff.) — in a well-known piece by Thomas Nagel[9] and the somewhat more thorough article by Adina Schwartz included here. The reprinted article by Allen Buchanan comes to Rawls's defense on this question.[10]

Rawls's appeal to the maximin principle made him vulnerable to the charge that he had attributed to his supposedly rational parties in the OP an irrational approach to uncertainty. The selections by David Gauthier (a philosopher) and by R.A. Musgrave and John C. Harsanyi (both economists) well represent the forcefulness of this attack and the variety of ways that it was couched. Binod Kumar Agarwala's article valiantly undertakes to defend Rawls on this point within the terms of *TJ*, as augmented somewhat by taking into account Rawls's own early reply to his critics on this point.[11] Joshua Cohen's defense draws more broadly on Rawls's more recent work, especially his exposition of the general ideal of mutual respect among free and equal citizens. Although this recent work stresses that maximin, or anything like it, has its proper place only within an attempt to articulate ideals of fair cooperation, Rawls's ideas have gained such broad influence that they have generated interesting attempts to determine, experimentally, whether actual humans in situations resembling the hypothetical one of the parties in the OP would or would not be drawn to the maximin principle. The reprinted article by Doug Bond and Jong-Chul Park provides a sample of this kind of social-scientific use of Rawlsian ideas.

Henry S. Richardson

Notes

[1] John Rawls, *A Theory of Justice* (Cambridge: Harvard University Press, Belknap, 1971).

[2] John Rawls, "Outline of a Decision Procedure for Ethics," *Philosophical Review* 60 (1951): 177–97; Rawls, "Two Concepts of Rules," *Philosophical Review* 64 (1955): 3–32. Almost all of Rawls's papers are now collected in his *Collected Papers*, ed. Samuel Freeman (Cambridge, Mass.: Harvard University Press, 1999).

[3] John Rawls, "Justice as Fairness," *Journal of Philosophy* 54 (1957): 653–62; John Rawls, "Justice as Fairness," *Philosophical Review* 67 (1958): 164–94.

[4] Isaiah Berlin, *Concepts and Categories: Philosophical Essays*, ed. Henry Hardy (N.Y.: Viking, 1979), p. viii.

[5] John Rawls, "Review of Stephen Toulmin, An Examination of the Place of Reason in Ethics," *Philosophical Review* 60 (1950): 572–80.

[6] See, e.g., Robert Paul Wolff, "A Refutation of Rawls' Theorem on Justice," *Journal of Philosophy* 63 (1966): 179–90; Brian Barry, "On Social Justice," *The Oxford Review* 55 (Trinity Term 1967): 29–52; Michael Lessnoff, "John Rawls' Theory of Justice," *Political Studies* 19 (1971): 65–80.

[7] Peter J. Hammond, "Equity, Arrow's Conditions, and Rawls' Difference Principle," *Econometrica* 44 (1976): 793–804. Stephen Strasnick, "Social Choice and the Derivation of Rawls's Difference Principle,"

Journal of Philosophy 73 (1976): 85–99. The contributions of Hammond and Strasnick are summarized in Amartya Sen's article reprinted in Vol. 2. For "fairness theory," see e.g. Elisha A. Pazner and David Schmeidler, "Social Contract Theory and Ordinal Distributive Equity," *Journal of Public Economics* 5 (1976): 261–68.

[8] For a distinguished American philosopher's thoughts on this question, see Marcus G. Singer, "The Methods of Justice: Reflections on Rawls," *Journal of Value Inquiry* 10 (1976): 286–316.

[9] Thomas Nagel, "Rawls on Justice," *Philosophical Review* 82 (1973): 220–34, reprinted in Norman Daniels, *Reading Rawls* (N.Y.: Basic Books, 1975).

[10] For a more recent critical discussion of primary goods, see Richard J. Arneson, "Primary Goods Reconsidered," *Nous* 24 (1990): 429–54. For an intermediate statement of Rawls's view of the basis of interpersonal comparison, see John Rawls, "Social Unity and Primary Goods," in *Utilitarianism and Beyond*, eds. Amartya Sen and Bernard Williams (Cambridge: Cambridge University Press, 1982), 159–85.

[11] John Rawls, "Some Reasons for the Maximin Criterion," *American Economic Review* 64 (1974): 141–46.

Further Reading

Arneson, Richard J. "Primary Goods Reconsidered." *Nous* 24 (1990): 429–54.

Barry, Brian. "On Social Justice." *The Oxford Review* 55 (Trinity Term 1967): 29–52.

Berlin, Isaiah. *Concepts and Categories: Philosophical Essays*. ed. Henry Hardy. N.Y.: Viking, 1979.

Daniels, Norman, ed., *Reading Rawls*. N.Y.: Basic Books, 1975.

Hammond, Peter J. "Equity, Arrow's Conditions, and Rawls' Difference Principle." *Econometrica* 44 (1976): 793–804.

Lessnoff, Michael. "John Rawls' Theory of Justice." *Political Studies* 19 (1971): 65–80.

Nagel, Thomas. "Rawls on Justice." *Philosophical Review* 82 (1973): 220–34.

Pazner, Elisha A., and David Schmeidler. "Social Contract Theory and Ordinal Distributive Equity." *Journal of Public Economics* 5 (1976): 261–68.

Rawls, John. *Collected Papers*. ed. Samuel Freeman. Cambridge, Mass.: Harvard University Press, 1999.

———. "Justice as Fairness." *Journal of Philosophy* 54 (1957): 653–62.

———. "Justice as Fairness." *Philosophical Review* 67 (1958): 164–94.

———. "Outline of a Decision Procedure for Ethics." *Philosophical Review* 60 (1951): 177–97.

———. "Review of Stephen Toulmin, An Examination of the Place of Reason in Ethics." *Philosophical Review* 60 (1950): 572–80.

———. "Social Unity and Primary Goods." In *Utilitarianism and Beyond*, eds. Amartya Sen and Bernard Williams, 159–85. Cambridge: Cambridge University Press, 1982.

———. "Some Reasons for the Maximin Criterion." *American Economic Review* 64 (1974): 141–46.

———. "Two Concepts of Rules." *Philosophical Review* 64 (1955): 3–32.

———. *A Theory of Justice*. Cambridge: Harvard University Press, Belknap, 1971.

Singer, Marcus G. "The Methods of Justice: Reflections on Rawls." *Journal of Value Inquiry* 10 (1976): 286–316.

Strasnick, Stephen. "Social Choice and the Derivation of Rawls's Difference Principle." *Journal of Philosophy* 73 (1976): 85–99.

Wolff, Robert Paul. "A Refutation of Rawls' Theorem on Justice." *Journal of Philosophy* 63 (1966): 179–90.

A Brief Sketch of Rawls's Life[1]

by Thomas Pogge

It is well known that Rawls's famous *A Theory of Justice* has induced a dramatic revival of interest in political philosophy and has stimulated many philosophers, economists, jurists, and political scientists to contribute to this field. The book has sold some quarter million copies in English alone and, translated into two dozen languages, has become a staple in North American and European universities and an inspiration to many in Latin America, China, and Japan. It is a true classic, likely to be read and taught for many decades to come. These matters can be amplified, but I will here concentrate on the life and personality of the man John Rawls whose work has had such a profound and worldwide impact.

Immediately striking about Rawls is his extraordinary intellectual and moral integrity. Over many years, he has developed a comprehensive and thorough understanding of moral and political philosophy by studying (especially) its important primary sources as well as much secondary literature about them. An attentive and critical reader, he retains clearly structured synopses of the texts he studies and of their various strengths and weaknesses. Rawls's works give ample evidence that he is equally strict and careful as a writer. He pays great attention to his choice of terms and phrases as well as to the clear exposition of his thoughts, often producing several thoroughly reworked versions over many months, even years, before he allows a text to be published. And the same care has been apparent also in his lectures, which were always superbly crafted and also so rich and concentrated that one could not fully absorb them even with utmost attention.

Rawls's extraordinary achievements as a scholar, author, and teacher can be traced to a variety of factors. He has great intellectual powers and virtues: an immense capacity for systematic thought, an excellent memory, a natural curiosity and fondness for books, and a critical attitude toward his own work which generates productive dissatisfactions and further progress. He has always been committed to contributing to the intellectual life of his students, colleagues, university, and society. In addition, Rawls has sharply focused his powers and efforts on two questions that are of great personal and moral significance to him: how it is possible for a social order to be just and for a human life to be worthwhile. He has pursued these questions in ethics and political philosophy and also beyond the traditional confines of these fields into economic theory and the study of the institutions

---

[1]This sketch is a slightly amended and revised translation of Chapter 1 of my book John Rawls (Munich: Verlag C.H. Beck 1994). The factual information it contains derives mostly from a series of conversations in the summer of 1993. I would like to thank Rawls for these conversations and him and his wife for checking the factual parts of this sketch for accuracy. I am grateful also for the good fortune of getting to know him personally during the time I spent at Harvard as his student and teaching fellow (1978-83).

and political history of the US (notably its constitution and important Supreme Court opinions). His profound aspiration to answer these questions, so apparent in his writings, has sustained Rawls during a lifetime of hard work.

His devotion to this great intellectual and moral task also reinforces Rawls's characteristic modesty, which has impressed so many. He is not unaware of his standing in the profession, of course, and he is surely glad that his work has proved so productive. But he always views his work in reference to the task to which he has dedicated his life. This perspective is indeed humbling.

Family and Schooling

John (Jack) Bordley Rawls was born on February 21, 1921 in Baltimore as the second of five sons of William Lee (1883–1946) and Anna Abell Rawls (née Stump, 1892–1954). His maternal grandparents came from affluent families residing in exclusive Greenspring Valley (immortalized in the movie "Diner") near Baltimore. Both had inherited some wealth consisting mainly of coal and oil holdings in Pennsylvania. The grandfather, Alexander Hamilton Stump, lost most of these inheritances however, and the grandparents were eventually divorced. They had four daughters, one of whom was married to man named Rawls.

The Rawls family hails from the South, and the Rawls name is still rather frequent there. Rawls's paternal grandfather, William Stowe Rawls, was a banker in Greenville, a small town in North Carolina. In 1896 he moved with his family to Baltimore. Suffering from tuberculosis, he wanted to live near the Johns Hopkins University Hospital. Some years after the move, Rawls's father also contracted tuberculosis, and his health continued to be poor throughout his adult life. He never went to college and started working at a young age as a "runner" for a law firm. This gave him the opportunity to use the firm's law books in the evenings and thereby to educate himself to the point of passing the bar exam without any formal studies. He went on to become a successful and respected corporate lawyer in the Marbury law firm — one of the best in Baltimore, its fame inaugurated by the important 1803 case *Marbury v. Madison*. In the earlier years after his bar exam, he also occasionally taught law at the Baltimore Law School.

Jack's parents both took a strong interest in politics. His father supported Woodrow Wilson and the League of Nations and also was a close friend and unofficial advisor of Albert Ritchie, the Democratic Governor of Maryland (1924–36). Ritchie even asked him to run for the US Senate — a proposal he declined for health reasons. He was a firm supporter of the New Deal as well, but his respect for Franklin D. Roosevelt ended abruptly with the Court Packing Crisis of 1937, when Roosevelt attempted to break the Supreme Court's resistance against his New Deal legislation through expanding the Court by six new judges to be appointed by himself. Jack's mother — a highly intelligent woman, who excelled both in bridge and portrait painting — was for some time president of the Baltimore chapter of the newly founded League of Women Voters. In 1940, she worked for the campaign of Wendell Willkie, who had quit the Democratic Party to run against Roosevelt as a Republican. While Jack was rather distant from his father, whom he remembers as somewhat cold and aloof from the family, he was very close to his mother and traces his lifelong interest in the equality of women to her influence (as well as to that of his wife and daughters).

The most important events in Jack's childhood were the losses of two younger brothers, who died of diseases contracted from Jack. The first of these incidents occurred in 1928, when Jack fell gravely ill. Although Robert Lee (Bobby), 21 months younger, had been sternly told not to enter Jack's room, he did so anyway a few times to keep Jack company. Soon both children were lying in bed with high fever. Because the family physician, a relative, initially misdiagnosed the disease, a long time passed until it was finally discovered that they were suffering from diphtheria. The correct diagnosis and antitoxin came too late to save Bobby. His death was a severe shock to Jack and may have (as their mother thought) triggered his stammer, which has been a serious, though gradually receding, handicap for him ever since that time.

Jack recovered from the diphtheria, but the very next winter caught a severe pneumonia, which soon infected his brother Thomas Hamilton (Tommy, born September 1927). The tragedy of the previous year repeated itself. While Jack was recovering slowly, his little brother died in February of 1929.

Jack's older brother William Stowe (Bill) was nearly six years his senior, and Jack followed him through several schools to Princeton College. Bill was considerably bigger and stronger than Jack and quite successful in football, wrestling, and tennis. Jack sought to follow his example in sports, but he also developed independent intellectual interests in the biographies of famous scientists and in chemistry. The latter interest had been encouraged by a godfather who was a chemist. As a child, Jack owned a chemistry set and, with the help of additional chemicals supplied by his uncle, produced all kinds of smells and explosions, preferably after Sunday school.

The brothers started out in the private Calvert School, where Jack completed a year of kindergarten and his elementary schooling (1927–33). The school was coeducational, but boys and girls were taught separately in the last three grades. There was an emphasis on public speaking and acting, and Jack learned with some joy that he could overcome his stammer when speaking in rhyme. (In one performance of Schiller's *William Tell*, he mixed up his lines and announced to the delighted audience that the apple had split the arrow in two.) Jack's outstanding record at Calvert led to his selection as valedictorian of his class. His performance and early IQ score also impressed his teacher, John Webster, who provided special support and much encouragement to the boy, even giving him private tutorials well after he had left Calvert to attend the Roland Park Junior High School. Jack was sent to this public school for two years (1933–35) because his father was then the (unpaid) president of Baltimore's school board and wanted to express support for the public school system. At the end of his father's term, Jack — as was not unusual among Baltimore's well-to-do — was sent to a private boarding school, where he completed the last four years of his schooling.

During his childhood, Jack's sense of justice was engaged through his mother's work for the rights of women. He also began to reflect on matters of race and class. Even then Baltimore had a large black population (ca. 40 percent), and Jack noticed early on that blacks were living in quite different circumstances and that black children were attending separate schools. He also remembers vividly how his mother was not pleased when he made friends with a black boy, Ernest, even visiting him at his home in one of the small back-alley houses that were then typical abodes for Baltimore's black population.

In order to escape the hot and humid Baltimore summers, the Rawls family spent their vacations up in Maine, in their summer home near Blue Hill (affording a beautiful view of Mt. Desert and the bay) where they also kept a motorboat used to visit the outlying islands. Here Jack was confronted with poor whites, the so-called "natives," some of whom worked as caretakers of the summer residence. He had some native playmates and noticed that their educational opportunities and life prospects in their tiny impoverished village were much inferior to his own. These childhood experiences made a lasting impression on Jack by awakening his sense of justice, but also by deepening his lifelong feeling of having been terribly lucky. He had survived the diseases that killed two of his brothers and enjoyed great undeserved privileges of affluence and education. (Later, he made it through the war without a scratch and was also quite fortunate in his chosen career.)

The boarding school Jack attended from 1935 to 1939, as had his brother six years earlier, was the Kent School in western Connecticut, a strictly religious boys' school in the High Church Episcopal tradition headed by a monk of the Poughkeepsie-based Order of the Holy Cross. This principal was a severe and dogmatic man, who left little freedom to his teachers and students. Except for vacations, the students were never allowed, for example, to leave the school grounds and thus could not visit the nearby village or watch a movie. All students had to do house chores for about an hour every day and had to attend religious services daily, and twice on Sundays. Intellectually, the school at that time did not have much to offer, and so it is not surprising that Rawls remembers his time there as unhappy and unproductive.

College and War

After completing boarding school, Rawls — like his brother Bill before him and his youngest brother Richard Howland (1933–67) after him — was admitted to Princeton University, a member of the class of 1943, which consisted of some 630 young men. In those days, applicants were rarely rejected, so getting in was easy for those whose parents, like his, could afford the tuition. For the less affluent, it was a different story: Scholarships were quite scarce and awarded mostly to athletes needed for intercollegiate sports competitions.

The beginning of his first semester at Princeton coincided with the German attack on Poland, and Rawls recalls that most students in his class assumed that they would have to fight in a war. A large fraction of the class immediately signed up for the Reserve Officers' Training Corps (ROTC), thereby securing the opportunity for a quick officer career after graduation. Rawls did not sign up, but was moved by the imminent war to read up on World War I in the university library. Although no one was eager for war, those around Rawls (both at home and at Princeton) all agreed that the US should defend Great Britain. There was isolationist opposition ("America First") in some circles, but not among Rawls's family, friends, and acquaintances.

In his first year at Princeton, Rawls tried to emulate the brilliant athletic example of his brother Bill, who had made the Princeton varsity team in three sports (football, wrestling, tennis) and had been captain of the tennis team. He was indeed accepted into the freshmen football team. But wrestling turned out to be a tougher challenge. Rawls was not good enough for a safe place in the weight class up to 165 lbs. and therefore tried to compete in the next lower class (up to 155 lbs.). This meant however that he had to lose a good bit of weight before each contest, which weakened him in the competition itself. Not particularly successful and increasingly averse to individual contests, Rawls quit the team even before the end of the season. He also gave up football after the first year. But he continued to enjoy baseball, though not as a member of any official team.

Fraternities were banned at Princeton, and social life revolved around the eating clubs, consisting of juniors and seniors. Students could apply (through a process of "bicker") for membership at the end of their sophomore year and, if admitted, could then eat all their meals at their club and also spend their evenings there, talking or playing pool. The clubs also organized parties, especially on house party weekend, which was celebrated by all eating clubs simultaneously and attracted many young ladies from near and far. Propriety was, however, strictly enforced. Women were not allowed to spend the night at an eating club, and had to break off visits to the dormitories at 7pm. All sexual contacts were strictly prohibited, and students found guilty of such, or even merely found out to be married, were summarily expelled from the college. Once more in the footsteps of his brother, Rawls was admitted into the prestigious Ivy Club, which traditionally favored students from Baltimore.

At first, Rawls was not sure what major to choose. He tried chemistry, mathematics and even art history, but, finding himself insufficiently interested or talented in these subjects, he finally ended up in philosophy. In this choice he did not follow his brother Bill, who went on to Harvard Law School and later became a lawyer in Philadelphia.

Rawls's first teachers in philosophy were Walter T. Stace, David Bowers, and Norman Malcolm. In his sophomore year, Rawls took a course in moral philosophy with the utilitarian Stace, in which Kant's *Groundwork*, John Stuart Mill's "Utilitarianism," and Stace's own work *The Concept of Morals* (1937) were discussed. Bowers (who died tragically during the war in an attempt to jump onto a departing train) was teaching Kant. The most important influence was however exercised by Malcolm, who was only some ten years older than Rawls.

After a period of study in Cambridge (England), where he worked with Wittgenstein, Malcolm had returned to Harvard in order to complete his dissertation under C.I. Lewis. On the basis of a strong recommendation from Lewis, he had already been offered a position at Princeton. Lewis came to regret this recommendation, however. The reason had to do with Malcolm's attitude toward phenomenalism which, championed by Lewis, was then prevalent in American epistemology. Under Wittgenstein's influence, Malcolm had come to dismiss this approach — a fact that became painfully obvious during the public defense of his thesis. Quite upset, Lewis fired off a retraction of his recommendation, but the Princeton Philosophy Department felt obligated to Malcolm and maintained its offer, thus enabling him to become the most important of Rawls's teachers during his college years.

The first meeting of the two was unpleasant, at least for Rawls. In the fall of 1941, Rawls gave Malcolm a philosophical essay which he himself thought rather good. Malcolm, however, subjected this essay to very severe criticism and asked Rawls to "take it back" and to "think about what you are doing!" Though temporarily disheartening, this sharp criticism contributed to a gradual deepening of Rawls's interest in philosophy, and he credits Malcolm's personal example with exerting a large influence on the development of his own way of doing philosophy.

During the spring term of 1942, Rawls took another course with Malcolm about the (as Rawls says) quasi-religious topic of human evil, with readings from Plato, Augustine, Bishop Butler, Reinhold Niebuhr, and Philip Leon. This topic was not among Malcolm's ordinary philosophical concerns, and his interest in it may have been inspired by the war. When Rawls mentioned the course to him much later (during Malcolm's term as president of the APA), he could not remember ever having taught it at all. This lack of memory may also be due to the fact that Malcolm joined the navy in April and thus did not conclude the course. Rawls was nevertheless deeply impressed by it. His interest in religion was rekindled for the next three years. He wrote his senior thesis on this topic, and his doctoral dissertation, too, was devoted to related questions of character assessment.

Rawls received his AB a semester faster than usual, in January 1943, after he had completed a special summer term in 1942, which had been added on account of the war. He graduated *summa cum laude* in philosophy, for which he (not untypically) credits his good memory as well as his habit of taking accurate and detailed notes. In February, Rawls reported to the army and, after basic infantry training, completed a course in the signal corps. He was then sent to the Pacific theater for two years, where he served in New Guinea, in the Philippines, and finally four months among the forces occupying Japan. During his time overseas, Rawls belonged to the 128th regiment of the 32nd infantry division and served both in the regimental headquarters company and in an Intelligence and Reconnaissance (I&R) unit that, in squads of seven or eight men, was reconnoitering enemy positions. He did not see much combat, but once narrowly escaped an ambush when the Japanese fired early. Having passed up the opportunity to become an officer toward the end of the war because he did not want to stay longer than necessary in what he considered a "dismal institution," Rawls left the army in January 1946, still an enlisted man. As he wrote in a little autobiographical sketch (composed on the occasion of a Kent School reunion marking the 50th anniversary of his graduation), he viewed his army career as "singularly undistinguished." And so it may well appear in comparison to that of his brother Bill, who had volunteered for the air force even before Pearl Harbor and had piloted four-engine Liberator bombers, flying many sorties from Italy over southern Germany, Austria, and Poland.

In early 1946, Rawls began his graduate studies of philosophy, on the GI Bill, again at Princeton University. After three semesters, he spent one year (1947–48) on a fellowship at Cornell University, where Malcolm and also Max Black were working on Wittgenstein. The following year (1948–49), he was back in Princeton, writing his dissertation under the supervision of Walter Stace. After completing his philosophical education in Dublin, Stace had become mayor of Colombo (capital of Ceylon, today Sri Lanka) and, despite his official duties, had continued his philosophical studies, especially of Berkeley and Hegel, and even written a book, *The Theory of Knowledge and Existence* (Oxford 1932). Rawls's thesis develops an anti-foundationalist procedure — somewhat similar to his later idea of reflective equilibrium — for checking (and perhaps correcting) our initial considered moral judgments about particular cases by trying to explicate them all through a set of moral principles. (His first publication, "Outline of a Decision Procedure for Ethics," summarizes parts of this work.) While completing his thesis, Rawls met, in late 1948, his wife-to-be, Margaret (Mardy) Warfield Fox (born 1927), who was then a senior at Pembroke College in Brown University. They were married in June 1949 and spent the summer in Princeton, producing the index to Walter Arnold Kaufmann's book *Nietzsche: Philosopher, Psychologist and Anti-Christ* (Princeton 1950) in exchange for the tidy sum of $500.

Drawn mainly to art and art history, in which Rawls, too, has had a lifelong interest, Mardy has also taken an active role in her husband's work, helping him with proofreading, stylistic suggestions, and increasingly with the editing of his books and papers as well. She has also brought home to him the importance of equality of opportunity for women. When they were married — they had known each other only six months — she told him that her parents had wanted to finance a college education only for her two brothers, not for herself and her younger sister. Mardy had then successfully applied for a scholarship and had managed, with its help and through various jobs, to pay for her own BA. The young couple agreed that they would provide the same opportunities to their daughters as to their sons. (And so they did: All four children studied with their parents' support — two at the University of Massachusetts at Amherst, the two others at Reed College and Boston University.)

Rawls had won a fellowship for the 1949–50 academic year, and it made sense, therefore, to spend another year as a student at Princeton, even though his thesis was essentially done. During that year, he worked mainly outside the philosophy department: In the fall term, he participated in an economics seminar with Jacob Viner and in the spring he took a seminar with Alpheus T. Mason on the history of US political thought and constitutional law, in which the main text was an anthology edited by Mason: *Free Government in the Making: Readings in American Political Thought* (Oxford 1949). In the course of this seminar, Rawls studied all the more important views on political justice that had been articulated in the course of US history, and tried to develop each of them into a systematic conception of justice.

Academic Career

Rawls taught the following two years (1950–52) as an instructor in the Princeton Philosophy Department. This was during the McCarthy era, from which Princeton was, however, largely insulated. Despite his teaching obligations, Rawls continued his studies outside philosophy. In the fall of 1950, he attended a seminar of the (later well-known) economist William J. Baumol, which focused mainly on J.R. Hicks' *Value and Capital* and Paul A. Samuelson's *Foundations of Economic Analysis*. In the following spring, these discussions were continued in an unofficial study group. Rawls also studied Leon Walras's *Elements of Pure Economics* and John von Neumann and Oskar Morgenstern's

Theory of Games and Economic Behavior. At the same time, he made friends with J.O. Urmson, an Oxford philosopher who was a visiting professor at Princeton in 1950–51. From Urmson he first learned about all the interesting developments in British and particularly Oxford philosophy which — with J.L. Austin, Gilbert Ryle, H.L.A. Hart, Isaiah Berlin, Stuart Hampshire, Peter Strawson, H. Paul Grice and R.M. Hare — was then in an especially creative phase. Following Urmson's advice, Rawls applied for a Fulbright fellowship and spent the 1952–53 year in Oxford as a member of the high table of Urmson's Christchurch College.

The year in Oxford was the philosophically most important for Rawls since 1941–42 (his first year as a philosophy student, under the influence of Malcolm). Through Urmson he got to know Oxford's most important philosophers. He attended a lecture course by H.L.A. Hart who, freshly promoted to a professorship, was expounding some of the ideas he would later publish in *The Concept of Law.* Rawls was especially impressed with a seminar, taught by Berlin and Hampshire, with Hart's active participation, in the winter of 1953, which covered Condorcet, Rousseau's *Social Contract,* John Stuart Mill's "On Liberty," Alexander Herzen, G.E. Moore, and two essays by John Maynard Keynes. Rawls continued to think of this seminar as an exemplar of excellent teaching that he should seek to emulate.

During this period, Rawls began developing the idea of justifying substantive moral principles by reference to an appropriately constructed deliberative procedure. He believes that the inspiration for this idea may have come from an essay by Frank Knight, which mentions the organization of a reasonable communicative situation. ("Economic Theory and Nationalism" in *The Ethics of Competition and Other Essays,* London 1935, pp. 345–359, esp. the footnote on pp. 345–347.) Rawls's initial idea was that the participants should deliberate independently of one another and should forward their proposals for moral principles to an umpire. This process was to continue until agreement would be achieved. As with later versions of the original position, Rawls was hoping that he could, from an exact and elaborately justified specification of the initial situation and its rules, derive substantive results hypothetically, i.e. without implementing the procedure with actual participants.

After his return from Oxford (1953) Rawls accepted an assistant professorship at Cornell University, where he was promoted to associate professor with tenure in 1956. In the 1950's, Cornell had a rather attractive philosophy department whose character was shaped by Malcolm and Black. Among his other colleagues were Rogers Albritton and David Sachs, who had been Rawls's fellow students at Princeton. The department published (as it still does today) a highly acclaimed journal, the *Philosophical Review,* and Rawls became one of its editors.

Though professionally quite content at Cornell, Rawls considered the university's location a major disadvantage. Ithaca is a small town in upstate New York, hundreds of miles away from the nearest cultural centers of New York City, Princeton, Philadelphia, Baltimore, and Boston. While the region is quite beautiful, it has severe winters, which tend to intensify the feeling of isolation. This disadvantage seemed all the more weighty as the Rawls family quickly gained four new members: Anne Warfield (born November 1950), today professor of sociology at Wayne University in Detroit with two sons; Robert Lee (born March 1954), production manager and designer of fitness machines in Seattle with one son and one daughter; Alexander (Alec) Emory (born December 1955), studying economics at Stanford and a carpenter and foreman in the construction of buildings; and Elizabeth (Liz) Fox (born June 1957), a writer, fashion designer, and championship ballroom dancer in New York.

The opportunity to leave Ithaca at least temporarily arose in 1959, when Rawls, who had meanwhile published several important essays, was invited to a one-year visiting professorship at Harvard, where his former colleague Albritton had taken up a permanent position. Rawls impressed many local philosophers during this year (1959–60), and MIT proceeded to offer him a professorship with tenure. MIT was then heavily concentrated in the sciences and economics, but also beginning to build a presence in philosophy, with one associate professor, Irving Singer, and two assistant professors, Hubert Dreyfus and Samuel Todes. There was no separate department, however, and the philosophers were part of a much larger humanities faculty. Rawls decided to accept the offer to become the only tenured philosopher at MIT. This enabled him to develop his friendships at Harvard (especially with Burton Dreben) and to continue his old friendships with Albritton and with Sachs, who was now teaching at Brandeis.

The MIT administration understandably wanted to concentrate its philosophy presence on the history and philosophy of science. With the help of Noam Chomsky and others, Rawls was to build up a humanities subdivision in this field. He did so by hiring James Thomson and then Hilary Putnam. Having spent considerable time and energy on mostly administrative service to a field in which he himself had little interest, Rawls was happy to receive an offer from Harvard in the spring of 1961. He nevertheless decided to postpone the move by a year in order to bring the changes at MIT to a successful conclusion. Rawls proceeded to teach in the Harvard Philosophy Department from 1962 until his retirement in 1991.

A Decade of Ferment: 1962–71

The following years were devoted mainly to the completion of *A Theory of Justice* ("TJ"). Rawls sought to combine the work on this book with his teaching duties as much as possible. Some of his courses were based, in part, on drafts of the book, which were sometimes distributed to the students. Rawls also used his courses for the study of the great historical figures of political philosophy, beginning in his first year at Harvard with a course on Kant and Hegel for which he composed an extensive lecture script on Hegel's philosophy.

Politically, the late 1960's were dominated by the Vietnam War. From the very beginning Rawls believed this war to be unjust and repeatedly defended his assessment in public. Together with his colleague Roderick Firth he took part, for example, in a Washington anti-war conference in May 1967. In the spring term of 1969, he taught a course "Problems of War," in which he discussed various positions on *ius ad bellum* and *ius in bello* in reference to the Vietnam War. (The last quarter of this course was canceled due to a general strike of the Harvard student body.)

Rawls was deeply concerned to understand what flaws in his society might account for its prosecuting a plainly unjust war with such ferocity and what citizens might do to oppose this war. In regard to the first question, he sees the main problem in the fact that wealth is very unevenly distributed and easily converted into political influence. The US political process is structured so as to allow wealthy individuals and corporations (notably including those in the defense industry) to dominate the political competition through their contributions to political parties and organizations. Written during that time, TJ shows traces of these thoughts: "Those similarly endowed and motivated should have roughly the same chance of attaining positions of political authority irrespective of their economic and social class. ... Historically one of the main defects of constitutional government has been the failure to ensure the fair value of the political liberties. ... Disparities in property and wealth that far exceed what is compatible with political equality have generally been tolerated by the legal system" (TJ 225f.). This critique is much expanded in a later essay, "The Basic Liberties and their Priority" (1983), which also severely reproaches the Supreme Court for blocking campaign reform legislation in *Buckley v. Valeo*.

In regard to the second question, Rawls deems it important to foster a public culture where civil disobedience and conscientious refusal are understood and respected as minority appeals to the conscience of the majority (TJ §§56–59). In the context of this discussion, Rawls offers a very brief account of international ethics (TJ 377–79), which is much elaborated (and somewhat revised) in his later book *The Law of Peoples* (1999).

It was the second question that confronted Rawls most immediately. Many young people were unwilling to perform their military service, which was compulsory for men up to the age of 26. The Department of Defense had decided not to conscript students in good standing, thereby giving professors an unusual power and responsibility; one failing grade could cause a student to be called up. Rawls thought that these "2-S deferments" for students were unjust, quite apart from the injustice of the war itself. Why should students be treated better than others — especially when rich parents have a significant advantage in securing a place for their sons at one educational institution or another? If young men are to be forced to participate in the war at all, then at least the sons of the rich and well-connected should share this fate equally with the rest. If not all fit young men are needed, then the requisite number should be selected by lot. With seven colleagues from the Philosophy Department — Albritton, Dreben, Firth, Putnam (who had joined Harvard after Rawls), Stanley Cavell, G.E.L. Owen, and Morton White, *not* Willard V. Quine or Nelson Goodman — and another eight from Political Science — including Judith (Dita) Shklar, Michael Walzer, Stanley Hoffmann, Harvey Mansfield, and Edward Banfield — Rawls defended this position and proposed its adoption at two faculty meetings in late 1966 and early 1967. The proposal was opposed by some of his colleagues and also by the university administration (headed by the conservative President Nathan Pusey) as an inappropriate interference with affairs outside the university. In response to this charge, the proponents were able to point out that the Attorney General himself, Burke Marshall, had asked the universities for their views on the matter. A vote was finally taken, and the proposal was defeated. But intense disagreement relating to the Vietnam War continued at Harvard for many years.

Rawls spent the academic year 1969–70 at the Center for Advanced Study at Stanford University so as finally to complete his great *Theory of Justice*. He arrived there with a typescript of about 200 single-spaced pages, which he was continuously revising through additions and substitutions. The revised parts were retyped by a secretary, Anna Tower, and so the typescript grew and proliferated (with alphabetized insert pages) in a way that was hard to survey. Can we still imagine, a mere 30 years later, how people wrote books without computers? It is easier for us electronic folk to imagine the sudden loss of a book in progress. This is what almost happened to Rawls toward the end of his Stanford year. In early April, the Center's director called him around 6am with the terrible news that a few incendiary bombs had been exploded in the Center overnight, concluding: "You have been wiped out." Rawls had left the latest version of the typescript on his desk in his office. The only other extant version was the initial one of the summer of 1969. Eight months of intensive labor seemed irretrievably lost. But Rawls was lucky once again. His office had largely been spared by the flames and had merely sustained severe water damage. Though the precious typescript was wet through and through, it was still quite readable. Rawls laid it out to dry and then used it as the basis for further modifications.

In September of 1970, Rawls returned to Harvard and became chairman of its philosophy department. This tough and time-consuming job was made even harder by the political circumstances. The members of the department had quite diverse views on the war and on the issues it raised within the university. Putnam, for instance, was a member of the Maoist Progressive Labor Party, while Quine and Goodman held conservative views. These intradepartmental differences — though dealt with in a polite and civilized manner — required extra time and energy from Rawls. Since he also had to take care of his courses, he had to use evenings and nights for the final polishing of the typescript.

Rawls remembers this academic year as the hardest of his career. But at its end he had a text that he was satisfied with. Since the typescript was full of insertions, he had no idea of its true length and was amazed when Harvard University Press sent him 587 pages of proof for corrections and indexing. Rawls prepared the index himself, and the long and widely anticipated book appeared in the US in late 1971.

After *A Theory of Justice*

The following decades passed rather more calmly. Since 1960, the Rawls family has lived in Lexington, some eight miles from Cambridge. This town is governed by five elected, unpaid selectmen, who serve as a policy-making board, and by a representative Town Meeting of 189 elected delegates, who serve as the local legislature. Ms. Rawls has been a Town Meeting member for about 30 years. In this capacity, she focused her efforts on matters of land use planning and environmental protection, and she has on occasion also engaged in environmental protection work professionally, for the state of Massachusetts. Recently, she has been pursuing her artistic career, originally begun at Brown University. Her watercolors have been on display in various places (including Harvard University), and one of them, a portrait of Lincoln, adorns Rawls's Harvard office.

Rawls himself has continued to devote most of his time to his intellectual work, which he does mostly at home. He has also continued to take an interest in the artistic work of his wife, and has enjoyed various sailing trips along the Maine coast. He tries to keep himself in good health by maintaining a strict dietary regimen and regular exercise. In 1983 he had to discontinue his hour-long jogs, however, because he had damaged a tendon while jumping rope. He switched to bicycling which, thanks to a stationary exercise bike, he can keep up year round.

In 1979, Rawls was promoted to the highest academic rank at Harvard, that of university professor. Members of this exclusive group receive not merely an especially high salary, but also complete freedom in regard to their teaching: They may offer courses in other departments, if they like, or skip a term to pursue research (though Rawls did not avail himself of these opportunities). Harvard had eight university professorships at the time, and Rawls was given the James Bryant Conant University Professorship (named for a former Harvard president), in which his predecessor had been the Nobel-laureate economist Kenneth Arrow.

Rawls taught at Harvard until 1991. His closest colleagues there were Albritton (who soon left for Los Angeles) and Dreben, as well as Firth, Cavell, Dita Shklar, Charles Fried, and in later years also the newcomers Thomas M. (Tim) Scanlon, Amartya K. Sen, and Christine Korsgaard. He left Massachusetts only for a sabbatical year at the University of Michigan (1974–75), a term at the Princeton Institute for Advanced Study (fall 1977), and a term at Oxford (spring 1986). In Michigan he made friends with William K. Frankena and Richard B. Brandt; in Oxford he spent time, once again, with many of his old friends from 1952–53 (in particular, Hart, Hampshire, and Berlin) as well as Philippa Foot, who had held a visiting professorship at MIT in the early 1960's.

As before, Rawls invested much effort into his courses (normally three per year, divided over two semesters), which have always been well attended and respected. Two mostly historical courses he offered regularly, though with somewhat variable readings, were Moral Philosophy (Butler, Hume, Kant, Sidgwick) and Social and Political Philosophy (Hobbes, Locke, Rousseau, Mill, Marx, and sometimes also "TJ"). These courses were open to graduate students and advanced undergraduates, and generally had an enrollment of 30-50 students. They consisted of two excellent lectures per week (which Rawls often summarized for the students on a single hand-written page) plus a one-hour discussion session which for the graduate students was conducted by Rawls himself and for the undergraduates by an advanced graduate student. Even if it had been given many times before, he would prepare each class lecture afresh, looking once more through the primary texts and familiarizing himself with any new and important secondary sources. Many graduate students sat through the same course year after year to deepen their understanding of the field and to partake in the development of Rawls's thinking.

Rawls has always found it difficult to function in larger groups, especially with strangers, and even more so when he himself is the center of attention. On such occasions he may seem shy or ill at ease and is sometimes still bothered by his stammer. In a Harvard lecture room, however, these problems were barely noticeable, especially after the first one or two weeks of term. By then the audience had become familiar, and Rawls would even make an occasional joke — invariably with deadpan delivery, so the students took some time to catch on. In informal settings, with just one interlocutor (or a few) whom he knows well, Rawls can be quite at ease and may talk with sensitivity and warmth about the other's life and problems or about any of a wide range of topics such as politics, meteorology, academic life, healthy nutrition, or a recent movie. On such occasions he can be animated, even playful, and really enjoy himself.

Rawls also regularly taught graduate seminars and tutorials (seminar-like courses for 4-6 advanced undergraduate philosophy majors) in which he discussed important new works in ethics and political philosophy as well as other related topics such as the freedom and strength of the will (Kant and Donald Davidson).

He also, of course, supervised dissertations and has trained an impressive group of philosophers over the years, including David Lyons (now Boston University), Tom Nagel (New York University), Tim Scanlon (Harvard), Onora O'Neill (Cambridge), Alan Gibbard (Michigan), and Sissela Bok (Harvard) in the 1960's; Norman Daniels (Tufts), Michael Stocker (Syracuse), Tom Hill (Chapel Hill), Barbara Herman (University of California in Los Angeles), Steven Strasnik, Josh Cohen (MIT), Marcia Homiak (Occidental), and Christine Korsgaard (Harvard) in the 1970's; and since then Jean Hampton (deceased, last at the University of Arizona), Adrian Piper (Wellesley), Arnold Davidson (Chicago), Andrews Reath (University of California in Riverside), Nancy Sherman (Georgetown), Thomas Pogge (Columbia), Daniel Brudney (Chicago), Sam Freeman (Pennsylvania), Susan Neiman (Tel Aviv), Sibyl Schwarzenbach (City University of New York), Elizabeth Anderson (Michigan), Hannah Ginsborg (University of California in Berkeley), Henry Richardson (Georgetown), Paul Weithman (Notre Dame), Sharon Lloyd (University of Southern California), Michele Moody-Adams (Indiana University), Peter de Marneffe (Arizona State), Hilary Bok (Johns Hopkins), Erin Kelly (Tufts), and Anthony Laden (University of Illinois at Chicago).

This list shows that Rawls has done much to make a professional career in philosophy possible and attractive for women. It also shows that most good philosophy departments in the US now have at least one prominent Rawls student. It is remarkable that these students have produced not only creative and original texts in moral and political philosophy, but also excellent works of historical scholarship. Although Rawls himself has published thus far only one of his many historical writings (an essay on Kant), he has done much to broaden and improve the study of the history of moral and political philosophy in the US. This achievement of his teaching is celebrated (and exemplified) in a volume of essays by his students, *Reclaiming the History of Ethics — Essays for John Rawls*, which they presented to him for his 75th birthday.

Through his quality as a teacher and the interdisciplinary focus and presentation of his work, Rawls has also had a lasting impact on many other students who took his classes as undergraduates or as graduate students in political science, law, or economics. They have carried the influence of his teaching and writing into these neighboring disciplines and helped to make its reception there more sympathetic and accurate.

In the years since his main work, Rawls has published various essays in which he has further explicated, defended, extended and also revised his theory of justice. His new book *Political Liberalism* includes many of these additions and improvements, but, unlike *A Theory of Justice,* mainly addresses the relation between religion and democracy and the conditions for their being compatible. This concern is most clearly expressed in "The Idea of Public Reason Revisited" (*Chicago Law Review*, 1997). Rawls is now rewriting *Political Liberalism* to fit this latest essay. Other recent and current projects include *Collected*

Papers (1999, containing most of his published essays); *The Law of Peoples* (1999, greatly expanding and improving an identically titled lecture he gave for Amnesty International six years earlier); *Lectures in Moral Philosophy* (2000, containing previously unpublished lectures on Leibniz, Hume, Kant, and Hegel); and *Justice as Fairness — A Restatement.*

The Meaning of Rawls's Project

All his life, Rawls has been interested in the question whether and to what extent human life is redeemable — whether it is possible for human beings, individually and collectively, to live so that their lives are worth living (or, in Kant's words, so that there is value in human beings' living on the earth). This question is closely related to that of evil in human character, with which Rawls, still under the influence of his religious upbringing, had been so fascinated during his student years. But even the life of someone whose conduct and character are above reproach may seem to lack worth. So much human time and energy are wasted on professional and personal projects that are ultimately pointless, and do not really promote human excellence and flourishing. In light of such thoughts, Rawls has tried to lead a worthwhile life in part by trying to show what might make human life worthwhile.

He has focused these contributions to the political plane: Is it possible to envision a social order under which the collective life of human beings would be worthwhile? One can imagine all sorts of things, of course. To be significant, the question must be understood in a realistic sense, that is, within the context of the empirical circumstances of this world and of our human nature. The question is then whether we can envision a *realistic* utopia, an ideal social order that is reachable from the present on a credible path of transition and, once reached, could sustain itself in the world as it is. By constructing such a realistic utopia, Rawls has sought to show that the world is good at least in this respect of making a worthwhile collective life of human beings possible.

Now one might think that our estimation of the goodness of the world should not be affected by a merely theoretical demonstration of a social order that would be just and stable, even reachable from where we are; what matters is the moral quality of our actual collective life. Against this, Rawls would certainly not maintain that the actual political achievement of justice is irrelevant, but he does hold that a well-grounded belief in its achievability can reconcile us to the world. So long as we are reasonably confident that a self-sustaining and just social order among human beings is realistically possible, we can hope that we or others will someday, somewhere, achieve it and can then also work toward this achievement. By modeling a fairly realistic utopia as a final moral goal for our collective life, political philosophy can provide an inspiration that can banish the dangers of resignation and cynicism and can enhance the value of our lives even today.

1921   Birth of John Bordley Rawls on February 21 in Baltimore, Maryland, as the second of five sons of William Lee and Anna Abell Rawls (née Stump).
1939–43 Studies at Princeton University concluded with an AB degree.
1943–45 Military training and service in the Pacific.
1946–50 Graduate study at Princeton University concluded with a Ph.D. in philosophy.

1947–48 Fellowship student at Cornell University.

1949   Marriage to Margaret Warfield Fox.

1950   Ph.D., dissertation *A Study in the Grounds of Ethical Knowledge: Considered with Reference to Judgements on the Moral Worth of Character.*
         Birth of his first child: Anne Warfield.

1950–52 Instructor in the Princeton Philosophy Department.

1952–53 Fulbright fellow at Christchurch College, Oxford.

1953   Appointment as Assistant Professor of Philosophy at Cornell University.

1954   Birth of his second child: Robert Lee.

1955   "Two Concepts of Rules," proposing to confine the principle of utility to the assessment of practices.
         Birth of his third child: Alexander Emory.

1956   Promotion to Associate Professor, with tenure, at Cornell University.

1957/58 "Justice as Fairness," introducing an early version of his two principles of justice, by which persons should agree to assess and reform their shared practices.
         Birth of his youngest child: Elizabeth Fox.

1959–60 Visiting professor at Harvard University.

1960   Appointment as Professor at the Massachusetts Institute of Technology.

1962   Appointment as Professor of Philosophy at Harvard University.

1969–70 Fellowship at the Stanford University Center for Advanced Study in the Behavioral Sciences.

1971   *A Theory of Justice.*

1974   Appointment as John Cowles Professor.

1974–75 Sabbatical at the University of Michigan.

1977   Sabbatical (fall) at the Institute for Advanced Study in Princeton.

1979   Appointment as James Bryant Conant University Professor, succeeding Nobel Prize winner Kenneth Arrow.

1980   John Dewey Lectures: "Kantian Constructivism in Moral Theory."

1983   Honorary doctorate from Oxford University.

1986   Sabbatical (spring) in Oxford.

1987   Honorary doctorate from Princeton University.

1991   Retirement.

1993   *Political Liberalism.*

1996   *Political Liberalism,* revised and expanded edition.

1997   "The Idea of Public Reason Revisited."
         Honorary doctorate from Harvard University.

1999   *Collected Papers.*
         The Law of Peoples.
         A Theory of Justice, second edition, with revisions made in 1974 for the German and subsequent translations.
         Rolf Schock Prize in the Field of Logic and Philosophy, awarded by the Royal Swedish Academy.
         National Humanities Medal of Excellence.

2000   *Lectures in Moral Philosophy.*

Amy Gutmann

THE CENTRAL ROLE OF RAWLS'S THEORY

When John Rawls began writing *A Theory of Justice* in the 1950s, philosophers were busy lamenting the death of political philosophy. Grand political theories, Bernard Crick observed, were treated like "corpses for students to practice dissection upon." Some philosophers, calling themselves "emotivists," elaborated versions of the view that morality is just a matter of opinion. If any systematic view could claim adherents in the academy, it was utilitarianism, which asserted the seemingly simple principle, "maximize social welfare." Utilitarianism was also extremely influential outside the academy. It seemed to provide a straightforward and rigorous method by which public officials could solve hard political problems: for every policy alternative, add up the social benefits, subtract the social costs, and implement the alternative that maximizes net benefits.

The common intuition that the rights of individuals should not be sacrificed for the sake of social welfare somehow persisted alongside the academic ascendancy of utilitarianism—a testimony, perhaps, to the tenacity of our moral intuitions. But believers in rights lacked systematic philosophical arguments against the opposing Benthamite intuition that rights are nothing more than "nonsense on stilts." Rights advocates also lacked a convincing response to the enduring Marxist critique of rights as—nòt nonsense—but the common sense of capitalism, confusing the class interests of the bourgeoisie with the universal interests of humanity.

Political thinking in the academy has changed since the 1950s and early 1960s in at least three significant ways. First, most rights advocates now embrace part of the Marxist critique and defend not only the traditional list of civil and political liberties but also more equal distributions of income, wealth, education, job opportunities, health care, and other goods essential to secure the welfare and dignity of the disadvantaged. Second, most prominent political philosophers are now rights theorists. Utilitarianism is everywhere on the defensive. Third, grand political theory is once again alive in the academy.

All three of these changes are attributable to the influence of *A Theory of Justice*. Of course, reading Rawls did not suddenly convert utility maximizers and "emotivists" into rights theorists. Some scholars were already searching for a systematic alternative to utilitarianism and emotivism. Many students read Rawls in their philosophically formative years and grew up, as it were, with strong Rawlsian sympathies. Still other, more established scholars first criticized *A Theory of Justice* and then constructed systematic theories to replace it. Most of these (like Ronald Dworkin's theory of equality) resemble Rawls's theory in significant ways, but even those that are radically different would not have been conceived, as Michael Walzer acknowledges in *Spheres of Justice*, without Rawls's work. Rawls's critics pay the greatest tribute to *A Theory of Justice* by affirming Henry James's view that "to criticize is to appreciate, to appropriate, to take intellectual possession, to establish in fine a relation with the criticized thing and to make it one's own." Among twentieth-century philosophical works Rawls's theory may be our most common possession.

Joining Socialist Criticism and Liberal Theory

To appreciate the political substance of Rawls's theory, it is best to begin with the first and most specific change that Rawls has wrought: the integration of socialist criticism into liberal theory. *A Theory of Justice* offers no philosophical rationalizations for the interests of any dominant class or group. The first principle of Rawlsian justice — the equal liberty principle — gives priority to securing basic liberal freedoms: freedom of thought, conscience, speech, assembly, universal suffrage, freedom from arbitrary arrest and seizure, the right to hold public office and personal property. Conspicuously absent from these basic liberties are capitalist market freedoms: to own commercial property, to appropriate what one has produced, to inherit or to pass on one's possessions. The absence of these freedoms from the list of basic liberties is no oversight or inconsistency on Rawls's part. Unlike the parties to Locke's social contract, Rawlsian "contractors" must choose distributive principles without knowing their relative wealth or their social class. Unaware of whether they are capitalists or workers, they will care more about securing a decent life for themselves and their children than about protecting the profits of property owners.

The second principle of Rawlsian justice has two parts. The first (and most famous) part — the "difference principle" — justifies only those social and economic inequalities that maximize benefits to the least advantaged citizens. The second part requires "fair equality of opportunity" for all, equalizing not only job opportunities but life chances. People with "similar abilities and skills should have similar life chances . . . irrespective of the income class into which they are born."

This is a liberalism for the least advantaged, a liberalism that pays a moral tribute to the socialist critique. The "difference principle" prevents the poor from falling (even into a safety net) so long as it is possible to raise their life prospects higher. Nothing short of securing their highest practicable life prospects will satisfy Rawlsian demands. Similarly, fair equality of opportunity goes far beyond the classical liberal ideal of careers open to talents. It also requires compensatory education and limits on economic inequalities so that "in all sectors of society there should be roughly equal prospects of culture and achievement for everyone similarly motivated and endowed."

Liberals can consistently support the theory's egalitarian economic implications because the first principle, the liberal core of Rawls's theory, rejects equalization at the expense of the basic liberties of any citizen. The income of the least advantaged may not be maximized, for example, by denying freedom of association to professionals or freedom of speech to neoconservatives. Socialists can consistently support the liberalism of the first principle because the second principle (the socialist core of Rawlsian justice) renders liberal freedoms far more than mere formalities for the disadvantaged.

This integration of liberal and socialist principle explains the appeal of Rawlsian principles to left-liberals. Although they find flaws and suggest revisions in the Rawlsian framework, most consider the principles a stimulus to their own thinking about justice. It also explains why *other* liberals and socialists have been more critical of Rawls's theory. Liberals who believe in distribution according to the market or individual desert (or both) have criticized Rawls for not counting the freedom to appropriate the fruits of one's own labor as among the basic liberties. Socialists who believe capitalist ownership of large-scale enterprises to be a postfeudal form of private government have criticized Rawls for leaving the choice between private and collective ownership of large-scale industry open to empirical argument rather than settling it on moral grounds.

Why both libertarians (like Robert Nozick) and democratic socialists (like Walzer) would criticize Rawls's theory is clear enough. Harder to justify are the rejections of Rawls based upon contradictory misrepresentations of Rawlsian principles. Many liberal critics have

17

followed Robert Nisbet's reading of Rawls's theory as a radically egalitarian rejection of liberal freedom (reminiscent of Rousseau), while many socialist scholars have followed Norman Daniel's first reading of the theory as yet another liberal rationalization of large-scale inequalities in income, wealth, and power between classes (reminiscent of Locke). It is curious that both sets of critics misrepresent the substance of Rawls's theory in a direction opposite to their own political sympathies. The result has been to stir up old ideological debates between partisans of liberty and equality, individual and community, equality of opportunity and equality of results.

Communitarian Critique

The most recent misrepresentation of Rawls is the communitarian critique. Michael Sandel's *Liberalism and the Limits of Justice* and Alasdair MacIntyre's *After Virtue* suggest that we must choose between a Rawlsian politics of individual rights, in which atomistic individuals languish without a shared morality, and an Aristotelian politics of the common good, in which solidaristic citizens fare well without the protection of individual rights. It is doubtful that our political alternatives are, or ever were, so stark and simple.

Were Rawls the first philosopher to suggest a way of narrowing the gap between classical liberalism and socialism, the misinterpretation of Rawlsian principles would be less surprising. But he follows a long line of liberal philosophers—John Stuart Mill, Henry Sidgwick, T.H. Green, L.T. Hobhouse, R.H. Tawney, John Dewey, among others—who defend a politics explicitly more egalitarian than Lockeanism and explicitly more libertarian than Marxism. The reluctance to accept the political meaning of Rawlsian principles is even harder to explain because on a wide range of political issues—such as compensatory education, equal pay for equal work, national health insurance, antitrust, and plant-closing legislation—many of Rawls's critics support positions that are both politically liberal and economically egalitarian. Ideological divisions of the past die harder in academic discourse than in actual politics.

Yet new philosophical ideas also catch on faster in the academy than in the real world. The Rawlsian idea that was accepted most readily is the "original position," a hypothetical situation in which a "veil of ignorance" deprives us of all knowledge of our natural talents, moral views, and place in the social order so that we can rationally choose principles of justice that are not biased in our own favor. Not knowing my own religion, I will choose a principle of religious toleration to govern society. Not knowing my social class, I will choose principles that guarantee fair equality of opportunity and maximize my life prospects if I turn out to be among the least advantaged citizens. And so will you and so will every other rational person, because in the "original position" there is nothing to distinguish us from each other. There we are all rational choosers. Here (in everyday social life) we are all "free and equal moral persons," led by our sense of "justice as fairness" to accept the "original position" as the fairest way to agree about political principles, to forge a new social contract.

Rawls's revival (and revision) of contract theory gave rise to the second significant change in political thinking in the academy: the ascendancy of rights over utility. Rawls's conception of justice as fairness challenged the dominant utilitarian understanding of how to treat people as equals. Thomas Nagel, T.M. Scanlon, Bernard Williams, and (most recently) Will Kymlicka have elaborated the challenge. Although utilitarians and social-contract theorists are both committed to equality, their commitments differ dramatically. For utilitarians, treating people as equals means counting each person's interests equally in calculations of social welfare. For social contract theorists, it means securing each person's basic interests *against* routine calculations of welfare. Philosophers still contend over which understanding is morally correct, but utilitarianism is now on the defensive against Rawls's argument that contract theory is a better *public* philosophy for a democratic society governed by a bill of rights. Many of our constitutionally guaranteed rights—free speech, religion, press, suffrage, and so on—

are among those that would be chosen by people in the "original position."

But what about the large bundle of rights necessary to secure fair equality of opportunity and the "difference principle"? Where are these rights to be found in our Constitution? The enormous interest in *A Theory of Justice* among legal scholars has been plausibly attributed to the opportunity it seems to offer American courts to expand the domain of individual rights. Democratic critics point out that such an expansion carries serious moral costs and reveals a significant tension within Rawls's theory: to the extent that courts read more rights into the Constitution, they narrow the domain of democratic decision making created by the fundamental political rights of citizens (to vote, to hold office, to influence public policy, and so on). If Rawls's theory requires such an expansive reading of our rights, the courts could put Congress into receivership. Judges would decide cases in the name of hypothetical rather than actual people.

Scholars allied with the critical legal studies movement carry this challenge one step further. Mark Tushnet and others question whether abstract rights derived from the "original position" (or any other philosophical position) can be translated into something as specific as a legally enforceable right to health care, housing, or a minimum income in the United States today. How much health care, housing, and guaranteed income would satisfy the presumed Rawlsian right? Whom would the courts hold responsible for providing the necessary goods and services? These are not questions that Rawls ever claims to answer. He recognizes, as some of his admirers do not, the intellectual gap that exists between an ideal theory of justice and a theory applicable to any nonideal society.

What, then, is the relevance of justice as fairness for American politics? Does the duty to further Rawlsian principles apply in some special way to judges? Since judges have more political power than the rest of us but less accountability than legislators, a Rawlsian philosopher (concerned to preserve the priority of equal political liberty) might discourage them from recognizing new welfare rights

against legislative will. If this is a practical implication of Rawls's theory, then it is more compatible with democratic decision making than its critics suggest. But it is also a less critical conception, at least in its legal implications, than some admirers of Rawls's theory hope.

Or, it may be that Rawlsian judges should be more "activist" and read a defense of welfare rights into the equal protection clause of the Constitution. On this view, the greater power of judges brings with it a greater responsibility than that of ordinary citizens to act on behalf of relatively powerless and poor citizens, especially when legislators fail to fulfill their responsibility to the least advantaged. The legal theorist Frank Michelman concludes that it is quite unclear what Rawlsian judges should do. Michelman's inconclusive conclusion seems correct. The absolute priority of liberty holds only for the ideal world. In our nonideal world, where inadequate education, housing, health care, and income may deprive the disadvantaged of their self-respect (a "primary good" to which Rawls also gives the highest priority), Rawlsian judges face a hard choice between deferring to legislative will (for the sake of equal political liberty) and enforcing welfare rights (for the sake of self-respect, the difference principle, fair equality of opportunity, and the fair value of liberty).

Although Rawls says little about the obligations of judges, legislators, or ordinary citizens in our society, his silence has stimulated scholars in many disciplines—law, philosophy, political science, economics, education, and medicine among others—to delve into issues of practical ethics in the spirit of Rawls's goal "to guide the course of social reform." To be sure, scholars stimulated by Rawls's theory have not singlehandedly (or together) guided the course of social reform. But they have broadly influenced public debates on a wide variety of controversial issues, among them affirmative action for minorities and women, legalization of abortion, distribution of health care and education, prevention of international famine, conscientious objection, civil disobedience, nuclear deterrence and foreign aid, and qualifi-

19

cations for appointments to the Supreme Court. Their forays into practical ethics invoke moral considerations similar to Rawls's—what it means to treat people as equals, what kinds of claims can legitimately count as moral arguments in a public forum, whether individual rights or only matters of public policy are at stake, whether a policy endangers the self-respect of citizens—but they rarely reach their conclusions in specific cases without generating new moral distinctions and priority rules, distinctions and rules tailored to the case at hand rather than derivable from an ideal theory of justice, Rawls's or even their own.

A Theory of Justice is still a triumph within the tradition of grand political theory. The triumph rests on more than the philosophical richness, originality, and wisdom that Rawls's work manifests to a degree not seen since John Stuart Mill. It rests on more than its influence in renewing philosophical defenses of human rights. Rawls's most distinctive contribution to the tradition of grand theory is his defense of a method of justification, which he calls "reflective equilibrium."

Grand theorists as different as Plato, Hobbes, and Mill wrote as if their conceptions of justice were justified for all people at all times. They searched for a set of eternal forms, a self-evident truth, or a very simple first principle from which to derive all practical moral imperatives. In defending the method of "reflective equilibrium," Rawls is the most modest, and in this respect wisest, of the grand philosophers. He argues that we have no better way of justifying principles that meet the minimum standards of moral reason (logical consistency, generality, and so on) than by translating the principles into social practices and judging whether the practices are consistent with our moral convictions. If a practice derived from the principles conflicts with a conviction, then we must either reformulate the principle or change our conviction. To decide which course to take, we must use our practical judgment to weigh a variety of considerations (the firmness and consistency of our convictions, the certainty of the principles and of the evidence underlying the practice, and so on).

When philosophers sidestep this process of approaching reflective equilibrium, they act on faith rather than reason.

Most philosophers today accept some version of Rawls's method of "reflective equilibrium," but few—including Rawls himself—actually practice it, at least in public. In *A Theory of Justice* and subsequent writings, Rawls stops short of translating his two principles into specific social practices and judging the principles in light of common convictions concerning the practices, even though this step is essential to the method of justification that he defends. The most distinctive principle of Rawls's theory, the "difference principle," is also the most counterintuitive. Is a society unjust if it falls short of *maximizing* benefits to the least advantaged? Outside the "original position," it seems more reasonable to call a society unjust if it fails to provide everyone with decent life prospects (adequate not optimal health care, housing, education, and income) and with the freedoms necessary to participate as an equal citizen in influencing the remaining distributions. The "difference principle" seems not to leave enough moral room for democratic decision making, or for distributions according to desert—not even for Nobel Prizes or Most Valuable Player awards (unless they can be shown to maximize the life prospects of the least advantaged).

But to invoke my intuitions, or anyone else's, against Rawls's does not constitute a devastating criticism of his theory—not only because his intuitions may be morally better, but more important because the method of "reflective equilibrium" welcomes just this kind of criticism. It challenges every critic to offer constructive revisions of justice as fairness, to defend another systematic theory whose premises and conclusions are more intuitively compelling, or to justify something other than a systematic theory (such as a plurality of principles refined and balanced by our practical judgment of particular cases). This is a formidable but fair challenge. An extraordinary number of philosophers, political scientists, economists, and constitutional lawyers have accepted it. □

20

A CIRCULAR PROCEDURE IN ETHICS

IN THE April, 1951, issue of this REVIEW, Mr. Rawls attempts to outline a reasonable procedure for making ethical decisions. Although I feel sympathy for some of Mr. Rawls's aims in this respect, I cannot agree that he is successful in carrying them out and I therefore wish to make the following critical comments.

What Mr. Rawls says seems to me best understood as an attempt to rehabilitate intuitionism in ethics. His program is first of all to define a class of competent moral judges, then to discover what moral judgements they actually intuit (cf. p. 183, 2.5 [vii]) and then finally, using these intuitions as a basis, to work out a set of moral principles.

Thus Mr. Rawls's procedure is really an attempt to answer the awkward questions posed to intuitionists: How can you tell whether your moral intuitions are true or false? Since intuitions differ, what is the test of their validity?

Mr. Rawls's reply is to the effect that we may presume that competent moral judges make correct intuitions and that from these we may derive general principles which we may then use to test the intuitions of ordinary erring mortals.

Mr. Rawls defends this procedure by drawing an analogy with inductive logic. But *is* this how we arrive at the principles of inductive logic (or deductive logic for that matter)? I for one have never read a book on logical principles which proceeded in this fashion: "X is a competent thinker. One day when X was particularly clearheaded and disinterested he pronounced such and such an argument to be satisfactory. The form of this argument is so-and-so; therefore we may assert that arguments of this form are good inductive arguments," etc.

Perhaps Mr. Rawls is prepared to give up his analogy but to maintain nevertheless that this is a suitable procedure for ethics. If so my next complaint is that he does not in fact carry out this procedure himself — in fact he does not take his own described procedure seriously. Thus having defined his class of competent judges and described how moral principles are explicated from their decisions, he then (p. 191,5.5) provisionally enunciates these principles. But the justification of these principles according to his own described method is lacking, and I can no more find his method of procedure in his own article than

21

I can find the analogous procedure in logic books. I had looked forward to reading, for instance, that on a famous occasion George Washington refused to tell a lie and that from this, together with similar tales, we could explicate the moral principle that one should not lie in order to get out of a difficult situation. However, in this expectation, I was disappointed. Mr. Rawls produces his moral principles but cites no actual cases of the moral intuitions upon which we are to presume that they are based.

More important is my further contention that Mr. Rawls's procedure is circular. This is so because the criteria by which the competent moral judges are selected are either inadequate for the task or else they already contain explicitly or implicitly the moral standards that are later to be found by explication from the judges' decisions. The characteristics of Mr. Rawls's judges, such as intelligence, reasonableness, impartiality, sympathy, are already moral or quasi-moral criteria — they already contain the moral standards which are later to be derived from the judges' decisions. The moral principles enunciated by Mr. Rawls are just the sort that one would expect a reasonable, intelligent, impartial man to act upon. If a man did not act upon these principles, then he would not deserve these laudatory qualifying adjectives and he would not be a morally competent judge. One can go directly from the criteria which determine the judges to the principles their decisions will exemplify *without examining actual judges or considering their actual decisions* and this is just what Mr. Rawls does, and that is why he does not bother to tell us delightful stories about George Washington and other moral heroes.

Mr. Rawls's procedure establishes moral principles only by assuming them at the beginning in a slightly different form, and of course this could not be avoided. If one is going to select morally competent judges one must use moral criteria — if one uses nonmoral criteria then there are no grounds for believing that the persons selected are morally competent. Thus they may be selected on the basis of their wealth, class, degree of education or physical development, but these criteria are inadequate; and, if anyone tries to argue that they are adequate, he can only do so by trying to show that these nonmoral characteristics are at least closely correlated with the possession of certain moral characteristics.

Mr. Rawls anticipates and tries to refute the charge of circularity by saying that the competent judge is not defined by what he says in particular cases, nor by what principles he expresses or adopts. He says that competence is determined solely by the possession of certain characteristics, some of which may be said to be capacities and achievements, while others may be said to be virtues (p. 180,2.4).

Concerning this defence two things may be said. Firstly, even if Mr. Rawls's statement be accepted, it does not touch the criticism I have leveled at his argument. No matter what procedure one uses to select the judges the criteria must involve moral characteristics, and whatever moral characteristics one chooses they will be reflected in the moral principles that are finally explicated. Secondly, the kind of distinction that Mr. Rawls makes between a man's characteristics and virtues and his particular acts and decisions will not do, for there is no other way of knowing a man's characteristics and virtues than that of observing what he says and does. One cannot legitimately say, "I know X is intelligent although I am completely unacquainted with his words and deeds."

Therefore, although I find much of Mr. Rawls's article interesting and suggestive, I conclude from the above analysis that his central thesis is valueless, being merely a complicated way of saying: Virtue is what is intuited to be virtue by the virtuous man.

ANTHONY M. MARDIROS

University of Alberta

RULE-UTILITARIANISM

By Joseph Margolis

The care and feeding of the utilitarian principle is one of the abiding concerns of ethical theory. It has been defended against egoism and against intuitionism and, most recently, against itself. Ideal utilitarianism has had to contend with hedonic utilitarianism, and rule-utilitarianism with act-utilitarianism. I am concerned here primarily with the last of these quarrels and with the possible implications of carrying it one step further.

W. D. Ross had, in his *The Right and the Good*,[1] decisively challenged all efforts to make act-utilitarianism a comprehensive principle on which to judge ethical issues. The reason one ought to keep a promise, he explained, is simply that one had made a promise, not consideration of the possible consequences (bonific or optimific) of doing so. He added also that the question of consequences did not even arise as a *prima facie* consideration and that, if it were raised, it could not be said to be self-evident that doing what was right would produce bonific or optimific consequences.[2] His arguments, direct and telling, collected the scattered objections of an earlier tradition, notably incorporating the views of Butler, and were accepted by more recent utilitarian-minded theorists not prepared to accept his intuitionism.

---

[1] Oxford, 1930.
[2] Cf. *op. cit.*, Ch. 2.

This was a considerable tribute. Current utilitarianism tends to agree that, following a distinction advanced by John Rawls, utilitarian considerations are not eligible in offering reasons for right acts.[3] Rawls correctly points out that one cannot defend his keeping a promise because it would have good consequences—the outcome would be that one might defend his breaking a promise because it too might have good consequences; but he insists that, though an act cannot be so defended, a practice can be (and reasonably may be required to be) defended on utilitarian grounds. This is what is meant by rule-utilitarianism. In fact, Rawls offers the ingenious (and convincing) explanation that "there are obvious utilitarian advantages in having a practice which denies to the promisor, as a defence, any general appeal to the utilitarian principle in accordance with which the practice itself may be justified".[4] Rawls thereby outflanks by adoption, the anti-utilitarian arguments of Ross.

The question needs to be asked whether Rawl's manoeuvre, attractive in itself, is put forward in a defensible form and, further, whether it is in principle possible to formulate it adequately. To state the same in another way: Is act-utilitarianism altogether indefensible and can rule-utilitarianism be sufficiently distinguished from act-utilitarianism? I am inclined to answer both these questions, No. The importance of the counter-argument is not so much that it exhibits certain difficulties inherent in rule-utilitarianism as it is that it suggests the impossibility of formulating a comprehensive principle on which all ethical judgments can be defended.

The strategy I adopt is this. I first identify certain kinds of cases in which utilitarian considerations are relevant. If these can be supported, Rawl's restriction about the eligibility of such considerations falls. I next consider Rawl's own formulation of rule-utilitarianism and show why these kinds of cases cannot be managed on his account and, further, why it is inherently impossible to distinguish rule-utilitarianism from act-utilitarianism. I then consider how, if the matter were pressed, it might be shown to be extremely difficult to distinguish rule- or act-utilitarianism from intuitionism (at least that form of intuitionism advocated by Ross).

I ask you to consider the case of the thalidomide babies. One of our ethical practices holds that we ought not to take the life of another human being. The practice is to be construed, and may be shown, to provide that certain excuses and exceptions and the

---

[3] "Two Concepts of Rules", *Philosophical Review*, LXIV (1955), 3-22.
[4] Ibid., 16.

like are part of the sense of the practice. Killing enemy soldiers during wartime, self-defence, accidental homicide are all comprehended within the practice of not taking another's life. The killing of thalidomide babies is not obviously provided for in the practice (in the sense in which a rule would provide for its defensibility). One cannot simply say that the killing of these babies is *right* as one can say that the killing of the enemy is *right*. I think we are prepared to concede, however, that though it is *wrong* to take another's life, it might have very significant bonific (or even optimific) consequences to end the lives of such terribly handicapped infants; that, furthermore, since such an act would have such *good* consequences (and avoid such evil consequences) it might therefore be right. I am not saying that it would be right or wrong but only that we would regard the debate as *eligible*. For if it were eligible, it would follow that utilitarian considerations are *sometimes* open in the defence of an act that otherwise falls under a practice defining what is right. I am saying that if we construe a practice as open to utilitarian defence, we should be obliged to admit such a defence for acts as well. I am not insisting that practices require utilitarian defence.

I am arguing from what are known as "hard cases". Breaking a promise under certain extraordinary circumstances, the killing of a moral monster, the taking of life of thalidomide babies, acts of mercy killing and the like *sometimes* may be so construed that *utilitarian considerations rather than the provisions implicit in the practice itself* may be entitled to a hearing. Under such circumstances, I am saying, Rawls' distinction between justifying an act and justifying a practice founders. Furthermore, we may suspect that the difference between utilitarian consequences and provisions inherent in a practice cannot be easily formulated; and that, if they cannot, the distinction between intuitionist grounds for particular acts and utilitarian grounds also cannot be sharply drawn.

Consider now Rawls' own account. One of the requirements for the defence of rule-utilitarianism, as he rightly sees, is the provision of an adequate conception of a rule. Rawls rejects one possible way of construing a rule, that is, as a summary of past decisions and acts that may serve as a guide for future conduct. The difficulty with this view is that, in principle, utilitarian considerations will have been employed in judging the individual cases on which the rule itself is based; Ross' objections will then be unanswerable. Also, it will not be possible to formulate what is to count as a breach of the rule. Rawls' own preference is for what he calls "the practice conception", that is, the view that "rules are pictured as defining a practice".[5] As he says further (and fairly): "it is essential to the notion of a practice that the rules are publicly known and understood as definitive".[6] This is not to say that excuses and exceptions and the like are not eligible but rather that they are provided for in the formulation of the full rule. From this point of view, appeal to an exception is an appeal to a rule and not to utilitarian considerations; the latter apply only to the justification of the practice, never to acts that fall under a practice.

It needs to be said that Rawls is, in a way, the first to notice the strain of this second conception of rules. He does say, for instance:

> utilitarians would be inclined to hold that some reliance on people's *good sense* and some concession to *hard cases* is necessary. They would hold that a practice is justified by serving the interests of those who take part in it; and as with any set of rules there is understood a background of circumstances under which it is expected to be applied and which need not—indeed which *cannot*—be fully stated. Should these circumstances change, then *even if there is no rule* which provides for the case, it may still be in accordance with the practice that one be released from one's obligation. But this sort of defence allowed by a practice must not be confused with the general option to weight each particular case on utilitarian grounds . . .[7]

I have italicized the important phrases, the phrases that show us that act- and rule-utilitarianism cannot be sharply distinguished and, even that (Ross') intuitionism and utilitarianism cannot be sharply distinguished. Though Rawls sees a possible objection to rule-utilitarianism, he does not think it is a telling one. I think he is mistaken.

Hard cases, like the case of the thalidomide babies, are not clearly subsumable under the rule defining a practice; they constitute a challenge to any formulated rule—that is their precise contribution. If one were to hold that hard cases are comprehended under a practice, even if not under a rule defining a practice (as Rawls says), rule-utilitarianism would fall and we would have to admit that utilitarian considerations directly at times apply to the judging of particular acts. Alternatively put, if no adequate rule can in principle be formulated for a given practice, then

---

[5] Ibid., 24.
[6] Ibid., 24.
[7] Ibid., 17.

(without raising any questions whatsoever about the proper account of what a rule is)[8] it would not be possible to distinguish completely between act-utilitarianism and rule-utilitarianism. *A fortiori*, there would be no rule for deciding which were the hard cases in which utilitarian considerations would apply and which ordinary cases where (following Ross) they would not apply. In short, what Rawls chooses to call "good sense" in judging "hard cases" may, in the absence of rules governing acts (granting, with him, the inappropriateness of utilitarian reasons in defending particular acts), be just as readily construed in intuitionist terms (in Ross' manner) as in terms of practices defended on utilitarian grounds.

An intuitionist like Ross might in fact very well claim that taking the life of a thalidomide baby was right, that it was *prima facie* right not to allow such senseless handicap and likelihood of suffering. By such a move, he would absorb allegedly utilitarian considerations into his own view. We should still be able to distinguish the intuitionist and utilitarian conceptions but it would no longer be pertinent to distinguish the justification of acts and practices on the eligibility of utilitarian reasons; it could no longer be maintained that suitable rules could be formulated on which to judge acts, and the very concept of a defence of a practice would therefore collapse. Only if a rule could be formulated on which to judge acts in accord with a practice, could it make sense to ask for a defence of the practice. For without such a rule, the so-called practice would merely be a summary of the kinds of properties right actions exhibit rather than of the kinds of reasons that make right actions right. The *reasons* a utilitarian might give for judging a *practice* might, by an intuitionist, be construed as the characteristic *properties* that right *acts* possess. There would then be no practice, in any sense independently formulable, to be defended at all—nothing but the acts themselves, which may exhibit a significant uniformity.

It may be added that Rawls' proposal regarding rule-utilitarianism is "bracketed" by him in an important way. He wishes to hold that the utilitarian position may be strengthened by his proposal, not that the view is "completely defensible".[9] The fact is that Rawls is primarily interested in the question of justifying a practice and not, narrowly, in a utilitarian defence. What we have attempted to show is the weakness inherent in contrasting the defence of an act and of a practice defined by a rule. But it needs also to be mentioned, what is, however, no part of the present

---

[8] Cf. B. J. Diggs, "Rules and Utilitarianism", *American Philosophical Quarterly*, I (1964), 1-13.

[9] *Op. cit.*, 24.

issue, that even if a practice calls for defence, utilitarian defence is by no means the only one available. And, in fact, Rawls himself pointedly draws our attention elsewhere to this new possibility.[10]

University of Cincinnati, Ohio.

---

[10] Cf. "Justice as Fairness", *Philosophical Review*, LXVII (1958), 164-194.

DISCUSSIONS

"TWO CONCEPTS OF RULES"—A NOTE

BY H. J. McCLOSKEY

In his article, " Two Concepts of Rules ",[1] John Rawls, by reference to the distinction between two types of rules, summary rules and rules defining a practice, claims to be able to set out a form of utilitarianism which will escape certain of the standard objections to utilitarianism. He illustrates his contention by reference to punishment and promise-keeping. This article has attracted a good deal of attention during the past 16 years, and is treated as essential reading for any serious student of utilitarianism. I wish here to argue that the argument of the article rests on a simple and evident fallacy.

Rawls' contention is that rules which define a practice, by contrast with summary rules which are generalizations about past decisions and past experience, are logically prior to the practice, and such that an act falling under the rule cannot be described without reference to the rule. Clearly there are rules of this kind, even though it may be disputed whether either of the examples Rawls gives, is an example of such a rule. (It is not my purpose here to discuss the latter issue. It is discussed fully enough in my article " An Examination of Restricted Utilitarianism ").[2] Rawls is correct too in pointing to rules in games, e.g. in chess or in football, as examples of such rules, and to acts of the players, *qua* players, as examples of acts which can be described only by reference to the relevant rules. Consider the statement : ' Smith scored a goal '. Until we know the game concerned and its rules—football, soccer, hockey, or basketball—i.e., until we know the rules which define the act of scoring a goal, we do not know what Smith did.

Rawls uses this distinction to argue that exceptions to rules in practice which appear to have a utilitarian justification, cannot really have a utilitarian justification. Thus he argues that Carritt's example of an act of framing an innocent person in order to combat an outbreak of cruel crimes which appears to have a utilitarian justification, cannot in fact be justified even if Carritt's factual claim that such a murder would really reduce the occurrence of the crime in that particular situation were correct. Similarly a breach of a promise which appears to have good utilitarian consequences and which does not fall under one of the types of exceptions allowed by the rule in practice (which itself has a utilitarian justification as such) would in fact have no utilitarian justification. Rawls' argument is that such exceptions would change the practice to being a practice of a significantly different

[1]*Philosophical Review*, Vol. 64 (1955), pp. 3-32. Page references are to this article.
[2]*Philosophical Review*, Vol. 66 (1957), pp. 466-85.

kind, and one which would not have the same utilitarian justification. Punishment would be changed to telishment, where the latter lacks the utilitarian justification of the former (pp. 11-12), and the practice of promise-keeping, the point of which is " to abdicate one's title to act in accordance with utilitarian and prudential considerations in order that the future may be tied down and plans co-ordinated in advance " (p. 16) would become a different and less useful practice. Rawls supports these contentions with impressive reasons. None the less his claims here are also open to question, as I have argued in the article cited above. However, this too is not the issue I wish to press here.

The claim I am concerned to question, and that which is essential if Rawls' argument is to succeed is that to make an exception to the rule in practice is to change the practice. Here, possibly because he is misled by an analogy with chess (where the players are also the officials, adjudicators and legislators concerning the rules if they so choose), Rawls seems to confuse a number of types of exceptions with the least usual type of exception which occurs in respect of rules which define a practice. This can best be illustrated by reference to punishment and rules in games such as Australian Rules football. The types of exceptions which he assimilates to the one type, and which need to be distinguished are : (i) Exceptions permitted by the legislators and written into the rules by way of giving discretionary powers to the police and/or the judiciary. Rawls must, if his argument is to succeed, treat all exceptions by officials and private individuals as being of this type. (ii) Exceptions made by some, few, individual officials (umpires) without the knowledge or consent of the legislators and the majority of other officials, and where the individuals publicly express profound respect for the rule in practice as one which ought not to be infringed. (iii) Exceptions to the rule which defines the practice by some individual officials (umpires) which are in no way concealed but which are publicly known. (iv) Exceptions made in secret by private individuals (players of the game). (v) Exceptions made publicly by private individuals (players of the game).

Only exceptions of type (i) *must* involve a change in the rule in practice. Exceptions of type (ii), provided they are as described, the exception and not common practice, would not alter the nature of the practice nor the rule defining the practice. Exceptions of type (iii) would affect the rule in practice only if they were likely to be generally imitated. If they are not of common occurrence such imitation is unlikely. In any case, the practice, and the rule defining it, would change only after imitation of the exception became commonplace. Further, such exceptions as of kinds (ii) and (iii) are possible under the kind of rule of punishment (and promise-keeping) for which Rawls argues as being justifiable utilitarian rules. Consider the institution of punishment. Rawls defines punishment thus :

> A person is said to suffer punishment whenever he is legally deprived of some of the normal rights of a citizen on the grounds that he has violated a rule of law, the violation having been established by trial according to the due pro-

cess of law, provided that the deprivation is carried out by the recognized legal authorities of the state, that the courts construe the statutes strictly, and that the statute was on the books prior to the time of the offense. (p. 10)

We know that under our rule in practice concerning punishment, which is one of a large range of very different institutions of punishments which would come under the description or definition of punishment set out by Rawls, some of which are just and some unjust, discretionary power cannot be withheld from the judiciary and the police. We know that under Australian rules concerning the institution of punishment, the judge can and even must at times use his discretion, and that he can use it unfairly to influence the jury against the accused whilst keeping his comments within what is permitted by the law. We know how easy it is or would be for an unscrupulous policeman to frame an individual, for example, by planting a drug on him, and arresting him for possessing the drug. One does not have to be a cynic to believe that some such immoral acts occur in one or other of the Western democracies, all of whose systems of punishment conform roughly with Rawls' definition of punishment. It is true that Rawls would not call the punishment which results from such abuses of office by the judge or policeman, punishment, but what is important here is that the institution allows the exercise of such discretionary powers to the officials, and cannot avoid doing so. Yet, unless abuses of power are widespread, the institution, the rules which define the practice, do not change.

A reference to the game of football will illustrate the point that such exceptions (abuses) do not change the practice, or in this case, the game. An umpire, for example, a goal umpire, may as a result of accepting a bribe decide for one match to count every doubtful goal or near miss by the Eagles as a goal, and to score every doubtful goal by the Falcons as a point. This is possible in a game such as Australian Rules football where the ball may be kicked higher than the posts and still be deemed a goal if its course falls between the line of the goal posts. It is deemed a behind—a point—if it passes between the goal and point posts. Many decisions are very difficult for the honest, conscientious umpire. The goal umpire is in the best position to make the judgment, and because of the honesty of these umpires, their judgment is generally respected by players and spectators alike even though it is accepted that from time to time honest mistakes are made. Our corrupt umpire would not alter the practice, in this case, the game. Examples of type (iii) are evidently more common than the foregoing type in Australian football. Some umpires deliberately do not penalize certain breaches of the rules—this may be so as to keep the game flowing. Others interpret such a rule as that the ball cannot be carried for more than 10 yards without bouncing it, generously and allow the players to run 15 or even 20 yards without penalty. Spectators and players accept such " interpretations " of the rules, provided they are consistently applied. The rules of football have not changed simply because one umpire at one ground has used his discretion—a discretion inseparable from his role as umpire—to interpret and apply the rules in a certain way. It may be true that the game he umpires that day is not football as defined by the rules, and that it is different from the game played at another ground as a game of football. However, the rules in practice of Australian football remain what the legislators define them as being, and in the next round of games the players will, by and large, conform with and the umpires will, by and large, look upon the rules formulated by the legislators as standards or norms to obey or enforce as the case may be. To press the claim that the fact that the umpire cannot but have discretionary powers which may be mistakenly exercised changes the game, would involve allowing that perhaps the game of Australian football is never played—and similarly with the " games " of punishment and promise-making and keeping. Hart's discussion of what it is for legal and social rules to exist is relevant here.[3]

Exceptions of types (iv) and (v) are of the kind that most critics of utilitarianism, including possibly Carritt, have had in mind, especially in respect of punishment. (It is true that Carritt's wording of his example gives the impression that he is prepared to argue for discretionary power being given to the judiciary and/or the police, but his example need not be construed in that way. Certainly, it readily admits of restatement in terms of it being an individual utilitarian, a sincere and dedicated utilitarian such as Henry Sidgwick who is prepared to accept hypocrisy when it is demanded by utilitarian considerations, and who therefore is, as a private citizen, prepared to frame an innocent person to prevent evil consequences, whilst at the same time severely condemning perjury.) Such exceptions by no means alter the nature of the rule in practice. This is equally true of the publicly known exception as of the secret exception to the rule in practice. Publicly known exceptions to the rule, where the exception is based on utilitarian considerations, no more alter the rule than do prudential or selfish exceptions, which may be crimes, and punished as such.

The games analogy helps to bring this out. It is contrary to a rule of Australian football for one player to hold another except when the player held possesses the ball. It is a common practice for full-backs covertly to hold full-forwards by their shorts, and this, in order to promote what they see as the good, victory for their side. They commonly escape detection by the umpires. Yet this does not alter the rule in practice which defines the game, Australian football, for when detected, as with offences against the criminal law, the rule is applied. The ordinary citizen is in the position of the player and his secret or public illegal acts no more alter the rule than do the undetected or detected breaches of the rules of players of a game.

Players commonly infringe rules of the game, hopefully that they will not be penalized by the umpire, in order to win, just as ordinary citizens, for instance the doctor who in his own car and without police permission exceeds the speed limit in order to get a dying child to hospital, does in

[3] H. L. A. Hart, *The Concept of Law* (Oxford, 1961), Chs. IV and V.

respect of the law. Such acts—and there are many violators of traffic laws on utilitarian grounds—in no way alter the rule in practice, provided that there remains a general convergence of behaviour in conformity with the rule and provided the officials generally, usually, accept the rule as a norm or standard.

It is essential for Rawls' argument if it is to establish what Rawls seeks to establish, that exceptions of types (ii) to (v) be not simply assimilated to but identified with exceptions of type (i). The foregoing arguments would suggest that there is a vast difference between these types of exceptions, and hence that the version of rule utilitarianism which rests its case on Rawls' contention fails to establish what it seeks to establish, namely that it avoids certain of the difficulties of act utilitarianism.

La Trobe University.

CONTRACTUALISM AND MORAL CRITICISM

NORMAN S. CARE

I

W<small>HAT FOLLOWS IS A LIMITED STUDY</small> of a recent view in moral and political philosophy as it has been developed by John Rawls and applied by W. G. Runciman.[1] I will call the view "contractualism." In general I argue that its structure is such that contractualism cannot achieve certain aims it might seem to be directed toward securing. My hope is that in particular the discussion clarifies the sense in which contractualism is a moral theory, and provides some assessment of it as a normative account of moral criticism. I hesitate to say that the discussion provides a criticism of contractualism, since the intended comprehensiveness of that view as regards different questions of moral philosophy is not yet plain. But even if the discussion does not provide a criticism, such clarification and assessment as it affords may be useful, for it is always desirable to understand about a theory that concerns social morality what its resources are regarding competing accounts of the nature of morality and regarding the objectivity of moral criticism.

---

[1] I will use initials to refer to Rawls' papers, which are as follows: "Outline of a Decision-Procedure for Ethics," in *The Philosophical Review,* LX (1951) [ODPE]; "Justice as Fairness," in *The Philosophical Review,* LXVII (1958), reprinted (slightly revised) in Peter Laslett and W. G. Runciman (eds.), *Philosophy, Politics, and Society,* Second Series (Oxford, 1962; my page references are to the reprint in Laslett and Runciman) [JF]; "Constitutional Liberty and the Concept of Justice," in Carl J. Friedrich and John W. Chapman (eds.), *Nomos VI: Justice* (New York, 1963) [CLCJ]; "The Sense of Justice," in *The Philosophical Review,* LXXII (1963) [SJ]; and "Distributive Justice," in Peter Laslett and W. G. Runciman (eds.), *Philosophy, Politics, and Society,* Third Series (Oxford, 1967) [DJ]. Part Four of W. G. Runciman's *Relative Deprivation and Social Justice* (Berkeley and Los Angeles, 1966) is a detailed attempt to apply contractualism normatively.

II

I begin by offering a reading of a proposition which Rawls refers to as a "theorem," and which he intends to be construed as a necessary truth. This theorem, I take it, lies at the heart of contractualism, and its structure is what suggests those limitations of the view which I wish to bring out. The interest of the theorem is that it is proffered as a general way of grounding or accounting for moral principles that is an alternative to recourse to intuition or a priori factors (cf. JF, p. 136). The form of the theorem may be set out in this way:

(T)   When persons are of a certain nature (P), and their circumstances are of a certain kind (C), and they accept (or have imposed on them) a certain deliberating-procedure (D-M), these persons will acknowledge, i.e., accept, moral principles of a certain type, e.g., (J_1) and (J_2).

The following remarks provide some description of the contents which Rawls' contractualism gives to (T).

Very briefly: (P) is to be thought of as a set of statements providing a characterization of persons as we know them: e.g., persons are characterized as beings who have needs, interests, and desires, some of which they have in common so that cooperation among them is possible, and who are rational in the sense that goes with the capacity to assess and criticize the social system of practices and institutions they possess. The characterization given in (P) is not meant to be technical or artificial in the sense of claiming any philosophically controversial properties for men, such as their possessing "natural rights" in the quasi-factual sense associated with Locke's account of men in the state of nature. (C) is to be thought of similarly as a set of statements, in this case providing a description of the social circumstances in which the persons described in (P) find themselves. In particular, these circumstances (which Rawls calls "typical circumstances of justice") are such that persons have conflicting claims on the design of their social system in the sense that not all the demands the system places on any one of them are always in his interest.

Finally, the element (D-M) is meant to represent the response we may imagine these persons making to the conflict they experience in their social circumstances. We are in effect to picture them (all) engaging in deliberations to the end of establishing standards (not practices) in light of which they may assess their practices and institutions and thus enable themselves to attempt reform where necessary. But since deliberations do not take place either automatically or efficiently when persons with a problem of mutual interest gather together, it is of major importance to note that the persons in question structure their deliberations. That is, they first of all accept (or have imposed on them)[2] a *procedure* under which they carry on their deliberations. Rawls describes this procedure as "expressing the constraints of morality," and specifies it as follows: all parties accept (or have imposed on them) as guides for their deliberations:

(a)   that the standards any one of them proposes for mutual acceptance by all be thought of as applicable to all, including the proposer,

(b)   that the standards be accepted by all as binding forever (and hence on their children as well as themselves),

(c)   that the standards be proposed from behind a "veil of ignorance" respecting the proposer's personal needs, interests, social station, etc.[3]

Given this set of antecedent conditions, i.e., given the truth of descriptions (P) and (C) together with the stipulation of acceptance (or imposition) of a deliberation-procedure expressing moral constraints (D-M), it is claimed that the product of the deliberations of these persons will be their acceptance of (something like) the following "principles of justice" as standards for the assessment of their practices and institutions:

---

[2] Rawls sometimes uses the language of acceptance and sometimes the language of imposition. Cf., JF, pp. 138-139; CLCJ, p. 103; and SJ, p. 282.
    [3] The graphic phrase "veil of ignorance" appears in DJ, p. 60, though words to its effect appear elsewhere; for example, in JF, p. 138, persons agree to be bound by the standards "in future circumstances, the peculiarities of which cannot be known," and in JF, p. 138, CLCJ, p. 104, and SJ, p. 283, they agree that none of them is to be "given the opportunity to tailor the canons of a legitimate complaint to fit his own condition."

(J₁)   An equal-liberty principle: "each person participating in a
        practice, or affected by it, has an equal right to the most
        extensive liberty compatible with a like liberty for all" (JF,
        p. 133).

(J₂)   a. A "difference" principle: inequalities involved in practices
        are tolerable provided "they are part of a larger system in
        which they work out to the advantage of the most unfortunate
        representative man" (DJ, p. 67).[4]
        b. An open-offices principle: inequalities involved in practices
        are tolerable "provided the positions and offices to which they
        attach, or from which they may be gained, are open to all"
        (JF, p. 133).[5]

I note just two points about this reading of contractualism
before proceeding. First, Rawls refers to the large number of
conditions briefly sketched here as forming an "analytic construction," [6] and he claims that (T) is a theorem, or necessary truth,
in the sense that when persons do not possess principles like
(J_1) and (J_2) we may infer that some condition(s) in the antecedent of (T) is (are) not fulfilled (JF, p. 141). Second, I place
some emphasis (as others have not) upon the fact that the antecedent of (T) contains the stipulation of acceptance (or imposition)
of (D-M), for it is only when this element accompanies the descriptive accounts (P) and (C), I think, that one is at least prompted
to think of something of the order of principles as ensuing from
the specified conditions. It is at the heart of my reading of contractualism that (T) expresses the intuitive idea that procedural
constraints may be relied upon to produce mutual agreement on
first principles among (so to speak) men of good will. In what

---

[4] I think the difference principle has the status, for Rawls, of an
interpretation of a "greatest-advantage" principle. In JF, p. 133, Rawls
expresses the principle he interprets as the difference principle in DJ,
pp. 66-68 in these words: "inequalities are arbitrary unless it is reasonable
to expect that they will work out for everyone's advantage." The important
point is that the difference principle, like the others in the set, is to be
thought of as a product of the deliberations in question. Cf., DJ, p. 68.

[5] The two principles in (J_2) are designed to show when it is tolerable
to violate the original position of equal liberty specified in (J_1). That is
why they are grouped together, rather than set out independently. Inci-
dentally, I see no commitment in Rawls' development of contractualism
to the effect that a and b exhaust the principles by which inequalities are
judged tolerable or not.

[6] In CLCJ and SJ.

follows I will not challenge either this idea or the claim that the contents which Rawls' contractualism gives to (T) express this idea successfully. That is, I will accept the view that (T), when filled out in the way Rawls suggests, is a necessary truth, and I will consider certain of the aims of contractualism in light of this understanding of (T).

III

One of the most important critical aims of contractualism is to show how, "as an interpretation of the basis of the principles of justice, classical utilitarianism is mistaken" (JF, p. 152). The mistake in the utilitarian account, according to Rawls, is that it is "unable to account" for a central element in the concept of justice, namely, the idea of fairness (JF, p. 132). And it is precisely this element that is emphasized by contractualism, for the theorem sketched above is meant to express fairness as "the possibility of mutual acknowledgement of principles by free persons who have no authority over one another," and it is this concept of fairness which is "fundamental to justice" (JF, p. 144).

But reflection upon the structure of contractualism indicates that this critique of classical utilitarianism is premature. The way in which it is premature is given in these points: first, that the structure of contractualism is compatible with utilitarianism; second, that therefore the idea of fairness is compatible with utilitarianism; and third, that the question of what procedure expresses the "constraints of morality" is not obvious and hence cannot be specified without argument.

What makes it possible to suppose that contractualism is compatible with utilitarianism is, first, that contractualism is at bottom a vehicle by which views concerning the nature of morality may be expressed, and second, that utilitarianism can be construed as at bottom a view about the nature of morality—in the classical language, a view about what is the "foundation" of morality. Insofar as the deliberating-procedure which is accepted (or imposed) as part of the antecedent of (T) is given by stipulation, one may suppose that there are possible alternative deliberating-procedures equally open to stipulation. This possibility seems implicit in Rawls' own description of his view as the contract doctrine "in its Kantian formulation" (DJ, p. 60). This description permits us to suppose that there may be other "formulations" of the contract doctrine, one of which might be recognizably utilitarian. Insofar as the nature of morality is concerned the issue does not turn on contractualism *per se*, but rather on which of its formulations provides an adequate account of morality.'

If this is so, then one may suppose that utilitarianism need not be construed as precluding in any strict way the notion of fairness which Rawls specifies. For that notion, as I understand it, concerns how moral standards are arrived at rather than what they are,' but its concern is such as not to dictate what in particular is the procedure which persons must be thought of as accepting (or having imposed upon them) to structure their deliberations. Rawls writes that classical utilitarianism assimilated justice "to a higher order executive decision" (JF, p. 151), which brings to mind a picture in which standards for the assessment of a social system are laid down from on high by administrators concerned to secure utility. But this assimilation is *not* a necessary feature of utilitarianism.' The natural point at which the utilitarian will take issue with contractualism "in its Kantian formulation" is that point at which the latter formulation is distinctively Kantian. And where Rawls' contractualism is distinctively Kantian is in its account of what procedure it is that expresses the constraints of morality. For example, the third part of that procedure, according to which standards are proposed from behind a "veil of ignorance," is designed to express the typically Kantian objection to "heteronomy" in the determination of right.

While my purpose here is not to defend a utilitarian formulation of the contract doctrine, its possibility does not seem excessively remote. The main point is that the difference between

---

' Rawls sometimes speaks of the theory of the social contract as the "traditional rival" of utilitarianism, e.g., in DJ, p. 59. I am suggesting that it is the social-contract theory "in its Kantian formulation" which is the rival of utilitarianism.

' It follows that it is a mistake to think that utilitarianism must deny that principles such as (J_1) and (J_2) are principles of justice.

' Cf., Everett W. Hall, "Justice as Fairness: A Modernized Version of the Social Contract," in *The Journal of Philosophy*, LIV (1957), p. 668. Hall's paper is a discussion of Rawls' earlier version of "Justice as Fairness," published in *The Journal of Philosophy*, LIV (1957).

contractualism in its Kantian and utilitarian formulations will be a difference in accounts of what procedures may be said to express moral constraints. One may speculate that in contrast with part (c) of Rawls' Kantian account of such a procedure, and perhaps with part (b) as well, a recognizably utilitarian procedure might involve persons in proposing standards *from* an explicit concern for the needs and interests of all parties to the deliberations (including those of the proposer), so far as they can be known to them; and it might commit them to such standards only for agreed-upon periods of time, such as a generation, followed by systematic review of their adequacy. It is plain at least that such a procedure will differ from the procedure which Rawls specifies; and it is not plain that such notions as those of deliberating from a concern for the needs and interests of both oneself and others,[19] and of subjecting standards to periodic review, have no moral credentials. In general: the idea of a procedure for deliberations is the idea of something to which there are alternatives, and it is not obvious that some one procedure, and no other(s), may be said to express the constraints of morality; if contractualism requires that we stipulate the procedure which is accepted by (or imposed upon) persons, then it does not itself determine what procedure is to be stipulated; and if it is thus open to different stipulations of procedures, it does not itself decide between them. In this sense the contractualist claim that utilitarianism is mistaken as regards the interpretation of the basis of the principles of justice is premature. For utilitarianism, like Kantian moral philosophy, may be viewed as a theory about what are the constraints of morality, in which case it is independent of, and not in competition with, contractualism *per se.*

---

[19] Proposing standards from an explicit concern for persons' needs and interests, including those of the proposer, need not preclude their being proposed disinterestedly. Cf. the chapter "Moral Theory" in S. I. Benn and R. S. Peters, *The Principles of Political Thought* (British title: *Social Principles and the Democratic State*) (New York, 1959; London, 1959), for the view that disinterestedness is a "formal" criterion of morality. Benn and Peters describe themselves as espousing a "cautious utilitarianism" (p. 5).

IV

The most important positive aim of contractualism, according to Rawls, is to provide an account of ordinary judgments concerning the justice of practices and institutions "made by competent persons upon deliberation and reflection" (JF, p. 157).[11] Now, such an account may be viewed as either an analysis of our ordinary judgments, or as a normative theory regarding them, or as both. That is, it may either set out what our judgments come to in the sense of showing what they presuppose and what principles are implicit in them, or it may attempt to show how certain of our ordinary judgments may be justified, or it may do both of these. It has been my hope that contractualism could be understood as a normative theory as well as an analysis of our ordinary judgments, and there is some evidence to suggest that Rawls and others, such as W. G. Runciman, have thought it could be so understood.[12] But reflection upon its structure suggests that contractualism has important limits as a normative theory.

Consider judgments which criticize, say, the practices associated with racial separatism as unjust. We would expect a normative theory of such criticisms to provide an account which shows how they may be justified. In general, contractualism would show this by referring us first to the principles upon which our criticisms rest, and then to the fact that these principles may be construed as the product of the deliberations of rational men in typical circumstances of justice under the constraints of morality. The point we must note is that although this account has a hopeful

---

[11] Rawls gives a full discussion of the idea of a "competent moral judge" in ODPE, p. 178-181.

[12] I have in mind Rawls' claim that "where the conception of justice as fairness applies, slavery is *always* unjust" in JF, p. 152 (Rawls' emphasis); this claim seems to be modified in CLCJ, p. 111, though for reasons that are not relevant to the present discussion. The most detailed application of contractualism qua normative theory that I know is Part Four of W. G. Runciman's *Relative Deprivation and Social Justice* (*op. cit.*); in "Runciman on Social Inequality" in *The Philosophical Quarterly*, XVIII (1968), I discussed the portion of Runciman's book which appeared as " 'Social' Equality" in *The Philosophical Quarterly*, XVII (1967); the present paper develops some points I attempted to bring against Runciman in that discussion.

"objectivist" ring to it, the reading I offered suggests that in fact moral criticisms which meet the terms of the account are relative so far as they rest on principles the acceptance of which is the result of deliberations structured by a procedure which is controversial. The importance of the point is that it permits us to imagine a variety of cases in which contractualism provides no helpful account of how moral criticism of practices and institutions may be justified.

It is not difficult to imagine men who are proponents of a system of practices (perhaps, again, those associated with racial separatism) which is unjust by (J_1) and (J_2), who prosper under that system, who are not at all vicious (they may have acquired their system as a part of their heritage and have been raised to think it natural), and who are, and even take pride in being, rational in the sense that they would move away from their system if they were given good reason to do so.[13] The question is whether the contractualist account shows how criticism of their system as unjust provides them with good reason for moving away from their system.

Consider what it would be to provide them with such reason. The structure of contractualism suggests that, in effect, they must be shown (i) that they are persons describable by (P), (ii) that their social circumstances are similar in relevant respects to those described in (C), and (iii) that they may be thought of as constrained in a sense that can be elucidated in terms of their being under just that deliberating-procedure which, together with the truth of accounts (P) and (C) for their case, insures (logically) their acceptance of the principles underlying our criticisms of their system. For present purposes we may assume that they can be shown (i) and (ii), for the contractualist accounts of persons and social circumstances, we have noted, are not intended to be controversial. It is important to consider what it would be to show them (iii), however, for this will help us determine the strength of contractualism as a normative theory.

We may distinguish at least three widely differing tasks for the

---

[13] It seems plausible to suppose that this use of "rational" would be among those involved in the concept of rationality which is included in the characterization of persons given in (P).

moral critic.   One of these is uninteresting from the standpoint
of normative moral theory, while the others are important from
that standpoint.   The latter two cases indicate some limits of
contractualism as a normative theory.

   A.   The first case is that in which the proponent of an unjust
system is in possession of moral constraints, but does not see, or is
unaware, that he is thereby in possession of principles in light of
which his system may be criticized as unjust.   Here the task for
the critic is not one of persuasion but one of getting the proponent
to see the implications of what he already acknowledges.[14]   This
case is important and common in practical life, but it is not of
special interest to normative moral philosophy, just because there
is in it no real problem of providing reasons for the proponent of
a system to move away from it.   The critic's task is not to provide
reasons, but to make explicit the reasons that are already present
in the thinking of the proponent.

   B.   We may next imagine a case in which the proponent may
acknowledge, and wish to acknowledge, being under moral constraints, but then make clear that the constraints he regards himself as under are not those specified by the contractualist critic.
The difficulty here concerns what constraints are moral constraints,
and, as my previous discussion suggests, arguments relevant to this
difficulty would have to be found outside the framework of contractualism as expressed in (T).   We may note in passing that it is
logically possible that this kind of difficulty would have no practical
sting.   It may be that different sets of conditions are sufficient to
yield acceptance of principles like (J_1) and (J_2), and thus the
critic may be able to show that the constraints acknowledged by
the proponent (and claimed by him to be moral constraints) themselves commit him to acceptance of the principles in light of which
his system is unjust.   In such a case the critic's task becomes like
that in case A, and hence normatively uninteresting.

   But the critic's task in this connection becomes normatively
interesting when the constraints acknowledged by the proponent
commit him to principles different from the critic's, or to no
principles relevant to the assessment of society at all.   For in cases
of this general kind he must provide a reason for change that

------

[14] Assuming, as I did above, that (T) is a theorem.

consists of arguments showing what are moral constraints and how acceptance of them in the proponent's circumstances commits him to principles which show his system to be unjust. Presuming for the moment that this latter could be shown,[14] and that the proponent in question does indeed wish to acknowledge moral constraints, the normative task is chiefly to identify these constraints, and this task lies outside the contractualist view as it is formulated in (T).

C. A third case is suggested by the language of contractualism itself. In this case the critic faces a proponent of injustice whose attention is fastened not so much on the problem of what are and what are not moral constraints, but on the idea that the justification of the criticisms of his system involves his being thought of as a follower of a certain deliberating-procedure which is said to express moral constraints (whatever exactly they are). His question concerns why he should be regarded, or should regard himself, in this way, i.e., why in the theoretical deliberating-situation he should be thought of as accepting (or allowing to be imposed upon him) the guides for deliberation that the contractualist sets out.

I do not know whether anything relevantly like this question arises in practical life, but it is clear that contractualism as it is expressed in (T) allows it to arise. It is an interesting question just because the contractualist critic cannot accuse the proponent who raises it either of issue-dodging or of moral ill-will. For example, the proponent's question need not be construed as the question "Why be moral?" for it may be that he can think of himself as in possession of morality, yet not see why he should think of himself as subscribing to the deliberation-procedure set out by the contractualist. It is the contractualist who proposes to understand the idea of possession of morality in terms of the idea of acceptance of certain guides for deliberation. If the contractualist can provide an answer to the question of why the guides he proposes should be accepted, it may be that he will thereby provide an answer to the question why one should be moral. But regardless whether the answer to the former question is an answer to the latter, the former question is intelligible, and an answer to it is needed if the proponent, in this case, is to be given a reason for moving away from

---

[14] In accordance, again, with the assumption that (T) is a theorem.

his system. Clearly, the task of providing such a reason again lies
outside the contractualism as expressed in (T).

V

Cases such as B and C bring to light the difficulty that when
contractualism as formulated in (T) is viewed as a normative
theory of moral criticism, it is incomplete. There are cases (important cases) in which contractualism cannot show how criticisms of
a set of practices and institutions as unjust according to principles
like (J_1) and (J_2) are justified. With respect to case C it would be
natural to attempt to remedy the incompleteness by exploring
the possibility of a further, more basic theorem—one that would
express the idea that men of a certain nature in social circumstances
in which interests collide may be expected to accept (or allow to be
imposed upon them) the guides for deliberation that the contractualist claims express the constraints of morality.

Suppose the contractualist proposes to explore this possibility
in such a way as to parallel his procedure in (T). To do this he
would seek to find a certain procedure (call it the S-procedure)
which, when followed by ordinary men in social circumstances,
yields (necessarily) their acceptance of the deliberation-guides that
express the constraints of morality, and which in turn yields their
acceptance of principles like (J_1) and (J_2). This is an interesting
proposal, for it would give the contractualist a way of completing
his theory that preserves and utilizes its attractive structural
arrangement at crucial points without reference to intuition or
a priori factors. But there are objections to it which incline one
not to attempt to work out its details, even though it may be possible in principle to construct the appropriate S-procedure.

In the first place, to parallel the structure of (T) we must
view the S-procedure (whatever exactly it is) as accepted by (or
imposed upon) persons in their social circumstances. But this
only gives rise to a question that parallels our present question
about acceptance of the deliberation-guides that express the constraints of morality, namely, the question of how it could be shown
that persons may be thought of, or ought to be thought of, as
accepting the procedure that expresses constraints tantamount to

the deliberation-guides. Second, his proposal thus leaves the contractualist not only with a problem of the same sort as that which his proposal was designed to handle, but also with the handicap of an evident regress if he should then deal with that problem in the way his present maneuver suggests. Third, if the regress is stopped (in the interests, perhaps, of securing objectivity for moral criticism), and the contractualist structure is preserved, then it would have to be stopped by recourse to some procedure which we must imagine persons "necessarily" accepting. But this is unsatisfactory for three reasons: (i) it would have the effect of ultimately guaranteeing the possession of morality, which simply seems too strong; (ii) it would appear to involve recourse to intuition or a priori factors if some account were to be ventured of how acceptance of the S-procedure is "necessary" (the contractualist wishes to avoid this recourse (cf. JF, p. 136)); (iii) it is not clear that the notion of a procedure which is "necessarily" accepted is even intelligible, for it is doubtful that there is such a thing as a procedure which cannot in principle be rejected either simply or in favor of some alternative.

With respect to a case like C the contractualist cannot complete his theory in a way that parallels his strategy in (T). It might be objected that the contractualist is not logically precluded from supplementing his theory with some account of acceptance of a deliberating-procedure expressing moral constraints that is not modeled upon the workings of (T). This is so, but I think certain familiar accounts that come to mind, exclusive of those involving recourse to intuition or a priori factors, must be unacceptable to the contractualist. One might, for example, attempt to account for acceptance by emphasis upon human self-interest, the point being that mutually self-interested persons in circumstances in which their interests collide have in those facts alone good reason to adopt a procedure which would provide them all with principles of justice. But, aside from the difficulty that self-interest *per se* is uninformative regarding what are moral constraints, this way of accounting for their acceptance fails just when we think of the persons involved as rational and benefiting proponents of an unjust system, for it is precisely these persons who cannot be moved by considerations of self-interest. *Ex hypothesi*, their interests are served by the (unjust) system they have.

The utilitarian tradition itself suggests that the presence of moral constraints (if not their acceptance *via* deliberations) can be accounted for by reference to what Mill called the "internal sanction" of morality, namely, the natural sentiment of sympathy.[16] Again, reference to sympathy cannot itself determine what are moral constraints, at least not if we follow Mill, for on his account the internal sanction is a condition of any morality, not just utilitarian morality. In any event, there is a dilemma of sorts for the contractualist who would appropriate any such account of how we are in possession of moral constraints. If we understand the internal sanction to be of the nature of a human disposition toward possession of moral constraints, then either that disposition is developed and cultivated by life in a moral society or it is not. If the former, then possession of moral constraints is logically posterior to the existence of a social system that meets (more or less) the moral standards that ensue from the contractualist's (T), and the idea of persons thus in possession of moral constraints deliberating to produce moral standards by which to assess their society is the idea of a trivial exercize in affirmation of the status quo.[17] If the latter, the disposition toward possession of moral constraints is not "conditioned" by social life, but the question arises as to how we are to understand this disposition: if it is a kind of innate moral attribute of men, as it would appear to be, then at a minimum the contractualist account of persons becomes philosophically controversial.

But even when natural sympathy is present among proponents of an unjust system it does not follow that moral criticism which meets the terms of a contractualist account thereby provides good reason for them to move away from their system. We can imagine the case in which the proponent is a member of a privileged class, and his being characterized by natural sympathy is, so to speak, class-restricted in its range of objects. In such a case, moral criticism that meets the terms of a contractualist account is futile, for it provides no reason for the proponent to enlarge the range of

---

[16] *Utilitarianism*, Ch. III.

[17] The "sense of justice" which Rawls views as the product of an elaborate set of "psychological constructions" in SJ is this kind of dispositional fact about persons, i.e., a fact whose presence depends upon the prior existence of a just social system.

objects of his sympathy. And this point holds even if the proponent acknowledges principles like (J_1) and (J_2), so long as he is consistent and class-restricts his application of such principles.[18]

This is not to claim that there is nothing to be said to rational and benefiting proponents of an unjust social system. As regards the problem of the range of objects of his sympathy, it may be that the proponent does not recognize that certain beings are like him in relevant respects, i.e., he does not recognize that certain beings are persons, and hence proper objects of his sympathy; or it may be that he does not recognize the persons who are like him in relevant respects, in the way some people can travel daily through urban ghettos and not notice the people and conditions there; or it may be that he believes that there are natural ranks among the beings we uncritically call persons, such that the system that turns out unjust by standards like (J_1) and (J_2) reflects in an accurate way an innate hierarchy in nature. In each of these cases the task of showing how a criticism is justified is difficult, and for none of them does contractualism begin to provide the various conceptual and factual resources needed to perform that task.

VI

My discussion yields these points:

(a) Contractualism supposes (without argument) the presence of certain moral constraints in the antecedent of (T). Depending upon what these constraints are, contractualism provides an attractive way of formulating rival moral theories, but it is not itself a way of arguing for any moral theory.

(b) It may be that the contractualist idea of fairness as the mutual recognition of principles by men with no special authority over one another is at the heart of the concept of justice. But it does not follow that contractualism is a rival to, say, utilitarianism in the sense that the latter precludes this idea. Rivalry exists between different formulations of contractualism, not between contractualism and its formulations.

(c) Contractualism is limited when viewed as a normative

------

[18] This point seems acknowledged by Rawls in JF, p. 157.

theory of moral criticism, insofar as it cannot itself specify what are the constraints of morality or provide an account of their acceptance or possession.   The theory thus lacks the capacity to show how important criticisms of systems of practices and institutions as unjust provide good reasons for rational and benefiting proponents of such systems to move away from them.

My concluding suggestion is that the source of these points is just the fact that contractualism holds that (T) is a theorem, a necessary truth.   For then the move from antecedent conditions to acceptance of such principles as (J_1) and (J_2) is broadly deductive in character, which is to say that the claim that these principles would be accepted is a way of setting out what is contained in the complex of elements "[(P) & (C) accept/impose (D-M)]" so arranged to express the conditions and circumstances which make up the antecedent of (T).   It should also be noted that if this is so then the question of whether these principles *would* be accepted is relatively uninteresting, for it implies that every counter-example could be met by some elaboration of the parts of the description which formulates the antecedent conditions."   When the move from antecedent conditions to acceptance of principles is logically automatic in this way, and the antecedent conditions themselves include the presence of moral constraints, then (T) becomes an elaborate device for expressing views about the nature of morality that are logically prior to it.   The theory itself thus becomes uninstructive with respect to the nature of morality and the justification of moral criticisms of practices and institutions.   The alternative, of course, would be to view the move from antecedent conditions to the acceptance of certain principles as non-deductive in character, such that the acceptance of them is a non-automatic result of deliberations in a sense of "deliberations" that is more readily seen to characterize ordinary practice.   But then (T) is no longer entitled to be a necessary truth in the sense that the absence

---

[19] For a discussion which argues that (T) is not a theorem, see Robert Paul Wolff, "Refutation of Rawls' Theorem on Justice," in *The Journal of Philosophy*, LXIII (1966).   Rawls' DJ is in part a reply to points such as those brought against the claim that (T) is a theorem by Wolff.

of the principles permits the inference that some part(s) of the antecedent is (are) not satisfied; and at the same time the central idea of contractualism is lost."[20]

Oberlin College.

[20] My thanks to Alfred F. MacKay for much help with an earlier draft of this discussion, and to John Rawls for encouragement regarding the general line of assessment expressed in it.

THE PRINCIPLES OF JUSTICE

Rawls' Theory of Justice[1]

T. M. SCANLON[*]

A leading characteristic of the ideal of social life underlying Rawls' theory is the primary role assigned to a shared conception of justice as the basis of social cooperation. Rawls says,

> Now let us say that a society is well-ordered when it is not only designed to advance the good of its members but when it is also effectively regulated by a public conception of justice. That is, it is a society in which (1) everyone accepts and knows that the others accept the same principles of justice, and (2) the basic social institutions generally satisfy and are generally known to satisfy these principles. In this case while men may put forth excessive demands on one another, they nevertheless acknowledge a common point of view from which their claims may be adjudicated. If men's inclination to self-interest makes their vigilance against one another necessary, their public sense of justice makes their secure association together possible. Among individuals with disparate aims and purposes a shared conception of justice establishes the bonds of civic friendship; the general desire for justice limits the pursuit of other ends. One may think of a public conception of justice as constituting the fundamental charter of a well-ordered human association [pp. 4–5].

The task of the parties to Rawls' hypothetical Original Position

---

[1] A slightly revised version of Parts II and IV of my 'Rawls' Theory of Justice', *University of Pennsylvania Law Review*, Vol. 121 (1973), pp. 1020–69.

[*] Associate Professor of Philosophy, Princeton University.

is to choose principles of justice which well play this central role in their own society. As is well-known, Rawls puts forward the following Two Principles as those the parties would prefer.

[*First Principle*]
Each person is to have an equal right to the most extensive total system of basic liberties compatible with a similar system of liberty for all [p. 250].

[*Second Principle*]
Social and economic inequalities are to be arranged so that they are both (a) to the greatest benefit of the least advantaged and (b) attached to offices and positions open to all under conditions of fair equality of opportunity [p. 83].²

In what follows I will discuss two leading features of Rawls' theory: the special place assigned to the basic liberties protected by the First Principle and the particular formula of distributive justice presented in the Second Principle. In each instance I will try to show how the case for the conclusions Rawls wishes to defend is related not only to the details of the Original Position construction but also to features of the ideal of social cooperation that underlies his theory.

I. *Liberty*

The ideal of social life expressed in Rawls' notion of a well-ordered society is strongly pluralistic: mutually accepted principles of justice are to provide a common bond for cooperation between persons with disparate aims and purposes, and these principles are to be accepted as limiting conditions on the pursuit of these other ends. It is not obvious that the parties to a social contract would assign this kind of priority to any principles of justice. Rather, it might be expected that they would insist on principles grounded in their own most firmly held values, e.g. in their religious ideals or in their conception of human excellence.

² This principle is advanced as the favored interpretation of the more ambiguous principle that 'social and economic inequalities are to be arranged so that they are both (a) reasonably expected to be to everyone's advantage, and (b) attached to positions and offices open to all' (p. 60). On the relation of these two formulations of clause (a), see note 15 *infra*.

Rawls seeks to prevent the parties to his Original Position from making such a choice by depriving them of the knowledge of their own religious beliefs and conceptions of the good. Forced to choose behind such a veil of ignorance, it is argued, the best way for them to secure a place for their own ideals and values will be to choose principles of toleration.

But the idea of principles chosen behind a veil of ignorance itself requires justification. If the best that can be said for Rawls' principles of justice and for the conception of social cooperation on which they are based is that they would be preferred by parties forced to choose without the knowledge of factors which many would consider to be of crucial importance, then the case for these principles has scarcely been made. To complete the argument some motivation for the construction of the Original Position is required, ideally a motivation which connects the device of choice behind a veil of ignorance with intuitively plausible arguments for a pluralist form of social cooperation. I believe that this further motivation can be found in Rawls' theory in the notion that a person's good is to be identified not with the particular goals and commitments which he may at any given time have adopted but rather with his continuing status as a rational agent able to adopt and modify these goals. In Section A below I will discuss this notion as it figures in Rawls' defense of his theory against that class of alternative theories that he calls perfectionist. Then, in Section B, I will examine the connection between this rather abstract notion and Rawls' argument for the priority of specific constitutional liberties.

A. THE ARGUMENT AGAINST PERFECTIONISM

Those theories which Rawls calls perfectionist direct us 'to arrange institutions and to define the duties and obligations of individuals so as to maximize the achievement of human excellence in art, science, and culture' (p. 325). In my previous remarks I have grouped such theories together with theories which take as the ruling aim of social institutions the promotion of a particular religious ideal. This grouping may seem somewhat unfair since there is in theories of the first sort a strong tendency toward elitism—i.e., toward placing much greater emphasis on the needs and interests of some members of society than on those of others—and while some religious-based theories may exhibit a tendency of this kind in singling out a small group (e.g., 'the elect' or the clergy) for special privileges, this need not be regarded as a characteristic feature of the type.

What all of these theories, religious and secular, share is first of all a teleological structure:[8] once the value of a certain end is established, social institutions are to be appraised strictly on the basis of their tendency to promote this end. In addition, quite apart from tendencies to elitism, all of these theories raise serious problems concerning individual liberty: institutions which preserve the opportunity for each person to adopt and pursue his own interests and ideals and to try to persuade others to follow him will be justified on perfectionist grounds only to the extent that they are the most effective means to the promotion of the given end.

Now it would be possible to reject theories of this kind simply on the basis of their tendency to support institutions which conflict with our considered judgments of justice, and then to design the Original Position in such a way that the offending theories are ruled out. Adopted alone, however, this strategy is not wholly satisfying. If we can give no independent rationale for the design of the Original Position then this manoeuver appears somewhat *ad hoc*. To provide such a rationale, based on a non-perfectionist ideal of social cooperation, would not constitute a refutation of perfectionism; but without such a rationale we are left with no response to the basic theoretical challenge which these theories raise: If there is an objective difference in the intrinsic value of different talents, goals and pursuits why should not information about these differences be used by the parties in the Original Position as the basis for their choice of the principles by which social institutions will be judged? How, in short, can we defend an egalitarian or libertarian position without embracing some form of skepticism about values?

Rawls' response to this challenge (and his rationale for the design of the Original Position) is grounded in the notion that social institutions are just only if they can be defended to each of their members on the basis of the contribution they make to his good as assessed from his point of view. We must be able to say to each member that the arrangements he is asked to accept provide as well for him as they possibly can, consistent with satisfying the parallel demands of others. In order to spell out this idea more fully it is necessary first to consider Rawls' analysis of the notion of an individual person's good (see pp. 60–5).

[8] The notion of a teleological theory is discussed more fully in Section II *infra*.

Those experiences, ends and activities are components in the good for a particular individual, Rawls argues, which have an important place in a plan of life which it would be rational for him to choose. Now it may seem that a person could be said rationally to choose a plan of life (if at all) only after he has developed a conception of his own good, on the basis of which he can judge and rank alternative plans of life. But Rawls argues, persuasively I think, that this is not the case. In real life our deliberations about those actual choices which, taken together, determine our plan of life proceed on the basis of knowledge of our present tastes and capacities, knowledge of what things we have in the past found satisfying, and knowledge of general principles governing the ways in which our tastes and capacities are subject to growth and change over time. This information allows us to decide on course of action not only with the aim of satisfying our current desires but also with the knowledge and intent that our choices will be instrumental in determining what interests, talents and desires we will come to have in the future. Long-range choices such as the choice of a career or a place to live give perhaps the best example of choices which, because they may be foreseen to have far-reaching effects on our interests and objectives, must be made on some basis which goes beyond the satisfaction of our current desires and specific interests.

Rawls puts forward a negative and a positive thesis about this process of deliberation. The negative thesis consists of an attack on the idea that there must be some single overriding general goal (e.g., the maximization of satisfaction or happiness) which underlies all of our deliberations and explains how we can compare and choose between disparate alternatives (see sect. 83–4).[4] The positive thesis consists of a sketch of standards of rationality with reference to which our choices, particularly those most general and far-reaching choices described as choices between alternative life plans, can be criticized. This sketch consists of two parts. First, there are general principles of rational choice according to which it is irrational, e.g., for anyone to prefer plan of life A to plan of life B if B involves the development of exactly the same interests and desires as A and provides for their satisfaction at a markedly higher level. Not all of these principles, which

[4] This negative thesis has an important role in Rawls' argument against utilitarianism. See Sect. 83–5, esp. 562–3. This argument is discussed in Scanlon, 'Rawls' Theory', pp. 1046–56.

Rawls calls 'counting principles', are as uncontroversial as this example, but are all fairly weak, and taken together they by no means can be expected to determine a unique plan as the only rational choice for a person to make. A choice from among the plans not ruled out by these principles (the set of maximal plans) will involve such things as comparing the relative intensity of different desires and the relative value for us of different kinds of accomplishments. For this choice there are on Rawls' view no principles of rationality which directly require a choice of some plans over others. The only relevant standards concern the manner in which the choice is made—whether the relevant evidence has been duly weighed, the possible sources of uncertainty and error properly discounted for, etc. These criteria are grouped together by Rawls under the heading 'deliberative rationality'.

Thus, to say that a certain thing is, objectively, a good for a certain person is, on Rawls' analysis (p. 417), to say that it would be a prominent feature in a plan of life which that person would hypothetically choose, with deliberative rationality, from among the class of maximal plans. Under any actual conditions, of course, not only the means for attaining those things which are good for us, but also ideal conditions for determining what things are such goods, will in some measure be lacking. What the parties in Rawls' Original Position look for in a society is not only the means for securing those things, whatever they may be, which are objectively components of their good, but also the conditions necessary for determining what these goods are.

From the fact that the parties in Rawls' Original Position suppose that as members of a society they will choose their own plan of life, and hence also determine their own conception of the good, it should not be thought that they suppose themselves to be independent of social forces which will in large part shape and influence the choices they make. It would be idle to deny that such influences exist, and irrational to object to all such influences as interfering with one's liberty. But it is still reasonable to prefer some institutions to others on grounds of the conditions they provide for rationally forming a conception of one's good. Obviously one may reasonably object, simply on grounds of efficiency, to institutions which place arbitrary obstacles and difficulties in the way of individuals' attempts to get a clear view of the alternatives open to them, of their own potentialities, and of what they and others can expect from various courses of action.

A more difficult case is presented by the fact that some features of institutions will not merely be random inferences but can be seen clearly to favor certain choices and to discourage others, and to do this not by just enlarging people's views or by approaching 'ideal conditions' thereby favoring 'the correct answer', but rather by skewing the evidence available or by restricting the alternatives likely to be considered, or by affecting people's deliberations in other more subtle and indirect ways. Systematic inference of this kind might be the result of relatively fixed impersonal features of institutional arrangements. Alternatively, certain individuals may be charged with overseeing and maintaining these influences through censorship or other devices.

It is one of the features of perfectionist views which strike us intuitively as objectionable that such views may authorize the use of means of this sort in order to produce individuals conforming to a particular ideal. Now we cannot simply reject as involving unacceptable 'conditioning' all social institutions which mold a person's choices and beliefs without his consent with the aim of bringing him closer to some ideal. Certainly Rawls cannot do this. For as he himself says, his own view involves a certain ideal of the person, and he is at some pains to show (sect. 51–9) that there are psychological laws which give us reason to believe that persons growing up in a well-ordered society governed by his Two Principles of justice will naturally acquire what he calls a sense of justice—the tendency to understand and be motivated by considerations of justice as specified by those principles. The action of these psychological laws is in part dependent upon the intellectual activity of the person on whom they are acting, but is also in large part something which happens to a person without his knowledge or rational scrutiny.

How then is one to distinguish among the various ways in which social institutions may be arranged to influence the choices and beliefs of their members without each member's consent? Can one distinguish acceptable from unacceptable influences of this kind on any basis other than an appraisal of the relative value of the particular types of persons these influences produce? The appropriate standards for making this distinction on Rawls' theory seem to me to be suggested by the criteria he offers for distinguishing justifiable from unjustifiable paternalism (pp. 249–250). The relevant principles here require first that paternalistic interventions, i.e., interventions in a person's life 'for his own sake' which are pursued contrary to his wishes or without his knowledge, have to be rationally justifiable *to him* after the fact. Second, such interventions must be justified on the grounds that the subject's evident failure or absence of reason and will at the time rules out a direct presentation of the issues to him for his own rational consideration and decision. A third requirement is that the intervention 'must be guided by the principles of justice and what is known about the subject's more permanent aims and preferences' or, failing such knowledge, by some neutral standard such as that provided by the primary goods.

While Rawls formulates these requirements specifically for the case of paternalistic action by one person toward another, they seem to be applicable as well to the broader class of interventions we are considering. This is indicated, for example, in the fact that Rawls' defense of the process by which a sense of justice is inculcated in persons who grow up in a well-ordered society governed by his Two Principles of justice advances considerations essentially parallel to these requirements (pp. 514–15). One can maintain here, first, that the principles which form the content of this sense of justice are ones the person can later come to see as justified. (This fact alone, of course, would not be an adequate defense since any successful piece of indoctrination, or at least any successful indoctrination of justifiable beliefs, could make this claim.) Further, the practices of moral education in a well-ordered society proceed as far as possible by appeal to the subject's reason, and rely upon other factors only insofar as the natural limitations of childhood make necessary. Finally, the acquisition of a sense of justice is, it is argued, not inconsistent with a person's good. Since the conception of justice (i.e. Rawls') which is the content of the sense of justice in question provides a secure protection for each person's interests and for his desire to determine his own conception of the good, the acquisition of such a sense of justice is not something which leaves a person open to exploitation or manipulation by others. In addition, having a sense of justice is a necessary condition for sharing fully in the life of a well-ordered society (p. 571) and a necessary condition as well for susceptibility to the natural attitudes of friendship, love and trust (p. 570). These are things, Rawls argues, which almost[5] anyone has reason to want.

Without going fully into the arguments for these claims, we may compare them to the case which might be made on per-

[5] Rawls does allow for the possibility that there may be 'some persons for whom the affirmation of their sense of justice is not a good' (p. 575).

fectionist grounds for features of social institutions designed to mold or restrict the choices of their members so as to promote a particular secular or religious ideal. There is a clear sense in which such features will have a rational justification: they will be justifiable on the basis of the objective value of the particular ideal in question. A perfectionist might thus maintain that the interferences with a person's liberty which these features represent are ones which he should, rationally, come to accept. But the justification which is offered by the perfectionist will not necessarily be one which claims that these features promote the good of the person whose liberty is restricted or which claims that they are consistent with his desire to determine his own conception of the good; it is apt to appeal instead to some impersonal scheme of values. Moreover, this justification need not be based on considerations which would be agreed upon by almost anyone regardless of his conception of the good. Rather, it is likely to be based on one specific conception of the good which, even if it is objectively correct, may nonetheless be something which is a matter of some disagreement among rational adults in the society in question. Indeed, it is just the fact that this conception of the good, though correct, does not compel general agreement, which may be taken on perfectionist grounds to make necessary the intervention in question. On Rawls' theory, however, such interventions are permitted only when there is 'evident failure or absence of reason and will', a phrase intended to cover cases such as infancy, insanity or coma which involve major diminution of rational capacities relative to the standard of 'a normal adult in full possession of his faculties'.

Thus, while Rawls' theory bases principles of justice on a hypothetical choice made by persons who may appear to be standing temporarily outside any particular society, the point of view which the theory takes as fundamental is actually that of a person *in* society. The parties in the Original Position do not act from special wisdom or knowledge which enables them to make choices which they later, as persons under the limiting and distorting conditions of real life in an actual society, will have to take on faith. Rather, the parties' aim is to make choices which they, as real citizens, will have reason to accept. Each party therefore regards his own judgment as a real citizen as sovereign—not as infallible or immune from limitations, but as the basis from which his life will be lived, his choices made and his work as ideal contractor appraised.

Rawls remarks that 'embedded in the principles of justice there is an ideal of the person that provides an Archimedean Point for judging the basic structure of society, (pp. 261–5, 584). Although I have not described this ideal in full, the preceding argument seems to me to illustrate part of the force of this remark. The ideal of each person as a rational chooser of his own ends and plans provides an Archimedean Point partly in virtue of the fact that this conception of a person is taken to be prior to any particular independently-determined conception of his good. One need not be a skeptic about values or truth to hold that each of us does in fact look at himself in this way. If this is so, then the assumption that the parties in the Original Position adopt this view of themselves should seem a natural one, and the fact that certain principles of social cooperation involve the recognition of each member of society as in this sense a sovereign equal, while others involve the denial of this status to at least some members, should seem a fact of some importance.

The conception of the person described by Rawls is of course not an Archimedean Point in the sense of being itself a notion formed outside of or independent of particular social and historical circumstances. It may well be that this conception of the person and the ideal of social cooperation founded on it are typical of particular historical eras and civilizations. But this is not in itself an objection to Rawls' theory, particularly if, as it seems to me, the conception of the person in question is one that has a particularly deep hold on us and is not a matter of great controversy or of significant variation across the range of societies to which the theory should be expected to apply. The question is not whether this conception of the person is in some sense absolute, but whether the particular features of this conception that are appealed to in Rawls' argument are more controversial than the conclusions they are used to support.

Certainly this conception of the person involves a number of important parameters which must be fixed before the notion can be appealed to in support of conclusions about the justice or injustice of particular institutions. The most obvious of these is the standard of rationality: what is to count, for example, as 'evident failure or absence or reason or will'? Other parameters are represented by the general facts of social science which the parties in the Original Position use in reaching their conclusions, by the notion of the primary social goods, and by other appeals to the idea that certain goods or circumstances are to be desired 'no matter what one's conception of the good may be'. The latter appeals depend upon some idea of the normal range of variation in conceptions of the good and upon some idea of the means and conditions required for the pursuit of these goods. All of these may be subject to some variation over time and social circumstances. But here again the theory need make no claim to *absoluteness* in these matters. It is sufficient to ask whether the appeals the theory makes to facts about persons and the circumstances of human life are controversial *for us*; in particular, whether the facts appealed to are more controversial than the conclusions at issue; and finally, whether the ways in which conclusions about the justice of institutions are made to depend on such facts strike us as plausible.

Much of the preceding discussion has been internal to Rawls' particular conception of social cooperation and is thus not in any proper sense a *refutation* of perfectionism. It is, rather, a description of an alternative ideal of social life, one which might be called 'cooperation on a footing of justice'. The development of this ideal enables Rawls to move beyond the observation that perfectionism seems to support arrangements which are at variance with our intuitive judgments of justice to a theory which explains why this should be so and provides a point of view from which we can see how the perfectionist challenge can be answered.

B. THE PRIORITY OF LIBERTY

I turn now from these theoretical issues to consideration of Rawls' more specific conclusions concerning the place of liberty in just institutions. Rawls' substantive account of justice is put forward in two forms which he calls respectively the General Conception and the Special Conception of Justice as Fairness. The General Conception of Justice as Fairness provides that '[a]ll social primary goods—liberty and opportunity, income and wealth, and the bases of self-respect—are to be distributed equally unless an unequal distribution of any or all of these goods is to the advantage of the least favored' (p. 303). The Special Conception is expressed in the two principles of justice stated earlier, with the proviso that the First Principle is to be held prior to the Second in a sense to be discussed more fully below. The Second Principle allows for inequalities in the distribution of goods other than basic liberties on terms similar to those specified by the General Conception, but the First Principle lays down a more stringent requirement of equality in basic liberties, a requirement which is not to be set aside for the sake of greater economic or social benefits. This principle and the rule specifying its priority receive their final statement in the following form.

First Principle
Each person is to have equal right to the most extensive total system of equal basic liberties compatible with a similar system of liberty for all.

Priority Rule
The principles of justice are to be ranked in lexical order[6] and therefore liberty can be restricted only for the sake of liberty. There are two cases: (a) a less extensive liberty must strengthen the total system of liberty shared by all, and (b) a less than equal liberty must be acceptable to those citizens with the lesser liberty [p. 250].

The 'basic liberties' with which the First Principle is concerned are specified by Rawls as follows.

The basic liberties are, roughly speaking, political liberty (the right to vote and to be eligible for public office) together with the freedom of speech and assembly; liberty of conscience and freedom of thought; freedom of the person along with the right to hold (personal) property; and freedom from arbitrary arrest and seizure as defined by the concept of the rule of law. These liberties are all required to be equal by the first principle, since citizens of a just society are to have the same basic rights [p. 61].

A liberty in the sense in which Rawls uses the term is defined by a complex of rights along with correlative duties of others to aid or not to interfere. Thus, by a restriction on liberty or an unequal liberty he means a restriction or inequality in what people are legally entitled to do (or, perhaps, entitled to do by the non-legal rules defining the basic institutions of their society). In-

---

[6] 'This is an order which requires us to satisfy the first principle in the ordering before we can move on to the second . . . A principle does not come into play until those previous to it are either fully met or do not apply' (p. 43). For Rawls' initial statement of the Second Principle, see text accompanying note 2 *supra*.

equalities in people's ability to take advantage of their rights due, e.g., to unequal economic means do not count as inequalities in liberty for Rawls but rather as inequalities in what he calls the 'worth' or 'value' of liberty. While the basic liberties must be held equally, the worth of these liberties may vary since any significant inequality in wealth, income or authority (allowed under the Second Principle) will represent an inequality in the ability of citizens to make use of their liberty in order to advance their ends (p. 204). Rawls stresses at a number of points (e.g., pp. 224–6, 277–8) the importance of preserving 'the fair value' of the basic liberties, particularly political liberties, but strict equality in the worth of these liberties is not required by the First Principle itself.

Two examples, frequently cited by Rawls, of restrictions on basic liberties that are justified on the ground that they strengthen the total system of basic liberty are the restrictions on the scope of majority rule imposed by a bill of rights and the restrictions on the freedom to speak imposed by a system of rules of order. In the first case a restriction of the legal powers of citizens is justified by the fact that more extensive powers could legally erase other basic liberties. In the second case what are sometimes called restrictions as to time, place and manner are imposed on the exercise of a basic liberty in order, Rawls says, to preserve the worth of that liberty to all (p. 204). Thus it appears that while equal worth of the basic liberties is not required by the First Principle, securing the worth of these liberties is one of the goals which can justify restrictions on basic liberties under the Priority Rule.[7]

1. The Preference for Basic Liberties over Other Primary Goods
Given the degree to which the content of the Priority Rule, and hence the claim of Rawls' theory to provide a secure basis for liberty, depends upon the distinction between the basic liberties and other goods and opportunities, it may seem surprising that no theoretical account of this distinction is offered. The list of familiar constitutional categories given above is offered by Rawls not as a precise enumeration of the class of basic liberties but

[7] Both of the cases considered here are examples of a lesser but still equal liberty as provided for by clause (a) of the Priority Rule. Primary examples of unequal liberty allowed by clause (b) seem to be cases of 'justifiable paternalism' in which a less than equal liberty is 'acceptable to those whose liberty is restricted' in the sense spelled out in the requirements discussed above.

only as indicating 'roughly speaking' what this class is to include. I suspect that here, as with the class of primary goods itself, no precise theoretical demarcation can be given. What is claimed for these liberties is just that, due both to the importance for anyone of the interests they safeguard and to their great instrumental value for the enjoyment of other goods, they are not only things it is rational for anyone to want but also things it is rational for anyone to value particularly highly relative to other primary social goods.

It is not claimed that these liberties are always to be valued more highly than any other goods. Rawls allows that under particularly dire conditions, when bare survival or the pursuit of the means for a minimally comfortable life is the dominant concern, and when the necessary prerequisites for the effective exercise of the basic liberties are lacking, it may be rational to sacrifice basic liberties for the sake of other goods such as increased security or economic development. It is under such conditions that the General Conception of Justice as Fairness applies. Rawls argues (sect. 82), however, that as conditions improve and the possibility for the effective exercise of the basic liberties becomes real, people will set an increasingly high marginal value on basic liberties relative to other goods. After the most urgent wants are satisfied, people come to set greater importance on the liberty to determine and pursue their own plans of life. They will therefore insist on the right to pursue their own spiritual and cultural interests, seek to 'secure the free internal life of the various communities of interests in which persons and groups seek to achieve . . . the ends and excellences to which they are drawn' and, in addition, 'come to aspire to some control over the laws and rules that regulate their association, either by directly taking part themselves in its affairs or indirectly through representatives with whom they are affiliated by ties of culture and social situation' (p. 543). Recognizing these tendencies, the parties in the Original Position will see that '[b]eyond some point it becomes and then remains irrational [for them] . . . to acknowledge a lesser liberty for the sake of greater material means and amenities. . . .' (p. 542). Thus the position of liberty under the Special Conception makes explicit the priority that emerges under the General Conception as the natural preference for basic liberties over increases in other primary social goods asserts itself.

There are a number of questions one might raise concerning this argument. First, since the appeal to an increasing preference for basic liberties over other primary social goods represents Rawls' most detailed claim about the way in which the parties in the Original Position would order bundles of primary social goods, it naturally gives rise to questions of the sort considered above under the heading of 'parameters'. Rather than to consider the general question of whether this preference is in some suitable sense 'universal', however, it seems to me more profitable to ask whether an appeal to such a preference provides adequate and interesting answers to those questions about liberty (and about the particular basic liberties listed by Rawls) that one would want a philosophical theory of liberty to answer.

Foremost among these is the question to what extent the basic liberties have some kind of absolute status and to what extent, and within what limits, they are to be understood and interpreted in terms of a balancing of competing interests. Rawls appears to have two answers to this question. The first, given by the Priority Rule, makes the limitation on acceptable balancing depend upon the distinction between basic liberties and other primary social goods: basic liberties are to be limited only for the sake of the total system of basic liberty itself. The second answer, and the one most often used by Rawls to indicate when a lesser but still equal liberty is just, is given by what he calls the Principle of the Common Interest:

> According to this principle institutions are ranked by how effectively they guarantee the conditions necessary for all equally to further their aims, or by how efficiently they advance shared ends that will similarly benefit everyone. Thus reasonable regulations to maintain public order and security, or efficient measures for public health and safety, promote the common interest in this sense. So do collective efforts for national defence in a just war [p. 97].

Rawls does not formulate this principle explicitly, but his discussion (p. 213–14) suggests the following formulation: basic liberties may be restricted only when methods of reasoning acceptable to all make it clear that unrestricted liberties will lead to consequences generally agreed to be harmful for all.

Rawls seems to hold (pp. 246–7, 212–13) that these two doctrines are consistent, i.e., that cases in which a restriction of basic liberties is justified by the Principle of the Common Interest are also cases in which basic liberty is being limited for the sake of the total system of basic liberty itself. This appears to be true in the most apocalyptic cases, e.g., cases in which a restriction of basic liberties is necessary as part of the common defense against an invasion. It may be true as well in some more mundane cases, such as Rawls' example of the restrictions imposed upon the right to speak by fair rules of order (taking into account, as was noted above, that what is protected in this case is not, strictly speaking, liberty but rather the worth of liberty). But if the restrictions on utterances imposed by such a set of rules count as restrictions on a basic liberty, then so also must similar restrictions on the time, place and manner of political demonstrations, religious festivals, parades, the placing of posters and the use of loudspeakers and sound trucks. Regulation of these activities is normally thought to be acceptable, and appears to be justified by something like the Principle of the Common Interest, but it seems to me difficult to maintain (without considerable stretching of the notion of a basic liberty) that in these cases basic liberties are being restricted only for the sake of the same or other basic liberties. It seems to me much more plausible and straightforward to say that in order to arrive at a policy in these cases we must balance the value of certain modes of exercise of a basic liberty not only against the exercise of other basic liberties but also against the enjoyment of other goods (uninterrupted sleep, undefaced public buildings, etc.). Something like this is surely true in the case of the restriction of expression by laws against defamation: different standards of defamation for, on the one hand, private, artistic or cultural expression and, on the other, political debate, seem to me obviously appropriate, and I take this to be the reflection of the differing values we place on the unfettered exercise of these forms of expression relative to, among other things, the value placed on safeguarding the primary good of self-respect.

One could of course maintain that what is balanced against liberty in these cases is not liberty itself but the *worth* of liberty. Since almost anything, including any significant increase or decrease in material well-being, can affect the worth of liberty, the general principle that basic liberties may be restricted only when this brings an increase (or is necessary to avoid a decrease) in the worth of the total system of basic liberties appears to be a weaker principle than Rawls wishes to defend. I suggest that Rawls' response here would be that while a great number of things can contribute to the worth of liberty, not every restriction of basic liberty yields gains in other goods or will yield sufficient gains to constitute a net increase in the worth of the total system of such liberties. This is what a restriction must do in order to be acceptable.

Conceivably, this principle can be made to fit the most obvious cases in which a restriction of basic liberty is justified. Given the rather diffuse character of the notion of 'the worth of the total system of basic liberties', however, it is not a principle that is easy to apply. Under any account the decision as to when a restriction on basic liberty is justified will involve some difficult balancing, but I do not think that a clear guideline between acceptable and unacceptable balancing is obtained by describing everything in terms of 'the worth of liberty'. Such an approach might seem inviting if one thought that the notion of an increasing preference for basic liberties over other goods represented the most important theoretical element in the case for liberty. But I do not think that this is so. On the contrary it seems to me that the idea of an increasing preference for basic liberties leaves out or obscures the most important factors in the case for certain of the basic liberties, factors which Rawls' own discussion of these particular basic liberties brings out quite clearly.

2. Freedom of the Person

The argument from the increasing marginal preference for liberties over the other primary goods is most appropriate as an account of the basis of freedom of the person. It is not completely clear from Rawls' discussion what this category of basic liberties is to encompass other than the protections against arrest and seizure embodied under 'the rule of law', but I take it to include at least freedom of movement within the country and across its borders, freedom of choice in aspects of one's personal life, and perhaps also freedom from surveillance. The increasing preference for these liberties claimed by Rawls can be seen as deriving in part from the fact that they represent important conditions for the use and enjoyment of other goods. Beyond this, however, there is the fact that the interventions these liberties are intended to preclude constitute particularly deep intrusions into a person's life which anyone has strong reasons to want to avoid, both because of the real disruption they cause and because of their great symbolic impact.

We can of course imagine people who felt quite differently about these matters. To the extent that such differences are not merely the object of speculative imagination but the subject of real disagreement and controversy, the force of Rawls' argument for the priority of freedom of the person will be seriously weakened. But in such an event it seems clear that the case for these liberties will be genuinely in doubt. Rawls' analysis of the case for the freedoms of the person as a matter of relative preference thus seems quite appropriate; there is no obvious theoretical element in the case for these liberties that his analysis leaves out.

3.   Liberties of Expression, Thought and Conscience

Freedom of speech and assembly, liberty of conscience and freedom of thought present a slightly different case. The argument for the priority of these liberties rests upon the recognition by the parties in the Original Position that as material conditions improve there will be a 'growing insistence upon the right to pursue our spiritual and cultural interests' (p. 543). As Rawls says in arguing for freedom of conscience, the parties 'must assume that they may have moral, religious, or philosophical interests' which they cannot put in jeopardy unless there is no alternative' (p. 206).

Now this argument contains two distinguishable elements. The first is the recognition by the parties in the Original Position that, for the reasons discussed in connection with the argument against perfectionism, they cannot concede to the government any authority in matters of religious, moral or philosophic doctrine. As Rawls says,

> The government has no authority to render religious associations either legitimate or illegitimate any more than it has this authority in regard to art and science. These matters are simply not within its competence as defined by a just constitution. Rather, given the principles of justice, the state must be understood as the association consisting of equal citizens. It does not concern itself with philosophical and religious doctrine but regulates individuals' pursuit of their moral and spiritual interests in accordance with principles to which they themselves would agree in an initial situation of equality [p. 212].

The second element is the recognition by the parties that they will come to set a particularly high value on the pursuit of their 'spiritual and cultural interest'.

These two elements are clearly independent. To take the case of religion, the value that a group of people place on keeping their religious commitments will be reflected in such things as the amount of economic loss and disruption of the pattern of life they are willing to undergo to allow everyone to observe the holidays of his religion, attend services, etc. and in the lengths to which they are prepared to go to recognize and respect the religious scruples of individual members against taking part in certain necessary tasks and activities. It is certainly possible that the cost a society is willing to bear in order to allow full freedom of religious observance might vary widely while the principle of the lack of governmental authority to decide between particular religious doctrines remained quite fixed.

This kind of variation in the value attached to religious observance, while possible, may in fact be unlikely if, as Rawls says, '[a]n individual recognizing religious and moral obligations regards them as binding absolutely in the sense that he cannot qualify his fulfillment of them for the sake of greater means for promoting his other interests' (p. 207). This extraordinary importance attached to religious matters tends to overshadow the distinction I have tried to draw and makes it inviting to rest the case for toleration entirely on the claim that the parties in the Original Position can forsee that they will come to set an incomparably higher value on religious liberty (i.e., on the freedom to meet their religious commitments) than on other primary social goods. But this approach becomes less attractive if we think not only of religious liberty but of freedom of thought and expression more broadly construed. A society is apt to set rather different values on the fulfillment of religious commitments, the pursuit of scientific knowledge and the pursuit and enjoyment of excellence in the arts, and these differences will be reflected in the price the society is willing to bear in order to allow these activities to go forward. But in a society which recognizes freedom of thought and expression the regulation of these pursuits will be guided by a common principle that governments lack the authority to decide matters of moral, religious or philosophic doctrine (or of scientific truth) and hence also lack the authority to restrict certain activities on the grounds that they promulgate false or corrupting doctrines. Let me call this principle, which I have formulated only very crudely, the Principle of Limited Authority.

Taken alone such a principle does not constitute a complete doctrine of liberty or even of freedom of thought and expression.

But it seems to me that this principle is the most important element in such a doctrine that can be established from the point of view of the Original Position. It is not possible to determine from that standpoint exactly what relative values are to be assigned to these pursuits and to other interests with which they may conflict. Nor is it possible to forsee from that standpoint what will be the best way of regulating these pursuits so that they do not conflict. These are problems that can be dealt with only at a later stage when the full facts about a society and the preferences of its members are known. (I suspect that this process of balancing and coordination is what Rawls has in mind when he speaks of restricting particular basic liberties in order to strengthen the total system of basic liberties.) While it may be possible for the parties in the Original Position to forsee that in general they will attach a high value to their spiritual and cultural interests, such a general preference, or a resultant general principle that in the balancing process these liberties are to take precedence over other goods, seems to me to be less useful as the basis for a doctrine of freedom of thought and expression than the idea that the process of balancing must take place within the constraints imposed by something like the Principle of Limited Authority.

A doctrine of freedom of expression founded on this idea is suggested by Rawls on a number of occasions, in particular in his principle of the common interest, with its emphasis on the distinction between what might be called 'neutral' and 'non-neutral' grounds for restricting liberty. I think that some account of freedom of expression of this general type must be correct, although there are a number of difficulties in formulating such a view.[8] While I have some misgivings about Rawls' particular formulation (misgivings, e.g., as to whether too much may be conceded to the doctrine of clear and present danger by his blanket allowance that liberty of conscience may be limited 'when there is a reasonable expectation that not doing so well will damage the public order which the government should maintain' (p. 213), it seems to me one of the strong points of Rawls' theory (as described in the first part of this section) that it provides a philosophical basis for an account of liberty of this type. It therefore seems to me important to ask whether this strength is adequately represented in his doctrine of the priority of liberty.

[8] I have myself put forward a view of this kind in 'A Theory of Freedom of Expression', *Philosophy and Public Affairs*, Vol. 1 (1972).

While it is not explicitly stated in the Priority Rule, the Principle of Limited Authority will be implied by clause (b) of that rule if (as seems plausible on the basis of the argument of the preceding section) we take governmental authority over matters of religion, etc., to represent an unequal liberty which would not be acceptable to those whose liberty is restricted. It is unclear, however, how this principle is related to the argument for the priority rule based on the increasing marginal value of liberty. There seem to be two possible interpretations of this argument.

While the parties in the Original Position might readily agree that there are conditions under which the pursuit of spiritual and cultural interests may be severely curtailed for the sake of other more pressing needs, it may seem unlikely, given the close relation between the Principle of Limited Authority and the conception of individual autonomy underlying the argument against perfectionism, that the parties would ever concede to a government the right to decide matters of moral, religious or philosophic doctrine. This suggests an interpretation of Rawls' argument according to which the Principle of Limited Authority applies under the General Conception of Justice as Fairness as well as under the Special Conception. What distinguishes the Special Conception, on this view, is just the increased importance that is attached to spiritual and cultural interests as the opportunity to pursue these interests presents itself and the demands of mere survival become less pressing. This interpretation is faithful to Rawls' description of the transition from the General Conception to the Special Conception as consisting of a shift in the ordering of primary social goods. But the Principal of Limited Authority is not a factor in this shift; it stands instead as a constant element of the theory. Given the importance of his principle from Rawls' point of view, it seems somewhat surprising on this interpretation that nothing resembling this principle is either stated or implied in Rawls' account of the General Conception.

An alternative, somewhat more extreme interpretation, and one which seems to me more likely to represent Rawls' view, would identify the Principle of Limited Authority as one of the distinguishing elements of the Special Conception. This means that there must be circumstances to which the General Conception of Justice as Fairness applies but in which the parties in the Original Position would not only allow the severe curtailment of expression on the grounds allowed under the Principle of the Common

Interest but would also suspend the Principle of Limited Authority itself. I am not quite certain what such situations would be like. Presumably they would be situations in which cooperation on certain common tasks is not merely mutually advantageous but essential for survival or for the amelioration of intolerable conditions. If deep disagreements were to exist which made the basis of this cooperation fragile, and if close and uninterrupted cooperation were required to avoid consequences that would be disastrous for all, then perhaps it would be rational not only to accept rigid regulation on the time, place and manner of expression to prevent interference with essential work, but also to grant to the government the power to ban the expression of views likely to give rise to dangerous controversy or to dissension and doubt.

It seems to me most accurate to describe such situations as ones in which the circumstances of justice would be present only to a limited degree. Cooperation in certain tasks may be feasible and profitable and in these areas of common purpose considerations of justice may apply, dictating, e.g., that the benefits and burdens of this cooperation (including liberties and constraints) should be shared in accordance with Rawls' Second Principle of Justice. But if the basis of this cooperation is quite shaky, and if the ends at which it aims are truly vital, then it might be rational for the parties involved to regard each other primarily as means to these ends. This attitude would be reflected, for example, in the parties' placing the smooth functioning of their institutions ahead of the right of individual members to raise and discuss with each other questions about the wisdom, viability or propriety of these institutions. I have some inclination to say that such a case would not represent cooperation on a footing of justice at all; collective actions to quell controversy in such circumstances are best seen not as the exercise of the distinctive authority of a just government in the sense defined by the Original Position, but rather as acts which must be justified on a case-by-case basis by appeal to the residual rights of the individuals involved to undertake those measures necessary to their self-defence and survival.[9]

However this may be, it is at least clear that the justification I have offered for limited tolerance in what might be called situations of partial justice depends upon the presence of conditions under which anything which undermines effective cooperation represents an immediate threat to all. When these conditions are

[9] Such a view is suggested in Scanlon, 'A Theory of Freedom of Expression', pp. 224–6.

lacking, such justification is also lacking and in addition it be-comes rational for people to seek to establish cooperation on a footing that gives full recognition to the status of the participants as autonomous equals, i.e., to something like Rawls' Special Con-ception.

One thing making this transition rational is the fact that under improving conditions individuals will develop religious, moral and philosophical interests and will want their institutions to safeguard their pursuit of these interests. But on the interpretation I have been discussing the Special Conception of Justice as Fairness can no longer be seen simply as what emerges under the General Con-ception once these interests begin to develop. For the transition to the Special Conception involves a fundamental change in the basis of cooperation, namely a move to what I called in the first part of this section cooperation on a footing of justice. Coopera-tion on this basis would be less apt to be rational for people if they did not place a high value on certain kinds of opportunity, but the defining elements of this form of cooperation go beyond this configuration of preferences, just as the defining elements of cooperation in the economic sphere go beyond the structure of needs and interests that make such cooperation inviting.

II. *Distributive Justice and the Difference Principle*

Rawls is concerned with justice in only one of the many senses of the term. For him, questions of justice are questions of how the benefits and burdens of social cooperation are to be shared, and the principles of justice he develops are to apply in the first instance not to arbitrary distributions of goods but to the basic institutions of society which determine 'the assignment of rights and duties and . . . regulate the distribution of social and economic advantages' (p. 61). Rawls' principles apply to particular distribu-tions only indirectly: a distribution may be called just if it is the result of just institutions working properly, but the principles provide no standard for appraising the justice of distributions independent of the institutions effecting them (p. 88). Conceived of in this way, principles of justice are analogous to a specification of what constitutes a fair gamble. If a gamble is fair then its out-come, whatever it may be, is fair and cannot be complained of. But the notion of a fair gamble provides no standard for judging particular distributions (Smith and Harris win five dollars, Jones loses ten dollars) as fair or unfair when these are considered in isolation from particular gambles which bring them about.

The principle which Rawls offers for appraising the distributive aspects of the basic structure of a society is his Second Principle of Justice which, considerations of the priority of liberty aside, is equivalent to what he calls the General Conception of Justice as Fairness. This principle is stated as follows: 'Social and economic inequalities are to be arranged so that they are both (a) to the greatest benefit of the least advantaged and (b) attached to offices and positions open to all under conditions of fair equality of opportunity' (p. 83).[10]

According to clause (a) of this principle, which Rawls refers to as the Difference Principle, a system of social and economic inequalities is just only if there is no feasible alternative institution under which the expectations of the worst-off group would be greater. The phrase 'fair equality of opportunity' in clause (b) requires not only that no one be formally excluded from positions to which special benefits attach, but also that persons with similar talents and inclinations should have similar prospects of attaining these benefits 'regardless of their initial place in the social system, that is, irrespective of the income class into which they are born' (p. 73). The rationale behind this principle, particularly the motivation for clause (a), will be discussed at length below. First, however, I will consider briefly how the principle is to be applied.

A. DIFFERENCE PRINCIPLE AND ITS APPLICATION

The most natural examples of inequalities to which Rawls' principle might be applied involve the creation of new jobs or offices to which special economic rewards are attached or an increase in the income associated with an existing job. But the intended application of the principle is much broader than this. It is to apply not only to inequalities in wealth and income but to all inequalities in primary social goods, e.g., to the creation of positions of special political authority. Further, its application is not limited to 'jobs' or 'offices' in the narrow sense but includes all the most general features of the basic structure of a society that give rise to unequal shares of primary social goods. In the case of economic goods these will include the system of money and

10 Rawls' final formulation of this principle (p. 312) incorporates considerations of justice between generations which the present discussion leaves aside.

credit, the laws of contract, the system of property rights and the laws governing the exchange and inheritance of property, the system of taxation, the institutions for the provision of public goods, etc.

It is fairly clear how Rawls' principle is to apply to the creation of one new office to which special rewards are attached (or to the assignment of new rewards to one existing position) in an otherwise egalitarian society: such an equality is just only of those who do not directly benefit from this inequality by occupying the office benefit indirectly with the result that they too are better off than they were before (and than they would be if the benefits in question were distributed in any alternative way). It is less obvious how the principle is to apply in the more general case of complex institutions with many separable inequality-generating features. Rawls deals with this problem by specifying that institutions are to be appraised as a whole from the perspective of representative members of each relevant social position. The Difference Principle requires that the total system of inequalities be so arranged as to maximize the expectations of a representative member of the class which the system leaves worst off.

The notions of relevant social position and the expectations of a representative person in such a position require explanation. Relevant social positions in Rawls' sense are those places in the basic structure of society which correspond to the main divisions in the distribution of primary social goods. (He mentions the role of 'unskilled worker' as constituting such a position (p. 98).) Rawls believes that the distribution of other primary social goods will be closely enough correlated with income and wealth that the latter can be taken as an index for identifying the least advantaged group. Accordingly, he suggests that the class of least advantaged persons may be taken to include everyone whose income is no greater than the average income of persons in the lowest relevant social position (or alternatively everyone with less than half the median income and wealth in the society (p. 98)). To compute the expectations of a representative member of a given social position one takes the average of the shares of primary social goods enjoyed by persons in that position. Thus, while the parties in the Original Position do not estimate the value to them of becoming a member of a given society by taking the likelihood of their being a member of a particular social position to be represented by the proportion of the total population that is in that position, they do estimate the expected value (in primary social goods) of being a member of a particular social position by taking the likelihood that they will have any particular feature affecting the distribution of primary social goods within that position to be represented by the fraction of persons in the position who have that feature. Rawls does not explicitly discuss his reasons for allowing averaging within a social position when he has rejected it in the more general case. A more extreme position eschewing averaging would require maximizing the expectations of the worst-off individual in society. The Difference Principle occupies a position somewhere between this extreme and the principle of maximizing the average share of primary social goods across the society as a whole, its exact position within this range depending on how broadly or narrowly the relevant social positions are defined. The resort to averaging seems to some extent to be dictated by practical considerations: a coherent and manageable theory cannot take into account literally every position in a society (p. 98). In addition, the theoretical case against the use of averaging (as opposed to some more conservative method of choice) is weaker when we are concerned with differences in expectation within a single social position rather than differences between such positions. For here we are not concerned with a single 'gamble' with incomparably high stakes: intraposition differences are, by definition, limited, and each person's allotment is determined by a large number of independent factors, many of which are of approximately equal magnitude (cf. 169–71).

There is a further problem about the notion of expectations which requires consideration. Rawls refers to the relevant social positions as 'starting places', i.e., as the places in society people are born into (p. 96). Now the expectations of a person born into a family in a certain social position can be thought of as consisting of two components. First, there is the level of well-being he can expect to enjoy as a child. Presumably we may identify this with his parents' allotment of primary social goods. Second, there are his long term prospects as a member of society in his own right. If perfect fair equality of opportunity were attained then this latter component would not be substantially affected by the social and economic position of one's parents. As Rawls notes, however, such perfect equality of opportunity is unlikely, at least as long as the family is maintained (pp. 74, 301), so we may suppose that in general the second component will be heavily influenced by the first. One might conclude that the second component can be neglected entirely, reasoning that the distribution of social and economic advantages will influence the long term life prospects of a representative person born into the worst-off class mainly through its effect on the conditions in which such a person grows up. Taking this course would have the same consequences as deciding that what should be considered in applying the Difference Principle are not the expectations of a representative person born into the worst-off social position but the expectations of a representative person who winds up in that position after the social mechanism for assigning people to social roles has run its course.

But the principle which results from ignoring long term expectations seems to me unsatisfactory. Suppose we have a society in which there are 100 people in the lowest social position and twenty-five people in each of the two higher positions, and suppose it becomes known that the basic institutions of the society could be altered so that in later generations there would be fifty people in each of the three social positions, with the levels of wealth, income, authority, etc., associated with these positions remaining the same as they are now. Now it seems to me that a person in the lowest social position in this society is apt to be strongly in favor of this change. And such a person could plausibly support this preference by saying that the expectations of a representative person born into this social position (in particular, the expectations of his children) would be better if this change were made than if it were not. This increase in expectations will not be captured by the interpretation of the Difference Principle just suggested or by any principle which focuses only on the levels of income, wealth, etc., associated with various positions in society while ignoring the way in which the population is distributed among these positions. Examples of this kind convince me that considerations of population distribution have to be incorporated in some way into Rawls' theory, and the most natural way to do this seems to me to be to bring them in through the notion of long term expectations.

But how is this to be done? The rule mentioned above that the expectations of a representative person in a given social position are to be determined by averaging the benefits enjoyed by persons in that position suggests that in a society with three relevant social positions whose average levels of income, wealth, authority, etc., can be indexed by p_1, p_2 and p_3, the long term prospect of a person born into the worst-off position should be represented by

$a_1p_1 + a_2p_2 + a_3p_3$, where a_1, a_2 and a_3 are the fractions of people born into the worst-off position who wind up in each of the three places.

But the adoption of averaging as the method for computing long term expectations has unpleasant consequences for Rawls' theory. To the extent that the inequalities in childhood expectations resulting from the unequal economic and social positions of different families are eliminated (perhaps by eliminating the institution of the family itself), the first component in the expectations of a representative person will become the same for everyone regardless of the social position into which he is born, and Rawls' requirement that the expectations of a representative person in the lowest social position be maximized becomes the requirement that we maximize the second component of these expectations, i.e., the long term expectation $a_1p_1 + a_2p_2 + a_3p_3$. Moreover, to the extent that fair equality of opportunity is achieved (and barring the formation of a genetic elite) the co-efficients a_1, a_2 and a_3 in this polynomial will become the same for every representative person regardless of social class, and the polynomial will thus come to express the average share of primary goods enjoyed by members of the society in question. It follows that on the interpretation just suggested Rawls' Difference Principle will be distinct from the principle requiring us to maximize the average share of primary social goods only so long as the inequalities resulting from the institution of the family persist or the fair equality of opportunity required by clause (b) of the Second Principle is otherwise not achieved. Even if fair equality of opportunity is an unattainable ideal this conclusion seems to me unacceptable for Rawls' theory. The principle of maximum average primary social goods is an extremely implausible one, much less plausible than the principle of maximum average utility.[11] I see no reason to think that this principle would be acceptable even if perfect equality of opportunity were to obtain.

The problem here is how to give some weight to the way in which the population is distributed across social positions without introducing aggregative considerations in such a way that they take over the theory altogether (or would do so but for the 'friction' introduced by imperfect equality of opportunity). One way of dealing with this problem which seems to me in the spirit of Rawls' theory would be to modify the Difference Principle to require the following:

11 See Scanlon, 'Rawls' Theory', p. 1050.

First maximize the income, wealth, etc. of the worst-off representative person, then seek to minimize the number of people in his position (by moving them upwards); then proceed to do the same for the next worst-off social position, then the next and so on, finally seeking to maximize the benefits of those in the best-off position (as long as this does not affect the others).[12]

This seems to me a natural elaboration of what Rawls calls the Lexical Difference Principle (p. 83).[13] It also has the advantage of dealing with the problem of population distribution without introducing the summing or averaging of benefits across relevant social positions. There are obviously many variations on this theme as well as many altogether different approaches.[14]

B. THE ARGUMENT FOR THE DIFFERENCE PRINCIPLE

I return now to the central question of the rationale behind the Difference Principle. The intuitive idea here is that a system of inequalities is just only if we can say to each person in the society, 'Eliminating the advantages of those who have more than you would not enable us to improve the lot of any or all of the people in your position (or beneath it). Thus it is unavoidable that a certain number of people will have expectations no greater than yours, and no unfairness is involved in your being one of these people.' The requirement that we be able to say this to *every* member of society, and not just to those in the worst-off group, corresponds to what Rawls calls the Lexical Difference Principle:

[I]n a basic structure within n relevant representatives, first maximize the welfare of the worst-off representative man;

---

[12] This solution was suggested to me by Bruce Ackerman.

[13] See text accompanying note 15, *infra*.

[14] One would be to take the position a person is 'born into' to be defined not only by the social and economic status of his family but also by his inborn talents and liabilities, i.e., those features which will enable him to prosper in the society or prevent him from doing so. Given this definition of the 'starting places', one could employ averaging as a method for representing the long term expectations of a representative person born into the worst-off such place without fear that the theory would collapse into the doctrine of maximum average primary social goods if the institution of the family were eliminated. Modifying the Difference Principle in this way would bring Rawls closer (perhaps too close) to what he calls 'the principle of redress', the principle that the distribution of social advantages must be arranged to compensate for undeserved inequalities such as the inequalities of birth and natural endowment. See pp. 100–2.

second, for equal welfare of the worst-off representative maximize the welfare of the second worst-off representative man, and so on until the last case which is, for equal welfare of all the preceding n-1 representatives, maximize the welfare of the best-off representative man [p. 83].[15]

This form of the principle is called 'lexical' since 'lexical priority' is given to the expectations of the worse-off: the fate of the second worst-off group is considered only to decide between arrangements which do equally well for the worst-off, and so on for the higher groups, working always from the bottom up. This asymmetry of concern in favor of the worse-off is a central feature of the theory. Rawls remarks a number of times in contrasting his theory with utilitarianism that under the Difference Principle no one is 'expected . . . to accept lower prospects of life for the sake of others' (pp. 178, 180). But what this means, as Rawls himself notes (p. 103), is that no one is expected to take *less than others receive* in order that the others may have a greater share. It seems likely, however, that those who are endowed with talents which are much in demand will receive less in a society governed by Rawls' Difference Principle than they would if allowed to press for all they could get on a free market. Thus, in a Rawlsian society these people will be asked to accept less than they might otherwise have had, and there is a clear sense in which they will be asked to accept these smaller shares 'for the sake of others'. What, then, can be said to these people?

Rawls' stated answer to this question consists in pointing out that the well-being of the better endowed, no less than that of the other members of society, depends on the existence of social cooperation, and that they can 'ask for the willing cooperation of everyone only if the terms of the scheme are reasonable'. The Difference Principle, Rawls holds, represents the most favorable basis of cooperation the well-endowed could expect others to

---

[15] I will regard this as the canonical formulation of Rawls' principle. When this version of the principle is fulfilled there is a clear sense in which prevailing inequalities are 'to everyone's advantage' since there is no one who would benefit from their removal. Fulfillment of the simple Difference Principle (that inequalities must benefit the worst-off) insures fulfillment of the lexical principle only if expectations of members of the society are 'close knit'—it is impossible to alter the expectations of one representative person without affecting the expectations of every other representative person—and 'chain connected'—if an inequality favoring group A raises the expectations of the worst-off representative person B then it also raises the expectations of every representative person between B and A (pp. 80–2).

accept. Taken by itself this does not seem an adequate response
to the complaint of the better endowed, for the question at issue
is just what terms of cooperation are 'reasonable'.

The particular notion of 'reasonable terms' that Rawls is
appealing to here is one that is founded in the conception of
social cooperation which he is propounding. The basis of this
conception lies not in a particular bias in favor of the less
advantaged but in the idea that economic institutions are reciprocal arrangements for mutual advantage in which the parties
cooperate on a footing of equality. Their cooperative enterprise
may be more or less efficient depending on the talents of the
members and how fully these are developed, but since the value
of these talents is something that is realized only in cooperation
the benefits derived from these talents are seen as a common
product on which all have an equal claim. Thus Rawls says of
his Two Principles that they 'are equivalent . . . to an undertaking
to regard the distribution of natural abilities as a collective asset
so that the more fortunate are to benefit only in ways that help
those who have lost out' (p. 179).

This same notion of the equality of the parties in a cooperative scheme is invoked in the following argument for the
Difference Principle.

Now looking at the situation from the standpoint of one
person selected arbitrarily, there is no way for him to win
special advantages for himself. Nor, on the other hand, are
there grounds for his acquiescing in special disadvantages.
Since it is not reasonable for him to expect more than an
equal share in the division of social goods, and since it is
not rational for him to agree to less, the sensible thing for him
to do is to acknowledge as the first principle of justice one requiring an equal distribution. Indeed, this principle is so
obvious that we would expect it to occur to anyone immediately.

Thus, the parties start with a principle establishing equal
liberty for all, including equality of opportunity, as well as an
equal distribution of income and wealth. But there is no reason
why this acknowledgment should be final. If there are
inequalities in the basic structure that work to make everyone
better off in comparison with the benchmark of initial equality,
why not permit them [p. 150–1]?

If one accepts equality as the natural first solution to the problem of justice then this argument strongly supports the conclusion that the Difference Principle marks the limit of acceptable inequality. More surprisingly, it also appears to show (whether or not one accepts equality as a first solution) that the Difference Principle is the most egalitarian principle it would be rational to adopt from the perspective of parties in the Original Position. It is of course a difficult empirical question how much inequality in income and wealth the Difference Principle will in fact allow, i.e., how many economic inequalities will be efficient enough to 'pay their own way' as the principle requires. The only theoretical limitation on such inequalities provided by Rawls' theory appears to be the possibility that glaring inequalities in material circumstances may give rise to (justified) feelings of loss of self-respect[16] on the part of those less advantaged, offsetting the material gains these inequalities bring them. One can thus make the Difference Principle more (or less) egalitarian by introducing a psychological premiss positing greater (or lesser) sensitivity to perceived inequality. But as far as I am able to determine there is no plausible candidate for adoption in the Original Position which is distinct from the Difference Principle and intermediate between it and strict equality. Since the inequalities allowed by the Difference Principle, while not great, may nonetheless be significant, this strikes me as a surprising fact. What it shows, perhaps, is that if one wishes to defend a position more egalitarian than Rawls' then one must abandon distributive justice as the cardinal virtue of social institutions, i.e., one must abandon the perspective which takes as the dominant moral problem of social cooperation that of justifying distributive institutions to mutually disinterested persons each of whom has a fundamental interest in receiving the greatest possible share of the distributed goods.[17]

---

[16] Inequalities give rise to loss of self-respect in Rawls' sense to the extent that they give a person reason for lack of confidence in his own worth and in his abilities to carry out his life plans (p. 535). Whether given inequalities have this effect will depend not only on their magnitude but also on the public reasons offered to justify them. Rawls believes that effects of this kind will not be a factor in a society governed by the Difference Principle since the inequalities in wealth and income in such a society will not be extreme and will 'probably [be] less than those that have often prevailed' (p. 536). In addition, the justification offered for those inequalities that do prevail will be one which supports the self-esteem of the less advantaged since this justification must appeal to the tendency of these inequalities to advance their good.

[17] A position of this kind was put forward, for example, by Kropotkin. See

The ideal of social cooperation which Rawls presents is naturally contrasted with two alternative conceptions of justice. The first of these is what Rawls calls the system of natural liberty (p. 72). This conception presupposes background institutions which guarantee equal liberties of citizenship in the sense of the First Principle and preserve formal equality of opportunity, i.e., 'that all have at least the same legal rights of access to all advantaged social positions' (p. 72). But no effort is made to compensate for the advantages of birth, i.e., of inherited wealth. Against the background provided by these institutions individuals compete in a free market and are free to press upon one another whatever competitive advantages derive from their different abilities and circumstances.

The second alternative is that of utilitarianism, understood broadly to include the two modified views presented at the end of the last section. The last of those two views differed from the versions of utilitarianism criticized by Rawls in that it incorporated Rawls' principle that no one may be asked to accept a less than equal share in order that some others may enjoy correspondingly greater benefits. But even though it is not simply a maximizing conception, this view is like other forms of utilitarianism in holding it to be the duty of each person to make the greatest possible contribution to the welfare of mankind. Any asset one may have control over, whether a personal talent or a transferable good, one is bound to disburse in such a way as to make the greatest contribution to human well-being.[18] Utilitarianism is in this sense an asocial view; the relation taken as fundamental by the theory is that which holds between any two people when one has the capacity to aid the other. Relations between persons deriving from their position in common institutions, e.g., institutions of production and exchange, are in themselves irrelevant. It would be possible to maintain a view of this kind which focused only on the well-being of members of a particular society, but such a restriction would appear arbitrary.

P. Kropotkin, *The Conquest of Bread*, ch. 13, p. 62, *et passim* (Penguin ed. 1972). Kropotkin holds that if one accepts, as Rawls appears to, the view that the productive capacities of a society must be seen as the common property of its members, then one must reject the idea of wages (or any other way of tying distribution to social roles). Rather, the social product is to be held in common and used to provide facilities which meet the basic needs of all.

[18] This aspect of utilitarianism is most clearly emphasized by William Godwin. See W. Godwin, *Enquiry Concerning Political Justice*, Bk. VIII (3d ed., 1797) (facsim. ed., F. Priestley, 1946).

The natural tendency of utilitarian theories is to be global in their application.

Rawls' Difference Principle can be seen as occupying a position intermediate between these two extremes. Like the system of natural liberty and unlike utilitarianism, Rawls' conception of justice applies only to persons who are related to one another under common institutions. The problem of justice arises, according to Rawls, for people who are engaged in a cooperative enterprise for mutual benefit, and it is the problem of how *the benefits of their cooperation* are to be shared. What the parties in a cooperative scheme owe one another as a matter of justice is an equitable share of this social product, and neither the maximum attainable level of satisfaction nor the goods and services necessary, given their needs and disabilities, to bring them up to a certain level of well-being.

The qualification 'as a matter of justice' is essential here since justice, central though it is, is not the only moral notion for Rawls, and other moral notions take account of need and satisfaction in a way that justice does not. Rawls speaks, for example, of the duty of mutual aid, 'the duty of helping one another when he is in need or jeopardy, provided that one can do so without excessive risk or loss to oneself' (p. 114). Now it seems likely that those to whom we are bound by ties of justice will fare better at our hands (or at least have a stronger claim on us) than those to whom we owe only duties of mutual aid; for justice, which requires that our institutions be arranged so as to maximize the expectations of the worst-off group in our society, says nothing about others elsewhere with whom we stand in no institutional relation but who may be worse off than anyone in our society. If this is so, then it may make a great deal of difference on Rawls' theory where the boundary of society is drawn. Are our relations with the people of South Asia, for example (or the people in isolated rural areas of our own country), governed by considerations of justice or only by the duties which hold between any one human being and another? The only satisfactory solution to this problem seems to me to be to hold that considerations of justice apply at least wherever there is systematic economic interaction; for whenever there is regularized commerce there is an institution in Rawls' sense, i.e., a public system of rules defining rights and duties etc. (p. 55). Thus the Difference Principle would apply to the world economic system taken as a whole as well as as to particular societies within it.

In distinguishing justice from altruism and benevolence and taking it to apply only to arrangements for reciprocal advantage Rawls' theory is like the system of natural liberty. But a proponent of natural liberty takes 'arrangements for reciprocal advantage' in the relevant sense to be arrangements arising out of explicit agreements. Such arrangements are just if they were in fact freely agreed to by the parties involved, and the background institutions of the system of natural liberty are designed to ensure justice in this sense. Since Rawls' Difference Principle constrains people to cooperate on terms other than those they would arrive at through a process of free bargaining on the basis of their natural assets, it is to be rejected. As Rawls says, the terms of this principle are equivalent to an undertaking to regard natural abilities as a common asset, and a proponent of natural liberty would say, I believe, that the terms of the principle apply only where such an undertaking has in fact been made.

Rawls holds, on the other hand, that one is born into a set of institutions whose basic structure largely determines one's prospects and opportunities. Background institutions of the kind described in the system of natural liberty are one example of such institutions; the various institutions satisfying the Difference Principle are another. Within the framework of such institutions one may enter into specific contractual arrangements with others, but these institutions themselves are not established by explicit agreement; they are present from birth and their legitimacy must have some other foundation. The test of legitimacy which Rawls proposes is, of course, the idea of hypothetical contract, as it is embodied in his Original Position construction.

The argument sketched here is obviously parallel to a familiar controversy about the bases of political obligation. The doctrine of natural liberty corresponds to the doctrine which seeks to found all political ties on explicit consent, and seems to me to inherit many of the problems of that view. For Rawls, on the other hand, the legitimacy of both political and economic institutions is to be analyzed in terms of merely hypothetical agreement. (Indeed, Rawls does not separate the two cases.) The parallel between the problems of political institutions and those of economic institutions is often obscured because the political problem is thought of in terms of *obligation* while economic justice is thought of in terms of *distribution.*[19] But

[19] For a discussion of political obligation relevant to economic contribution as well, see M. Walzer, *Obligations* (1970).

economic institutions, no less than political ones, must be capable of generating obligations, viz. obligations to cooperate on the terms these institutions provide in order to produce shares to which others are entitled (p. 313).[20]

The idea of such economic obligations raises a number of interesting issues which I can only mention here. Such an obligation to contribute would be violated, e.g., by a person who, while wishing to receive benefits derived from the participation of others in a scheme of cooperation satisfying the Difference Principle, refused to contribute his own skills on the same terms, holding out for a higher level of compensation than the scheme provided. Presumably obligations of this kind do not in general prevent a person from opting out of a scheme of economic cooperation, any more than political obligation constitutes a general bar to emigration; but this does not mean (in either case) that people are always free to simply pick up and go. Further, there obviously are limits to what a just scheme can demand of those born into it and limits to how far their freedom to choose among different forms of contribution can be restricted. It seems likely that these limits would be defended, on Rawls' view, by appeal to an increasing marginal preference for various species of liberty in the economic sphere relative to other goods. Thus one might claim, following Rawls' argument in Sect. 82, that as soon as a certain level of basic well-being is attained it becomes and then remains irrational for persons to accept lesser control over the terms and conditions of their working lives 'for the sake of greater material means and amenities'. Indeed, such an appeal to increasing preference seems to me more satisfactory as an argument for industrial democracy than as an account of the priority of traditional constitutional liberties.

As I have argued above, the central thesis underlying the Difference Principle is the idea that the basic institutions of society are a cooperative enterprise in which the citizens stand as equal partners. This notion of equality is reflected in Rawls' particular Original Position construction in the fact that these parties are prevented by the veil of ignorance and the requirement that the principles they choose be general (i.e., contain no proper names or token reflexives) from framing prin-

[20] The contribution side of the problem of economic justice is forcefully emphasized in R. Nozick, *Anarchy, State and Utopia* (New York and Oxford, 1974). Nozick criticizes Rawls from the prospective of a purely contractarian view much more sophisticated and subtle than the system of natural liberty I have crudely described here.

ciples which ensure them special advantages.[21] But the fact that it would be chosen under these conditions is not a conclusive argument for the Difference Principle since a person who favored the system of natural liberty would undoubtedly reject the notion that principles of justice must be chosen under these particular constraints. The situation here is similar to that of the argument against perfectionism: Rawls' defense of the Difference Principle must proceed in the main by setting out the ideal of social cooperation of which this principle is the natural expression. The advantages of this ideal—e.g., the fact that institutions founded on this ideal support the self-esteem of their members and provide a public expression of their respect for one another—can be set out, and its ability to account for our considered judgments of justice can be demonstrated, but in the end the adoption of an alternative view is not wholly precluded. A person who, finding that he has less valuable talents, wishes to opt for the system of natural liberty is analogous to the person who, knowing his own conception of the good, prefers a perfectionist system organized around this conception to what I have called 'cooperation on a footing of justice'. In both cases one can offer reasons why cooperation with others on a basis all could agree to in a situation of initial equality is an important good, but one cannot expect to offer arguments which meet the objections of such a person and defeat them on their own grounds.

I do not regard this residual indeterminacy as a failing of Rawls' book or as a source for skepticism. The conception of justice which Rawls describes has an important place in our thought, and to have presented this conception as fully and displayed its deepest features as clearly as Rawls has done is a rare and valuable accomplishment. Almost no one will read the book without finding himself strongly drawn to Rawls' view at many points, and even for those who do not share Rawls' conclusions will come to a deeper understanding of their own views as a result of his work.

[21] These considerations alone, of course, do not ensure that the parties in the Original Position will arrive at a principle of equal distribution even as a first solution. Given that they have no way to ensure a larger share for themselves the question remains whether they should settle for the maximum solution represented by the Difference Principle or gamble on receiving a larger share under some other rule.

SOCIAL JUSTICE AND SOCIAL INSTITUTIONS

HUGO ADAM BEDAU

W HAT is a theory of social justice about? What sort of thing is the primary bearer, so to speak, of the attribute of justice or injustice? What is it that is supposed to conform to the principles of justice? How does our answer to these questions affect our views about the principles of justice themselves, the moral rules in terms of which we distinguish between the just and the unjust in human affairs? Do some theories of justice have an edge over their rivals because of the answers to these questions they require or allow?

For whatever reasons, these questions seem not to have been much asked. It is one of the many virtues of Rawls's *Theory of Justice* [1] that these questions are now easily asked and can be seen to be of interest for the development and appraisal of theories of justice. According to Rawls, the answer to the questions posed above is that a theory of social justice is best thought of as a theory about "the basic institutions of society," [2] of institutions that constitute "the basic structure of society." [3] That the basic structure of society is institutional and that this structure is the primary subject of a theory of justice — that the principles of justice refer first and foremost to the design of this institutional structure — is the thesis I shall refer to, for brevity's sake, as the *institutional* thesis and as Rawls's *institutionalism*. [4] My purpose is to examine this thesis in order to see how it affects the theory of justice as Rawls develops it. To do so, I shall look first at some traditional theories of justice, especially Aristotle's (§1), and then at the views of some contemporary theorists (§2). Next, I shall conjecture explanations for the neglect of the institutional thesis (§3), and examine possible alternatives to it (§4). Finally, I shall turn to some problems in Rawls's own theory to which the institutional thesis gives rise (§§ 5–6).

§1. How widespread among theories of social justice is institutionalism? Is it a familiar and prominent feature of these theories? It is somewhat difficult to get a correct picture of the matter from Rawls's own comments, because he has not bothered

91

to discuss it in detail and because his passing remarks are at best misleading. When he introduces the idea that the basic structure of society is the primary subject of a theory of social justice, he comments that this "may not seem to tally with tradition."[5] But he quickly goes on to mention Aristotle in particular as one who would have accepted the institutional thesis.

Whether this is so, as distinct from whether it would have been better for Aristotle and others if their views had been developed in accord with this thesis, is doubtful. Rawls cites virtually nothing from Aristotle to support his claim, and evidence from the views of those who followed Aristotle and undertook to give us explicit but alternative accounts of justice is conspicuously missing. Indeed, when Rawls mentions Aristotle's examination of the concept of justice, he correctly reminds us that Aristotle shows he thinks of injustice primarily in terms of unfair advantage of one person over another in daily relationships. Accordingly, his conception of justice is "framed to apply to actions."[6] If so, then it is not primarily institutional, since the actions or transactions in question between persons do not involve or depend upon any such institutions. (When Rawls later mentions Kant in a similar context, he concedes that Kant also nowhere spoke of basic institutions as the primary subject of his theory of justice.)[7]

Quite apart from anything Rawls says, it can also be argued that there is little or no evidence that Aristotle has a concept of *social* justice as distinct from *distributive* justice. It is true that most writers, including many recent ones (see below, §2), treat these two concepts as interchangeable, as though the problem of justice is to fit the allocation of goods and services, benefits and advantages, in society to some governing principle. But such an orientation is too primitive. For a society as complex as ours, the fundamental insight to be worked with throughout the theory of justice is that the goods and services to be distributed are in the first instance a direct or indirect product of social cooperation. Without social institutions there cannot be any structure, permanence, or predictability to social cooperation, and without cooperation in the production of goods and services there is little to distribute. Furthermore the institutional constraints on conduct required to attain a given level of productivity are greater than are required to distribute the fruits of that productivity. It is for this reason that Rawls can rightly say that, on his or any adequate theory, "distributive justice as frequently understood, justice in the relative shares of material means, is relegated to a subordinate place."[8] But the collapse of social justice into traditional distributive justice, or the irrelevance of distinguishing the two, is a direct outgrowth of the Aristotelian analysis of justice. It is in fact the traditional view.

So how is Rawls able to persuade himself that his position is nonetheless continuous with tradition? He argues:[9] (a) in Aristotle, fair as distinct from unfair advantage in individual actions is determined by a conception or principle of "what property belongs to a person and of what is due him;" (b) such a principle is "very often derived from social institutions and the legitimate expectations to which they give rise." Before turning to criticize this argument, let us note that a principle such as Aristotle's on fair division or apportionment might usefully be called a "secondary" principle of justice, because it has no direct or explicit reference to the structure of basic social institutions (as the fundamental principles of justice are supposed to have) and because its status can therefore be likened to that of the moral principles (including the "standards" and "maxims" of justice) John Stuart Mill called "secondary" by contrast to his principle of utility.[10]

Premise (b) in the above argument is too weak for Rawls's purpose. His argument as it stands does not entail that Aristotle's theory of justice is really about the basic structure of social institutions, unless there is no other way — or no alternative that is plausible — to account for the secondary principles in question. Rawls has not asserted nor has he tried to establish that there is no other way to account for them; I do not believe that it could be established. If I am right, the alleged continuity with Aristotle is unwarranted on the evidence Rawls himself has offered, and it would be more accurate to regard Rawls as having given us a rational reconstruction of part of Aristotle's views of justice so that it can be seen as a foreshadowing of Rawls's own theory.

In this vein, we might notice that there is a better argument than the one Rawls gives for the conclusion he tries to establish. In *Politics*, Book III, Aristotle stresses the connection between justice in society — legal and distributive justice — and alternative types of political constitution (democratic, oligarchic, monarchic). It could be argued that justice, on such a view, is at least in part constitution-relative. Since a society's constitution is its most important institutional determinant, Aristotle's view of what counts as a just distribution or as lawful in any given society rests on the nature or structure of that society's most basic institutions as defined by its constitution. Aristotle himself does not advance any argument such as this; he never tries to connect his constitutionalism with a doctrine that the basic structure of society is the primary subject of justice. But then it is doubtful whether any philosopher prior to Rawls has *argued* for this view. For reasons I consider below, however, I think that this possible argument Aristotle might have developed has to be put to one side because of other features of his views that orient us in a different direction. Even so, I think this argument is a better one than the one Rawls actually gives and on which he based his claim of continuity with the tradition that begins with Aristotle.

One more consideration counts against Rawls's claim of continuity with the tradition, namely, his criticism of theories of justice, such as Mill and Marx provide, that are built mainly around "commonsense precepts of justice."[11] Rawls objects that such precepts, for example, "to each according to his effort," cannot be the fundamental principles of justice because they are formulated "at the wrong level of generality."[12] They cannot be readily connected with the features of "the background system"[13] — the basic social institutions whose structure and function determine who gets what. I think this criticism is persuasive and revealing of what is wrong with all those theories that place great weight on such maxims or precepts.[14] Not their least fault is the way they tend to end up with an arbitrary and pluralistic doctrine of justice. But criticism of theories along these lines does not sit well with Rawls's contention that his own institutional emphasis is, after all, only the traditional one. If we can say of Aristotle, as we must, that although he never explicitly ties his notions of unfair advantage in distribution to any features of basic institutions, nevertheless (as Rawls would have it) he recognizes that his precepts of justice are to be understood as derived from a conception of these institutions, then why can't we make the same maneuver on behalf of Mill and Marx? Either there is something special about Aristotle's precepts of distributive justice, something Rawls has not identified and to which I cannot point, that ties them in to features of the basic structure of society, or Rawls's criticism of Mill and Marx for being content with precepts that lack such a tie is unnecessary and unimaginative. A better view of the whole matter, as I have already suggested, is that Rawls's institutionalism departs from tradition more than he is willing to acknowledge, and constitutes a rational reconstruction of part of that tradition. It may be, as he says, that "any ethical theory recognizes the importance of the basic structure as a subject of justice."[15] But if we are convinced that this structure is the primary subject of a theory of justice, it is likely to be only after thorough exposure to Rawls's views and the implicit invitation they contain to rethink and reconstruct traditional ethical theories in this way.

§2. Essentially the same conclusions can be reached by a different route. With the wisdom of hindsight, we can now see that an institutional emphasis in the theory of social justice is implicit (occasionally explicit) in the series of papers Rawls wrote prior to his treatise and beginning with his widely read paper of twenty years ago, "Justice as Fairness." But how prominent was this emphasis in the views of others during the same two decades? Because institutionalism may now seem so plausible and attractive, we might not realize how relatively novel it is even today. To prove the point would require an extensive and tedious examination, but a brief consideration of six recent discussions of justice should illustrate it convincingly.

Shortly after Rawls's "Justice as Fairness" appeared, the influential volume of essays on social justice edited by Richard B. Brandt was published.[16] In the opening essay, William K. Frankena set out an account of "the concept of social justice" in which he pointed out that "social justice" is "not . . . a property of individuals and their actions, but . . . a predicate of societies . . . and of their acts and institutions."[17] Furthermore, lest social justice collapse into one of its proper parts, political justice, Frankena refused to identify it with the "formal" to the exclusion of the "informal" features of society. By the "informal" aspects of society properly part of social justice he meant a society's "cultural institutions, conventions, moral rules, and moral sanctions."[18] But once moral rules have been mentioned, Frankena says nothing more about institutions. It is as though the institutions will take care of themselves once we identify the correct moral rules that constitute the principles of justice.

In a later essay,[19] Frankena discusses both egalitarian (democratic) and inegalitarian (oligarchic, aristocratic) conceptions of justice. His purpose is to show that these alternative ideas of the place of equality in justice turn on general conceptions of society, which in turn depend upon and reflect different views about basic social (in this instance, mainly political) institutions. However, in this essay as in the earlier one, there is no emphasis on any of the institutions necessary to implement the principles that define justice. The idea that the principles of justice do their work in society primarily by dictating the design of basic social institutions is nowhere to be found. It is not denied, but it is not asserted or even considered.

Concurrent with the publication of Brandt's book on social justice, A. M. Honoré published the initial version of his essay on social justice.[20] Honoré makes much out of the intuitive contrast between "individual" and "social" justice.[21] One might think this contrast would be developed in terms of relations among individuals that do not involve social institutions, and those that do. No such contrast is drawn. Instead, we are offered vague ideas about what differentiates social justice from individual justice: It concerns the claims of an individual "against other members of society as a whole,"[22] "the claims of man as man," in contrast to the claims between persons that involve "special relations" between them.[23] These ideas are difficult and perhaps impossible to use in this form; they could have been usefully reformulated in terms of what gives structure to "society as a whole" and to "man as man," *viz.*, basic social institutions. Honoré's emphasis on the principle of equal opportunity as one of the principles of social justice and his recognition of the complexity of equal opportunity[24] make his silence on the need for close attention to social institutions all the more distressing.

Probably the most widely read recent monograph on justice prior to the appearance of Rawls's own treatise was Nicholas Rescher's book, *Distributive Justice*. Rescher rightly stresses at the very outset that "social justice . . . has both a political and an economic dimension" and that the latter concerns "the entire question of the proper distribution of goods and services within the society."[25] One might expect that this would naturally lead Rescher to emphasize the role of economic and political institutions in terms of which distributions will proceed, but it does not. He immediately abandons any reference to society or the state and its institutions as essential to the concept of social justice, because "the scope of our concept will include the distribution of goods and evils generally, without regard to whether the distributing agent is an individual or person proper, or a collective individual or 'person' such as a corporation or state."[26] It is unclear why it should be assumed, as it seems Rescher does, that the very same principles govern justice in society in the production and distribution of goods and services, and the individual in personal transactions with other persons. But once such an assumption is made, there is no possibility that any special weight can be given to the existence, role, structure, and function of basic social institutions in the elucidation of social justice. Accordingly, one finds no further discussion of such institutions in Rescher's monograph.

Consider, finally, three of the most recent discussions: The essay-length book by N. M. L. Nathan, *The Concept of Justice*, which appeared a few months before Rawls's treatise; the first major alternative theory to Rawls's, Robert Nozick's "entitlement theory of distributive justice"; and the most recent book of all, David Miller's *Social Justice*.

Nathan, perhaps uniquely among writers on justice, self-consciously addresses himself to the kinds of "objects" to which the term, "just," "can be sensibly applied."[27] His list of these objects is a very short one: "actions, persons or states of affairs."[28] Taken literally, it looks as if Nathan has committed himself to the view that reference to just or unjust *institutions* is strictly senseless, because the semantics of "just" forbid such reference. This seems so absurdly implausible that one is bound to search for a way out. One such way is to relax what counts as a state of affairs. Instead of saying that talk about the injustice of an institution, for example, slavery, is senseless or never occurs at all, one might say that such talk is shorthand for reference to the unjust states of affairs that constitute or result from the institution of slavery, or to the unjust actions this institution permits, or to the unjust persons (the masters) that this institution essentially involves. No doubt slavery involves injustice in all these ways, but what is the point of the maneuver in the first place? If talk about the justice of institutions is an unfortunate or unilluminating or unnecessary way to formulate the issues, then by all means let that be argued. But if such talk is not only desirable but (as Rawls claims) necessary to the development of an adequate theory of justice, then any such semantic doctrines as Nathan's, which imply that the domain of the just/unjust simply does not include any institutions, and a fortiori not any "basic" institutions, is misguided from the start.

It could be argued in reply that nowhere in his essay does Nathan (unlike Frankena, Honoré, and Rescher) purport to be telling us anything about *social* justice. This is true enough, but it is a weak line of defense all the same. Given Nathan's opening declaration of purpose ("My first aim in this essay is to describe the range of senses of 'just' and the even wider range of conceivable principles of justice"),[29] the only conclusion we can draw from the fact that he nowhere discusses or uses the term "social justice" is that he thinks this term is not used at all or that it is used only as an inconsequential term of art or that the sense of this term is identical with one of the senses of the term "just" that he does identify. The result, in any case, is the total neglect of any reference to social institutions in his overall account.

Of all of Rawls's early critics, none understands better than Nozick that Rawls's theory of justice is an institutional theory in the sense in which I have been using the phrase. Yet it is one of the curious features of his own "entitlement theory of distributive justice" that it is extremely difficult to see how much or little of this Rawlsian viewpoint is retained. Nozick's central doctrine is that the justice of a person's "holdings" at any given time is entirely a function of the way the person got them. They could be obtained rightfully only in three ways: by "acquisition" from the stock of non-holdings, by "transfer" from someone else's holdings, or by "rectification" from a third party acting to correct a prior unjust acquisition or transfer.[30] How acts manipulating holdings in these ways are to be regulated and implemented in practice is not something Nozick discusses. What institutions, if any, this theory requires is also not discussed. The theory, of course, is quite reminiscent of Hobbes's, because it looks as if the only government institutions needed will be the traditional ones of the "minimal" or "nightwatchman" state, viz., the police and the courts. Their function will be to protect the most important institution of them all: private property. All other social institutions presumably will serve and implement these. But no special role is allotted to them in the entitlement theory. They bear no noticeable burdens, discharge no identified functions, and their structure is never mentioned. What if any special features are required by the police powers and the institution of private property are also ignored, as though these things do not matter to the practice of justice where justice is defined through entitlements. Whether Nozick even thinks of his theory as one in which there is an answer to the question, What is the primary subject of a theory of justice, is unclear. It is clear that if he thinks the answer is the basic institutions of society, then he has failed to make this answer explicit and to tell us what those institutions are.

The situation with David Miller is quite different. When Miller tells us what social justice is, his definition is obviously Rawlsian: "Social justice . . . concerns the distribution of benefits and burdens throughout a society, as it results from the major social institutions — property systems, public organizations, etc."[31] But as Miller's subsequent discussion shows, his arguments (including his criticisms of Rawls) do not focus on this institutional aspect, central to his definition. Rawls is criticized for everything but the way his principles are addressed to the design of social institutions, with the result that Miller (along with most of Rawls's critics so far) does not see the way in which Rawls's attack on desert,[32] on the commonsense precepts of justice,[33] and his defense of pure procedural justice,[34] to cite but three examples, are all intimately tied to his emphasis on social justice as a property first and foremost of basic social institutions. The bulk of Miller's book is devoted to contrasting the different conceptions of justice to be found in Hume, Herbert Spencer, and the anarchist utopian Kropotkin. Here it can be said of Miller's book that it does tend to apply the institutional emphasis consistent with his own definition of social justice quoted above. What the reader is offered is an account of the different social, political, and economic institutions appropriate to the views of these three thinkers. One could even argue that to the degree Miller is successful in accomplishing his major purpose — to show that "substantive ideas of social justice . . . take radically different forms in different types of society"[35] — he presents us with a case study of the fruitful consequences of the institutional thesis in the examination of alternative conceptions of social justice. Thus Miller's book is both an exception to the prevailing practice that neglects the importance of social institutions in the theory of social justice, and (at least in his criticism of Rawls's theory) an illustration of it as well.

§3. The discussion so far of Aristotle and representative contemporary thinkers yields a common conclusion: None of these philosophers explicitly takes the basic structure as the primary subject of his theory of justice. Why is this so? It is not as though one finds arguments from these philosophers to the effect that one should not take the basic structure as the primary subject. If my account is correct, it is mainly the uniform neglect of this idea that needs explaining.

After reading Rawls's treatise, one's inclination may be to think that this neglect is simply owing to a persistent and widespread failure of analysis among philosophers. Perhaps so. It would hardly be the first time that an essential ingredient of any true theory on a topic turns out to be missing in the accounts provided by reputable thinkers. Another possibility is that by committing themselves to the view that the principles of justice refer mainly to something else, philosophers have blinded themselves to the possibility or desirability of the institutional emphasis found in Rawls. I shall examine this further in §4. Yet another possibility is that most philosophers, classic and recent, write as if they had an independent criterion for the justice or injustice of the distribution of goods in society, so that it does not matter much what the character of social institutions is, so long as the outcome of their operation satisfies the criterion. Because Rawls denies that any such criterion exists, he is driven to a position in which the basic institutional structure in conjunction with "pure procedural justice" alone must suffice. I shall examine this point further in §6.

There is a further possibility worth considering. May it not be, at least for some philosophers, that they see all basic social institutions as a relatively fixed and irrelevant background against which the morally relevant aspects of our lives — including justice and injustice in human affairs — are played out? In Hobbes, for example, we are presented with a conception of justice defined in terms of the keeping of valid covenants, a definition that confines justice to the relatively superficial and narrow sphere of interpersonal transactions. Laws as such, Hobbes explicitly informs us, and by implication all institutions and practices that depend on sovereign decision, are neither just nor unjust.[36] Can it be that Hobbes thinks (exactly the reverse of Rawls) that if we look after the pennies — particular transactions between morally equal persons — the pounds will take care of themselves? It is unlikely. It is more probable that Hobbes's narrow view of the scope of justice is owing to his beliefs about human nature and moral psychology, the necessity for strong centralized government, and the immunity of basic social institutions to design and redesign.

Such an interpretation as this may not be persuasive without further evidence marshalled from a close reading of the relevant texts. Still, it illustrates the possibility that the absence of any prominent assertion and analysis of the institutional thesis in the philosophical literature on justice prior to Rawls may be owing to important but unavowed ideas and assumptions relating to other matters. If nothing else, bringing the institutional thesis into prominence may help bring these latent conceptions and beliefs incompatible with it to the surface, where they can be evaluated for their impact on the theory of justice.

§4. In order to get a better grasp on the institutional thesis, it may be useful to consider directly the alternatives. If we ask, What could be the primary subject of a theory of justice?, all the answers we are likely to get can be sorted into one or another of a few categories: *Persons*, in virtue of their character or their acts, the *acts* themselves, the *character* of persons manifested and developed by those acts, the *pattern* of possessions distributed among persons, or the *basic social institutions* that control and supply the distribution of possessions (the institutional thesis). Let us look briefly at these alternatives to institutionalism.

Justice, insofar as it is thought of as a virtue, can be treated like the other virtues, as a trait of character of persons who are just. Justice, on this view, is the virtue that makes just men act justly; it is the virtue that just men exhibit when they act according to character. Philosophers, however, seem not to have regarded either the virtue itself or the persons who have it as strong candidates for the primary subject of a theory of justice. It is easy to see why. Aristotle's theory of moral education, for example, incorporates the notion that a person acquires moral virtues by imitating and extrapolating from the conduct of those who already have the virtue.[37] A person has a virtue only if he has a settled trait of character to act in accord with certain principles. For the moral beginner, it is as though the task of becoming a just person were to begin with such things as standing patiently with one's parents in a queue, as an instance of compliance with a precept of justice (first come, first served), or being awarded a prize for placing first in a race, as an instance of another precept of justice (to the winner belongs the spoils). In due course, the character trait of being just is acquired by conducting oneself in accord with the relevant precepts in the relevant situations. The explanatory role of the virtue of justice is thus secure. It accounts for the promptness with which the just person does the right thing in the right way at the right time. But the subject of justice, the bearer of the attribute itself, is the *act*, whether of a person who is just or of one who is only learning to be just. This also explains why it is not primarily the person that is just. For a person who is not just can perform a just act, and we can characterize the just without reference to the person who is just. Logical priority for the subject of justice thus falls elsewhere than on the character trait or on the person who has it. It belongs to the acts that conform to the precepts and principles of justice. Hobbes is another philosopher who defines justice in such a way that it becomes a predicate of actions, *viz.*, of performances on valid covenants. On such a view, it is only natural to imply that the primary subject of justice is such performances.

One of the advantages of the view shared by Aristotle, Hobbes, and others is that it implies that it is possible to reach a correct and final judgment on the justice or injustice of particular acts — transactions, exchanges, undertakings, acquisitions, transfers, purchases, sales, payments, and so forth — and to do so by virtue of some feature of the act itself (its history, Nozick would say). This is surely the intuitive view as well, and almost every critic of Rawls has relied on it to some extent, because most of the commonsense counter-examples to Rawls's principles of justice are generated by considerations of these sorts.[38] Oddly enough, however, few of these critics seem to have noticed that if Rawls is right, there are insuperable difficulties in generalizing over the discontinuous and heterogeneous judgments of particular justice (as we might call them), and that in any case counter-examples of this sort cannot refute a theory of justice that makes the basic social structure, and not any individual acts, the primary subject. This is not to deny the attractiveness of theories that share the view to be found in philosophers as different as Aristotle and Hobbes. The perennial ideas of a fair wage, fair price, fair compensation, fair opportunity and the like have usually been built up out of models drawn from fair agreements, fair division of a fixed stock of goods, fair contests — all examples of familiar situations where the focus is on some individual act (winning a race, slicing a cake, tossing a coin) and where it is implausible to refocus on any underlying institutional structure. But if Rawls is right, intuitive paradigms of justice drawn from such quarters are of limited utility for a theory of social justice, and a theory based upon them to the exclusion or subordination of other considerations will turn out to be wrong-headed, superficial, and unworkable.

The remaining alternative — that justice is fundamentally lodged in the distribution pattern of things (goods, rights) that persons possess — is one toward which radically egalitarian and utilitarian theories of justice are inevitably driven. Following Nozick, we can say that the principle of utility is a "patterned principle" because "it specifies that a distribution is to vary along with some natural dimension,"[39] *viz.*, the aggregate or average level of satisfaction. The resulting distribution is patterned if it accords with some such principle. As critics of utilitarianism have pointed out, once the focus of attention shifts to maximizing (total or average) happiness, satisfaction or whatever, which persons are the ones who happen to have what satisfactions, and therefore what goods and rights, is of no significance in itself. If there are moral rules developed and enforced to insure continuity in the ownership of things and the possession of rights, this is merely because such continuities are instrumental in achieving the desired maximization. It is not an essential feature required by the theory. Social justice on such an outlook cannot attach pre-eminent significance to any acts or virtues of persons, or to the persons themselves, as they are all only so many centers of satisfaction.[40] Thus Nozick's comment that "all that needs to be looked at, in judging the justice of a distribution [under a patterned principle], is who ends up with what"[41] is at best misleading, so far as utilitarianism is concerned, because this theory "does not take seriously the distinction between persons."[42] What alone matters, as Nozick himself makes clear elsewhere, is simply the pattern constituting "the current time-slice" or "the end-result" or "end-state."[43] Where aggregates or averages rule, the fact that some particular individuals and not others do or have certain things is incidental. Similarly, the fact (if it is a fact) that without certain basic social institutions this aggregate or average cannot be created, preserved, or enlarged over time is a secondary consideration. It merely shows again that such institutions are necessary conditions of a just society. The justice of the society does not attach to them, but to the aggregate of whatever it is that they yield and that the utilitarian principle in question counts as good.

These alternatives to institutionalism, including Rawls's version of that thesis, are consistent with certain assumptions or possibilities that are inconsistent with institutionalism and that Rawls implicitly or explicitly rejects. (1) It is possible that there are no major or basic social institutions, in Rawls's sense, at all. (N. B. What this sense is has yet to be stated, and examples of such institutions have yet to be given; see §§5–6 below). Despite the absence of such institutions, judgments of justice and injustice might make sense, so long as persons are in social contact and not in social isolation. (Hobbes, as is known, explicitly requires more, but he is an exception.) (2) It is also possible that although there are basic institutions in society, we do not know which ones are basic and which are not. Either we lack a criterion for the distinction, or we lack adequate evidence to apply it. (Strictly, of course such systematic ignorance does not invalidate institutionalism, but it would nullify the usefulness of developing a theory of justice of that sort.) (3) Even if there are major social institutions and we know which they are, their effects on the traits of persons, their acts, or the patterns of distribution, could be relatively insignificant. In any case, these effects could always be isolated and disregarded in theory from what makes for the justice or injustice of the primary subject (a move crucial to Nozick's criticism of Rawls).[44] If so, then we can judge the justice of particular persons, acts, and distribution patterns without first (or ever) establishing the justice of the basic institutions themselves. Likewise, stability or instability of the basic institutions does not matter very much, because what is just and why it is just (except for the justice of institutions) does not depend upon the structure of these institutions. Similarly, justice in society can be increased or decreased without significantly altering the basic institutions, whatever they are. (4) Insofar as the basic institutions themselves can be judged to be just or unjust, it is because of the ways they facilitate or impede the development of justice in persons, their deeds or their possessions. There is no way independently of these effects to bring about the justice of institutions. (5) Given that persons differ in their natural endowments and the opportunities that come to them in terms of which their talents are exercised and cultivated, or neglected and frustrated, there is nothing wrong with permitting the consequences of luck and talent to work out over time unaffected by the design of institutions. Since justice is nothing but the working out over time of natural endowments, the only institutions that justice allows are those that implement or express the interaction of these endowments and the opportunities for their exercise.

If Rawls is correct, *all* of these assumptions must be false. Institutionalism in the theory of social justice assumes from the start that such possibilities as the above must be rejected. In the end, they are part of the articulation of a different view of man and society. To challenge Rawls's institutionalism, therefore, it is sufficient to establish at least one of these views. Whether this can be done — most of the several assumptions listed above seem to me ill-suited to play any role in explaining ourselves as social creatures — I leave for others to examine in detail.

§5. One way to motivate concern for our interest in the institutional thesis (apart from the weakness of alternatives to it, explored above) is to consider the following line of reasoning. On any theory of social justice, a given action of a person either depends upon (as when, for example, it amounts to administration of) the basic social structure, or it does not. Where it does, then the structure of the institution in question is decisive because the action simply transmits or applies in a particular instance the features of the institution itself. Where it does not, if the institutional thesis is correct, the action of the individual is of no great consequence one way or the other so far as social justice is concerned, because its effects will in time be blunted or effaced by interference from the basic social institutions. On any alternative, therefore, the powerful impact upon individual action from the basic social institutions is inescapable. If justice is to prevail in society, then the principles of justice cannot ignore the structure of the basic social institutions. Since these institutions also serve as the basis for ongoing social cooperation, and since it is this cooperation that is the source of most of the goods at the disposal of society, a parallel argument to the one already given can easily be constructed to yield the same conclusion.

Considerable interest, therefore, attaches to how we are to answer a variety of questions about the nature of these basic institutions. Great weight has to rest upon our knowledge, for example, of history, anthropology, political economy, and political sociology to assure us that the actual functions of basic social institutions are not subtly dependent upon factors that will frustrate instead of foster the requirements of social justice, human freedom, natural equality, and the right to equal regard as persons. (These ideals and principles are prominent in Rawls's theory of justice as fairness though not necessary to every possible institutionalist approach to social justice.) We also have to be able to identify and measure the effects of the basic institutions upon persons and to construct the appropriate counterfactual generalizations of what personal character, aspiration, and conduct would be like in the absence of actual basic social institutions and in the presence of a different set. Unless these matters can be handled relatively reliably, we will have reason to doubt whether a theory of social justice ought to be primarily about the basic institutional structure of society, or — what is worse — reason to doubt whether a theory of social justice can be developed at all or actually implemented to any great extent in human life.

5.1 These desiderata and others can be illustrated by reference to certain features of Rawls's own theory. (a) Rawls nowhere gives a list of all and only the institutions that he regards as basic, nor does he give a criterion for a basic social institution. What appears to be his definition of "the basic structure" (*viz.*, "a public system of rules defining a scheme of activities that leads men to act together so as to produce a greater sum of benefits and assigns to each certain recognized claims to a share in the proceeds")[45] is not easily connected with actual institutions. The examples he gives initially of basic institutions — "the legal protection of freedom of thought and conscience, competitive markets, private property in the means of production, and the monogamous family"[46] — are all familiar institutions of *our* society. But they are not equally basic even for us, and they certainly have not all been basic throughout recorded history. Moreover, why any of these institutions is basic and what the evidence is for its basic status is not discussed. This lack raises the question whether Rawls has, or thinks he has, enough empirical information to give us this necessary information about basic social institutions. (b) Rawls does define the concept of an institution,[47] and his discussion shows that he does so at least in part so that he can characterize the basic structure of society. Yet his definition is framed to include among institutions "games and rituals, trials and parliaments, markets and systems of property."[48] Since games and rituals would never be basic social institutions (Rawls himself implies they would not), his definition is at least intended to be broader than what is wanted for the proper characterization of all and only basic institutions. One might also be uncomfortable with the unsociological notion of institution that Rawls defines, a notion of "social practice" that he has long favored.[49] At the very least, one would like assurance that there is a close fit between what Rawls regards as a "basic" social institution and what a social scientist might identify under this rubric. (c) Rawls devotes nearly a third of his treatise to discussing the nature of institutions (*viz.*, Part II, "Institutions," especially Chapters IV and V), and it is presumably basic institutions exclusively to which his discussion is directed. The foremost such institution, he says, is the political constitution, because "the constitution is the foundation of the social structure."[50] But Rawls's idea of a constitution and what counts as the actual constitution of an actual state are not identical. The reason is not merely that every actual constitution has some features of injustice in it, although it should not be forgotten that actual constitutions of actual states are at least in part the product of considerations other than social justice, as the study of our own constitutional history amply confirms. The reason is that Rawls in effect defines the constitution as whatever institutions are necessary and sufficient to implement the principles of justice. The interdefined nature of the idea of a basic institution, the constitution, and the principles of justice leaves us still uncertain what these institutions are, just as the gap between what Rawls means by "constitution" and the actual constitutions of actual states entails that we cannot be sure that by the study of the institutions basic to any given constitution we are studying what Rawls would regard as basic institutions.

5.2 Let us approach all this in another way. If Rawls's thesis about the primary subject of justice and the social structure is true and interesting, then it ought to be possible to divide all institutions into two groups, *viz.*, those that are basic and all the others. Since Rawls clearly denies that his theory is the only possible theory of justice, we also ought to be able to make a further independent division of institutions into three groups, viz., those basic institutions required by *any* theory of justice, the additional ones required by Rawls's theory, and all other institutions (some of which will be required by other theories of justice, and the rest of which will be required by none). It would be a bit of an exercise to take every identifiable social institution and sort it by means of the cells of this matrix. It is also doubtful whether the task could even be completed successfully because the whole concept of basic institutions in Rawls's theory is vaguer than one might expect, given the role he insists they are supposed to play in any adequate theory of social justice.

It will suffice to illustrate some of the problems encountered if we attend to the part of this large task that consists of identifying the basic institutions required by Rawls's own theory. As we have seen, these will be all and only the institutions necessary and sufficient to implement the principles of greatest equal liberty, with fair equality of opportunity, and the difference principle, in lexical order.[51] What, exactly, are these institutions? One expects to see Rawls say, as he does, that they are "those of a constitutional democracy."[52] But all he really says is that these institutions suffice; he explicitly denies he gives any argument that they are necessary, and suggests that perhaps they are not.[53] Such caution is praiseworthy, but it is troubling not to be told whether, for example, political parties or a system of regular elections or jury trial or an independent judiciary is *necessary* to implement the principles of justice in a constitutional democracy. It is difficult to believe that none of these institutions is necessary, and it is also difficult to believe that there is no argument that shows they are necessary.

Given Rawls's emphasis on the rules that define a social practice, it is not surprising that when he undertakes to talk about a basic social institution it is these rules or principles on which he concentrates. Thus, whether or not there are any churches in a society is a genuine question about the existence and function of certain social institutions, *viz.*, the religious ones. This is apparently of no importance to Rawls's theory. Instead, what is important is only that *if* there are churches then they must be free of interference on ideological grounds, and *if* there are churches then there must be as many or as few as the religious aspirations of persons dictate.[54] In short, what Rawls offers to us under the name of basic social institutions tends to reduce to how certain institutions must embody certain principles (for example, toleration of religious belief) appropriate to the first principles of justice.

5.3 A good illustration of a further problem, the non-neutrality of the basic social institutions to various other features of the overall theory, can be seen if we look at Rawls's account of the background institutions needed for economic justice. Rawls mentions as appropriate and sufficient, but not as necessary or inevitable, four or five "branches" of government, with relatively distinct functions that enable them to fulfill the requirements of the difference principle, *viz.*, the "allocative," "stabilization," "transfer," "distributive," and "exchange" branches.[55] All the details about the structure and function of these institutions, however, are left out. Two reasons are offered. One is that Rawls believes his theory of social justice is neutral between socialist and capitalist economies.[56] The other is that he believes the missing details relate to "questions of political judgment" and not to the theory of justice.[57] At some point or other, one must concede the latter claim, so I shall not pursue it further here. But the former is more fundamental, and warrants comment.

First of all, the five branches of government themselves already involve economic functions no classical capitalist would allow. Rawls can think of his principles of justice as neutral between socialist and capitalist economies only with respect to residual issues; he has already turned over to government major functions of what could otherwise be in the private sphere. Second, if Rawls's principles of justice are neutral between socialist and capitalist economics, it is only on certain assumptions. *A priori*, it seems unlikely that it does not matter to social justice whether a society uses the economic institution of the market place broadly or narrowly and whether it encourages or discourages public ownership of its major industries. For instance, it has lately been argued that for a society such as ours, a shift to a wholly collectivized economy would achieve "only a small improvement in equality at the expense of a significant worsening of efficiency."[58] Under Rawls's principles of justice, any argument for significant institutional change (such as the shift from private to public ownership represents) must be tested not only by reference to the difference principle but by the principle of greatest equal liberty as well. If the economic judgment quoted above is sound, the difference principle suffices to reject the institutional change, since the worst off would have little if anything to gain and perhaps much to lose whenever overall economic efficiency drops significantly with a slight decrease in their distance from the socio-economic mean. If, in addition, it is empirically true that "a market economy helps to safeguard political rights against encroachment by the state" [59] — that is, helps to stabilize the operation of the first principle of justice — then it looks as if the choice for a market over a socialist economy is *required* by the principles of justice themselves. In this case, Rawls would be wrong in thinking that his principles of justice are consistent with socialist economic institutions. Much turns, therefore, on whether the empirical economic judgments quoted above are special cases or are among "the general facts about human society" that figure in the calculations from "the original position." [60]

5.4 Finally, we must consider the one basic non-governmental institution that Rawls mentions, the family. I would suppose that in almost any anthropology and sociology, the family emerges as an important social institution. Rawls, as we saw, cites "the monogamous family" as a "major social institution." [61] But is it a basic institution in the sense in which he says that it is the structure of such institutions that the principles of justice are primarily about? Rawls gives no reason for an affirmative answer, and I can think of none. If the idea is that the theory of justice as fairness dictates a preference for the monogamous family, in contrast to families based on polygamy, polandry, unisexual or unmarried heterosexual liaisons, and the like, then the inference eludes me. It also elevates the monogamous family to a status that is probably not endorsed by most behavioral, social, and clinical scientists. If, however, the idea is that the theory of justice as fairness dictates a need for the family in some form, rather than either the cessation of procreation and child-rearing or the conduct of these activities without any socially recognizable family forms, then agreement might be more readily forthcoming. Even so, however, it is difficult to see how the existence and structure of the family as a social institution is *required* by the principles of justice taken severally or together. It is, after all, the requirement or the necessity of certain institutions that is at issue, [62] not merely their consistency with the principles of justice. If the argument is that the family must be regulated by the principles of justice, not because these principles require this institution but because the structure and function of the family have such far-reaching and permanent effects upon all aspects of social life, then new considerations come into play. For one thing, we now have need of a criterion of basic institutions that will make them independent of the constitution of society (as Rawls understands that term) and of the principles of justice. While this certainly caters to our initial intuitions, according to which institutions are going to be more or less basic as a function of the permanence and prominence of their effects on social relationships, it goes against the main thrust of Rawls's apparent conception of what makes a basic institution basic. The case of the family, therefore, emerges as an interesting test for several of the fundamental ideas surrounding Rawls's institutional approach to the theory of justice.

§6. From a theoretical point of view, the reason it is important to defend and clarify the institutional thesis is that if Rawls is correct, any judgment on the justice or injustice of the actual distribution of goods and services in society must be the product of a judgment on the justice of the basic structure itself. If there were an independent criterion for the fair division of all goods and services in society, then it would be simply a question of finding a set of institutions to guarantee or at least progressively approximate the requirements of the criterion. Social justice would then be a case of "perfect procedural justice." Rawls believes that this is impossible, except in simple cases (his example is dividing a cake fairly among a few persons),[63] and they provide no solution and not even any guidance for the problem of justice in society. Instead, as in cases of fair gambling or a fair lottery, the best that can be done is to set up a fair procedure and apply it, secure in the knowledge that whatever the outcome is, no one has any complaint against it on grounds of fairness. In such cases, "the background circumstances define a fair procedure."[64] In society, the background circumstances are the basic social institutions, and their regular operation amounts to the toss of the dice in the game of social life.[65] Social justice is thus a case of "pure procedural justice."

Insofar as Rawls has an argument for his view that social justice is a case of pure procedural justice, its fundamental form is a simple disjunctive syllogism. There are, he implies, only three possibilities to start with, viz., pure, perfect, and imperfect procedural justice. Two of them can be directly eliminated because they depend on the availability of an independent criterion for what counts as a fair division of the social product. Presumably, an independent criterion of the sort in question would be something that would tell each person in a society at any given time exactly what fraction of goods and services he or she deserves as a fair share of the whole. Rawls nowhere directly addresses himself to the proof that no such criterion exists, but throughout his discussion of other points the difficulty, perhaps the utter impossibility, of arriving at any such criterion is implied. Once this basic point is granted, and so long as utter scepticism over the very possibility of a theory of social justice does not take over, the only alternative seems to be the one he defends.

There is a troubling lapse, however, in his account. In a few passages in his treatise, he comments to the effect that at the level of policy, "the best attainable scheme is one of imperfect procedural justice."[66] One way to take this remark is to take it literally, that is, as a judgment about the availability of what is defined elsewhere as "imperfect procedural justice." This leads straight to a fundamental contradiction, because imperfect procedural justice involves (a) an independent criterion of the just outcome or result of a practice, but (b) no procedures sufficient to guarantee such an outcome (the example is of a criminal trial, where innocent persons, defined as those who are not guilty as charged, are nevertheless sometimes convicted).[67] Rawls's fundamental position is that where social justice is concerned, we lack the independent criterion but fortunately have just procedures. So politics can never involve "imperfect procedural justice" in this sense. If it could, then the whole argument for the crucial importance of the basic structure, tied in as it is with the necessity of "pure procedural justice," would collapse.

There is another not implausible way to understand these passages. Presumably when Rawls says that in politics all we can hope for is imperfect procedural justice he really means that we must not expect to achieve results that satisfy the exact requirements of pure procedural justice, much less those that define perfect procedural justice (viz., where we have both an independent criterion of the just and procedures sufficient to achieve outcomes that square with the criterion). If all this means is that in the real world we should not hope to achieve ideally just results, even if we could realize the theory Rawls develops, this is no occasion for despair. There is no theory of social justice in which we can hope to close completely the gap between what the theory requires and what we can actually bring about.

Rawls's actual view, however, is not the above. It is different and deeper and amounts to a concession that, even in the abstract, the theory of social justice Rawls develops does not give us actually just distributions or outcomes of the basic structure because we cannot in theory hope to view the system as one of pure procedural justice.

In at least one place this seems to be the point, for Rawls remarks, "So far at least there does not exist a theory of just constitutions as procedures leading to just legislation which corresponds to the theory of competitive markets as procedures resulting in efficiency."[68] Elsewhere he notes that even under a just constitution we will often have to adopt a socio-economic policy of which "the best we can say . . . is that it is at least not clearly unjust."[69] It is as if by cranking the political handle of our just structure to yield a just outcome (cf. a fair throw of unbiased dice), something goes wrong, because the structure underdetermines the outcome; while it suffices to reject some policies those that remain are not by that fact alone just. Elsewhere, Rawls remarks that "on many questions of social and economic policy we must fall back upon a notion of quasi-pure procedural justice."[70] The idea seems to be that there is a disjunction of several "not clearly unjust" policies, with no way to choose among them on the grounds of justice. Although it is not certain what he here calls "quasi-pure procedural justice" is what in the other passages under discussion he called "imperfect procedural justice," the reading offered above may be the best we can get.

Perhaps the problem can be put more simply. Rawls seems to argue initially that there is as much and as little sense in asserting that a weekly welfare check of $50 is unfairly large or small or just right as there is in asserting that getting the short straw instead of one of the longer ones is a fair or unfair outcome. It all depends on the "background circumstances." The parallel seems reasonable enough when judged from the standpoint of the absence of any "independent criterion" to tell us what outcome is the just one. But the parallel looks increasingly unreasonable from the standpoint of how the outcomes are actually connected to the rules, mechanism, or procedure that determines them. The procedure in the lottery case is more "pure" — more direct and less subject to the effects of delay and friction in the system — than in the welfare check case. So Rawls shifts his ground, or anyway his judgment, to accommodate this difference, and comes up with the conclusion that social justice is not ever even in theory quite what results, because the required "pure procedural justice" always turns out to be only "quasi-pure" or defectively pure (compare "imperfect") procedural justice. It is hardly any wonder that, in the wake of Rawls's analysis, his critics tend to divide into those who think that social justice is simply an impossible idea,[71] those who believe in the availability of an independent criterion that in effect ignores the basic structure altogether,[72] and the rest of us, those who are groping toward an as yet unformulated alternative theory.

§7. I have concentrated in the last two sections on some exegesis and criticism of Rawls's theory because at present it remains the clearest and most elaborate attempt to found a theory of social justice upon a conception of basic social institutions. The difficulties I have suggested in his theory may shed some light on it as well as on the general problems of trying to make an institutional approach work. A clear strategy of destructive internal criticism of Rawls's theory emerges from the discussion: Show that the notion of the basic structure cannot yield what it is supposed to yield, viz., a defensible notion of just allocations of the social product to individuals under varying conditions. One gambit in this direction has been partially explored: Show that the theory relies on pure procedural justice in a form or forms that yield results too remotely and too disjunctively related to the principles of social justice to leave much sense to the description of them as "not unjust." As for testing other features of an institutional emphasis in the theory of social justice, features not so directly tied to Rawls's own views, we must await the constructive efforts of some Marxist or utilitarian, that is, some theorist who will offer us a fundamentally different theory of society and of the person.[73]

FOOTNOTES

[1] John Rawls, *A Theory of Justice* (Cambridge, Mass.) 1971.

[2] *A Theory of Justice*, p. 4.

[3] *A Theory of Justice*, p. 7.

[4] For Rawls's latest comments on this topic, see his essay, "The Basic Structure as Subject," *American Philosophical Quarterly*, 14:2 (April 1977): 159–165.

[5] *A Theory of Justice*, p. 10.

[6] *A Theory of Justice*, pp. 10–11.

[7] *A Theory of Justice*, p. 252.

[8] *A Theory of Justice*, p. 546, and compare to p. 6, the last few lines.

[9] *A Theory of Justice*, pp. 10–11.

[10] John Stuart Mill, *Utilitarianism*, Parts II and V.

[11] *A Theory of Justice*, §47.

[12] *A Theory of Justice*, p. 308.

[13] *A Theory of Justice*, p. 307.

[14] The two best recent examples of such theories, although Rawls does not mention them in this connection, are Nicholas Rescher, *Distributive Justice* (Indiana, 1966), and Norman E. Bowie, *Towards a New Theory of Distributive Justice* (Amherst, Mass., 1971).

[15] *A Theory of Justice*, p. 84.

[16] Richard B. Brandt, ed. *Social Justice* (New Jersey, 1962).

[17] William K. Frankena, "The Concept of Social Justice," in Richard B. Brandt, ed., *Social Justice* (New Jersey, 1962), p. 1.

[18] "The Concept of Social Justice," p. 2.

[19] William K. Frankena, *Some Beliefs About Justice* (Kansas, 1966).

[20] A. M. Honoré, "Social Justice," *McGill Law Journal*, 8 (1962): 78–105, reprinted in a revised version in Robert S. Summers, ed., *Essays in Legal Philosophy* (Oxford, 1971), pp. 61–94. All page references here are to this version.

[21] "Social Justice," pp. 65–66.

[22] "Social Justice," p. 66, section 1 and compare to p. 72.

[23] "Social Justice," p. 66, section 2, and compare to p. 81, section 7.

[24] "Social Justice," p. 89–91.

[25] *Distributive Justice*, p. 1.

[26] *Distributive Justice*, p. 6.

[27] N. M. L. Nathan, *The Concept of Justice* (London, 1971), p. 5.

[28] *Ibid.*

[29] *The Concept of Justice*, p. 1.

[30] Robert Nozick, *Anarchy, State and Utopia* (New York, 1974), pp. 150–153.

[31] David Miller, *Social Justice* (Oxford, 1976), p. 22.

[32] Compare *A Theory of Justice*, §48, and *Social Justice*, pp. 46f.

[33] Compare *A Theory of Justice*, §47, and *Social Justice*, p. 44f.

[34] Compare *A Theory of Justice*, §14, and *Social Justice*, p. 45.

[35] *Social Justice*, p. 253.

[36] Thomas Hobbes, *Leviathan*, Part II, chapter 30.

[37] Aristotle, *Nichomachean Ethics*, Book II, chapters 4, 9; Book Xm chapter 9.

[38] An excellent example will be found in Walter A. Kaufmann, *Without Guilt and Justice* (New York, 1973), pp. 66–92.

[39] *Anarchy, State and Utopia*, p. 156.

[40] David Lyons defends a very different view of rights and justice in Mill, and to that extent in utilitarianism. See his "Human Rights and the General Welfare," *Philosophy and Public Affairs*, 6:2 (Winter, 1977): 113–129.

[41] *Anarchy, State and Utopia*, p. 154.

[42] *A Theory of Justice*, p. 27.

[43] *Anarchy, State and Utopia*, p. 155.

[44] *Anarchy, State and Utopia*, pp. 183–189 esp.

[45] *A Theory of Justice,* p. 84.

[46] *A Theory of Justice*, p. 7.

[47] *A Theory of Justice*, p. 55.

[48] *Ibid.*

[49] See John Rawls, "Two Concepts of Rules," *The Philosophical Review*, 64:1 (January 1955): 3–32, p. 3 note 1. Compare the definition of "practice" given here with the definition of "institution" in *A Theory of Justice*, p. 55. By contrast, see the definition of "institution" to be found in any standard encyclopedia or dictionary of social science.

[50] *A Theory of Justice*, p. 227.

[51] *A Theory of Justice*, pp. 301–303.

[52] *A Theory of Justice*, p. 195.

[53] *Ibid.*

[54] *A Theory of Justice*, §§33–34.

[55] *A Theory of Justice*, §43.

[56] *A Theory of Justice*, pp. 258, 280, 309; but see 274, where "a property-owning democracy" is given preference under the theory, though allegedly only for illustrative and explanatory purposes.

[57] *A Theory of Justice*, p. 270.

[58] Arthur M. Okun, *Equality and Efficiency: The Big Trade-Off* (Washington, D.C., 1975), p. 61, compare to pp. 33–64 passim.

[59] *Equality and Efficiency: The Big Trade-Off*, p. 38.

[60] *A Theory of Justice*, p. 137.

[61] *A Theory of Justice*, p. 7.

[62] Compare to *A Theory of Justice*, pp. 261–262.

[63] *A Theory of Justice*, p. 85.

[64] *A Theory of Justice*, p. 86.

[65] A wag might say that Rawls's theory of justice as a pure procedure gives new meaning to the phrase, "You bet your life!"

[66] *A Theory of Justice*, p. 198, and compare to pp. 353, 360.

[67] *A Theory of Justice*, pp. 85–86.

[68] *A Theory of Justice*, p. 360.

[69] *A Theory of Justice*, p. 199.

[70] *A Theory of Justice*, p. 201.

[71] *Without Guilt and Justice*, p. 67.

[72] *Social Justice*, p. 44.

[73] This paper is a revised and expanded version of remarks originally presented as a commentary on the paper (cited *supra*, note 4) presented by John Rawls at the 51st Annual Meeting, American Philosophical Association, Pacific Division, March 27, 1977. I am grateful to Mark Bedau for comments and criticism on the final draft that helped me to avoid some errors and to improve the expression of my views in several places.

THE JOURNAL OF PHILOSOPHY

VOLUME LXXVII, NO. 6, JUNE 1980

CONTRACTS AND CHOICES:
DOES RAWLS HAVE A SOCIAL CONTRACT THEORY? *

I N *A Theory of Justice* ** John Rawls tells us he is presenting a social contract theory: "My aim," he writes, "is to present a conception of justice which generalizes and carries to a higher level of abstraction the familiar theory of the social contract as found in say, Locke, Rousseau, and Kant" (11). And indeed his many and various critics have generally assumed he has a contractarian position and have criticized him on that basis. However, it will be my contention in this paper that a contractual agreement on the two principles not only *does not* but *ought not* to occur in the original position, and that, although Rawls uses contract language in his book, there is another procedure outlined in Part One of *A Theory of Justice* through which the two principles are selected.

Clearly, a project of this kind has value insofar as it reveals the nature of Rawls's method. However, the importance of clarifying the decision-making process in the original position also derives from the fact that, according to Rawls, the reasons why the two principles are selected in the original position are the reasons why they are justified as the appropriate principles of justice for our society. Hence, following my argument, I will indicate how Rawls's actual, noncontractarian selection procedure provides a highly Kantian justification for his conception of justice.

* I would like to thank Israel Scheffler, John Rawls, Ruth Anna Putnam, and especially Richard Healey for their many useful criticisms of earlier drafts of this paper. Much of the work on the paper was made possible by the Mark de Wolfe Howe Fellowship granted by Harvard Law School during the summer of 1978.

** Cambridge, Mass.: Harvard, 1971; hereafter referred to as TJ. All future page references will appear in the body of the text.

0022-362X/80/7706/0315$02.40

I. RAWL'S ARGUMENT FOR THE EXISTENCE OF A CONTRACT
IN THE ORIGINAL POSITION

Rawls's guiding ideas behind the construction of the original position seem to accord with our "ethical intuitions." Most people would agree with him that the process of defining and administering justice depends upon the objectivity and impartiality of the members of a society, and this underlies

> . . . the somewhat unusual conditions which characterize the original position. The idea here is simply to make vivid to ourselves the restrictions that it seems reasonable to impose on arguments for principles of justice, and therefore on these principles themselves. Thus it seems reasonable and generally acceptable that no one should be advantaged or disadvantaged by natural fortune or social circumstances in the choice of principles. . . . We should insure further that particular inclinations and aspirations and persons' conceptions of their own good do not affect the principles adopted. . . . One excludes the knowledge of those contingencies which sets men at odds and allows them to be guided by their prejudices. In this way, the veil of ignorance is arrived at in a natural way (TJ 18/9).

However, once these ideas are built into the original position, we get a very peculiar selection environment where there are no conflicting interests that need to be mediated, where everyone prefers the same two principles, and where the agreement on these principles is unanimous.

The nature of this selection environment has caused Sidney Alexander to express some nervousness about Rawls's claim that the selection of the two principles comes about through a contract.[1] Instead, Alexander prefers to see that selection characterized as a rational "choice" by each party:

> . . . the contractarian aspect of Rawls' device is not essential. . . . it is even misleading. What is essential, I think, is the *choice* aspect. What-

---

[1] "Social Evaluation through Notional Choice," *Quarterly Journal of Economics*, LXXXVIII, 4 (November 1974): 597–624.

One can find the same nervousness in Robert Nozick's book *Anarchy, State and Utopia* (New York: Basic Books, 1974); see ch. 7, footnote on p. 197: "And what is thinking of what is a 'fair agreement' (section 3 [of TJ]) or a 'fair basis' (p. 103 [of TJ]) doing here anyway, in the midst of rational, self-interested calculations of persons in the original position, who do not knowingly possess, or at any rate utilize, particular moral notions?" Note that Nozick discusses in chapter 7 a contract model in TJ, alluded to by Rawls in section 1, which is unrelated to the original-position procedure and which involves negotiations between the "most" and the "least" advantaged. I do not discuss this contract model, however, because Nozick's own discussion indicates why it is an unsatisfactory justification for the two principles and because it is not the main method for legitimating the two principles in TJ.

ever worthwhile principles Rawls can validly deduce from his social contract method can also be deduced as the principles that a single rational man would choose, from behind the veil of ignorance, for a social system in which he was to be assigned a role after that choice (Alexander, *op. cit.*, p. 604).

In fact, Rawls himself seems to suggest precisely this interpretation of the selection procedure in *A Theory of Justice:*

> . . . it is clear that since the differences among the parties are un-known to them, and everyone is equally rational and similarly sit-uated, each is convinced by the same arguments. Therefore, *we can view the choice in the original position from the standpoint of one person selected at random.* If anyone after due reflection prefers a conception of justice to another, then they all do, and a unanimous agreement can be reached (TJ 139; my emphasis).

Unfortunately, Alexander never really explores in what sense the notion of a contract is "misleading" or "nonessential" to Rawls's theory. He assumes it is consistent to label the decision in the original position either a "contract" or a "choice," but believes that the "choice" characterization is preferable, on the basis of passages in TJ like the one cited above. Thus he does not expli-citly give arguments that *rule out* interpreting the selection of the two principles as an agreement.

In his reply to Alexander,[2] Rawls argues that Alexander's pref-erence ordering should be reversed, first, because the contract ex-emplifies important features of moral deliberation (for example, the way in which each party must take into consideration the needs of the other parties as free and equal rational beings) and, secondly, because the contract's requirements actually play a role in the *selection* of the two principles of justice by the original-position parties. Hence his view is that *only* the contract model correctly represents his argument in the book. Because of its im-portance, I will quote heavily from Rawls's presentation of the argument in his Reply:

> The agreement in the original position is unanimous and yet every-one is situated so that all are willing to adopt the same principles. Why, then, the need of an agreement when there are no differences to negotiate? The answer is that reaching a unanimous agreement without a binding vote is not the same thing as everyone's arriving at the same choice, or forming the same intention. . . .

[2] "Reply to Alexander and Musgrave," *Quarterly Journal of Economics,* LXXXVIII, 4 (November 1974): 633–655.

In general, the class of things that can be agreed to is included within, and is smaller than, the class of things that can be rationally chosen. We can decide to take a chance and· at the same time fully intend that, should things turn out badly, we shall do what we can to retrieve the situation. But if we make an agreement, we have to accept the outcome; and therefore to give an undertaking in good faith, we must not only intend to honor it but with reason believe that we can do so. Thus the contract condition is a significant further constraint.

. . . The idea is this: since everyone is to give an undertaking in good faith, and not simply to make the same choice, no one is permitted to agree to a principle if they have reason to doubt that they will be able to honor the consequences of its consistent application ("Reply," 651/2).

The argument seems to be this. A person who merely has to choose some action believes he can "retrieve" his situation if necessary; that is, he believes that circumstances can be altered or the choice reversed to avoid any damaging consequences that the choice might involve. But contracts have binding power over the people who make them—they are final, prescribe actions without exception, and prevent any party who has "signed his name" from changing his mind and going back on the decision reached. Thus, says Rawls, it follows from the contract requirement that the selection of a justice conception is "final and made in perpetuity, there is no second chance. . . . A person is choosing once and for all the standards which are to govern his life prospects" (TJ 176).

Rawls then maintains that this "irrevocability" involved in a contractual agreement generates another constraint on the parties' reasoning in the original position. Because each party knows his selection cannot be made over again, he knows he must select only those principles which he is sure he can always honor no matter how their consistent application might affect him. This is the "strains of commitment" constraint on the parties' reasoning, and Rawls argues that it plays a decisive role in the selection of the two principles over the principle of average utility when the two conceptions are in a pairwise contest:

. . . in view of the higher order interest in securing the basic liberties and other considerations, the two principles have to be acknowledged . . . . [They] always secure acceptable conditions for all, while the utility condition might not ("Reply," 652).

Thus, because the constraint from the strains of commitment helps to effect the selection of the two principles and because it is generated only by the irrevocability constraint following from the contract requirement, Rawls maintains that a choice characterization of the two principles' selection reflects a misunderstanding of the way the parties in the original position actually reason.

In order to make Rawls's argument as clear as possible, I would like to construct a model of the parties' reasoning for the two principles which his remarks suggest. In this way I hope to make clear the kind and nature of the premises and constraints Rawls says figure in their deliberations and cause them to select his theory of justice. This is certainly not meant to be a fully worked-out model of their deliberation, but rather a sketch of such a model, useful in revealing the character of the parties' reasoning processes:

MODEL M1: DELIBERATION OF A PARTY IN
THE ORIGINAL POSITION
After Rawls's Remarks in *A Theory of Justice* and
in "Reply to Alexander and Musgrave"

STEP ONE: I have assumed the original position in order to choose a conception of justice for my society. Thus, I am submitting myself to the following constraints and conditions in the original position:

STEP TWO: I am subject to the veil of ignorance. (See TJ, section 24.)

STEP THREE: I find myself defined solely as a "moral personality."
(This follows from step 2 and Rawls's conception of the nature of human beings. The veil of ignorance strips away everything not part of my fundamental moral personality which I possess as a human being; thus, I am rational, separate from others, nonenvious, possessing a normal risk aversion, possessing a sense of justice and a capability to pursue some plan that will further what I perceive to be my own good. See TJ, sections 3 and 4.)

STEP FOUR: I am desirous of the maximum amount possible of the primary goods.
(No matter what my conception of the good, these resources will be useful to me in my efforts to achieve it; hence I desire as many of them as possible.)

STEP FIVE: Because I know nothing about which specific identity I possess, "I" could be anyone in my society. (From step 3.)

STEP SIX: When I choose a conception of justice, I must take into consideration the general needs and interests of each person in the society, and each person's rights as a moral personality, no matter what his social position or conception of the good. (The restriction from ignorance, from steps 2, 4, and 5.)

STEP SEVEN: I know that the "circumstances of justice" apply in my society. (See TJ, section 22.)

STEP EIGHT: My choice is subject to the "constraints of the concept of right."
(—the conception I choose must be general, universal, and understand-

able; it must satisfy the publicity and finality conditions, and impose an
ordering on conflicting claims.)

STEP NINE: Everyone placed in the original position is required to contract
unanimously upon a conception of justice for a well-ordered society.
(The contract condition; see TJ, sections 3 and 20.)

STEP TEN: Everyone else in the original position, in virtue of being subject
to the same constraints and conditions as I am, is defined solely as a
moral personality desirous of the maximum amount of primary goods
possible. (From steps 2, 3, 4, and 5.)

STEP ELEVEN: Everyone else in the original position is my equal. (From
step 10.)

(This knowledge assures me that the contract can take place, because
I know that no one is in the position of being able to use his/her power
to impose a noncontractual decision through force.)

STEP TWELVE: The selection of a justice conception which I will make is
final and binding. (The irrevocability constraint, following from the
contract condition. See "Reply," pp. 651–653; and TJ, section 25 and
section 29—particularly pp. 175 ff.)

STEP THIRTEEN: Therefore, from (12), (6), and (3), I must ensure that we
agree on a conception of justice which, when actualized, will always
allow me to express my essential nature as defined by (3), no matter
what social position I will find myself in (see step 6), because only then,
will I be able to promise, as required by (12), that I will abide by the
agreement. (The strains of commitment condition; see "Reply," pp.
651–653.)

STEP FOURTEEN: These conditions 1 to 13 lead me to reason according to
the maximin rule.

[i.e., I want to ensure that we select a theory of justice that will allow
me the *most* amount of the primary goods (which I know I will desire)
if I am the least advantaged person in the society. See TJ, section 26.]

. . . Leads to a contractual agreement on Rawls's conception of justice,
which, of all the conceptions of justice on the list, best fulfills the requirements of steps 1 to 14.

This model makes clear that the strains-of-commitment constraint
does not follow exclusively from the irrevocability constraint generated by the contract requirement, but depends also on the veil-
of-ignorance condition. Each party realizes that he must reject all
justice conceptions that would allow certain members in his society to have too few of the primary goods—because he knows he
might in fact turn out to *be* one of those people. According to
Rawls, it is a short step from here to the decision to reason according to the maximin rule, which in turn guarantees the selection of
the two principles over both forms of utilitarianism.[3]

[3] In order not to exceed the scope of the issues considered in this paper, I am
assuming throughout that Rawls's argument for the appropriateness of the max-

Now the reader might have noticed something odd about this reasoning model. The contract seems to be playing a rather small role in the actual selection of the two principles, necessary only to ensure that each party realizes his decision is final. However, in many passages of TJ Rawls suggests, even asserts, that the contract condition is playing a much more direct and important role in the selection of the two principles. For example, in section 20 of TJ, Rawls writes that we are

> . . . to think of the first principles of justice as themselves the object of an original agreement in a suitably defined initial situation. These principles are those which rational persons concerned to advance their interests would accept in this position of equality to settle the basic terms of their association. . . . [G]iven the circumstances of the parties, and their knowledge, beliefs and interests, an agreement on these principles is the best way for each person to secure his ends in view of the alternatives available (TJ 118/9).

In many passages like this in TJ, what Rawls regards as crucial in the selection of the two principles is the restriction of each party's latitude of choice caused by the legitimate demands made by the other parties in the original position during the process of reach-

---

imin rule of choice actually works. But, of course, there has been a good deal of doubt about this. However, the discussions have often pin-pointed the source of the problem incorrectly. Rawls is not covertly maintaining that people are particularly risk averse, and then using this to explain why they invoke the maximin rule. Instead, in section 15 he maintains that they have a *normal* risk aversion, but that, because of the extensiveness of the losses they would suffer if they were the least advantaged in a society, they have good reason to be conservative. And notice how part of the argument goes:

> The person choosing has a conception of the good such that he cares very little, if anything, for what he might gain above the minimum stipend that he can, in fact, be sure of by following the maximin rule. It is not worthwhile for him to take a chance for the sake of a further advantage, especially when it may turn out that he loses much that is important to him (TJ, 154).

But how can Rawls characterize the parties' conception of the good in this way when they are supposed to be completely ignorant of it? And doesn't that characterization conflict with what Rawls says is the basic motivation of the parties in the original position, i.e., preferring more primary goods rather than less? Indeed, the whole point of introducing the primary goods was to provide a "thin" conception of the good, neutral between competing theories of justice, which could be used to construct the parties' motivation in the original position. But in justifying the maximin rule Rawls uses a conception of the good which not only conflicts with the basic desire for as many primary goods as possible, but also seems to incorporate some of the moral opinions that he says are forbidden in this environment by the veil of ignorance. Although I will not be discussing or drawing attention to this problem again in this paper, the reader will notice how this other conception of the good plays a role in generating the "strains of finality" constraint (step 9) in Model M3, and arises out of Rawls's conception of the human being as a "moral personality."

ing a contractual agreement. The idea is that no one party will be allowed by the other parties to advance a justice conception that either benefits himself exclusively or fails to answer somehow the needs of all of them. And because the parties are equal in strength and power, no party can forcibly impose his biased justice conception on the others. Therefore, a give-and-take process will take place, a *negotiation* of conflicting interests. And in these circumstances, argues Rawls, the two principles are the final result of the negotiation, because they represent the parties' best answer to the problem of satisfying each of them fairly.

This same characterization of the selection process is found in Rawls's earlier article "Justice as Reciprocity." [4] In this article, Rawls has the parties (who are at this point not subject to the veil of ignorance, although stripped of any power to impose a justice conception on the others) confront one another and follow a procedure whereby each party is allowed to "insist on an advantage to himself, and so on a common advantage, for none is willing to sacrifice anything for the others" (252). The two principles are finally acknowledged in this situation because only they satisfactorily meet the demands of all without sacrificing the needs of some; that is, only they meet the demands of reciprocity.

Thus, in some of his writings we find Rawls indicating that the constraint of taking into consideration other people's interests as well as one's own, which I will call the "restriction from the demands of reciprocity" (using the term Rawls employs in the early article), is instrumental in effecting the choice of the two principles, and is a natural outgrowth of the process of forging a contractual agreement. Hence in these passages he suggests another model of the parties' deliberation, one significantly different from M1 in that here the restriction from the demands of reciprocity is playing a major role in the selection of the two principles:

MODEL M2: DELIBERATION OF A PARTY IN
THE ORIGINAL POSITION
After Rawls's Remarks in Section 20 of *A Theory of Justice*

STEP ONE: I have assumed the original position in order to choose a conception of justice for my society. Thus, I am submitting myself to the following constraints and conditions of the original position.

STEP TWO: I am subject to the veil of ignorance.

STEP THREE: I find myself defined solely as a "moral personality."

---

[4] In Samuel Gorovitz, ed., *Utilitarianism: John Stuart Mill, with Critical Essays* (Indianapolis: Bobbs-Merrill, 1971), pp. 242–262.

STEP FOUR: I am desirous of the maximum amount of primary goods possible.

STEP FIVE: Because I know nothing about which specific identity I possess, "I" could be anyone in society.

STEP SIX: I know that the circumstances of justice apply in my society.

STEP SEVEN: I am subject to the constraints of the concept of right.

STEP EIGHT: Everyone placed in the original position is required to agree unanimously upon a conception of justice for a well-ordered society. (The contract condition.)

STEP NINE: Everyone else in the original position, in virtue of being subject to the same constraints and conditions as I am, is defined solely as a moral personality desirous of the maximum amount of primary goods possible.

STEP TEN: Everyone else in the original position is my equal.

STEP ELEVEN: The selection of a justice conception which I will make is final and binding. (The irrevocability constraint.)

STEP TWELVE: I am subject to the restriction from the demands of reciprocity.

[From steps 8, 9, 10, and 11. Because I must contract with my fellows (from 8), who are my equals in this situation (from 10), and as interested as I am in obtaining the greatest amount of primary goods possible (from step 9), I am forced to modify my demands in response to the demands of these others in order that an agreement can be reached; and to agree to only those modifications I know I will always be able to live with if they are incorporated into the final justice conception we select (from 11).]

STEP THIRTEEN: These conditions 1 to 12 lead me to reason according to the maximin rule.

. . . Leads to a contractual agreement on Rawls's conception of justice, which, of all the conceptions of justice on the list, best fulfills the requirements of steps 1 to 13.

The reader will note that the reciprocity restriction in M2 is taking the place of the "strains of commitment" restriction found in M1. In both models the irrevocability constraint following from the contract condition plays a role in determining the two principles' selection. However, whereas in M1 the party's choice is also affected by his concern (which his ignorance forces him to take) for the needs of everyone in the *society*, the restriction from ignorance is not even operative in M2; instead it is the demands of others *in the original position* which play a part in determining his choice. Each party in M2 is concerned not so much with his possible identity in society as with the pressure other parties in the original position will exert upon him to accept a conception of justice that will distribute primary goods fairly among them. Therefore, in Model M1 the veil of ignorance in conjunction with the irrevocability constraint forces the parties to accept the two principles because only these principles will allow them a decent share of primary goods if they find themselves in the lowest social stratum. But in M2 the parties accept the two principles both because of the effects of the irrevocability constraint and because they know the others in this position will not permit them more than a fair and reasonable distribution of resources.

Now the fact that we can come up with *two* models of the deliberation in the original position, which give different roles to the contract condition in the selection of the two principles, should be enough to indicate that the social contract notion in TJ is at least troublesome! Perhaps because Rawls used Model M1 in his "Reply to Alexander," he feels that M2 is incorrect. Certainly I will argue for the rejection of M2 as the correct deliberation model of the parties' deliberation in TJ. However, my argument will be extended to include M1 as well. And in the end I will be maintaining not only that agreements of all sorts are unnecessary in the original position, but also that no agreement on the two principles in this situation is even possible. The point of this paper is not merely to show that Rawls *need* not use the social contract method; more importantly I wish to show that he *cannot* use it if he wishes the two principles to be selected. In short, I wish to argue that these principles cannot be contractually justified.

II. WHY THE PARTIES DO NOT CONTRACT UPON THE TWO PRINCIPLES
IN THE ORIGINAL POSITION

In order to determine whether Model M1 or M2 is an accurate sketch of the deliberation process followed by the parties in the original position, that is, in order to determine whether the contract condition plays either of the roles these models assign to it, we should first be clear about what a contract really is. For this we should turn to legal theory, because the term 'contract' is used literally in this discourse, and an examination of its meaning in the law courts will shed light on what roles the term performs when it is used figuratively in philosophic discourse.

Legal theorists have isolated two essential features of contractual agreements. First, these agreements are distinguished by the fact that the parties involved in them give *promises* to one another. The action each agrees to undertake is therefore considered to be binding, unless the party to whom the promise is made in the agreement releases the other from his or her commitment; and the role of the law is to *enforce* these promises:

> A contract is a promise or set of promises for the breach of which the law gives a remedy, or the performance of which the law recognizes a duty.[5]

Second, contracts involve an *exchange;* they are *bargains:*

> . . . the typical contract is a two-sided affair, something being promised or done on the one side in return for something being promised or done on the other side.[6]

What are exchanged in these situations are called in the law "considerations." As it is frequently defined, a consideration is just the "price" for a promise: it is that benefit which I promise to confer or that detriment which I promise to suffer, in order to get you to promise to confer a benefit on me or to promise to impose a detriment on yourself which I find desirable.

Whereas Model M1 makes heavy use of only the first feature of contractual agreements, M2 relies on both features. The restriction from the demands of reciprocity just is the realization on the part of each person that, in addition to the fact that he must be able to commit himself to the decision reached, he must give adequate consideration to the others for the benefits he hopes to gain from the contract decision. And in section 20 Rawls argues that each party settles on the two principles because they are the best considerations available, allowing each to receive the benefits he desires and yet enabling each to pay a sufficient price to the other parties for these benefits. Therefore, because it makes the best use of the literal meaning of 'contract', let us first consider the claim Model M2 has to being the correct sketch of the parties' deliberation. We will do this by considering whether the exchange of considerations which M2 depicts is possible in the original position.

Our suspicions should be aroused by the fact that in M2 (as well as M1) reasoning from the maximin rule is directly responsible for the two principles' selection, and game theorists regard this criterion of choice as appropriate not for group decision-making nor for individual choice made in situations where others are present

---

[5] *American Restatement of the Law of Contracts (First)*, vol. 1, adopted and promulgated by the American Law Institute, May 6, 1932 (St. Paul: American Law Institute Publishers, 1932), p. 9. Technically, I will be referring in this discussion only to bilateral and not to unilateral contracts, since the latter are irrelevant to our concerns here.

[6] P. S. Atiyah, *An Introduction to the Law of Contracts* (New York: Oxford, 1971), p. 24/5.

(i.e., in the context of a game), but for individual choice under conditions of complete uncertainty.[7] When a decision-maker is completely ignorant of the relative probability of any particular circumstance being realized in the future, this rule instructs him to choose that act which affords him the best utility pay-off if the worst circumstances prevail. As Luce and Raiffa observe in their classic game-theory text *Games and Decisions*, this is an extremely conservative principle, but "It has the merit that it is extremely conservative in a context where conservatism might make good sense" (279).

Now it is clear that the original position is an "uncertain situation." Because of the veil of ignorance, the parties must choose between alternative conceptions of justice without knowing their identity in society and without being able even to compute the probability that they are any one person. Rawls argues (to the consternation of some of his critics) that this conservative rule of choice is appropriate in these circumstances (see fn 3, above); and thus the parties choose the conception of justice that gives the best pay-off to the worst-advantaged person. But how can a contract based on an exchange of considerations take place in an environment where the maximin rule is the appropriate criterion of choice? The veil of ignorance which introduces the uncertainty in this situation also makes impossible genuine competing preferences for any of the alternative conceptions of justice. None of the parties advocates a different conception because they are all ignorant of the different moral conceptions they hold and of personal facts that would make one of the alternatives preferable. Hence none of them "pays" anything to the others in order that the contract be made; none of them abandons his "favorite conception" and chooses the two principles as the best compromise. Instead, all of them, after reflection, prefer the same conception, because all of them are faced with the same problem of uncertainty, leading them *separately* and *independently* of one another to invoke the maximin rule in order to solve it. Hence no party's adoption of the two principles is made *in exchange for* the selection of the two principles by the other parties. No promises are ever traded in order to get any party to accept this conception of justice. There is only a series of independent but identical deliberations and decisions in this "uncertain" selection environment.

Thus, basically, the fault of M2 is this: it includes *two* sorts of

[7] Howard Luce and R. Raiffa (New York: Wiley, 1957), pp. 276–278.

decision procedures which are mutually exclusive. The contract procedure works when there are differing preferences over alternatives which need to be mediated; the maximin rule is invoked in circumstances of uncertainty. However, the original position, insofar as it includes the veil of ignorance, is clearly an uncertain situation. And because the veil prohibits disagreements among the parties over which alternative is preferable, it rules out the making of a contract based on an exchange of considerations and makes appropriate the invocation of the maximin rule which selects the two principles as the best justice conception in these circumstances.

So far we have shown only that a contract following from the reciprocity restriction *need* not take place in order for the two principles to be selected, not that it *cannot* take place there at all. Perhaps the two principles could be contractually selected if the veil of ignorance were lifted. So suppose we remove it and allow each party to know his own identity in society and thus his conception of the good, his social class, etc. Because of this knowledge, each has a clear idea which conception of justice will likely benefit him. Therefore, real conflicting preferences over alternative conceptions of justice arise, and a contract following from the effects of the demands of reciprocity takes place. (In fact it is because Rawls has no veil of ignorance in "Justice as Reciprocity" that it makes sense for him to invoke a contract to explain the selection of his conception of justice.) Note that the raising of the veil means that the maximin rule is no longer determining the two principles' selection. There is no longer any uncertainty in this position making the reasoning from that principle advisable. Instead, the reciprocity restriction is directly involved in the selection of a justice conception. And if we believe Rawls's arguments, the conception that will be the best answer to the demands of all and still give sufficient consideration to each party, will be his own.

However, as Rawls must have realized by the time he wrote TJ, the restriction from the demands of reciprocity is not strong enough to guarantee that the two principles are finally selected, for in these circumstances "we might imagine . . . one of the contractees threaten[ing] to hold out unless the others agree to principles favorable to him" (TJ 139/140). This means, as Robert Paul Wolff has observed, that either the bargaining process would never end in a contract and there would be no selection of a justice conception, or else, if a time limit were imposed such that the last proposal discussed would be adopted, the last party to make a proposal before time ran out would gain an unfair advantage, probably proposing a justice conception which would benefit himself over the others but which would have to be adopted by the other parties.[8] And even if a time limit were not imposed and the parties resolved instead to do their best in reaching a justice conception in an unspecified but "reasonable" length of time, who would decide when deliberations had gone on long enough? It would very likely be a majority or sizable minority who liked one particular justice conception and who would bring pressure to bear on all those withholding their support from it to end their opposition and accept the more popular conception in the interest of reaching an agreement. In such circumstances, a justice conception like Average Utilitarianism would seem more likely to win substantial popular support than Rawls's two principles, and hence stand a far greater chance of being selected. In any case, without the veil of ignorance the parties' deliberations would be subject to all sorts of prejudices, irrational desires, and inclinations, and it is difficult to imagine the two principles faring well in an environment where reason could easily be outshouted by the voices of emotion, prejudice, and natural inclination.

Indeed, what Rawls is doing in TJ when he invokes the veil of ignorance is admitting that an attempt to derive a fair justice conception from the circumstances of actual contractual agreements with actual people won't work. Such a selection can be achieved only if the veil of ignorance is placed over the parties, thus introducing uncertainty into the circumstances of choice and forcing the parties to reason from the maximin rule. But, given that the restriction from the demands of reciprocity and the maximin rule cannot cooperate as rules of choice in the original position, and given that reciprocity and the conditions making it possible cannot ensure the two principles' selection, whereas the maximin rule plus the condition (the veil of ignorance) making it possible *do* guarantee the selection of Rawls's justice conception, the maximin rule must be the actual rule of choice Rawls wants the parties to employ in their deliberation, and, as we have seen, this means that a contract on the two principles following from the reciprocity constraint simply cannot be made in the original position.

So much for the claim of M2 to be the correct model of the deliberation process in *A Theory of Justice*. Let us now consider

---

8 "On Strasnick's 'Derivation' of Rawls's 'Difference Principle'," this JOURNAL, LXXIII, 21 (Dec. 2, 1976): 849–858, p. 850; and *Understanding Rawls* (Princeton, N.J.: University Press, 1977), ch. 5, esp. pp. 47–56.

whether M1 can be granted this title. But before we begin, let us note that since we have already shown that the model of contractual agreement best fitting the legal definition does not correctly express the derivation of the two principles, we should be suspicious of M1's claim to do so from the start.

If Rawls wanted to defend M1 he could argue that it succeeds where M2 fails because, instead of stressing reciprocity, it emphasizes the commitment involved in forging a contract, in such a way that the "bargaining" among the parties occurs indirectly when each reasons from the "strains of commitment" constraint. The idea would be that, because each party knows he has to contract with his fellows, he knows he cannot change his mind about the conception of justice selected. This causes him to choose the two principles because he knows that only these will never place him in a social position he could not rationally accept. Therefore, Rawls could maintain that, although the parties still reason separately from one another in this model, the choice each makes is partially effected by the contract requirement, and this makes the parties' decision fundamentally contractarian.

It is worth while taking time to appreciate what Rawls has done by constructing M1. If it is right, he has introduced circumstances of uncertainty into the contractual situation which eliminate the restriction from the demands of reciprocity as an actual constraint on the deliberations, but which also make possible the constraint from the strains of commitment and, hence, reasoning from the maximin rule. That is, it looks as if he has done exactly what it appeared he could not do from our previous discussion—define a contract situation where it makes sense for the parties to invoke the maximin rule.

The reader should note, however, that, even if we accept M1 as the correct model of the parties' deliberations, Rawls's theory is contractarian only in a weak sense. All the contract condition does is prescribe that the parties must always be committed to the agreement and, hence, that their decision is irrevocable. Why not, the critic might ask, just drop the contract condition and build the irrevocability condition into the deliberation process outright? It appears that all the contract really *is* in M1 is an irrevocability condition; so why can't this constraint be stated directly, thus making appeals to a final contract unnecessary and thereby streamlining this circuitous contractarian route to the two principles?

Rawls might want to resist such streamlining, but this resistance would be fruitless, because, although he does not seem to be aware of it, there is a constraint operating *already* in the original position, independent of anything following from the contract requirement, which generates the strains-of-commitment condition. One of the "constraints of the concept of right" is the finality constraint, requiring that the conception of justice selected be composed of the highest and final principles used to arbitrate conflicts and distribute resources. It dictates, in Rawls's words, that "the parties are to assess [each] system of principles [on the list] as a final court of appeal in practical reasoning. There are no higher standards to which arguments in support of claims can be addressed" (TJ 135). Although this finality constraint doesn't sound at all like irrevocability, it successfully leads to the strains-of-commitment condition. Because the parties know that the conception of justice selected will be final, i.e., unconditionally applied, they realize they must evaluate each conception of justice with the idea that, if it is selected and actualized, there will be no argument any citizen can make to avoid the consequences of its application, and nothing will be able to "overrule" the ways it establishes of arbitrating conflicts and distributing resources. This constraint, combined with the effects of the veil of ignorance, causes the parties to realize that they might very well be "stuck" in one of society's worst positions with no way of avoiding the consequences of this conception's application. But this is the realization which, as we have already discussed, leads the parties to reason from the strains-of-commitment condition and adopt the maximin rule. However, in this case, it is the finality and "unavoidability" of the *application* of the justice conception selected, and not the irrevocability of their *decision*, which makes them refuse to gamble on a risky set of principles and choose the two principles as their best bet.

It is no accident that the finality constraint successfully leads to the strains-of-commitment condition. I will now argue that it is covertly involved in the irrevocability constraint and thus is the only condition doing the work for Rawls anyway. Whereas the finality constraint is a constraint on what will count as an appropriate conception of justice, the irrevocability constraint is a requirement concerning only the selection procedure. That is, what it dictates as "final" is not the conception of justice selected but the selection itself. However, a constraint on the latter produces a constraint on the former. Because the parties know that the selection procedure they are involved in cannot be repeated, they know that the justice conception selected can never be circumvented or avoided, i.e., that it is final. And it is this realization of "unavoidability" which causes the parties to reason from the strains-of-commitment condition. But, as we have already seen, this reasoning is already effected by a finality constraint existing in the original position independent of any irrevocability condition. Hence the latter condition and the contract requirement from which it follows are superfluous.

Rawls might want to respond to this argument by saying that, although we have shown that the two principles *need* not be contractually selected as M1 describes, we have not established that they *cannot* be so selected. Specifically, he might argue that the contract requirement and the irrevocability condition could always be substituted for the finality condition if a contract characterization of the two principles' selection was thought desirable on other grounds. However, there are two problems with this defense. First, the irrevocability condition is a bad way of introducing finality, because it simply isn't true that the original-position procedure cannot be repeated! *Rawls himself* explicitly maintains that this procedure may be repeated whenever a new justice conception is formulated [9] in order to see whether it would be preferred to the two principles. More fundamentally, it is inappropriate to introduce into the original position such a "temporal" condition, which suggests that the parties, insofar as they can make this choice only once, do so at a specific time. Such talk distorts the nature of the position itself, which is a timeless perspective, expressing how principles of justice would be selected no matter who occupied it or how often the procedure was repeated.

Second, even if Rawls (mistakenly) wanted to use the irrevocability constraint to imply finality, he could not derive this constraint from the contract requirement, because contractual agreements are not necessarily irrevocable. Recall that, when discussing the "binding nature" of contracts, we noted that the contractual commitment lasts only as long as at least one party continues to insist on the agreement. But if every party releases the others from the promise(s) they made to him, the commitment is abolished. That is, the parties can simply agree to call the whole thing off. Insofar as the making of a contract is voluntary, the ending of it is voluntary as well. Thus, although there is a commitment condition following from the contract requirement, it is not a commitment that makes the parties "finally" and "eternally" bound to the agreement. And this weaker "commitment" constraint is not

[9] See, for example, TJ, section 21.

enough to imply finality. Because the parties know that their decision can be redone if all parties agree to end the initial contract, each party knows there is a chance of retrieving his situation. In particular, each of them knows that if he finds the consequences of a justice conception's application too distasteful once he has resumed his place in society, he might be able to convince the others to renegotiate the contract, thereby avoiding those consequences. But this means that there would be arguments that would threaten the unconditional application of the justice conception selected and, therefore, that finality would not hold. And the parties in the original position might well decide that, given there is a chance of retrieving their situation if things went badly, the maximin rule would be too conservative, and another more risky rule leading to a conception like Average Utilitarianism would be preferable. Hence if Rawls were to substitute the contract constraint and the commitment condition following from it for the finality condition, he would decisively *change* the way the parties reason in the original position, to the point where the selection of the two principles would no longer be guaranteed and would actually be in doubt.

In the end, M1 fails as an alternative contractarian argument for the two principles, first, because the requirement in M1 that the contract be irrevocable doesn't even make sense insofar as the selection procedure in the original position is supposed to be a hypothetical, repeatable, justificatory device, and, second, because the commitment constraint that does follow is too weak to ensure the selection of the two principles.

One comes to the conclusion that Rawls is confused about the logic of his own thought. Neither of the contract models that his remarks suggest actually works as an account of the two principles' selection, and, thus, neither can be used to justify his political theory.[10]

III. THE CORRECT MODEL OF THE PARTIES' REASONING
IN THE ORIGINAL POSITION

I would now like to offer Model M3 as the appropriate representation of the parties' reasoning in the original position, a model

---

10 Some readers might believe that Rawls needs the notion of a contract in order to explain why we are bound to follow and apply the conception of justice selected in the original position. However, Rawls himself denies this and maintains that he needs the contract not to explain why we ought to be just, but rather to define the content of our "natural duty" to be just (see TJ, section 19). Thus, it is the contract's role in the definition of justice which I am challenging in this paper. However, note that even if there were a contract on the two principles among hypothetical parties in the original position, that contract could not explain why *we* ought to follow those principles.

which makes the selection of the two principles the result of a single party's choice. It is essentially the same as Model M1, only now purged of the contract condition, and containing the correct formulation of the finality constraint.

MODEL M3: DELIBERATION OF A PARTY IN THE ORIGINAL POSITION

STEP ONE: I have assumed the original position in order to choose a conception of justice for my society. Thus, I am submitting myself to the following constraints and conditions of the original position.

STEP TWO: I am subject to the veil of ignorance.

STEP THREE: I find myself defined solely as a moral personality.

STEP FOUR: I am desirous of the maximum amount of primary goods possible.

STEP FIVE: Because I know nothing about which specific identity I have, "I" could be anyone in my society.

STEP SIX: When I choose a conception of justice, I must take into consideration the general needs and interests of each person in the society, no matter what his social position is. (The restriction from ignorance.)

STEP SEVEN: I know that the circumstances of justice apply in my society.

STEP EIGHT: My choice is subject to the constraints of the concept of right, one of which is the finality constraint, which requires that the conception selected hold unconditionally in my society.

STEP NINE: Therefore, from steps 8, 6, and 3, I must choose a conception of justice which, when actualized, will always allow me to express my essential nature as defined by 3, no matter what social position I will find myself in (see 6), because only then will I always be able to accept the unconditional application of the conception.

STEP TEN: These conditions 1 to 9 lead me to reason according to the maximin rule.

. . . Leads to a *choice* of the conception of justice involving Rawls's two principles of justice, which, of all the conceptions of justice on the list, best fulfills the requirements of steps 1 to 10.

We see that Rawls was right to regard the "strains of commitment" (step 9) as the fundamental constraint on the parties' reasoning, but the title now seems inappropriate. The constraint is a result of the action of the restriction from ignorance and the finality condition, i.e., the realization that this conception would be unconditionally applied, and not from any irrevocability condition generated by the demands of contract making. Hence, a better name for this constraint is the "strains of finality."

Because M3 describes the reasoning process of anyone in the original position, it makes no theoretical sense to speak of there being more than one inhabitant of this position. Rawls induces us to think there is a multiplicity of parties by asking us to posit actual, highly individuated people and then to strip them of all their defining personal characteristics. But once they are "in" the original position, it is impossible to provide criteria that would allow us to individuate these parties. Their personalities, their reasoning processes, their final selection of a conception of justice —in short, *all* their characteristics are completely identical. Consequently, a philosopher like W. V. Quine would say that there is no reason to claim that more than one person exists in these circumstances. In "Identity, Ostension and Hypostasis," [11] Quine proposes the "Identification of Indiscernibles" maxim: "objects indistinguishable from one another within the terms of a given discourse should be construed as identical for that discourse." We have already shown that there is no theoretical reason to posit more than one party in the original position, nor can criteria for individuating these parties be provided. Hence we are forced to apply Quine's maxim and, for purposes of this discourse, construe the indistinguishable parties as *one* person reasoning as M3 dictates.[12]

The reader never finds the actual noncontractarian deduction of the two principles, i.e., Model M3, explicitly stated or straightforwardly discussed by Rawls. Instead, the contract terminology is ubiquitous. As we have seen, not only does Rawls constantly refer to the "contract" in the original position and talk about its power to effect the selection of the two principles; he also uses labels like 'strains of commitment' to describe steps of the procedure, and his referring to an original "position" inhabited by "parties" presupposes that he is deriving the two principles from a bargaining procedure. All of this, as I hope to have shown, is like dust in the eyes of the book's readers, who are thereby prevented from seeing clearly how the deduction really proceeds and why.

But why does Rawls get the logic of his argument wrong? It is an intriguing question, one that I don't have time to explore fully. Certainly he must have liked the way the contract imagery con-

---

[11] In *From a Logical Point of View* (New York: Harper & Row, 1961), pp. 65–79. For the idea of using Quine's maxim to discuss the individuation of the parties in TJ, I am indebted to Israel Scheffler.

[12] Model M3 ought to remind readers of John Harsanyi's bayesian representation of moral deliberation as the reasoning of a single individual in a situation of risk and uncertainty. Harsanyi recognizes the similarity of his and Rawls's approach; see, for example, his "Morality and the Theory of Rational Behavior," *Social Research*, XLIV (1977): 634. However, their fundamentally different conceptions of the nature of human beings generate different motivational assumptions, constraints, and rules of choice under uncertainty, such that Harsanyi's reasoning model justifies Utilitarianism, whereas Rawls's procedure selects only his two principles of justice.

veyed how the two principles acknowledge each person's free and equal nature, and thus, how it helped him argue that his conception is different from and preferable to Utilitarianism. But I believe there is a biographical explanation for his contract talk as well. In Rawls's earlier writings, before he conceived of the veil of ignorance, he believed that a person could be forced to take into consideration other people's needs when choosing a theory of justice only if other people were present and involved in his decisions, actively lobbying for a conception giving them as much of a share of society's resources as possible, and insisting on a certain minimum share. However, what Rawls does not appear to see clearly in TJ, and what M3 makes quite plain, is that the introduction of the veil of ignorance into the original position makes it possible to derive a conception of justice that takes into consideration every person's interests without having to appeal to such a contract situation and the demands of reciprocity following from it. With the veil, *it no longer matters to the inhabitant of the original position who, if anyone, occupies the position with him or what its occupants' interests are.* What matters to him are the desires and goals of every *actual* member of his society, because the veil forces him to reason *as if he were any one of them.* In this way, the veil is a theoretical device that makes the reciprocity restriction completely unnecessary (and, as we have argued earlier, impossible). Rawls keeps thinking it is the demands of other parties *in the original position* that play a role in the two principles' selection, but as M3 shows, it is the demands of other people *in the society* which force the principles' selection by a single deliberator subject to the original-position constraints.

Model M3 raises questions about what the actual justification of Rawls's two principles is. If it is not contractarian, and if M3 sketches the right derivation of the two principles, then what is it about M3 that should convince us the two principles correctly embody our justice concept? I regard the answering of this question as the real pay-off of our investigation; although the proof that Rawls has no contract in the original position is nice, unless we show why this sheds light on Rawls's actual justificational technique for his theory, we have been indulging in little more than a scholastic activity.

IV. THE JUSTIFICATION OF THE TWO PRINCIPLES

In this section I will be discussing the reasons Model M3 gives us for thinking the two principles are correct. What I will be contending, at bottom, is that Rawls, far from relying on the traditional social-contract argument, has constructed a new, highly Kantian device for legitimating a political theory.[13]

Rawls himself in section 40 of TJ indicates why his approach to defining justice is Kantian in nature. "The original position," he writes, "may be viewed . . . as a procedural interpretation of Kant's conception of autonomy and the categorical imperative" (TJ 256). It is useful to review these Kantian notions. The human being, according to Kant, although often pursuing goals set by the desires of the body, is also capable of seeking objects dictated by reason alone. The method of reasoning used for this self-legislation Kant calls the "moral law" or the "categorical imperative," and he formulates it in the *Foundations of the Metaphysics of Morals*[14] as follows: "I ought never to act except in such a way that I can will that my maxim will become a universal law." There are two important points to stress concerning this Kantian approach to morality. First, the moral law is a *method* of reasoning that tests an agent's maxim, constructed out of his interests and desires in particular situations, by turning it into a universal "law of nature" descriptive of the behavior of all human beings. Only if the agent is able to *understand* and *will* the maxim in this form can he consider the action it dictates to be moral. And second, this method of reasoning comes *prior* to the definition of the moral object, and therefore, according to Kant, prescribes a truly free choice.[15] Whereas men who act only from inclination allow their desires to define the object they seek and employ their reason only to determine the best way of achieving that object, the moral agent does the reverse, first accepting the moral law as his sole, authoritative reasoning procedure and then pursuing only those objects which this reasoning procedure dictates. According to Kant, men who have allowed their desires to define their objects of pursuit first, have enslaved their will to these objects and are,

[13] Many of the ideas in this section come from an interpretation of Rawls's remarks in section 40 of TJ. I have time here only to hint at some of the many ways Rawls's theory can be better understood when it is *dissociated* from the social contract tradition, and thus from the ideas about human nature and human motivation assumed by that tradition. I also believe Kant does not have a social contract theory either; again I cannot discuss this here, but J. W. Gough provides some arguments for this contention in his *The Social Contract* (New York: Oxford, 1957).

[14] Lewis White Beck, trans. (Indianapolis: Bobbs-Merrill, 1959). For a fine discussion of this law, see Onora Nell, *Acting on Principle: An Essay in Kantian Ethics* (New York: Columbia, 1975).

[15] For a discussion of this, see Immanuel Kant, *Critique of Practical Reason*, Beck, trans. (Indianapolis: Bobbs-Merrill, 1956), especially p. 65.

thus, able to act only heteronomously, whereas the moral agent who acts solely from a law *he* gives *himself*, is complete determiner of all the actions he takes, and thus acts *freely, autonomously*.

It should now be evident that Rawls is adopting a Kantian approach to defining justice. First of all, like Kant, he maintains that a moral object, in this case justice, is to be defined by looking at what kind of action an autonomous rational being would regard as moral, or in this case just, after following the appropriate method of practical reasoning. And the Rawlsian original-position deliberation is very similar to the "universalization" test of Kant's categorical-imperative procedure. In the same way that a moral agent using Kant's moral law tests a plan of action by considering what it would be like for him if *all* people acted that way, Rawls's M3 procedure tests a conception of justice by forcing the deliberator (through the veil-of-ignorance condition) to consider what a society ruled by this conception would be like for him if he were *anyone* in that society. Thus, both procedures transform a person's own-interested outlook into a perspective that considers every rational agent's interests. And both Kant and Rawls consider this sort of universalization procedure to be descriptive of the correct operation of our practical reason.

Second, Rawls follows Kant in using a method of reasoning to define a moral object, rather than vice versa, in order to show the way that object is something we freely pursue. Through the veil of ignorance, Rawls ensures that our personal desires and inclinations do not define the conception of justice for us, rendering our choice heteronomous. Instead, he defines justice through a procedure which represents practical reason and which thus models a truly *free* choice. He writes:

> The description of the original position interprets the point of view of noumenal selves, or what it means to be a free and equal rational being. Our nature as such beings is displayed when we act from the principles we would choose when this nature is reflected in the conditions determining the choice. Thus men exhibit their freedom, their independence from the contingencies of nature and society, by acting in ways they would acknowledge in the original position (TJ 255/6).

Therefore, understanding the deliberation in the original position as carried out by a single deliberator following the dictates of practical reason, rather than understanding it as carried out by many parties trying to forge a contract, is a far better way of showing how Rawls thinks a state organized according to the two principles is something to which we would *voluntarily* consent, its constraints and obligations recognized by us as *self-imposed*.

Rawls says in section 40 of *A Theory of Justice* that he has departed from Kant's views in several respects, in particular: "The person's choice as a noumenal self I have assumed to be a collective one" (TJ 257). I hope to have shown that Rawls is incorrect here, that he has been more fully Kantian than he realizes.

JEAN HAMPTON

Harvard University

On John Rawls' *A theory of justice:* Is a pure procedural theory of justice possible?

Paul Ricoeur

ohn Rawls' A Theory of Justice *(1971) is univer-
ally considered as one of the most important
ontemporary works of moral and political the-
ry. It offers a fundamental analysis of the uneasy
elations between social justice and economic
erformance, and provides powerful intellectual
ools to be used in the study of modern societies.
As such, it is of particular relevance to social
scientists. In the following articles, Paul Ricoeur
questions Rawls' theory from an ethical perspective, while Richard C. Bayer
proceeds to an empirical
application of the difference
principle developed by
Rawls.*

A.K.

What accounts for John
Rawls' decision to inquire
into the idea of justice?[1]
There are two main reasons.

Firstly, Rawls clearly
belongs to the tradition of
Kant rather than that of Aristotle. The justice seen by
Aristotle as a particular vir-
tue, namely distributive and corrective justice,
derives its meaning – like all other virtues –
from the *teleological* framework of thought that
links it to the good, at least as understood
by human beings. Kant reversed the order of
priority, attributing more importance to what is
right and less to what is good, so that justice
acquires its meaning from a *deontological* framework of thought.

Secondly, whereas Kant's conception of
justice applied primarily to the relations

Paul Ricoeur, an important contemporary French philosopher, is professor at
the Universities of Strasbourg, Paris I
(Sorbonne) and Paris X (Nanterre), as
well as professor emeritus, University of
Chicago. He has published numerous
books, including *Philosophie de la
volonté, Temps et récit* (3 vols) and *Du
texte à l'action*.

---

between individuals Rawls' applies primarily to
institutions – it is the virtue *par excellence* of
institutions – and only secondarily to individuals
and to nation-states viewed as individuals on
the stage of history. This deontological approach
to morality has managed to maintain itself at
the institutional level only by basing itself on
the fiction of a social contract by means of which
a collection of individuals manages to overcome
the supposedly primitive state of nature and
attain the state of law. This
conjunction of a resolutely
deontological approach to
moral questions and the
contractarian approach at
institutional level is the central subject tackled by
Rawls. The following questions may be asked: is the
connection contingent?
Does a deontological
approach to morality logically form an integral part
of a contractarian pro-
cedure when virtues are
applied to institutions
rather than individuals – as the virtue of justice
is? What sort of link exists between a deontological *viewpoint* and a contractarian *procedure*?

It is my hypothesis that this link is not at
all contingent, in that the purpose and function
of a contractarian *procedure* is to ensure the
primacy of the right over the good by substitut-
ing the deliberative procedure itself for any
commitment to a supposed common good.
According to this hypothesis it is the contractual
procedure that is assumed to engender the prin-

ISSJ 126/1990

133

ciple or principles of justice. If that is indeed the main point then the entire problem of providing a satisfactory explanation for the idea of justice hinges on the difficulty of determining whether a contractarian theory can replace with a procedural approach any attempt to base justice on a few prior convictions concerning the good of the whole, the common good of the *politeia*, the good of the republic or *commonwealth*.

It is to this central question that Rawls provides the best answer of recent times. He attempts to solve the problem left unsolved by Kant in the *Rechtslehre* paragraphs 46–7: how to proceed from the first principle of morality – autonomy in its etymological sense (liberty, being rational, lays down the law for itself as a rule for the universalization of its own maxims for conduct) – to the social contract by means of which a large number of people surrender their external liberty in order to recover it as members of a republic? In other words, what is the link between autonomy and the social contract? Such a link is assumed but not proved by Kant.

Now, if it were possible for Rawls' endeavour to succeed we would have to say that a pure procedural conception of justice can have a sense without any assumption about the good and that it can even liberate the right from the tutelage of the good, firstly as it relates to institutions and secondly, by implication, as it relates to individuals and nation-states regarded as individuals.

Anticipating what comes later I should like to say at this point that my main objection will be that a moral sense of justice, based on the golden rule 'Whatsoever ye would that men should do to you, do ye even so to them', is always assumed by the pure procedural proof of the principle of justice. But it must be clearly understood that this objection does not amount to a refutation of Rawls' theory of justice, which would be pointless and quite absurd.

On the contrary, it comes down to a sort of indirect defence of the primacy of this moral sense of justice in that Rawls' extraordinary construct borrows its underlying thrust from the very principle he claims to generate by his pure contractual procedure. In other words, the circularity of Rawls' argument actually constitutes, in my view, an indirect plea for the pursuit of an ethical foundation for the concept of justice.

Consequently it is this circularity that will be at issue throughout my investigation of Rawls' theory of justice.

It is quite clear that Rawls' theory of justice assumes the primacy of the right over the good: indeed this is openly professed by the author. What must now be shown is that the revival of the contractarian tradition ensures this primacy by equating the right with a specific procedure considered to be fair.

What must be said at the outset is that his entire theory is directed against another version of the teleological conception of justice – utilitarianism – which held sway for two centuries in the English-speaking world and found in John Stuart Mill and in Henry Sidgwick their most eloquent advocates. This point should never be forgotten in the following discussion. When Rawls speaks of a teleological approach he is thinking not of Plato or Aristotle, who seldom give rise to more than a few footnotes, but of the utilitarian concept of justice. Utilitarianism is, in fact, a teleological doctrine in that it defines justice as the greatest good for the greatest number. When applied to institutions this good is no more than the extrapolation of a principle of choice established for the individual whereby a simple pleasure, an immediate satisfaction, should be *sacrificed* for a greater but remote pleasure or satisfaction. We shall see later on how Rawls' second principle of justice is diametrically opposed to the utilitarian version of justice: *maxi*mizing the *min*imum share in a situation of unequal apportionment – which we will call the *maximin* rule – is completely at odds with the rule of the greatest benefit of the greatest number. The first idea that springs to mind is that there is an ethical gap between utilitarianism as a teleological view and the deontological view in general: when we extrapolate from the individual to society as a whole, as utilitarianism does, the notion of sacrifice takes on an alarming aspect. It is no longer a personal pleasure that is being *sacrificed* but an entire social stratum: as Jean-Pierre Dupuy (a French disciple of René Girard) maintains, utilitarianism tacitly implies a principle of sacrifice that is equivalent to legitimizing a scapegoat strategy. The Kantian rejoinder would be that the less or least advantaged party in an unequal apportionment of benefits is a person and should not be sacrificed, which is one way of saying that under the sacrificial principle the potential victim of such an apportionment would be treated as a means and not as an end. In a sense this is also Rawls' conviction, as I shall attempt to demonstrate below, but it is not his argument, which is what counts. The entire book is an attempt to shift the emphasis from the question of foundation to a question of mutual agreement, which is the very essence of any contractarian theory of justice. Rawls' theory of justice is undoubtedly a deontological theory in that it is opposed to the teleological approach of utilitarianism, but his brand of deontology has no transcendental foundation. That is because the purpose of the social contract is to derive the content of the principles of justice from a fair procedure without making any commitment to a few objective criteria of what is just – for fear of ultimately reintroducing, according to Rawls, some assumptions with regard to the good. The declared aim of Rawls' *Theory of Justice* is to provide a procedural method of achieving the right. A *fair* procedure for the *just* ordering of institutions is exactly what is meant by the title of Chapter 1: 'Justice as Fairness'.

Fairness is first and foremost characteristic of the deliberative procedure that should lead to selection of the principles of justice advocated by Rawls, whereas *justice* designates the content of the principles chosen. Thus the entire book seeks to provide a contractarian version of Kantian autonomy. The law for Kant is the law liberty would adopt if it were free from the influence of desires and pleasure. For Rawls a just institution would be the institution chosen by a relative majority of reasonable and disinterested individuals if they were free to deliberate in an equitable situation; we shall shortly be examining the conditions for and constraints acting on such a situation. Let me repeat, the book's main purpose is to replace a foundational approach to the question of justice as far as possible by a procedural approach. Hence the constructivist or even 'artificialist' form the book shares with the rest of the contractarian tradition. When the just is subordinate to the good it must be discovered; when it is engendered by purely procedural means it must be constructed: it is not anticipated but is assumed to follow from deliberation in conditions of complete fairness. In order to dramatize the issues I propose to say that justice as fairness – as procedural fairness – attempts to solve the difficulty of

Rousseau's famous paradoxical legislator. In Book II, Chapter 7 of *The Social Contract* we read that: 'In order to discover the rules of society best suited to nations, a superior intelligence beholding all the passions of men without experiencing any of them would be needed. This intelligence would have to be wholly unrelated to our nature, while knowing it through and through; its happiness would have to be independent of us, and yet ready to occupy itself with ours; and lastly, it would have, in the march of time, to look forward to a distant glory, and, working in one century, to be able to enjoy in the next. It would take gods to give men laws.'*

Justice as fairness may be understood as the *earthly* solution to this paradox. The awesome magnitude of the attempt to devise such a solution may explain the fascination Rawls' book has exerted for nearly 20 years over friends and adversaries alike.

After this long introduction I now intend to present the answers Rawls provides to the following three questions:

1. What would ensure *the fairness* of the deliberative situation that could lead to an agreement concerning a *just* arrangement of institutions?

The idea of the 'original position' and the famous allegory accompanying it, the 'veil of ignorance', is Rawls' answer to this question.

2. What *principles* would be chosen behind the veil of ignorance?

The reply to this question is to be found in the description, interpretation and correct ordering of the two 'principles of justice'.

3. What *argument* could persuade the deliberating parties to choose unanimously

Editor's note

J. J. Rousseau, *The Social Contract*. London: J. M. Dent and Sons Limited, 1946 , p. 32. See also, on p. 33: 'He, therefore, who draws up the laws has, or should have, no right of legislation'; and also, on p. 34: 'an enterprise too difficult for human powers, and, for its execution, an authority that is no authority'. Further still the paradox becomes a circular argument: 'the effect would have to become the cause; the social spirit, which should be created by these institutions, would have to preside over their very foundation; and men would have to be before law what they should become by means of law. The legislator therefore . . . must have recourse to an authority of a different order, capable of constraining without violence and persuading without convincing'. That was why in Rousseau's view (ibid., p. 34) divine intervention was necessary.

Rawls' principles of justice rather than, say, some version of utilitarianism? The answer lies in the so-called *maximin* argument borrowed from game theory and transposed to the sphere of economics.

Only after presenting these three cardinal theses in the most neutral terms possible can we return to the philosophical question posed above: whether and to what extent a purely procedural conception of justice can replace the ethical foundation of our socio-political sense of justice.

1. The original position

As we have already said, an agreement is fair if the circumstances of the choice are fair. Therefore justice as fairness is based on the fairness of what Rawls calls the original situation or position. Two points must be made at the outset. Firstly, this position is not historical but hypothetical or imaginary: 'Thus, we are to imagine that those who engage in social co-operation choose together, in one joint act, the principles which are to assign basic rights and duties and to determine the division of social benefits.' (I shall return in the next section to the underlying conception of social justice as a process or procedure of distribution, as is suggested by the terms assign and divide). My emphasis is on the phrase 'Thus we are to imagine . . .'. This leads me to my second introductory remark: 'In justice as fairness the original position of equality corresponds to the state of nature in the traditional theory of the social contract'. In fact the original position replaces the state of nature in that it is a position of equality. It will be remembered that for Hobbes the state of nature was described as the war of all against all and, as Léo Strauss emphasizes, as the state in which every individual is motivated by the fear of violent death. The issue for Hobbes is not justice but security. Rousseau and Kant, while not sharing the anthropological pessimism of Hobbes, describe the state of nature as lawless, that is to say as possessing no power of arbitration between opposing claims. But the principles of justice can be selected by common accord if and only if the original position is fair, that is to say equal – and it can be fair only in a purely hypothetical situation.

A great deal of speculation is necessary in order to identify the constraints with which the original condition would have to comply in order to be considered equal in every respect, and this speculation finds intuitive support in the fable of the 'veil of ignorance' to which Rawls owes much of his reputation.

The idea is the following:

Among the essential features of this situation is that no one knows his place in society, his class position or social status, nor does anyone know his fortune in the distribution of natural assets and abilities, his intelligence, strength, and the like. I shall even assume that the parties do not know their conceptions of the good or their special psychological propensities.

It might be thought that this imaginary state of ignorance reintroduces something equivalent to Kant's transcendental will, which is also independent of any empirical basis and consequently of any reference to ends and values, being, in short, devoid of all teleological implications. But the comparison is misleading. According to Rawls the subject has worldly interests but does not know what they will actually be. One could speak in this connection of a philosophical position that is intermediate between transcendentalism and empiricism, but that does not simplify the task of describing exactly what Rawls means by the original position. The difficulty can be seen chiefly in what Rawls postulates the parties *should know* behind the veil of ignorance if their choice is to have a bearing on the things of this world, that is to say not only on rights and duties but on the apportionment of social advantages. To put in another way, inasmuch as the choice will concern conflicting interests the parties placed behind the veil of ignorance must know what it means 'to have an interest'. For a question of justice arises whenever the appropriate apportionment of social *advantages* is at issue. At that point the parties must be not only free and rational beings but individuals concerned to promote their own interests. Hence the first constraint imposed on the initial situation: each partner must have a sufficient knowledge of the general psychology of humankind in regard to its passions and fundamental motivations. Rawls frankly admits that his philosophical anthropology comes very close to that of Hume in *A Treatise of Human Nature*, Book III, with regard to needs, interests, ends, plans and conflicting claims, including 'the interests of a self that regards its conception of the good as worthy of recognition and that advances claims in its behalf as deserving satisfaction'. Rawls calls these constraints 'the circumstances of justice' (para. 22).

Secondly, the parties must know what any rational being presumably wishes to possess, that is to say the *primary social goods* without which the exercise of liberty would be an empty claim. In this connection it is important to note that *self-respect* figures on the list of primary goods. Hence a purely deontological approach to the notion of the just is not devoid of teleological considerations, since they are already present in the original position (see para. 15), 'Primary Social Goods as the Basis of Expectations'). The persons in the original position do not know what their own conception of the good will be, but they do know that human beings prefer to have more rather than less of the primary social goods.

Thirdly, as the choice is to be made between several conceptions of justice the parties deliberating behind the veil of ignorance must possess appropriate information about the competing principles of justice. They must know the utilitarian arguments and, ironically, they must also be familiar with Rawls' principles of justice, for the choice is not between particular laws but between global conceptions of justice. It is for that reason that the principles of justice are described and interpreted in Rawls' book *before* the thematic treatment of the original position (we shall return in the critical part of this presentation to the problem I refer to as the 'order of reasons'). The alternatives open to the persons in the original position must be presented in detail with all their applications (see para. 21, 'The Presentation of Alternatives'). The contract is precisely an ordering of the alternative theories of justice (*ranking options*).

Nor is that the end of the matter: Rawls also wishes to add what he calls 'the formal constraints of the concept of right', that is to say the constraints that apply to the choice of any ethical principle and not only those of justice. The most important of these constraints is *publicity*. We shall see below that utilitarianism does not tolerate this sort of *glasnost*, as Mr Gorbachev would call it, inasmuch as the principle of sacrifice it implies must remain hidden and not be made public. All the parties must be equally well informed, and that is why the presentation of the alternatives and arguments must be public. Another constraint is what Rawls calls the *stability* of the contract,

that is to say the expectation that it will have a constraining effect in real life whatever the prevailing circumstances.

In sum:

(a) The basic idea behind the veil of ignorance is 'to set up a fair procedure so that any principles agreed to will be just. The aim is to use the notion of pure procedural justice as a basis of theory'. The link between the concept of the veil of ignorance and the search for a pure procedural conception of justice should not be underestimated. Procedural justice presents a complete alternative to substantive justice, which is governed by shared presuppositions concerning the common good.

(b) Procedural justice is justice, inasmuch as the effects of specific contingency are cancelled behind a veil of ignorance that ensures that the situation of choice is fair.

(c) The argument then continues as follows: 'since the differences among the parties are unknown to them, and everyone is equally rational and similarly situated, each is convinced by the same arguments . . . if anyone after due reflection prefers a conception of justice to another, then they all do, and a unanimous agreement can be reached.'

I would sum up by saying that in the original situation there is a perfect equation between 'each' and 'all'.

2. Which principles of justice would be chosen behind the veil of ignorance?

Before looking in detail at the precise formulation of the two principles of justice I shall make two general observations about 'the subject of justice'.

My first observation is that justice is not first and foremost an interpersonal virtue, a virtue governing bilateral relations, but rather a virtue governing social institutions. 'Justice is the first virtue of social institutions, as truth is of systems of thought.' This first assertion would appear to be more in keeping with the Platonic conception of justice than with that of Aristotle. Justice is the virtue of the whole (*Republic*, Book IV), whereas in the *Nicomachean Ethics*, Book V, Aristotle holds distributive justice to be a particular or partial form of justice in relation to justice in general, which is nothing other than obedience to the laws of the city. Why partial or particular? Firstly because it is linked to a specific situation: the distribution or apportionment of goods, honours and advantages. Moreover, the sort of equality that is an attribute of justice is not arithmetic but proportional equality, that is to say an equality of relations, of parties and shares; the relation of one party to one share must be equal to the relation of the other party to the other share. Thus, in so far as Plato appears more holistic than Aristotle, Rawls seems to carry on the work of Plato rather than that of Aristotle. But my second observation will rectify this conclusion: Rawls' conception of justice is both holistic and distributive. Rawls thus joins Aristotle without betraying Plato. The following quotation explains the point I am trying to make: 'The primary subject of justice is the basic structure of society, or, more exactly, the way in which the major social institutions distribute fundamental rights and duties and determine the division of advantages from social co-operation.' Thus the social system is primarily a distributive process, distributing roles, status, advantages and disadvantages, benefits and burdens, obligations and duties. Individuals are partners: they *participate*, inasmuch as society distributes *shares*. This conception of society as a distributive process enables us to transcend the classical opposition between a holistic conception of society such as that of Durkheim and the epistemological individualism of Max Weber. If there were any value in this opposition there would be a clear contradiction between the claim that the primary subject of justice is the basic structure of society and the attempt to derive the basic rules of society from a contract. Inasmuch as society is 'a co-operative venture for mutual advantage' it must be pictured simultaneously as an irreducible whole and as a system of interrelations between individuals. Justice may then be considered the virtue of institutions, but of institutions that seek to promote the good of those participating in them. Participation is not a marginal feature, for institutions have a distributive role, and individuals are defined as partners. This is why the rational choice must be made jointly, with a view to ultimate agreement on the best manner of governing society. It also explains the sense in which justice as distributive justice can have the basic structure of society as its primary

subject: this basic structure is itself a distributive phenomenon. (This renders inoperative the objections advanced by R. P. Wolff,[2] who wrongly sees distribution as a purely economic phenomenon opposed to production in quasi-Marxist fashion.) Moreover, society is problematic, an area of possible alternatives, insofar as it is, as a system, a distributive phenomenon: since there are several ways of distributing advantages and disadvantages society is from the outset a consensual–conflictual phenomenon. On the one hand any apportionment may be challenged, especially, as we shall see, in an unequal distribution; on the other hand, stable distribution demands a consensus as regards the procedures for arbitrating between competing claims. The principles of justice we shall now consider bear precisely on this problematic situation created by the requirement of fair and stable distribution.

Having made these points, we may now consider the two principles of justice.

I shall put on one side the definitive and complete formulation, the product of the complex proof that will be the subject of the third part of my presentation. Quoting Rawls (p. 60),

The first statement of the two principles reads as follows. *First: each person is to have an equal right to the most extensive basic liberty compatible with a similar liberty for others. Second: social and economic inequalities are to be arranged so that they are both (a) reasonably expected to be to everyone's advantage, and (b) attached to positions and offices open to all.*

The first principle thus ensures the equal liberties of citizens (such as freedom of speech and assembly, freedom to vote and eligibility for public office). The second principle applies to a state of inequality and assumes that certain inequalities must be considered preferable even to an egalitarian distribution. We read further, on page 61, that 'The second principle applies, in the first approximation, to the distribution of income and wealth and to the design of organizations that make use of *differences* in authority and responsibility' (hence the name of the difference principle) ' . . . While the distribution of wealth and income need not be equal it must be to everyone's advantage, and, at the same time, positions of authority and offices of command must be accessible to all. One applies the second principle by holding positions open, and then, subject to this constraint, arranges social and economic inequalit-ies so that everyone benefits.'

As important as the content of these prin-ciples is the rule of priority that links them. Rawls speaks here of a serial order: 'These principles are to be arranged in a serial order with the first principle prior to the second. This ordering means that a departure from the institutions of equal liberty required by the first principle cannot be justified by, or compensated for, by greater social and economic advantages' (p. 61). This idea of serial or lexical order clashes head on with Marxism as well as utili-tarianism. Rawls calls this order lexical or lexico-graphical for a simple reason: in a dictionary the first letter is lexically first in the sense that no rearrangement of the subsequent letters can erase the harm caused by the substitution of any other letter for the first letter; the impossibility of any such substitution bestows immeasurable significance on the first letter. Nevertheless the subsequent order is not devoid of significance, as the following letters differentiate between two words which begin in the same way. A lexical order assigns a specific weight to all elements but does not make them interchange-able. Applied to the theory of justice this means that a loss of liberty, however small, cannot be compensated for by an increase in economic efficiency. Well-being cannot be purchased at the expense of liberty. Those commentators who have concentrated on the second principle, disregarding the lexical order, have made a serious error: the lexical order applies not only between the first two principles but also between the two parts of the second principle. The econ-omically least advantaged must be accorded lexical priority over all the other parties. This is what Jean-Pierre Dupuy refers to as the anti-sacrificial implication of Rawls' principle. A potential victim should not be sacrificed for the common good.

Now, why are there two principles instead of just one; why an egalitarian principle and a non-egalitarian principle? The answer is that in economics the total sum to be shared out is not determined in advance but depends on the nature of the distribution, which leads to differ-ences in productivity. Under a system of arith-metic equality productivity could be so low that even the interests of the least advantaged would be harmed. There is a point at which social transfers become counterproductive. And it is at that point that the difference principle comes into operation. Rawls is thus caught between two groups of opponents. From his right come accusations of egalitarianism (absolute priority for the least advantaged) whereas those to his left accuse him of justifying inequality. Rawls' answer to the first group is that in a situation of arbitrary inequality the advantages of the best off would be threatened by the resistance of the poor or simply by their lack of co-operation. To the second group he replies that a more egalitarian solution would be rejected unani-mously, because under it all would be losers. The difference principle selects the most nearly equal situation compatible with the rule of una-nimity.

This last assertion leads to a third question: for what reasons would the parties placed behind the veil of ignorance prefer these principles in their lexical order to any version of utilitarian-ism? The anti-sacrificial implication of Rawls' theory of justice comes to the fore at this point, which is also the starting point for my own argument.

3. Argument

The argument concerns chiefly the difference principle. Borrowed from the theory of decision-making in a context of uncertainty it is referred to by the term *maximin*: the parties choose the arrangement that *maxi*mizes the *mini*mum share. It is difficult here not to transpose the psychology of an individual, of a poker player let us say, to the original situation; but this is impossible as an awareness of personal psy-chology is precisely what all the parties lack. Hence the only remaining motivation in the original situation is that of parties with a mutual commitment to respect a contract whose terms have been publicly defined and unanimously accepted: the contract establishes links, and the commitment binds. No one with any doubts as to their ability to fulfil their promise will be prepared to bind themselves. The intention is all the more restricting in that the agreement must be final and that its subject is nothing less than the basic structure of society. If two conceptions of justice are in conflict and one of them permits a situation that someone could not accept whereas the other conception excludes such a possibility then the second will prevail. Rawls' entire bid turns on the proof that in the utilitarian scheme of things the person occupying the least advantaged position is the sacrificial victim, whereas the conception of justice defended by the author is the only one capable of making that person an equal partner. That is enough to prove the superiority of the second theory.

This point may be demonstrated without accepting all the intricacies of the maximin argument. In a society that publicly professed Rawls' principles the least advantaged would know that their position derived maximum benefit from the inequalities they perceived. Lesser inequalities would victimize them to an even greater extent. The most advantaged, who would appear to be less so than their counterparts in all known societies, would be convinced by the argument that their relative loss (in comparison with the more advantageous position a less equitable distribution would offer them) would be compensated for by the co-operation of their fellows, in the absence of which their relative privilege would be threatened. In a society that publicly declared itself to be utilitarian the least advantaged would find themselves in an entirely different situation. They would be asked to accept that the greatest well-being of the group was a sufficient reason to justify their unenviable lot. They would have to agree to see themselves and to be seen by others as the scapegoats of the system. In fact the situation would be worse, as a cynically utilitarian system is unable to satisfy the rule of publicity. The sacrificial principle implied by utilitarianism must remain hidden in order to be effective. That is one more reason for rejecting the utilitarian conception of justice in the original position.

Discussion

I can now come back to my first question. Is it possible to substitute a pure procedural conception of justice for an ethical foundation? For that is the issue in any contractarian theory of justice.

It is my contention that a procedural conception of justice provides at best a rationalization of a sense of justice that remains a presupposition. In arguing this it is not my intention to refute Rawls but simply to develop the presuppositions in his work that seem to me unavoidable. I shall proceed in three stages.

1. Let us look first at the '*order of reasons*' followed by Rawls' work (to employ the Cartesian expression). What prevails throughout the work is in my view not a *lexical* order such as the order that operates between the principles of justice but the *circular* order that, also in my view, is characteristic of all ethical reflection. The reader may be surprised by the fact that the principles of justice are defined and even developed (paras. 11 and 12) before the circumstances of the choice are examined (paras. 20-25), hence before the thematic treatment of the veil of ignorance (para. 24) and, more significantly, before the proof that these principles are the only rational principles (paras. 26–30). This does not prevent Rawls from describing the two principles of justice in advance as those that would be chosen in the original position. Indeed, as early as paragraph 3, Rawls asserts that the principles of justice are 'the principles that free and rational persons concerned to further their own interests would accept in an initial position of equality as defining the fundamental terms of their association'. The theory is thus presented as a whole independently of any genuinely serial order linking the formulation of the two principles, the original position, the veil of ignorance and the rational choice. Without this anticipation justice could not be identified as fairness: 'The original position is, one might say, the appropriate initial *status quo*, and thus the fundamental agreements reached in it are fair.' This explains the propriety of the title of Chapter 1 'Justice as Fairness': it conveys the idea that 'the principles of justice are agreed to in an initial situation that is fair'. It is necessary to anticipate not only the criterion of the original position but also its principal features, namely the idea that the parties have interests although they do not know what they are and the idea that, in addition, they are conceived as 'not taking an interest in one another's interests'.

Such is the curious state of the 'order of reasons'. On the one hand the principles of justice are broadly defined and interpreted before it is proved that they are the principles that would be chosen in the original position; on the other the original agreement must be anticipated for the formulation of the two principles to acquire some relevance. Rawls himself confirms this circularity when he introduces the principles of justice for the first time: 'I shall now state in a provisional form the two principles of justice that I believe would be chosen in the original position . . . the first formulation of these principles is tentative. As we go on I shall run through several formulations and approximate step by step the final statement to be given much later. I believe that doing this allows the exposition to proceed in a natural way' (page 60). My interpretation of the above statement is as follows: the definition of justice provided before the maximin argument is only exploratory; after the maximin argument it is definitive. Consequently we are looking not at a linear argument but at the gradual clarification of a preliminary understanding of what justice means.

2. This first consideration derived from the formal presentation of the argument leads on to the main argument, which is that the procedural definition of justice does not constitute an independent theory but rests on a preliminary understanding allowing us to define and interpret the two principles of justice before it is proved – if indeed it can be proved – that those are the principles that would be chosen in the original position, that is to say behind the veil of ignorance. This will be the second stage in my argument.

My objection would appear to constitute a challenge to any contractarian school for which the procedural dimension must be independent of any presupposition with regard to the good in a teleological approach to the concept of justice or even with regard to the right in a transcendental form of deontology. In this sense the entire exposition of *A Theory of Justice* may be understood as a gigantic effort to guarantee the independence of the two components in the argument: the theory of the original position and the reason for choosing the two principles rather than any utilitarian version of justice. It is my contention that circularity wins out over the linearity claimed by the theory of justice on behalf of the independence of the work's theoretical core.

(a) Let us consider first of all the original position: all the constraints that define it are of course constructed as an intellectual experiment and create an entirely hypothetical situation without roots in history or experience; but they have been devised in such a way that they satisfy the idea of fairness that represents the transcendental condition for the entire pro-

cedural development. Now, what is fairness but equality between the parties facing the demands of a rational choice? Is this not what is meant by *isotes*, as used by Isocrates and Aristotle, which, in turn, implies a respect for the other as an equal partner in the procedural process?

(b) This suspicion that a moral principle governs the apparently artificial construction is confirmed by the role played in practice by the maximin argument throughout the proof. Rawls seems to mean that the maximin rule as such provides an *independent* basis for choosing the two principles of justice in preference to the utilitarian concept of justice. He presents the argument as a heuristic process that enables us to conceive of the two principles as the maximin solution to the problem of how to achieve social justice. According to Rawls the two principles are analogous to the maximin rule as a means of making a choice in any situation of uncertainty. At first sight the argument appears completely rational, drawing an ethical conclusion from non-ethical premises. But on examining more closely the decisive argument deployed against utilitarianism – the fact that one must be willing to sacrifice a few disadvantaged individuals or groups if that is necessary for the greatest good of the greatest number – we cannot help thinking that what we are seeing is an ethical argument concealed by a technical argument borrowed from the theory of decision-making in its most elementary form, game theory, where there are winners and losers totally unconcerned by ethical considerations. The flaw in utilitarianism is precisely its extrapolation from the individual to society. It is one thing to say that an individual may have to sacrifice some tiny, immediate pleasure for the sake of a greater pleasure at a later date; it is quite another thing to say that the satisfaction of a minority must be sacrificed for the satisfaction of the majority. Moreover, the lexical order of the first and second principles and the maximin rule argue against the legitimacy of extrapolating from the individual to society as a whole. The argument is, it seems to me, a moral one. It is directed against what I – like Jean-Pierre Dupuy – refer to as the sacrificial principle, i.e. the logic of the scapegoat. In my view the argument is a moral one, and a Kantian one into the bargain: on the sacrificial principle some individuals are treated as means and not as ends in themselves in relation to the alleged good of the whole. We are thus brought back to the second formulation of the categorical imperative and, beyond that, to the golden rule: 'Whatsoever ye would that men should do to you, do ye even so to them.' I have pointed out elsewhere that the golden rule has an advantage over the Kantian formulation in that it takes account of the reference to several goods. This applies to Rawls, who differs from Kant on precisely this point: behind the veil of ignorance the parties know that human beings have interests. They are unaware only of what their own interests will be in real life.

This interpretation of the maximin rule as a tacitly ethical argument could be anticipated from the beginning of the book. We read on page 1:

Justice is the first virtue of social institutions, as truth is of systems of thought. A theory however elegant and economical must be rejected or revised if it is untrue; likewise laws and institutions no matter how efficient and well-arranged must be reformed or abolished if they are unjust. Each person possesses an inviolability founded on justice that even the welfare of society as a whole cannot override. For this reason justice denies that the loss of freedom for some is made right by a greater good shared by others.

After reading these lines we may wonder how it is possible to support both recognition of an ethical presupposition and a bid to release the procedural definition of justice from any presupposition concerning the good and even the right. Is there any element of mediation between what I shall call for the sake of brevity the *ethical* approach and the pure *procedural* approach of Rawls' theory of justice? This question leads me on to the third stage in my discussion.

3. The element of mediation sought between the ethical presupposition of the theory of justice taken as a whole and the purely technical maximin argument is suggested by Rawls himself in paragraph 4, when he introduces the idea of the original position for the first time. After declaring that the principles of justice should be defined as 'those which rational persons concerned to advance their interests would consent to as equals when none are known to be advantaged or disadvantaged by social and natural contingencies' (page 19), Rawls makes the following statement. 'There is, however, another side to justifying a particular description of the original position. This is to see if the principles which would be chosen match our considered convictions of justice or extend them in an acceptable way' (ibid.). Let us consider briefly this notion of 'considered convictions'. It sums up all the 'precomprehension' Rawls calls 'intuitive', that is to say the moral judgements 'in which we have the greatest confidence' (ibid.). Are not these considered convictions ultimately rooted in the sense of justice equivalent to the golden rule applied to institutions rather than to individuals in a face-to-face relationship: applied moreover to institutions considered in terms of their distributive role? In fact, our sense of injustice is usually more reliable than our sense of justice. For example, says Rawls. 'We are confident that religious intolerance and racial discrimination are unjust' (ibid.). In this connection. R. J. Lucas begins his excellent book *On Justice* with a chapter on what is held to be unjust.[3] The cry of injustice is the cry of the victim, the victim utilitarianism is willing to sacrifice for the sake of the general interest. While our sense of injustice is normally sound 'we have much less assurance as to what is the correct distribution of wealth and authority. Here we may be looking for a way to remove our doubts' (page 20). This is where rational arguments come in. But they cannot replace considered convictions: 'We can check an interpretation of the initial situation . . . by the capacity of its principles to accommodate our firmest convictions and to provide guidance where guidance is needed; (ibid.). We can even go so far as to say that the lexical order of the two principles of justice is virtually prefigured in our considered convictions. 'Thus it seems reasonable and generally acceptable that no one should be advantaged or disadvantaged by natural fortune or social circumstances in the choice of principles' (page 18). The entire system of argumentation may thus be considered a gradual rationalization of one's convictions when they are infected by prejudices or weakened by doubts. Rawls give a name to this mutual adjustment of conviction and theory:

By going back and forth, sometimes altering the conditions of the contractual circumstances, at others withdrawing our judgements and conforming them to principle, I assume that eventually we shall find a description of the initial situation that both expresses reasonable conditions and yields principles which match our considered judgements duly pruned and adjusted. *This state of affairs I refer to as reflective equilibrium*. It is an equilibrium because at last our principles and judgements coincide; and it is reflective since we know to what principles our judgements conform and the premises of their derivation. (page 20)

The entire book may thus be seen as a search for this reflective equilibrium. But if I have correctly understood the course of the argument the sort of circularity the search for reflective equilibrium seems to presume appears threatened by the centrifugal forces exerted by the contractarian hypothesis. At the beginning of this presentation we drew attention to the constructivist and even 'artificialist' tenor of both the theory of the original position and the maximin argument for the difference principle. Can we simultaneously maintain the adjustment between theory and conviction and the fully independent status of the argument for the two principles of justice? This is the element of ambivalence that seems to me to dominate Rawls' theory of justice. That theory tries to succeed on two counts, firstly by satisfying the principle of reflective equilibrium and secondly by constructing an independent argument introduced by the hypothetical course of the reflection. This explains the apparent lack of harmony between the initial statements assigning a regulatory role to considered convictions and the proud plea delivered at a later stage in support of an independent argument resembling the maximin rule. The millstone of any contractarian theory may be that it derives from a procedure approved by all the very principles of justice that, paradoxically, have already motivated the search for an independent argument

This ambiguity ultimately concerns the role of rational arguments in ethics. Can they be made to replace prior convictions by devising a hypothetical deliberative situation? Or is their role rather to throw a critical light on prior convictions? It seems to me that Rawls is trying to have the best of two worlds: to construct a pure procedural conception of justice without losing the security provided by a reflective equilibrium between conviction and theory. In my view it is our intuitive understanding of the unjust and the just that ensures the deontological aim of the allegedly independent argument, including the maximin rule. Once removed from the context of the golden rule the maximin rule would remain a purely prudential argument typical of any bargaining process. Neither the

deontological intention nor even the historical dimension of the sense of justice is simply intuitive: they are the result of a long process of *Bildung* originating in the Judaeo-Christian and Graeco-Roman traditions. Divorced from that cultural background the maximin rule would lose its ethical character. Instead of being quasi-economic, I mean analogous to an economic argument, it would tend to become a pseudo-economic argument, once it was deprived of its basis in our considered convictions.

But this first suggestion concerning the epistemological status of rational arguments in ethics has no sense except when taken in conjunction with the second. We cannot do without a critical assessment of our supposed sense of justice. The task would be to discover which components or aspects of our considered convictions require the constant eradication of prejudices and ideological biases. The first area to which this critical effort would be applied would be the prejudices hidden behind what moralists have referred to as 'specifying premises', for example the restriction of the principle of justice that for centuries meant that slaves were not classed as human beings. One may ask whether it is not pure Utopia to trust in the rationality of ordinary citizens, that is to say their capacity to put themselves in the place of others or better still to transcend their place. But without such an act of trust the philosophical fable of the original position would be no more than an unbelievable and irrelevant hypothesis. There is another reason that makes us think that this overcoming of prejudice, this openness to criticism is possible: it derives from what we said at the beginning about the problematic nature of a society defined in terms of its distributive function. Such a society is on principle open to a variety of possible institutional arrangements. It is for that very reason that justice can only be distributive and demands a highly refined form of reasoning such as Aristotle began to practise by distinguishing between arithmetic and proportional equality.

To conclude, the adjective 'considered' in the expression 'considered convictions' has as much weight as the noun 'convictions'. In this context *considered* means open to the criticism of others, or, as Apel and Habermas would say, subject to the rule of argumentation.

(Translated from French)

Notes

1. John Rawls, *A Theory of Justice*. Cambridge, Mass.: The Belknap Press of Harvard University Press, 1971.

2. R. P. Wolff, *Understanding Rawls*. Princeton: Princeton University Press, 1977.

3. R. J. Lucas, *On Justice*. Oxford: Oxford University Press, 1966.

THE JOURNAL OF PHILOSOPHY

VOLUME LXX, NO. 9, MAY 10, 1973

A THEORY OF JUSTICE BY JOHN RAWLS: TWO REVIEW ARTICLES *

SOME ORDINALIST-UTILITARIAN NOTES ON RAWLS'S THEORY OF JUSTICE †

RAWLS'S major work has been widely and correctly acclaimed as the most searching investigation of the notion of justice in modern times. It combines a genuine and fruitful originality of viewpoint with an extraordinary systematic evaluation of foundations, implications for action, and connections with other aspects of moral choice. The specific postulates for justice that Rawls enunciates are quite novel, and yet, once stated, they clearly have a strong claim on our attention as at least plausible candidates for the foundations of a theory of justice. The arguments for accepting these postulates are part of the contractarian tradition, but have been developed in many new and interesting ways. The implications of these postulates for specific aspects of the institutions of liberty, particularly civil liberty, and for the operations of the economic order are spelled out in considerable and thoughtful detail (as an economist accustomed to much elementary misunderstanding of the nature of an economy on the part of philosophers and social scientists, I must express my gratitude for the sophistication and knowledge which Rawls displays here). Finally, the relations between justice of social institutions and the notion of morally right behavior on the part of individuals is analyzed at considerable and intelligent length.

It will become clear in the sequel that I have a number of questions and objections to Rawls's theory. Indeed, it is not surprising that no theory of justice can be so compelling as to forestall some

* Cambridge, Mass.: The Belknap Press of the Harvard University Press, 1971. xv, 607 p. Cloth $15.00, paper $3.95.

† This note was prepared with assistance from Grant N.S.F. No. GS28626X.

objections; indeed, that very fact is disturbing to the quest for the concept of justice, as I shall briefly note in the last section of this paper. These questions are a tribute to the breadth and fruitfulness of Rawls's work.

My critical stance is derived from a particular tradition of thought: that of welfare economics. In the prescription of economic policy, questions of distributive justice inevitably arise (not *all* such questions arise, only some; in particular, justice in the allocation of freedoms rather than goods is not part of the formal analysis of welfare economics, though some economists have made strong informal and unanalyzed commitments to some aspects of freedom). The implicit ethical basis of economic policy judgment is some version of utilitarianism. At the same time, descriptive economics has relied heavily on a utilitarian psychology in explaining the choices made by consumers and other economic agents. The basic theorem of welfare economics: that, under certain conditions, the competitive economic system yields an outcome that is optimal or efficient (in a sense which requires careful definition), depends on the identification of the utility structures that motivate the choices made by economic agents with the utility structures used in judging the optimality of the outcome of the competitive system. As a result, the utility concepts which, in one form or another, underlie welfare judgments in economics as well as elsewhere (according to Rawls's and many other theories of justice) have been subjected to an intensive scrutiny by economists. There has been more emphasis on their operational meaning, but perhaps less on their specific content; philosophers have been more prone to analyze what individuals should want, where economists have been content to identify "should" with "is" for the individual (not for society).

I do not mean that all economists or even those who have concerned themselves with welfare judgments will agree with the following remarks, but I do want to suggest the background out of which these concerns originated.

In section I, I will highlight the basic assumptions of Rawls's theory and stress those aspects which especially intersect my interests. I will be brief, since by now the theory is doubtless reasonably familiar to the reader. In section II, I raise some specific questions about different aspects of the theory, in particular, the logic by which Rawls proceeds from the general point of view of the theory (the "original position," the "difference principle" in its general form) to more specific implications, such as the priority of liberty and the maximin principle for distribution of goods. Section III is the central section of this paper; in it I raise a number of the epistemological issues that seem to me to be crucial in the development of most kinds of ethical theory and in particular Rawls's: How do we know other peoples' welfare enough to apply a principle of justice? What knowledge is assumed to be possessed by those in Rawls's original position when they agree to a set of principles? In section IV, I state more explicitly what may be termed an *ordinalist* (i.e., epistemologically modest) version of utilitarianism and argue that, in these terms, Rawls's position does not differ sharply. A brief section V discusses the role of majority and other kinds of voting in a theory of justice, especially in light of the discussion in section IV. Section VI turns to a different line, an examination of the implication of Rawls's theory for economic policy. Finally, in section VII, some of the preceding discussions are applied and extended to raise some questions about the possibility of any theory of justice; the criterion of universalizability may be impossible to achieve when people are really different, particularly when different life experiences mean that they can never have the same information.

I. SOME BASIC ASPECTS OF RAWLS'S THEORY

The central part of Rawls's theory is a statement of fundamental propositions about the nature of a just society, what may be thought of as a system of axioms. On the one side, it is sought to justify these axioms as deriving from a contract made among rational potential members of society; on the other side, the implications of these axioms for the determination of social institutions are drawn.

The axioms themselves can be thought of as divided into two parts: one is a general statement of the notion of justice, the second a more detailed elaboration of more specific forms.

The general point of view is a strongly affirmed egalitarianism, to be departed from only when it is in the interest of all to do so. "All social values—liberty and opportunity, income and wealth, and the bases of self-respect—are to be distributed equally unless unequal distribution of any, or all, of these values is to everyone's disadvantage" (p. 62; parenthetical page references are to Rawls's book). This *generalized difference principle*, as Rawls terms it, is no tautology. In particular, it implies that even natural advantages, superiorities of intelligence or strength, do not in themselves create any claims to greater rewards. The principles of justice are "an agreement to regard the distribution of natural talents as a common asset and to share in the benefits of this distribution" (101).

Personally, I share fully this value judgment; and, indeed, it is implied by almost all attempts at full formalization of welfare economics.[1] But a contradictory proposition: that an individual is entitled to what he creates, is widely and unreflectively held; when teaching elementary economics, I have had considerable difficulty in persuading the students that this *productivity principle* was not completely self-evident.

It may be worth stressing that the assumption of what may be termed *asset egalitarianism*: that all the assets of society, including personal skills, are available as a common pool for whatever distribution justice calls for, is so much taken for granted that it is hardly argued for. All the alternatives to his principles of justice that Rawls considers imply asset egalitarianism (though some of them are very inegalitarian in result, since more goods are to be assigned to those most capable of using them). The productivity principle is not even considered. It must be said, on the other hand, that asset egalitarianism is certainly an implication of the "original position" contract. (The practical implications of asset egalitarianism are, however, severely modified in the direction of the productivity principle by incentive considerations; see section VI below).

But Rawls's theory is a much more specific statement of the concept of justice. This consists of two parts. First, among the goods distributed by the social order, liberty has a priority over others; no amount of material goods is considered to compensate for a loss of liberty. Second, among goods of a given priority class, inequalities should be permitted only if they increase the lot of the least well off. The first principle will be referred to as the *priority of liberty*, the second as the *maximin* principle (*max*imizing the welfare at its *min*imum level; Rawls himself refers to this as the *difference principle*).

Rawls argues for these two principles as being those which would be agreed to by rational individuals in a hypothetical *original position*, where they have full general knowledge of the world, but do not know which individual they will be. The idea of this "veil of ignorance" is that principles of justice must be universalizable; they must be such as to command assent by anyone who does not take account of his individual circumstances. If it is assumed that rational individuals under these circumstances have some degree of aversion to uncertainty, then they will find it desirable to enter into an insurance agreement: that the more successful will share

[1] See A. Bergson, *Essays in Normative Economics* (Cambridge, Mass.: Harvard, 1966), ch. I; P. A. Samuelson, *The Foundations of Economic Analysis* (Cambridge, Mass.: Harvard, 1947), pp. 230–248; or F. Y. Edgeworth (London: Kegan Paul, 1881), pp. 56–82.

with the less, though not so much as to make them both worse off. Thus, the original-position argument does lead to a generalized view of justice. Rawls then further argues that his more specific principles (priority of liberty and the maximin principle) also follow from the original-position argument, at least in the sense of being preferable to other principles advanced in the philosophical literature, such as classical utilitarianism.

Two final remarks on the general nature of Rawls's system: (1) The principles of justice are intended to apply to the choice of social institutions, not to the actual allocative decisions of society separately. (2) The principles are supposed to characterize an ideal state of justice. If the ideal state is not achieved, they do not in themselves supply any basis for deciding that one non-ideal state is more or less just than another. "Questions of strategy are not to be confused with those of justice. . . . The force of opposing attitudes has no bearing on the question of right but only on the feasibility of arrangements of liberty" (231). It is intended of course that a characterization of ideal or optimal states of justice is a first step in a complete ordering of alternative institutional arrangements as more or less just.

II. THE DERIVATION OF RAWLS'S SPECIFIC RULES

From the viewpoint of the logical structure of the theory, a central question is the extent to which the assumption of the original position really implies the highly specific forms of Rawls's two rules. Let me take the priority of liberty first. This is given a central place in presentation, and at a number of points the fact that the theory puts such emphasis on liberty is used to distinguish it favorably from utilitarianism; the latter, it is argued, might easily lead to sacrificing the liberty of a few for the benefit of many. "Each person possesses an inviolability founded on justice that even the welfare of society as a whole cannot override. For this reason justice denies that the loss of freedom for some is made right by a greater good shared by others" (3/4).

Despite its importance, the definitive argument for the priority of liberty is postponed to very late in the book (541–548). The key argument is that the priority of liberty is desired by every individual. In technical terms, each individual has a *lexicographical* (or "lexical" in Rawls's simplification) ordering of goods of all kinds, with liberty coming first; of any two possible states, an individual will always prefer that with the most liberty, regardless of other goods (such as income), and will choose according to income only among states with equal liberty. "The supposition is that . . . the persons

. . . will not exchange a lesser liberty for an improvement in their economic well-being, at least not once a certain level of wealth has been attained. . . . As the conditions of civilization improve, the marginal significance for our good of further economic and social advantages diminishes relative to the interests of liberty" (542).

The argument is clearly an empirical judgment, and the reader can decide for himself how much weight it will bear. I want to bring out another aspect, the relation to utilitarianism. If in fact each individual assigns priority to liberty in the lexicographical sense, then the most classical sum-of-utilities criterion will do the same for social choice; the rule will be for society to maximize the sum of individuals' liberties and then, among those states which accomplish this, choose that which maximizes the sum of satisfactions from other goods.

Let me now turn to the maximin rule (this is to be applied separately to liberty and to the nonpriority goods). The justification appears most explicitly on pages 155–158; it is mainly an argument for maximin as against the sum-of-utilities criterion. It should first be noted that the original-position assumption had also been put forth by the economists W. S. Vickrey [2] and J. C. Harsanyi [3]; but they use it to supply a contractarian foundation to a form of utilitarianism (discussed at considerable length by Rawls, 161–175). They start from the position, due to F. P. Ramsey, and J. von Neumann and O. Morgenstern, that choice under risky conditions can be described as the maximization of expected utility. In the original position, each individual may with equal probability be any member of the society. If there are n members of the society and if the ith member will have utility u_i under some given allocation decision, then the value of that allocation to any individual is $\Sigma u_i(1/n)$, since $1/n$ is the probability of being individual i. Thus, in choosing among alternative allocations of goods, each individual in the original position will want to maximize this expectation, or, what is the same thing for a given population, maximize the sum of utilities.

[2] "Measuring Marginal Utility by Reactions to Risk," *Econometrica*, XIII (1945): 319–333, p. 329; "Utility, Strategy, and Social Decision Rules," *Quarterly Journal of Economics*, LXXIV (1960): 507–535, pp. 523f.

Vickrey's 1945 statement has been overlooked by all subsequent writers, not surprisingly, since it received relatively little emphasis in a paper overtly devoted to a seemingly different subject. I read the paper before I was concerned with the theory of social choice; the implications for that theory were so easy to overlook that they did not occur to me at all when they would have been relevant.

[3] "Cardinal Utility in Welfare Economics and the Theory of Risk-taking," *Journal of Political Economy*, LXI (1953): 434/5; "Cardinal Welfare, Individualistic Ethics, and Personal Comparisons of Utility," *ibid.*, LXIII (1955): 309–321.

Rawls, however, starting from the same premises, derives the state-ment that society should maximize min u_i. The argument seems to have two parts: first, that in an original position, where the quality of an entire life is at stake, it is reasonable to have a high degree of aversion to risk, and being concerned with the worst possible out-come is an extreme form of risk aversion; and, second, that the probabilities are in fact ill defined and should not be employed in such a calculation. The first point raises some questions about the meaning of the utilities and does not do justice to the fact that, at least in Vickrey and Harsanyi, the utilities are already so measured as to reflect risk aversion (see some further discussion in section IV). The second point is a version of a recurrent and unresolved contro-versy in the theory of behavior under uncertainty; are all uncertain-ties expressible by probabilities? The view that they are has a long history and has been given an axiomatic justification by Ramsey [4] and by L. J. Savage.[5] The contrary view has been upheld by F. H. Knight [6] and by many writers who have held to an objective view of probability; the maximin theory of rational decision-making under uncertainty was set forth by A. Wald [7] specifically in the latter con-text. Among economists, G. L. S. Shackle [8] has been a noted advo-cate of a more general theory which includes maximin as a special case. L. Hurwicz and I [9] have given a set of axioms which imply that choice will be based on some function of the maximum and the minimum utility.

It has, however, long been remarked that the maximin theory has some implications that seem hardly acceptable. It implies that any benefit, no matter how small, to the worst-off member of society, will outweigh any loss to a better-off individual, provided it does not reduce the second below the level of the first. Thus, there can easily exist medical procedures which serve to keep people barely alive but with little satisfaction and which are yet so expensive as to reduce the rest of the population to poverty. A maximin prin-ciple would apparently imply that such procedures be adopted.

[4] F. P. Ramsey, "Truth and Probability," in *The Foundations of Mathe-matics and Other Logical Essays* (London: K. Paul, Trench, Trubner, 1931), p. 156–198.

[5] *The Foundations of Statistics* (New York: Wiley, 1954).

[6] *Risk, Uncertainty, and Profit* (New York: Houghton Mifflin, 1921).

[7] "Contributions to the Theory of Statistical Estimation and Testing Hypothe-ses," *Annals of Mathematical Statistics*, x (1939): 299–326.

[8] *Expectations in Economics* (Cambridge: University Press, 1949) and subse-quent works.

[9] "An Optimality Criterion for Decision-making under Ignorance," in C. F. Carter and J. L. Ford, eds., *Uncertainty and Expectation in Economics* (Oxford: Basil Blackwell, 1972), pp. 1–11.

Rawls considers this argument, but rejects it on the ground that it will not occur in practice. He fairly consistently assumes that the actual society has the property he calls *close-knittedness*: "As we raise the expectations of the more advantaged the situation of the worst off is continuously improved. . . . For the greater expections of the more favored presumably cover the costs of training and encourage better performance" (158). It is hard to analyze this argument fairly in short compass. On the face of it, it seems clearly false; there is nothing easier than to point out changes that benefit the well-off at the expense of the poor, including the least advantaged, e.g., simultaneous reduction of the income tax for high brackets and of welfare payments. Rawls holds that one must consider his principles in their totality, in particular, a strongly expressed demand for open access to all positions. But, even with perfect equality of opportunity, there will presumably remain inequalities due to biological and cultural inheritance (Rawls nowhere advocates abolition of the family) and chance events, and, once inequalities do exist, the harmony of interests seems to be less than all-pervasive. In any case, the assumption of close-knittedness undermines all the distinctions that Rawls is so careful to make. For, if it holds, there is no difference in policy implication between the maximin principle and the sum of utilities; if all satisfactions go up together, the conflict between the individual and the society disappears.

III. EPISTEMOLOGICAL ISSUES IN THE THEORY OF JUSTICE

Many theories of justice, including both Rawls's and utilitarianism, imply that the social institutions or their creators have access to some kinds of knowledge. This raises the question whether they can in fact or even in principle have such knowledge. In this section, two epistemological questions are raised, though there are others: (1) How can interpersonal comparisons of satisfaction be made? and (2) What knowledge is available in the original position?

1. The problem of interpersonal comparison of utilities seems to bother economists more than philosophers. As already indicated, utility or satisfaction or any other similar concept appears in economic theory as an explanation of individual behavior, for example, as a consumer. Specifically, it is hypothesized that the individual chooses his consumption so as to maximize his utility, subject to the constraints imposed by his budget. But, for this purpose, a quantitatively measurable utility is a superfluous concept. All that is needed is an ordering, that is, a statement for each pair of consumption patterns as to which is preferred. Any numerical function over

the possible consumption patterns having the property that it assigns larger numbers to preferred bundles could be thought of as a utility function. Clearly, then, any monotonic transformation of a utility function is also a utility function.

To turn the matter around, it might be asked, How can we have any evidence about the magnitude of utility? The only evidence on an individual's utility function is supplied by his observable behavior, specifically the choices he makes in the course of maximizing the function. But such choices are defined by the preference ordering and must therefore be the same for all utility functions compatible with that ordering. Hence, there is no quantitative meaning for utility for an individual. (This *ordinalist* position was introduced into economics by V. Pareto and I. Fisher and has become fairly orthodox in the last thirty years.)

If the utility of an individual is not measurable, then *a fortiori* the comparison of utilities of different individuals is not meaningful. In particular, the sum-of-utilities criterion becomes indefensible as it stands. Rawls's maximin criterion also implies interpersonal comparison, for we must pick out the least advantaged individual, and that requires statements of the form, "individual *A* is worse off than individual *B*." Unlike the sum-of-utilities approach, however, this does not require that the units in which different individuals' utilities are measured be comparable, only that we be able to rank different individuals according to some scale of satisfaction. But we do not have any underlying numerical magnitude to use for this purpose, and the question still remains, What is the operational meaning of the interpersonal comparison?

If one is to take the sum-of-utilities criterion seriously, then it would have to be considered possible for individuals to have different utility functions; in particular, they might derive different amounts of satisfaction from the same increments to their wealth. Then, the utilitarian would have to agree that the sum of utilities would be increased by shifting wealth to the more sensitive individuals. This does not occur in Rawls's theory, but something parallel to it does. Consider an individual who is incapable of deriving much pleasure from anything, whether because of psychological or physical limitations. He may well be the worst-off individual and, therefore, be the touchstone of distribution policy, even though he derives little satisfaction from the additional income.

In the usual applications of the sum-of-utilities approach, the problem of differing utilities is dodged by assuming it away; it is postulated that everyone has the same utility function. This avoids not only what may be thought of as the injustice of distributing income in favor of the more sensitive, but also the problem of ascertaining in detail what the utility functions are, a task which might be thought impossible, as argued above, or at least very difficult in practice, if the ordinalist position is not accepted. Rawls criticizes this utilitarian evasion, though cautiously; he does not wish to reject interpersonal comparisons (90/1). But in fact he winds up with a somewhat similar approach. He introduces the interesting concept of *primary goods*, those goods which are needed whatever an individual's preference relation ("rational plan of life," in Rawls's terms) is. These might be liberties, opportunities, and income and wealth. Then, even though individuals might have very different uses for these primary goods, we need consider only some simple index of them for purposes of interpersonal comparison. Thus, the fact that one individual was satisfied with water and soy flour, while another was desperate without pre-phylloxera clarets and plovers' eggs, would have no bearing on the interpersonal comparison; if they had the same income, they would be equally well off.

If this comparison appears facetious, consider the haemophiliac who needs about $4000 worth per annum of coagulant therapy to arrive at a state of security from bleeding at all comparable to that of the normal person. Does equal income mean equality? If not, then, to be consistent, Rawls would have to add health to the list of primary goods; but then there is a trade-off between health and wealth which involves all the conceptual problems of differing utility functions.

The restriction to some list of primary goods is probably essential. I have but two comments: (1) so long as there is more than one primary good, there is an index-number problem in commensurating the different goods, which is in principle as difficult as the problem of interpersonal comparability with which we started; (2) if we could resolve the problem of interpersonal comparability in Rawls's system by reducing everything in effect to a single primary good, we could do the same in the sum-of-utilities approach. To the last statement, however, there is a qualification: the maximin criterion requires only interpersonal ordinality, whereas the classical view requires interpersonally comparable units; to that extent, the Rawls system is epistemologically less demanding.

2. Let us turn from the epistemological problems of the current decision-maker for society to those in the original position. Individuals are supposed to know the laws of the physical and the

social worlds, but not to know who they are or will be. But empirical knowledge is after all uncertain, and even in the original position individuals may disagree about the facts and laws of the universe. For example, Rawls argues for religious toleration on the grounds that one doesn't know what religion one will have, and therefore one wants society to tolerate all religions. Operationally, a Catholic would have to recognize that in the original position he wouldn't know he would be a Catholic and would therefore have to tolerate Protestants or Jews or whatever, since he might well have been one. But suppose he replies that in fact Catholicism is the true religion, that it is part of the knowledge which all sensible people are supposed to have in the original position, and that he insists on it for the salvation of all mankind. How could this be refuted?

Indeed, just this sort of argument is raised by writers like Marcuse, not to mention any totalitarian state and, within wider limits, any state. Only those who correctly understand the laws of society should be allowed to express their political opinions. I feel I know that Marxism (or laissez-faire) is the truth; therefore, in the original position, I would have supported suppressing other positions. Even Rawls permits suppression of those who do not believe in freedom.

I hope it is needless to say that I am in favor of very wide toleration. But I am not convinced that the original position is a sufficient basis for this argument, for it transfers the problem to the area of factual disagreement.

There is another kind of knowledge problem in the original position: that about social preferences. Rawls assumes that individuals are egoistic, their social preferences being derived from the veil of ignorance. But why should there not be views of benevolence (or envy) even in the original position? All that is required is that they not refer to named individuals. But if these are admitted, then there can be disagreement over the degree of benevolence or malevolence, and the happy assumption, that there are no disagreements in the original position, disappears.

IV. SOME REMARKS ON UTILITARIANISM

It will already have been seen that my attitude toward utilitarianism is ambivalent. On the one hand, I find it difficult to ascribe operational meaning to the utilities to be added. On the other hand, I have suggested that the practical differences between the maximin and the sum-of-utilities criteria are not great, and indeed that the maximin principle would lead to unacceptable consequences if the world were such that they really differed.

In this section, I will take up several different points raised by Rawls, and try to defend utilitarianism against them.

First, let me extend a little the discussion of the Vickrey-Harsanyi position, which Rawls calls *average utilitarianism*. In part, this discussion continues the epistemological considerations of the last section. As Ramsey and von Newmann and Morgenstern have shown, if one considers choice among risky alternatives, there is a sense in which a quantitative utility can be given meaning. Specifically, if choice among probability distributions satisfies certain apparently natural rationality conditions, then it can be shown that there is a utility function (unique up to a positive linear transformation) on the outcomes such that probability distributions of outcomes are ordered in accordance with the mathematical expectation of the utility of the outcome.

By itself, this theorem does not establish any welfare implications for this utility function; after all, the choice among probability distributions of outcomes could equally well be described by any monotonic transformation of the expected utility. When I first wrote on this matter,[10] I therefore denied the welfare relevance of expected-utility theory. But the Vickrey-Harsanyi argument puts matters in a different perspective; if an individual assumes he may with equal probability be any member of society, then indeed he evaluates any policy by his expected utility, *where the utility function is specifically that defined by the von Neumann-Morgenstern theorem*. Rawls therefore errs when he argues that average utilitarianism assumes risk neutrality (165); on the contrary, the degree of risk aversion of the individuals is already incorporated in the utility function. This point may be given further strength by noting that the maximin criterion, far from being opposed to average utilitarianism, can be regarded as a limiting case of it. For let U be any utility function, in the sense of a function that represents preferences without uncertainty. Then, for any a > 0, $-U^{-a}$ is an increasing function of U and so also is a utility function. Any member of this family could be the von Neumann-Morgenstern utility function, i.e., that utility function for which it is true that the individual seeks to maximize expected utility. It is easy to see that, the larger the value of a, the higher the degree of risk aversion. Then, according to Vickrey, the value of a policy to an individual with a random stake in society would be

$$V = \Sigma(-U_i)^{-a} = -\Sigma U_i^{-a}$$

[10] *Social Choice and Individual Values* (New York: Wiley, 1951), first ed., pp. 9/10.

But a social-welfare function is only an index of choice and can itself be subject to monotonic transformation; hence, another criterion that would yield the same choice is

$$W = (-V)^{-1/a} = (\Sigma U_i^{-a})^{-1/a}$$

It can, however, easily be proved that, as a approaches infinity, representing increasing degrees of risk aversion, W approaches min U_i.

I do not wish to argue that average utilitarianism meets all the problems that can be raised. Rawls very properly points out that each individual may have a different utility function, so that, although each wishes to maximize a sum of utilities, each individual has a different utility function in his maximand (173); in addition, the use of equiprobability in this case is certainly not beyond cavil.

A second of Rawls's objections to utilitarianism is that it may require that some individuals sacrifice for the benefit of others, so that other men appear to be means, not only ends (181, 183). But I don't follow this argument at all. A maximin principle certainly seems to imply that the better off should sacrifice for the less well off, if that will in fact help. The talents of the more able are, in Rawls's system (and in my value judgments), to be used on behalf of the less able; is this not using some people as means?

A third criticism of classical utilitarianism is that it makes an illegitimate analogy between individuals and society. "The classical view results, then, in impersonality, in the conflation of all desires into one system of desire" (188). But it would appear to me a purely formal requirement of any theory of justice that it act as such a conflation. A theory of justice is presumably an ordering of alternative social states, and therefore is formally analogous to the individual's ordering of alternative social states. Further, Rawls and Bentham and I would certainly all agree that justice should reflect individual satisfactions; hence, the social choice made in accordance with any of these theories of justice is "a conflation of all desires." No doubt perfectionist theories or those based on religious considerations would not be so characterized; but Rawls is not defending *them*.

V. A REMARK ON VOTING

The expression and aggregation of individual preferences through voting does not have a high place in Rawls's system: "There is nothing to the view, then, that what the majority wills is right" (356). The legislators or voters are thought of as experts in justice and are not to vote in self-interest. The assumption seems to be simply that the workings of justice will not always be clear and that a pooling of opinions is worth while; a majority makes more sense from this point of view than a minority.

Clearly, there is something to Rawls's position, which indeed he shares with many political philosophers, as he notes. A political system in which there is no other-regardingness will not function at all. Further, Rawls is right in saying that the analogy with the market is imperfect. In the market, he agrees that selfish behavior is socially correct, but holds that the political process can never lead to perfect justice if based on self-seeking behavior. But I would argue that the analogy, though imperfect, is not completely wrong either. Political competition does serve some of the same functions in its sphere as economic competition. Further, the expression of one's own interests in voting seems to me an essential part of the information process needed for voting. Unless voters express their interests, how is anyone going to know if the ends of justice are in fact being carried out? "If I am not for myself, then who is for me?," said Hillel, though he continued in more Rawlsian terms, "and if I am not for others, then who am I?"

To put the matter more emotionally, I would hold that the notion of voting according to one's own beliefs and then submitting to the will of the majority represents a recognition of the essential autonomy and freedom of others. It recognizes that justice is a pooling of irreducibly different individuals, not the carrying out of policies already known in advance.

VI. ECONOMIC IMPLICATIONS OF RAWLS'S PRINCIPLES

Rawls's views have implications most directly for the redistribution of income, both among contemporaries and across generations. The maximin rule would seem on the face of it to lead to radical equalization of income. Indeed, so would the sum-of-utilities rule, if it is assumed that all individuals have the same utility function which displays decreasing marginal satisfactions from additional increments of income. Rawls, however, holds that the close-knittedness of members of the society means that perfect equality of income is not to the advantage of the least well-off, but that typically they will benefit by an increase in income to some higher up in the income scale. Rawls is rather brief on why one might expect this kind of relation, but economists have laid considerable stress on the *incentive* effects of taxation. Assume that each individual can produce a certain amount per hour worked, but that this productivity varies from individual to individual. In the absence of taxation, the least productive individual will be the worst off. Therefore, a Rawlsian (or even an old-fashioned utilitarian) may advocate a tax on the income of the more able to be paid out to the less able. This is, in fact, essentially the widespread proposal for a negative income tax. But since the effort to produce may in itself detract from satisfaction, an income tax will lead individuals to reduce the number of hours they work and therefore the amount they produce. If the tax rate on the more able is high enough, the amount of work will go down so much that the amount collected in taxes for redistribution to the worst off will actually decrease. It is at this stage that the economy becomes close knit.

The conflict between incentive and equity occurs in a utilitarian framework and was already noted by Edgeworth (who was really very conservative and was glad to escape from the rigorous egalitarianism to which his utilitarianism led). The mathematical problem of choosing a tax schedule to maximize the sum of utilities, taking account of the adverse incentive effects, is a very difficult one; it was broached by Vickrey in his 1945 paper (*op. cit.*) and analyzed by Mirrlees,[11] Fair,[12] and Sheshinski,[13] among others. More recently, the tax implications of the Rawls criterion have been analyzed along similar lines in forthcoming papers by Atkinson, Phelps, and Sheshinski. The practical implications of this research are as yet dubious, primarily because too little is known about the magnitude of the incentive effects, particularly in the upper brackets.

As I have indicated, Rawls is inexplicit about the incentive effects and so does not give clear guidance to the determination of tax rates. On pages 277–279 he argues for progressive income and inheritance taxes to achieve justice, but there is no indication how the rates should be chosen. Clearly, the philosophy of justice is under no obligation to tell us what the rates should be in a numerical sense; but it is supposed to define the rule that translates any given set of facts into a tax schedule. The maximin rule would, on the face of it, lead to perfect equalization, i.e., 100 per cent taxation above a certain level, with corresponding subsidies below it. As far as I can see, it is only the incentive question that prevents us from carrying this policy out.

The incentive question raises another issue with regard to the obligation of an individual to perform justice (Rawls has much to

[11] J. A. Mirrlees, "An Exploration in the Theory of Optimal Income Taxation," *Review of Economic Studies*, xxxviii (1971): 175–208.

[12] R. C. Fair, "The Optimal Distribution of Income," *Quarterly Journal of Economics*, lxxxv (1971): 551–579.

[13] E. Sheshinski, "The Optimum Linear Income Tax," *Review of Economic Studies*, xxxix (1972): 297–302.

say on the notion of duties and obligations on individuals, though I have slighted this discussion in this review). If each individual revealed his productivity (the amount he could produce per unit of time), it would be possible to achieve a perfect reconciliation of justice and incentives; namely, tax each individual according to his ability, not according to his actual output. Then he could not escape taxes by working less, and so the tax system would have no adverse incentive effects. Practical economists would reject this solution, because it would be taken for granted that no individual would be truthful if the consequences of truth-telling were so painful. But Rawls, like most social philosophers, takes it for granted that individuals are supposed to act justly, at least in certain contexts. For example, as legislators or voters, it is an obligation or duty to judge according to the principles of justice, not according to self-interest. If, then, an individual is supposed to assess his own potential for earning income, is there an obligation to be truthful?

One of the most difficult questions in allocative justice is the distribution of wealth over generations. To what extent is one generation obligated to save, so as to increase the welfare of the next generation? The traditional economic problem has been the general act of investment in productive land, machines, and buildings which produce goods in the future; more recently, we have become especially concerned with preservation of undisturbed environments and natural resources. The most straightforward utilitarian answer is that the utilities of future generations enter equally with those of the present. But since the present generation is a very small part of the total number of individuals over a horizon easily measurable in thousands of years, the policy conclusion would be that virtually everything should be saved and very little consumed, a conclusion which seems offensive to common sense. The most usual formulation has been to assert a criterion of maximizing a sum of *discounted* utilities, in which the utilities of future generations are given successively smaller weights. The implications of such policies seem to be more in accordance with common sense and practice, but the foundations of such a criterion seem arbitrary.

Rawls argues that the maximin criterion, properly interpreted, can be applied to the determination of a just rate of savings (284–292). In the original position, individuals do not know which generation they belong to and should therefore judge of a just rate on that basis. That is, they agree to leave a fixed fraction of their income to the next generation in return for receiving an equal frac-

RAWLS'S THEORY OF JUSTICE: TWO REVIEWS

tion of the previous generation's income. There are two difficulties with this argument: (1) Why should they agree on a *fraction* rather than some more complicated rule, for example, an increasing fraction as wealth increases? (2) More serious, it would appear that the maximin rule would most likely lead to zero as the agreed-on savings rate; for the first generation would lose under any positive savings rate, whereas the welfare of all future generations would increase. This point is reinforced strongly if one adds the empirical fact of technological progress, so that even in the absence of savings the successive generations are getting better off. Then a maximin policy would call for improving the lot of the earlier generations, which can only be done by negative saving (running down existing capital equipment) if at all possible. (To be precise, the above argument is valid only in the absence of population growth. If population is growing, then zero saving would mean less capital per person and therefore a falling income per capita. Hence, a maximin rule in the absence of technological progress would call for positive saving; it can easily be shown that the rule would be that the rate of savings equals the rate of population growth multiplied by the capital-output ratio.)

Rawls, however, modifies the motivations in the original position at this point in the argument. "The parties are regarded as representing family lines, say, with ties of sentiment between successive generations" (292). This is a major departure from the egoistic assumptions held up to this point about behavior and choice in the original position. It should be noted that so long as fathers think more highly of themselves than of their sons or even more highly of their sons than of subsequent generations, the effect of this modification is very much the same as that of discounting future utilities. Although my guess is that any justification for provision for the future will run somewhat along these lines, it cannot be said that the solution fully escapes all difficulties. (1) It introduces an element of altruism into the original position; if we introduce family sentiments, why not others (nation, tribal)? And why not elements of envy? (2) One might like a theory of justice in which the role of the family was derived rather than primitive. In a reexamination of social institutions, why should the family remain above scrutiny, its role being locked into the original assumptions? (3) Anyway, the family argument for saving has an implication that should be displayed and might be questioned. Presumably the burden of saving should fall only on those with children and perhaps in proportion to the number of children. Since education and public construction are essentially forms of saving, taxes to support them should fall only on those with children. In the original position, this is just the sort of contract that would be arrived at if the concern for the future were based solely on family ties.

VII. A CRITICAL NOTE ON THE POSSIBILITY OF JUSTICE

Rawls's work is based on the hypothesis that there is a meaningful universal concept of justice. If there is, it surely must, as he says, be universalizable in some sense, that is, based on principles that are symmetric among the particular accidents that distinguish one individual's position from another. But as I look around at the many conflicts that plague our humanity, I find many for which I can imagine no argument of a symmetric nature which would convince both sides.

One problem is that any actual individual must necessarily have limited information about the world, and different individuals have different information. Hence, they cannot possibly argue themselves back into an original position with common information, even if they succeed in "forgetting" who they are. Indeed, one of the most brilliant passages in Rawls's book is that on what he calls "social union" (520–530). He argues that no human life is enough to encounter more than a small fraction of the experiences needed for completeness, so that individuals have a natural complementarity with each other (a more mundane version of this idea is Adam Smith's stress on the importance of the division of labor). The social nature of man springs from this variegation of experience. But precisely the same differentiations imply differing and incompletely communicable life experiences and therewith the possible impossibility of agreeing on the just action in any concrete situation.

Indeed, the thrust of Rawls's work, particularly in its latter passages, is highly harmonistic; the principles of justice are stable, according to Rawls, because the moral education they induce reinforces them. But if the specific application of the principles is judged to be different according to different life experiences (and of course different genetic experiences), even as between parent and child, then the needed concordance of views may evaporate.

To put the matter somewhat differently, many sociologists would hold that, in a world of limited information, conflict unresolved by appeal to commonly accepted principles may have a positive value; it is the means by which information about others is conveyed. In its own sphere, this is the role assigned to competition by economists; if everyone attempted to act justly at every moment in his economic life, it might be difficult ever to find out what the true interests of anyone were.

To the extent that individuals are really individual, each an autonomous end in himself, to that extent they must be somewhat mysterious and inaccessible to each other. There cannot be any rule that is completely acceptable to all. There must, or so it now seems to me, be the possibility of unadjudicable conflict, which may show itself logically as paradoxes in the process of social decision-making.

KENNETH J. ARROW

Economics, Harvard University

Moral Neutrality and Primary Goods[*]

Adina Schwartz

The Rockefeller University

In this paper, I shall consider the use of the concept of primary goods in John Rawls's *A Theory of Justice*. I will aim to cast doubt on two claims which Rawls makes on behalf of his theory. I will argue that justice as fairness is more of a teleological ethical theory than Rawls would like to admit. I will also argue that Rawls's "original position" is not significantly more "minimal" than the initial situations of other contract theories. On this basis, I will suggest that, if one's most strongly held ethical judgments do not come close to those of a liberal democrat,[1] one may have very little reason for accepting Rawls's theory of justice.

I

One of the main aims of Rawls's book is to provide a viable alternative to teleological ethical theories. Rawls believes that any ethical theory which defines right conduct in terms of the maximization of some particular good is morally invalid. This is because "human good is heterogeneous because the aims of the self are heterogeneous."[2] Therefore, he claims that the valid path to the development of an ethical theory is first to derive principles of right conduct. These principles should then serve as constraints on definitions of various concepts involving the notion of moral good and on the things accepted as good for a particular man or man in general. This should be the case, since in a non-teleological theory "something is good only if it fits into ways of life consistent with the theory of right already on hand."[3]

[*] I am deeply grateful to Joel Feinberg and Howard Burdick for valuable discussion, criticism, and encouragement.

1. Throughout this paper, I will assume that Rawls's principles of justice and outline of a social structure provide a systematic encapsulation of the main ideas of the liberal democratic tradition. Therefore, the term "liberal democratic" will be applied to Rawls's theory of justice and to ethical views whose most important judgments agree with the judgments provided by Rawls's theory.

2. John Rawls, *A Theory of Justice* (Cambridge, Mass., 1971), p. 554.

3. Ibid., p. 396.

In developing his theory, Rawls is aware of the historic deontological pitfalls which have added to the persuasive impact of teleological theories. These are: (1) Deontological theories have often amounted to a scattering of precepts of right conduct providing no systematic or determinate guide for ethical decision. (2) These precepts of right conduct have often been presented with no justification beyond an appeal to intuition or common sense. Rawls believes that the contractual derivation of the two principles of justice enables his theory to escape these defects. This derivation justifies the two principles of justice by showing that "they are the principles that free and rational persons concerned to further their own interests would accept in an initial position of equality as defining the fundamental terms of their association."[4] In addition, the contract derivation is supposed to provide a systematic guide to ethical decision by establishing two principles of justice in lexical order and by identifying the initial choice situation as the relevant standpoint for decision making.

The significance of contractualism as a justifying and systematizing device is threatened, however, by Rawls's own admission that there are many possible contract theories of justice. Different conceptions of justice can be "contractually derived" if the initial choice situation for principles of justice is formulated in different ways. Each contract theory will presumably claim that its interpretation of the initial choice situation is the proper interpretation of the condition of having free, rational persons choose principles of justice in a situation of equality. Therefore, rival contract theories will each claim that the principles presented would be chosen by free, rational persons in a situation of equality and that the presented conception of the initial situation defines a relevant standpoint for ethical decision. However, Rawls does not think the possibility of rival contract theories seriously challenges his use of contractualism. He claims a choice between contract theories can be made by comparing formulations of the initial choice situation. According to Rawls, his theory's original position is more philosophically favored than rival contract theories' interpretations of the initial situation. One reason for this is that the original position leads to principles of justice which best accord with the considered judgments of competent moral judges in reflective equilibrium. According to Rawls, his two principles yield judgments matching those which would be made by competent moral judges who had considered rival ethical theories and adjusted and systematized their convictions on that basis. Another reason is that the conditions involved in the formulation of the original position are a "constrained minimum."[5] These conditions are strong enough to generate a "workable theory of justice,"[6] but they are weaker (in the sense of being more widely acceptable) than the

4. Ibid., p. 11.
5. Ibid., p. 583.
6. Ibid.

conditions involved in other theories' interpretations of the initial situation. I will try to show that the conditions in the formulation of the original position are not a constrained minimum. On this basis I will claim that Rawls's contract derivation is only justified by the method of reflective equilibrium.

Rawls's original position is formulated in terms of three main sets of conditions. First, the circumstances of justice obtain since there is a moderate scarcity of goods, and individuals put forth competing claims on the division of the advantages of social cooperation. Second, the parties to the deliberation are rational, moral agents. Each is moral since he has a conception of the good and is capable of developing a sense of justice. Each is rational since he is free from envy and chooses the options which are most likely to further more of his purposes. Third, moral constraints insure the validity of the principles of justice which result from the deliberation. The formal moral constraints of generality, universality, publicity, ordering, and finality limit the conceptions of justice available for choice. In addition, the imposition of the "veil of ignorance" insures that the choice of principles of justice will not rest on the social and natural contingencies which grant competitive advantages to certain men. The parties to the deliberation cannot choose principles of justice which further their particular interests since they are deprived of knowledge of their individual social statuses, abilities, conceptions of the good, and psychological propensities.

Rawls claims that this interpretation of the initial situation is particularly "minimal" and uncontroversial since it does not stipulate ideals of rationality, moral personality, or the good, and does not rest on questionable hypotheses about psychology or the working of societies. He claims that the initial situations of utilitarian or perfectionist contract theories are less widely acceptable since they either stipulate ideals or rest on questionable hypotheses. But a rejoinder might be that, by attempting to avoid the strong assumptions of the utilitarian or perfectionist, Rawls does not provide sufficient information for a rational choice of principles of justice. How can a rational individual choose principles to further his advantage if he is behind a "veil of ignorance" and does not know facts about himself and society and his conception of the good? Rawls's reply is that the "veil of ignorance" prevents individual interests, ideals, and theories from affecting the choice of principles of justice even if it is broken by knowledge of general facts about society and psychology. Although the "veil of ignorance" does not allow knowledge of particular conceptions of the good, it allows the knowledge that the parties share a preference for more rather than less of the primary goods. Since the primary goods ("liberty and opportunity, income and wealth and, above all, self-respect")[7] "are things which it is supposed a rational man wants whatever else he wants,"[8]

7. Ibid., p. 433.
8. Ibid., p. 92.

the assumption of a preference for them does not introduce a specific conception of the good. Thus, Rawls's "weak" original position is supposed to produce a rational choice of principles of justice on the basis of a preference for primary goods and general knowledge about psychology and society.

This paper will be directed to arguing that, in attempting to insert enough knowledge behind the "veil of ignorance" for rational choice, Rawls inserts moral ideals and hypotheses about psychology and society which are as controversial as those of the utilitarian or perfectionist. I shall not give a complete argument for this claim. I will only argue that Rawls's interpretation of the initial situation favors a particular range of conceptions of the good. In endowing the parties to the deliberation with a preference for more rather than less of the primary goods, Rawls gives them a preference which is not common to all rational individuals.

If this argument is successful, there will be strong grounds for the claim that Rawls's formulation of the initial situation is not particularly minimal. As we have seen, Rawls was led to contractualism by the desire to obtain the systematic virtues of teleological theories while avoiding the pitfall of basing principles of right on a conception of the good. Having admitted the possibility of contractual formulations of teleological theories, Rawls attempts to preserve contractualism as a deontological alternative. He does this by ruling out teleological contract theories on the ground that their interpretations of the initial situation rest on strong assumptions about the good. Therefore, if I can show that Rawls's original position also involves controversial assumptions about the good, I will defeat one of his central claims for the weakness of his interpretation of the initial situation. Doubt should also be cast on the minimality of Rawls's original position since my arguments against the preference for primary goods should show that he makes controversial assumptions about psychology and society.

If Rawls's formulation of the initial situation is not significantly more "minimal" than the formulations of rival contract theories, he can only justify it by claiming that the resulting principles of justice are most in accord with our judgments in reflective equilibrium. Therefore, if the original position is not minimal, the contract derivation will only justify the two principles of justice if these principles are already justified by the method of reflective equilibrium. If this is the case, Rawls's contractualism will be only of expository value. Instead of being a powerful device for refuting ethical skepticism, the contract derivation will be a mere appendage to the method of reflective equilibrium in justifying the two principles of justice. The value of Rawls's painstaking development of contractualism will lie in the fact that the contract derivation is a useful device for organizing the assumptions at the basis of our judgments of justice.

It is possible that Rawls believes that the method of reflective equilibrium is sufficient justification for any ethical theory and that no great harm is done to his theory if the contract derivation is only of expository value. However, some of us should find these beliefs hard to swallow. First, there seem to be good grounds for being wary of a justificatory use of the method of reflective equilibrium. Would not the judgments in reflective equilibrium of competent moral judges of Nazi society have accorded with Nazi principles of justice? If the method of reflective equilibrium is our only method of ethical justification, we can only defeat this claim for Nazi principles of justice by an unjustified decision to follow the judgments of our society's competent moral judges. Second, Rawls's two principles of justice do not seem to accord with many of the most firmly held convictions of certain utilitarians and perfectionists. Therefore, unless Rawls's principles are so superior that any rational utilitarian or perfectionist presented with them would abandon his most important views, the claim that Rawls's principles accord with the considered judgments in reflective equilibrium of competent moral judges is equivalent to the claim that his principles accord with the considered judgments in reflective equilibrium of competent liberal democrats. If this is the case, those not of liberal democratic persuasions may see little reason to study an ethical theory whose only justification is that it reflects liberal democratic beliefs. A nonliberal democrat may find Rawls's book of value as a clear and systematic exposition of the bases of liberal democratic thought. However, Rawls's theory of justice should not convert anyone whose basic beliefs differ radically from those of the liberal democrat.

II

In presenting the contract derivation, Rawls does not justify either the claim that there are primary goods (things which "rational individuals, whatever else they want, desire . . . as prerequisites for carrying out their plans of life")[9] or the enumeration of the primary goods. However, in chapter 7 of *A Theory of Justice*, he admits that a theory of the good is needed to justify both these claims. Rawls labels this theory the "thin theory of the good" and contrasts it with the "thick theory of the good." The thin theory is supposed to explain the preference for primary goods needed for the contract derivation by developing a morally neutral notion of the good, that is, a notion of the good acceptable to all rational individuals regardless of ethical persuasions. On the other hand, the thick theory is supposed to explain the various aspects of moral goodness by developing a moral notion of the good by combining the thin theory and the two principles of justice.

The distinction between the thin and thick theories of the good is of major importance in Rawls's theory. Rawls wants to deny that basing his principles of right on a preference for primary goods introduces a strong teleological element in his theory. He can do this if he can show that

9. Ibid., p. 396.

assuming a preference for primary goods does not commit him to claims about the moral validity of particular conceptions of the good. This can be done if Rawls can draw a distinction on grounds of moral controversiality between the thin and thick theories and show that the thin theory can justify the assumption of a preference for primary goods.

In the rest of this paper, I will argue that Rawls's attempt to distinguish between the thin and thick theories does not free him from the charge that his assumption about primary goods makes his theory strongly teleological. I will support this by offering two interpretations of what might be meant by the thin theory of the good. I will suggest that the thin theory might be taken as equivalent to Rawls's three-part definition of the good. Or the thin theory might be taken as composed of the three-part definition of the good and certain assumptions about human motivational structures. I will argue that, on the first interpretation, the thin theory of the good is morally neutral but does not justify the assumption of a preference for primary goods. On the second interpretation, the thin theory does justify that assumption, but it is not a morally neutral theory.

Rawls's thin definition of the good is based on the notion of "goodness as rationality." The thin definition states that "a person's good is determined by what is for him the most rational plan of life given reasonably favorable circumstances,"[10] and that "once we establish that an object has the properties that it is rational for someone with a rational plan of life to want, then we have shown that it is good for him."[11] In explaining this "thin" definition, Rawls must show that, in equating a person's good with a rational plan of life, he is not advocating the pursuit of a rationalistic ideal. He defends the moral neutrality of his use of the notion of rationality to define a person's good by developing a three-part definition of "good."

The three parts of the thin theory's definition correspond to three senses of the term "good"; (1) the sense in which we say that an object is good since it achieves what is commonly desired in objects of its kind; (2) the sense in which we say that an object is good for a person since it achieves what he desires in objects of that kind; and (3) the sense in which we say that an object serves a person's good since it achieves what he wants in objects of that kind, and his desire is part of a system of desires and aims which correctly reflects what he wants in life. The first two senses of good are instrumental. When we use one of them in evaluating an object, we ask whether the object achieves its designated purpose but do not question the value of the purpose. Rawls is able to use a purely instrumental sense of rationality in defining these senses of good. In the first part of the definition, an object is a good object of its kind if and only if it has the properties which it is rational to want in objects of its kind. In the second part, an object is a good object of its kind for a par-

10. Ibid., p. 395.
11. Ibid., p. 399.

ticular person if and only if it has the properties which it is rational for him to want in objects of its kind. In both cases, an object has the properties which it is rational to want just when it has the properties which achieve its designated end.

Since a person who uses the first two parts of Rawls's "rationalistic" definition of good is not committed to any particular criticism of ends, the first two parts of the definition are morally neutral. However, it might seem that the moral neutrality of these parts of Rawls's definition lends no support to the claim that the third part of his definition is morally neutral. In the third part of the definition, an object having the properties which it is rational for a person to want in view of his desires is not good if the desires are not part of a rational plan of life. This part of the definition surely seems to entail a rationalistic criticism of ends. Nevertheless, Rawls is able to use his definitions of the first two senses of "good" to show the moral neutrality of his definition of the third sense of "good."

In developing a nonmoral sense of rationality in the third part of the definition, Rawls "adopt[s] Royce's thought that a person may be regarded as a human life lived according to a plan."[12] Therefore, according to the second part of the definition, a person's good has the properties which it is rational for him to want in a plan. Since part three states that an X is a good X if and only if it satisfies part two of the definition and fits into a rational plan of life, Rawls obviously thinks that rationality is the property that it is rational to want in a plan. This claim can be understood by considering the purposes of plans. It seems evident that a plan is an ordering of desires and goals for the purpose of getting these achieved. Therefore, it is rational (in an instrumental sense of rationality) to want a plan to have the property of instrumental rationality, that is, the property which leads to the best achievement of desires and goals. In saying that a man's good is a rational plan of life and that an object is good for a person if and only if it "has the properties that it is rational for someone with a rational plan of life to want,"[13] Rawls is not stipulating a moral ideal. He is simply clarifying the commonly held notion that a person's good (at least in a nonmoral sense) is the achievement of his wants considered within the framework of the overall system of his desires.

Although the thin definition of the good is morally neutral, it cannot justify the assumption of a preference for primary goods. In his discussion of the third part of the thin definition, Rawls claims that "a person's plan of life is rational if and only if (1) it is one of the plans that is consistent with the principles of rational choice when these are applied to all the relevant features of his situation, and (2) it is that plan among those meeting this condition which would be chosen by him with full deliberative rationality, that is, with full awareness of the relevant facts and after a

12. Ibid., p. 408.
13. Ibid., p. 399.

careful consideration of the consequences."[14] It might seem that this speci-fication of the conditions for the rationality of plans would enable us to know the sorts of ends characteristic of rational plans. On the basis of this knowledge, we might be able to claim that certain things are primary goods since they are needed for the pursuit of all rational plans of life. However, as Rawls admits, "The definition of the good is purely formal" and "we still cannot derive from the definition of rational plans alone what sorts of ends these plans are likely to encourage."[15] Therefore, Rawls needs to provide grounds other than the thin definition of the good in order to justify his assumption of a preference for primary goods. He can show that that assumption is morally neutral only if he can show that these grounds can be part of a morally neutral theory of the good.

Rawls claims that the thin (morally neutral) theory of the good justi-fies his assumption about primary goods since "the list of primary goods can be accounted for by the conception of goodness as rationality in con-junction with the general facts about human wants and abilities, their characteristic phases and requirements of nurture, the Aristotelian Princi-ple, and the necessities of social interdependence."[16] At first sight, it seems plausible that facts about human motivational structures can be used to generate morally neutral lists of human goods. Certainly, we want to de-sign our ethics for men rather than for fictional constructs, and we can do this only by taking account of facts about men. On an intuitive level, it seems that all men have certain needs and motives in common and that specifying these will show that certain things (goods) are needed for the fulfillment of all plans of life. However, when one considers how one would employ psychological facts to arrive at a list of human goods, the moral neutrality of this kind of enterprise seems dubious. Human moti-vational patterns seem so diverse that any use of "facts" about motivation to arrive at a substantive list of human goods would seem to involve a controversial view of human nature.

It does seem possible to provide very general, morally neutral char-acterizations of primary goods. For example, since all men need food, clothing, and shelter, we can say that all rational individuals want a cer-tain amount of wealth. Similarly, since a person's good is a rational plan of life, we can say that all rational individuals want the liberty to pursue a plan of life. However, these characterizations are not specific enough to generate a choice of principles of justice. Although all rational indi-viduals want a certain amount of wealth, some rational individuals might always prefer a greater to a lesser amount of wealth, while other rational individuals might only want a certain minimal amount of wealth. Simi-larly, although all rational individuals want a certain amount of liberty, rational individuals might differ as to the kinds and amounts of liberty

14. Ibid., p. 408.
15. Ibid., p. 424.
16. Ibid., p. 434.

needed for the pursuit of their plans of life. While our general characterizations cannot be further specified without an ethical choice between
rational plans of life, principles of justice cannot be generated on the basis
of our general characterizations of primary goods. Rawls's assumptions
about primary goods are specific enough to generate a workable theory of
justice, but they commit him to a morally controversial account of the
good.

The problems involved in specifying the primary goods seem implicitly recognized in an equivocation on Rawls's part. In the original position, the assumption made is that all men have a preference for more
rather than less of the primary goods. However, Rawls equivocates on
whether the assumption is justified because, in real life, all rational individuals have this preference or because rational individuals generally have
this preference. He is forced to move to the second position once he admits that "of course, it may turn out, once the veil of ignorance is removed, that some of them [the parties to the deliberation] for religious
or other reasons may not, in fact, want more of these [primary] goods."[17]
But if Rawls justifies his assumption by the general preferences of rational individuals, is he not basing his assumption about primary goods
on an ethical decision to further the majority's preferences? Rawls tries
to counter this objection by claiming that "from the standpoint of the
original position, it is rational for the parties to suppose that they do want
a larger share [of the primary goods], since in any case they are not com-
pelled to accept more if they do not wish to, nor does a person suffer
from a greater liberty."[18] In the remaining portion of this paper I will
argue that (1) rational individuals without a preference for more rather
than less of Rawls's primary goods can claim that they would be harmed
by the furtherance of this preference, at least to the extent that they
would be better off in a society that did not further it; and (2) since it
is not rational for all individuals to assume they have this preference,
Rawls's assumption of a preference for primary goods in the original position is not morally neutral.

I will illustrate my case by drawing a picture of a rational individual
whose plan of life does not involve a preference for more rather than less
of Rawls's primary goods. Consider a socialist somewhat in the lines of
the early Marx. This individual believes that a good life must rest on self-
realization through labor, that the political structure of a society is determined by its economic structure, and that a person is morally harmed
by the possession of more than a certain minimal amount of wealth. This
individual's plan of life involves a preference for goods which can be
generally characterized as wealth and liberty. However, he does not have
a preference for the goods of wealth and liberty described in Rawls's
specification of the primary goods.

17. Ibid., p. 142.
18. Ibid., p. 143.

In enumerating the primary goods, Rawls claims that rational individuals have a preference for more rather than less of "the basic liberties of citizens." These are "roughly speaking, political liberty (the right to vote and to be eligible for public office), together with freedom of speech and assembly; liberty of conscience and freedom of thought; freedom of the person along with the right to hold (personal) property; and freedom from arbitrary arrest and seizure as defined by the rule of law."[19] As Rawls admits, this account of liberty is based on a conception of a social structure divided into two parts; one part concerned with political rights and liberties and another concerned with the distribution of economic wealth. Since he believes that the economic structure of a society determines the mode of operation of its political institutions, our socialist will not accept this two-part conception. He will justify his refusal to accept this conception by claiming that Rawls has not given any reason for it beyond conceptual simplicity. The socialist will then argue that Rawls's liberties do not further the pursuit of his plan of life or the plans of most men. Since Rawls's descriptions of the liberties are formulated without reference to the economic structure of society, the socialist will claim that there is no guarantee of the meaningfulness of the exercise of these liberties. In arguing that the furtherance of Rawls's primary good of liberty is not in his interest, the socialist will turn two of Rawls's own arguments for the priority of liberty against him.

According to Rawls, in the original position it is rational for individuals to assume they prefer liberty above the other primary goods. The grounds for this assumption are (1) the great importance of liberty of conscience and freedom of thought, and (2) the fact that the preference for liberty expresses the "central place of the primary good of self-respect and the desire of human beings to express their nature in a free social union with others."[20] The socialist will agree with Rawls's estimate of the importance of self-respect. However, he will claim that self-respect is best furthered by a different system of liberties than the one Rawls advocates. The socialist will claim that, for him, a strong sense of his own worth would depend on having the freedom to realize his nature as a laboring being. He will also claim that only a socialist, nonmarket economy could grant this freedom. The socialist might admit that, in a system which did not produce "alienation of labor," Rawls's liberties (or economically constrained analogs of these liberties) would further the pursuit of rational plans of life. However, he would claim that rational plans of life would not be furthered in a system which only furthered Rawls's liberties, that is, a system that did not guarantee freedom of labor. He would say that Rawls's noneconomic formulation of the descriptions of the liberties allows for a system to formally further liberty while producing economic and social disparities which make liberties of little value

19. Ibid., p. 61.
20. Ibid., p. 543.

to the more disadvantaged members of society. Furthermore, he could say that even a constrained free-enterprise system which furthered Rawls's liberties and limited social and economic disparities could produce a great amount of alienation of labor. Due to this alienation, many men might not be motivated to and might even be incapable of exercising their liberties to further their plans of life. On this basis, the socialist would claim that Rawls's description of liberty allows liberty to be of little worth to many men. Therefore, furthering the Rawlsian preference for liberty does not guarantee most persons a meaningful exercise of liberty of conscience and freedom of thought. The socialist would argue that a system of liberty based on the importance of freedom of labor would express the importance of self-respect and guarantee liberty of conscience and freedom of thought more firmly than a Rawlsian system of liberty. Therefore, he would claim that it is rational for him (and for most men) to prefer this type of liberty above Rawlsian liberty.

Our socialist will also object to Rawls's assumption that rational individuals share a preference for a greater rather than a lesser amount of wealth. He will claim that his good is furthered by just enough wealth so that he is decently fed, housed, and clothed. However, Rawls could argue against this objection to his specification of this primary good. He could claim that, even if the socialist's plan of life is furthered by a minimal amount of wealth, the socialist would not be harmed by a system based on a preference for a greater amount of wealth. Rawls could argue that, in actual life, the socialist could always refuse to accept any wealth he did not desire.

Our socialist could object to Rawls's argument by claiming that he would be harmed by living in a society based on a preference for a greater rather than a lesser amount of wealth. He could say that, living in such a society, he would devote valuable time to thinking about material wealth and trying to decide whether or not to avoid the temptation of attempting to acquire more possessions. Therefore, he could claim that he would be more able to pursue his good in a system based on a preference for a minimal amount of wealth. In addition, the socialist could claim that a system based on a preference for a greater amount of wealth would be against his interest since it would prevent him from forming strong ties of affection with other human beings. He could claim that, in such a system, people would tend to be more interested in wealth than in other people. He could also claim that a system which encouraged a preference for a greater amount of wealth might encourage envy of others' possessions. The socialist could argue that a system based on a preference for a minimal amount of wealth would encourage close personal ties. Therefore, he could claim that the assumption of a preference for a greater amount of wealth is against his interest since a system based on a preference for less wealth is more in his interest.

Nevertheless, despite our socialist, the derivation of the preference for Rawlsian primary goods from "general facts" of psychology might be relatively uncontroversial. Most persons with rational plans of life might, in fact, have preferences for these primary goods. Rawls might claim that his theory is only addressed to this large majority and that it does not apply to persons whose rational plans of life do not involve this preference. However, this does not seem to be a legitimate interpretation of Rawls. In the last chapter of his book, Rawls claims that affirming a Rawlsian sense of justice furthers the good (as defined by the thin theory) of most rational individuals. He also claims that the constraints of the two principles of justice are to apply even to those persons for whom "given their aims and wants and the peculiarities of their nature, the thin account of the good does not define reasons sufficient for them to maintain this regulative sentiment [the sense of justice]."[21] According to Rawls, "To justify a conception of justice we do not have to contend that everyone, whatever his capacities and desires, has a sufficient reason (as defined by the thin theory) to preserve his sense of justice."[22] At this point in his book, Rawls does not seem to equate persons who do not have sufficient reasons (as defined by the thin theory) to affirm the sense of justice with persons who do not have preferences for the Rawlsian primary goods. However, it seems reasonable to believe that, if Rawls admitted the possibility of rational individuals not having preferences for his primary goods, he would claim that the two principles of justice should apply to those individuals. But if it is possible to conceive of rational human beings who do not prefer more rather than less of Rawls's primary goods and if principles which further this preference do not only apply to those who have it, only two justifications for Rawls's assumptions about primary goods seem to remain. However, each of those justifications is morally controversial.

The first justification states that since any plan of life not involving a preference for Rawls's primary goods is not rational, this preference is involved in any person's good. However, this claim does not follow from Rawls's thin definition of the good. It seems that our socialist can have a life plan that fulfills the thin theory's criteria of rationality, that is, one that is consistent with the principles of rational choice and that could be chosen with deliberative rationality. However, Rawls might argue that our socialist's plan of life is not rational since it is based on false beliefs. Rawls could say that the socialist is wrong in thinking that the social structure cannot be conceived as divided into two parts and in thinking that self-realization as a laboring being is an important part of his good. But saying that these beliefs make the socialist's plan of life irrational would push Rawls to the point of claiming that only irrational persons could disagree with his ethical system. In his book, Rawls supports his two-part conception of the social structure by offering grounds of simplicity and by presenting a sketch of a society based on this conception. However, these

21. Ibid., p. 575.
22. Ibid., p. 576.

175

arguments are not strong enough to justify calling the socialist irrational (on a narrow definition of rationality) for not accepting a two-part conception. Similarly, no morally neutral notion of rationality can be used to label the socialist irrational on the basis of his conception of the good. The socialist's conception of the good is not irrational in the sense of either being logically inconsistent or based on obviously false beliefs. Therefore, in order to justify the claim that all rational plans of life involve a preference for Rawlsian primary goods, Rawls would need to develop a morally controversial notion of rationality. But any definition of "good" in terms of such a notion of rationality would be controversial. Furthermore, this method of justifying the assumption about primary goods goes against the spirit of Rawls's development of the thin theory of the good. Rawls wanted to use "general facts" of human motivation to justify his assumption just because he wanted to avoid inserting a rationalistic ideal in the thin definition.

The second justification is that most rational individuals share a preference for Rawls's primary goods. This seems to be the justification Rawls uses, and he seems to consider it a morally neutral one. As we have seen, Rawls claims his assumption about primary goods is morally neutral since persons without a preference for more of his primary goods are not harmed by more of these goods. However, I believe I have shown that furthering the preference for more rather than less of Rawls's primary goods is not in the interest of certain rational individuals. If my contention is justified, another assumption is needed in order to justify the assumption of a preference for Rawls's primary goods by the fact that most rational individuals have this preference. This is the assumption that the majority's conceptions of the good should determine the choice of principles of justice. On the face of it, this assumption seems far from ethically neutral. It seems possible for someone to ask why it is better to choose principles of justice on the basis of a preference common to the majority instead of on the basis of a peculiarly virtuous person's conception of the good. Surely, a perfectionist might argue that the majority are wrong in having conceptions of the good whose furtherance depends on the presence of Rawls's primary goods of liberty and wealth. He might claim that a religious conception of the good which advocates minimizing Rawlsian wealth and liberty for the glory of God is the right one and that a society which furthers this conception is a just society.

In the light of these arguments, it might not seem possible to justify the claim that a conception of the good based on motivational facts about the majority of men can be ethically neutral. However, one possible justification for this claim still remains. Rawls might claim that persons who do not prefer his primary goods are so odd that the majority in a society could never be like them. In Rawls's contract derivation, persons stripped of knowledge of their positions in society and their conceptions of the good are to choose principles of justice to further their interests. Given that only very odd individuals do not have a preference for Rawls's primary goods, it would seem rational (in a narrow sense of rationality) to choose principles of justice on the basis of this preference. But, this justification seems based on a controversial view of the "general facts" of human psychology. I believe Rawls has to admit that there can be rational persons whose plans of life are not furthered by his primary goods. He also has to admit that there have been long-lasting, stable societies, such as feudal societies, which have denied his primary good of liberty. Given these admissions, how can Rawls show that a preference for his primary goods is a feature of men (or most men) qua men rather than of men qua members of particular societies? If he cannot show this, he is left with a decision to rest principles of justice on the motivational structures of men qua members of particular societies. At best, this decision seems ethically controversial.

In short, one might argue that basing an ethical theory on human nature as we know it involves a controversial assumption about the immutability of human psychological structures. One might claim that, even if most persons in most societies have had a preference for more of Rawls's primary goods, this does not show that people must always have this preference. A perfectionist might argue that a society based on principles of justice which advanced a "best" conception of the good (one not furthering Rawls's primary goods) would produce men having this conception of the good. He might admit that techniques such as indoctrination would be needed to develop such men. However, he might claim these techniques could be ethically justified since their use would eventually result in good men. If there is nothing logically or physically inconceivable about producing a large number of persons who do not have preferences for Rawls's primary goods, Rawls's assumption of a preference for his primary goods in the original position is morally controversial.

CANADIAN JOURNAL OF PHILOSOPHY
Volume V, Number 3, November 1975

Revisability and Rational Choice*

ALLEN BUCHANAN, University of Minnesota

I

1.   There is no dearth of objections to Rawls's *A Theory of Justice*. Scores of articles and several books begin by praising the rigor and depth of Rawls's book — and end by concluding that it is thoroughly mistaken. In the present essay I will not add to the list of negative responses to *A Theory of Justice*. Instead I will attempt to reply to Rawls's critics in a way which makes a positive contribution to his theory.

2.   Among the many objections that have been raised against Rawls's theory, two are of paramount importance. It is these two objections I shall attempt to meet. They may be formulated as follows.
   (1)   The dominant preference for what Rawls calls *primary goods* is either arbitrary or at least not supportable by what Rawls calls the 'thin' theory of the good.
   (2)   The employment of a veil of ignorance in the choice of principles of justice is not adequately justified.
To grasp the importance of the first objection, one must understand the role which the theory of primary goods plays in Rawls's theory of justice. One must understand the sense in which the 'thin' theory of the good, as defined by what Rawls calls the principles of rational

---

*   In developing the ideas presented in this essay I am indebted to A. Kuflik and S. Darwall. Darwall was very helpful in steering me away from several errors in my discussion of revisability. It was Kuflik who first suggested to me that the strongest interpretation of Rawls's theory is the Kantian interpretation. It was this suggestion which prompted me to develop the arguments of the present essay. I would also like to thank the referees of the *Canadian Journal of Philosophy* for several helpful comments.

choice, is supposed to support the preference for primary goods. To appreciate the force of the second objection, one must understand the functions of the veil of ignorance.

According to Rawls, the correct principles of justice are those which free and rational persons, each concerned to further his own conception of the good, would accept "in an initial position of equality."[1] Though the parties to Rawls's ideal contract are behind a veil of ignorance which prevents them from knowing *what* their particular conceptions of the good or life plans are, each party knows that he *has* a conception of the good or life plan.

Rawls lists several principles of rational choice[2] which, when taken together, are said to explicate the sense in which the parties are rational choosers. For our purposes, what Rawls calls the Effective Means Principle will serve as a representative of the set of principles of rational choice. This principle states that

> One is to adopt that alternative which realizes the end in the best way . . . given the objectives, one is to achieve it with the least expenditure of means (whatever they are); or given the means, one is to fulfill the objective to the fullest possible extent.[3]

When applied to the notion of a life plan or conception of the good, these principles of rational choice are said to yield a 'thin' theory of the good.

According to this 'thin' theory of the good there are certain primary goods — things it is supposed "a rational man wants whatever else he wants."[4] This theory of the good is 'thin' in the sense that the principles of rational choice on which it is based do not include any controversial moral principles. If the preference for primary goods depended on sentiments of justice, for example, the use of the theory of primary goods to derive principles of justice would be circular.[5]

Rawls not only claims that there are primary goods; he also provides a list of which goods are primary. The primary goods, he contends, include[6]

---

1 Rawls, *A Theory of Justice* (Cambridge, Mass.: Belknap Press of Harvard University Press, 1971), p. 11.

2 *Ibid.*, pp. 408-15.

3 *Ibid.*, p. 412.

4 *Ibid.*, p. 92.

5 *Ibid.*, pp. 396-97.

6 *Ibid*, pp. 62, 92-93.

a. political participation liberties
b. freedom of thought, speech, and information
c. freedom of the person
d. freedom from arbitrary arrest and seizure
e. opportunities
f. wealth and income

This group of primary goods provides the *content* of Rawls's two principles of justice.[7] The goods listed fall into two classes. The various rights or freedoms are covered by Rawls's first principle of justice, the greatest equal liberty principle. The remaining goods are covered by his second principle of justice, which consists of the difference principle and a principle of fair equality of opportunity.

Those who raise the first objection contend that Rawls has failed to show that these particular goods, rather than others, are primary goods — goods for any rational human being. Adina Schwarz, for example, goes so far as to maintain that the preference for these particular liberties, as well as the preference for wealth, is arbitrary unless one is a liberal democrat.[8] Michael Teitleman agrees with Schwarz that some of Rawls's alleged primary goods are not primary goods at all, but merely goods which are fundamental in certain societies or for persons with certain ideologies or particular conceptions of the good. "Wealth and power," Teitleman says, "may be essential for the attainment of a person's ends in some kinds of societies but not in others."[9]

Unless these objections are met, Rawls's theory collapses. For unless the 'thin' theory of the good generates a common set of preferences, preferences for primary goods, no determinate principles of justice will be chosen.

The second objection is no less serious: it threatens to undercut an essential function of the original position. According to Rawls, the veil of ignorance is needed if the unanimous choice of a single determinate conception of justice is to be possible.[10] The veil of ignorance is an informational constraint in the original position, the circumstances in which the social contract is to be forged. Under the veil of ignorance, no one knows the content of his conception of the good,

---

7   The primary goods I list here are what Rawls calls the *social* primary goods: they are products of social cooperation. Among the *natural* primary goods, Rawls includes, vigor, imagination, health, and intelligence.

8   Schwarz, "Moral Neutrality and Primary Goods," *Ethics*, vol. 83, p. 294.

9   Teitleman, "The Limits of Individualism," *Journal of Philosophy*, vol. LXIX, no. 18, p. 551.

10 Rawls, pp. 139–40.

> his place in society, his . . . natural assets and ability, his intelligence, strength and the like.[11]

Some of Rawls's critics have complained that since we usuallly think of rational choices as choices made in the light of all the relevant facts, it is implausible to introduce such stringent constraints on information.

If Rawls's critics are right, if the veil of ignorance is not adequately justified, the consequences are disastrous. For without the veil of ignorance, Rawls concedes, there is no solution to the problem of choice in the original position. Knowledge of the "specific contingencies which put men at odds"[12] will preclude a unanimous agreement. It should now be clear why these two objections are of crucial importance.

II

3. Having articulated the two objections and explicated their dark implications for Rawls's theory, I should now like to show how they can be effectively met. My strategy can be outlined as follows. First, I will present a series of arguments to show that a strong preference for the goods Rawls lists as primary goods is not arbitrary, but uniquely rational. I will argue, that is, that Rawls's alleged primary goods are primary goods. Second, I will show that the principles on which these arguments are based should be added to the list of principles of rational choice, and that the resulting theory of the good is still 'thin' in the requisite sense. Third, I shall argue that these same principles of rational choice support Rawls's view that principle of justice are to be chosen from behind a veil of ignorance rather than from the standpoint of particular conceptions of the good.

4. The parties in the original position, we have seen, are characterized by Rawls as each desiring to further his life plan or conception of the good. Now any life plan, or conception of the good, like any theory, must be viewed as *revisable*. If one has a certain life plan or conception of the good and if one is rational, then one will realize that the acceptability of that conception, like the acceptability of a theory, is conditional on many factors. One will realize that conception-construction, like theory-construction, is a fallible enterprise. One will realize that one's life plan or conception of the good may eventually

---

11 *Ibid.*, p. 12.

12 *Ibid*, p. 136.

require serious modification, perhaps even abandonment, in the face of a successor-conception. No matter how unlikely one thinks it to be that one's conception of the good will turn out to be mistaken, one must nonetheless view one's conception as revisable in principle. One must at least remain open to the possibility that one's present conception is mistaken and that some competing conception — which may or may not be presently available — will be superior to one's present conception. We can express this notion of revisability somewhat more formally as the principle.

    R: One ought, *ceteris paribus*, to maintain an attitude of critical revisability toward one's own conception of the good (or life-plan) and of openmindedness toward competing conceptions.

5.   It might be thought that subscription to the thesis that one should regard one's conception of the good as revisable commits one to a very strong and controversial meta-practical thesis: the thesis of value realism. By value realism I mean the view that there are values which exist independently of us and of any valuing subjects. Or it might be thought that principle R at least commits one to the weaker but still controversial thesis of value objectivism. By value objectivism I mean the view that there are objective or intersubjectively valid modes of justification for value judgements, just as there are objective or intersubjectively valid modes of justification for theoretical or factual judgements.

Surprisingly enough, the principle that one ought to maintain an attitude of critical revisability toward one's life plan or conception of the good commits one to neither value realism nor to value objectivism. Indeed, all the principle of revisability commits one to, roughly, is the view that valuation is a rational enterprise. By the view that valuation is a rational enterprise, I mean the very minimal view that value judgements, and hence conceptions of the good, are subject to *rational assessment*. On the weakest interpretation of this view, rational assessment is limited to considerations of the consistency or coherence of one's value judgements with each other and with one's other beliefs. If rationality requires that we at least achieve consistency or coherence in our beliefs, and if achieving this may require revising some of our value judgements, then the minimal rational commitment to consistency and coherence commits us to maintaining an attitude of critical revisability toward our value judgements and hence toward our conception of the good. So even if the justifiability of a life plan is only a matter of achieving and maintaining the consistency or coherence of one's own system of belief, this is quite enough to commit one to the principle of revisability.

If one subscribes to a somewhat stronger interpretation of the thesis that value judgements are subject to rational assessment, the rationality of a commitment to principle R is even more apparent. On this stronger view, value judgements are justifiable, and the value of a thing depends on the facts about that thing. Now if the justifiability of value judgements about a thing depends upon the facts about that thing, then revisions in one's factual or perceptual — or, more broadly, one's theoretical beliefs — may require revisions in one's value judgements or practical beliefs. Since factual, or perceptual or theoretical beliefs should be regarded as revisable, and since the justification of value judgements depends upon factual, perceptual or theoretical beliefs, it follows that value judgements, and hence conceptions of the good, should be regarded as revisable as well. Thus the rationality of maintaining an attitude of critical revisability in matters theoretical requires the same attitude in the practical sphere.

Revisions in one's life plan or conception of the good might be required by revisions in
i. one's beliefs about the feasibility of certain goals,
ii. one's belief as to what is the most efficient means to a certain end,
iii. one's beliefs about what one will find satisfying, or
iv one's belief that a certain activity will lead to further satisfying pursuits.
Revisions in one's life plan may also be rationally required by revisions in one's moral judgements about the institution of marriage, one's beliefs about the proper role of religion in one's life, or by one's belated awareness of the diminishing number of jobs in philosophy.

6. We have seen that subscription to R does not commit one to any of several strong meta-practical theses. I should now like to show that to deny R is to commit oneself to a set of exceedingly strong and implausible epistemological theses.

If one is consistently to deny that one ought to maintain an attitude of critical revisability toward one's life plan, one must hold all of the following claims.
(a) One's theoretical judgement is infallible.
(b) One's judgement about the goodness of ends is infallible.
(c) One's judgement about the ranking of ends is infallible.
(d) One is infallible in one's judgement that (a), (b), and (c) are true.
Unless one's theoretical beliefs are infallible, then, as we saw above, one's practical judgements may require revision in the light of revisions in one's theoretical beliefs. Unless one's judgement about the goodness of ends and about the ranking of ends is infallible, one's conception of the good may require revision in the light of revisions in either of these sorts of judgements. So unless one enjoys infallibility with respect to both one's judgements about the goodness of ends

and the ranking of ends, one should regard one's conception of the good as revisable. Further, to deny that one ought to regard one's life-plan as revisable one must also claim that one is infallible in one's belief in the infallibility of one's theoretical beliefs, one's beliefs about the goodness of ends, and one's beliefs about the ranking of ends.

Even this will not suffice. If one is consistently to deny R one must also hold that

(e) Both the factual circumstances which one's theoretical-beliefs represent and the values expressed in one's judgements about ends and their ranking are immutable.

Unless this latter assumption holds, changes in circumstances, or changes in the value of things, or changes in the priority relations among values may require revisions in one's conception of the good.

Yet another assumption is required if R is to be consistently denied. One must maintain that:

(f) One is infallible with respect to one's belief that assumption (e) is true.

It is difficult to imagine a less plausible set of epistemological theses than (a)-(f). Yet if one is to reject the principle that one ought to maintain an attitude of critical revisability toward one's life-plan, one must embrace all of them. If this is so, then R is at least as plausible as these epistemological theses are implausible.

7. If it is rational to maintain an attitude of critical revisability toward one's conception of the good, then it is rational to attempt to satisfy the *conditions necessary for critical revision*. The rationality of an attitude of critical revisability toward one's conception of the good requires, then, that one attempt to satisfy the conditions in which defects in one's conception will be discovered and in which a rational comparison of one's conception with competing conceptions can be made. Thus principle R is seen to entail principle

R_e: One ought, *ceteris paribus*, to attempt to satisfy the epistemic conditions necessary for the effective expression of an attitude of critical revisability.

Note that I am not claiming that an attitude of critical revisability requires that one be constantly engaged in actively examining one's conception of the good. Nor am I claiming in R_e that one should constantly be striving to realize whatever epistemic conditions may be relevant to the active assessment of one's conception. R_e requires only that one attempt to satisfy those basic epistemic conditions which will allow one to determine when active criticism is indicated and which are necessary for effectively engaging in active criticism when it is indicated. Similarly, regarding a scientific theory as revisable does not require that one constantly be engaged in actively examining and testing a well-confirmed theory. It does require, however, that con-

185

ditions be maintained in which competing theories can emerge and in which errors will be discoverable. I shall say more about what these basic conditions are later on.

We can also add a second corollary of principle R, namely, principle

R_i: One ought, *ceteris paribus*, to attempt to provide for the implementation of those new or revised conceptions of the good which one may develop (as a result of one's commitment to R and R_e).

My contention is that a commitment to R, the principle of revisability, to its epistemic corollary R_e, and to its implementation corollary R_i, is a constituent of being practically rational. Further, it is important to note that principles R and R_e, when stated in their most general forms, are simply principles of rationality. They cut across the distinction between theoretical and practical rationality since they apply with equal cogency to conceptions (and theories) in general, whether practical or non-practical. In the non-practical, or theoretical sphere, the rationality of a commitment to general forms of principles R and R_e is perhaps more apparent than in the practical sphere. There are some things, at least, which the scientific realist and the scientific fictionalist can agree on. The first is that theories are revisable. The second is that rationality requires a critical attitude toward one's theories. A third point of agreement is that since it is rational to maintain a critical attitude toward one's theories, one must attempt to satisfy the epistemic conditions which make the active expression of this critical attitude possible. If one agrees that principles R and R_e are applicable to scientific theories, it is difficult to see how one can deny that they are applicable to practical conceptions or plans of action. My argument does not depend, however, upon the assumption that a conception of the good *is* a type of theory. It appeals only to the fact that both conceptions of the good and theories are revisable systems of belief which are subject to rational assessment.

8. Keeping these three principles in mind, let us now return to the question of whether Rawls's alleged primary goods *are* primary goods. Rawls's critics have overlooked the peculiar character of the goods he lists as primary goods. When Rawls says that a rational man wants these goods, whatever else he wants, his contention is that these are goods of a very general, higher-order type. Some of these goods, for example, freedom of the person and freedom from arbitrary arrest and seizure, are *conditions of the pursuit of ends in general*. Others, such as wealth, freedom of speech, educational opportunities, effective access to the benefits of the legal system, and the political participation liberties, are best thought of as *maximally flexible assets*. Still others, namely, freedom of speech, thought, assembly, and informa-

tion are *required for rationally formulating, criticizing, and revising one's life plan or conception of the good.*

9.   At this point the rationality of a preference for maximally flexible assets should be clear: this preference is required by one of the principles of rationality, the principle R_i. Since one ought to make provision for implementing the new or modified conceptions of the good one may develop, one ought to attempt to secure those things which will be useful for the implementation of as broad a range of conceptions as possible. So from R_i it follows that, other things equal, it is rational to prefer more rather than less of those primary goods which are maximally flexible assets. Some of the most important primary goods under the principle of greatest equal liberty (e.g., freedom of speech and information) and under the difference principle (e.g., wealth) are maximally flexible assets, and as such are required by R_i.

Since it is perhaps the best representative of this group of primary goods, and since Rawls's critics have focused their attack on the claim that it is a primary good, let us consider *wealth* more closely. Teitleman, Schwarz and others have failed to see that wealth is primary good because they have failed to see that it is a maximally flexible asset. They have failed to see that it is a maximally flexible asset because they have interpreted the concept of wealth too narrowly, or perhaps because they have confused having access to wealth with being wealthy, where the latter is construed as a kind of relative advantage or superior buying power over others. But in the following passage Rawls makes it clear that he is interpreting the concept of wealth very broadly, and that on this interpretation wealth is preeminently a maximally flexible asset.

> [Wealth] is not an easy concept to define, but I mean to use it in the sense understood by economists. . . . Wealth is the legal command over the material means [and personal services] in general necessary to realize peoples' needs and interests. . . .[13]

10.   The rationality of a preference for goods which are conditions of the pursuit of ends in general is even more evident. If it is rational to make provisions for implementing one's conception of the good, and especially if one is to provide for implementing new or revised conceptions of the good one may develop, then it is rational to secure the conditions of the pursuit of ends generally. Thus R_i also gives us an argument for the preference for another group of the primary goods,

---

13   Rawls, "Fairness to Goodness," (An unpublished essay) pp. 5 and 7. This passage is cited with the permission of the author.

namely, those such as freedom from arbitrary arrest and seizure, which are conditions of the pursuit of ends generally. And the fact that they are conditions of agency in general shows why at least these basic liberties should be accorded priority over other primary goods such as wealth, at least where an adequate minimum of the latter has already been secured.

It may be less than fully convincing to claim that political participation liberties are, like wealth, primary goods in virtue of being maximally flexible assets. Consequently I will suggest a familiar argument to support this claim by specifying perhaps the most important uses to which these assets can be put. The argument is that the effective exercise of political participation liberties is, in the long run, the best available means (1) for achieving and maintaining those other basic liberties, such as freedom of the person, which are conditions of agency in general, and (2) for securing an adequate share of maximally flexible assets such as wealth. In sum, the political participation liberties are best thought of as maximally flexible assets whose most important use is to help us get and preserve an adequate share of other primary goods.

11.   There is yet another line of justification for at least some of the more prominent primary goods included among the basic liberties. Yet it is a line which Rawls's critics have again overlooked. Rawls hints at this justification when he says that if a party in the original position failed to choose liberty of thought and conscience, and to accord them priority over the second principle of justice, this failure

> would show that one did not take one's religious or moral convictions seriously, or highly value *the liberty to examine one's beliefs.*[14] (emphasis added)

The rationality of the desire to examine one's religious and moral beliefs, indeed one's belief systems in general, is, as we have seen, a consequence of the rationality of viewing one's beliefs as revisable. I would now like to suggest that perhaps the strongest justification for at least some of Rawls's basic liberties — especially freedom of thought, speech, and religion — is that they are required by one of the principles of rationality, principle R_e, the epistemic corollary of the principle of revisability. In scientific inquiry the importance of guaranteeing freedom of thought, speech, and information is obvious and generally acknowledged. But once we view our conceptions of the good (and of the obligatory) as revisable, then the justification for placing a priority on the freedoms in question becomes equally apparent with respect to practical matters. The basic liberties cited are epistemic conditions

---

14   Rawls, p. 207.

of critical revision and of rationally informed conception-succession in practical reasoning.[15]

12.   Once it is seen that the preference for Rawls's primary goods is based on the fact that these goods are either (a) conditions of the pursuit of ends in general, or (b) maximally flexible assets, and hence required for implementing whatever new or modified conceptions one may develop (R_i), or (c) required for rationally formulating and criticizing one's conception (R_e), the claim that the preference for primary goods is arbitrary is seen to be quite spurious. The best justification for the strong preference for primary goods is that this preference is required by certain principles of rationality, specifically R, R_e, and R_i.

13.   So far I have presented certain arguments for the rationality of a preference for primary goods, and I have argued that they can meet a prevalent criticism of Rawls's theory. I will now argue that Rawls can and should consistently avail himself of these arguments by incorporating into his theory of rational choice the principles on which these arguments are based.

Rawls characterizes the persons in the original position as each being concerned to further his own conception of the good or life plan[16]

---

15   It is generally recognized that J.S. Mill gives a similar justification for liberties in general in Chapter III of *On Liberty*. The argument I have sketched is distinct from Mill's: it is at a higher level of abstraction and is not necessarily linked to Mill's radical value-empiricism nor to utilitarianism. Mill argues that liberty is required for the effective pursuit of one's own happiness through experimentation in practical experience and that social utility will be maximized by insuring equal liberty for all to engage in such experimentation. The difference is that while Mill views liberty as necessary for rationally informed conception-construction in the individual's conception of what is conducive to his own happiness, the argument I have presented views liberty as necessary for rationally informed construction and revision of the individual's conception of the good, where it is not assumed that the individual's conception is hedonistic or even egoistic.

16   It might be thought that this characterization of the parties implies that they are egoists. This is false. On p. 129 Rawls makes it clear that there is a distinction between *one's own conception of the good* and *one's own conception of one's own good* and that the parties know only that they have a conception of the good: "It should be noted that I make no restrictive assumptions about the parties' conceptions of the good except that they are rational long-term plans. While these plans determine the aims and interests of a self, the aims and interests are not presumed to be egoistic or selfish." Failure to attend to this passage has led many of Rawls's critics to make the mistake of describing the parties as being egoistically motivated.

by employing the principles of rational choice. I propose that this characterization of the rationality of the parties be modified to include the claim that each is concerned to further his own conception of the good *in a critical way*. More specifically, we can add R, R_e, and R_i to the set of principles of rational choice.

14.   What should be clear at this point is that the addition of R, R_e, and R_i to the list of principles of rational choice is quite consistent with still regarding the resulting theory of rational choice as definitive of a 'thin' theory of the good: so far, at least, no 'morally controversial' elements have been injected into the theory of the good. Or if they *are* morally controversial, then so much for the moral theories they controvert: the principles in question are principles of rationality in a fundamental sense. They are, as Kant would say, principles of practical reason.

III

15.   There is another reason for Rawls to expand his theory of rational choice to include the principles of revisability: doing so lends support to another of his basic tenets, the claim that a veil of ignorance is required for the choice of principles of justice. If this argument is successful, the second major objection to Rawls's theory ((2)) will be at least partly met.

It is usually assumed that the only functions of the veil of ignorance are to harmonize interests of *different* persons by avoiding clashes between individuals' disparate conceptions of the good and to prevent one individual or class from tailoring the principles of justice to fit his or its particular conception. And of course these are important functions of the veil of ignorance. There is, however, another distinct but related function which the veil of ignorance performs. On the interpersonal level, the veil of ignorance insures that principles of justice will be chosen within which diverse individuals may pursue quite disparate conceptions of the good. Similarly — and just as importantly — on the level of *the single individual*, viewed as a critical pursuer of ends over time, the veil of ignorance insures that the principles of justice will allow that individual maximum freedom to develop and implement new or modified conceptions of the good. Quite apart from the need to avoid collisions with other individuals' pursuits of their ends, and quite apart from the need to insure that the principles of justice do not favor certain individuals or classes, the principles of revisability give each individual good reason to avoid determining by his present life plan the entire framework within which he will pursue all the ends he ever will pursue.

Rawls may be suggesting a justification in terms of revisability when he says that the veil of ignorance expresses the Kantian notion of autonomy and that this notion in turn emphasizes the importance of "freedom in the choice of a system of final ends" or conception of the good.[17] Kant would agree that allowing one's particular conception of the good at a certain time to limit one's potential for developing and implementing future conceptions of the good would be irrational. It would be irrational because it would impose avoidable limitations on the exercise of one's practical rationality in the future.

There is a passage in his political writings in which Kant appeals to the possibility of revision as a reason for not tailoring public rules to one's particular value-conceptions. In the essay on "Theory and Practice" Kant argues that an official state religion with a fixed canon of orthodoxy is unacceptable — even if it accords with one's own particular religious views — because it prevents one "from making further progress in religious understanding or from correcting any past mistakes."[18] Limiting one's rational agency for the sake of one's present conception of the good is a subtler form of heteronomy than allowing one's conduct to be determined by a particular present desire one has not even integrated into one's present conception of the good. But it is heteronomy nonetheless.

Rawls's veil of ignorance prevents the contracting parties from choosing an institutional framework which restricts their freedom in this fashion. It appears, then, that once again the principles of revisability, R and R_i, lend support to one of Rawls's central theses: that principles of justice should be chosen from behind a veil of ignorance rather than from the temporally parochial standpoint of particular conceptions of the good.

Rawls's critics have overlooked these arguments from revisability, I believe, because they take a purely *synchronic* rather than a *diachronic* view of persons' needs and conceptions of the good. The arguments for the veil of ignorance and for the preference for primary goods I have offered are higher-order, *diachronic* justifications in that they appeal to principles which deal with conception-succession rather than merely with the implementation or choice of a particular conception at a particular time.

---

17   Rawls, p. 254.

18   Kant, *Band VIII*, p. 305. Academy Edition.

IV

16.   The chief conclusions of this essay can now be summarized. Rawls's critics have overlooked what appear to be the most cogent replies to two of their most fundamental objections. (i) Once the 'thin' theory of the good is strengthened by adding the principle of revisability (R) and its two corollaries (R_e and R_i) to the set of principles of rational choice, we can meet the first criticism by showing that the preference for Rawls's primary goods is uniquely rational. (ii) The strengthened 'thin' theory of the good also provides a reply to the second major objection by showing that there is good reason for choosing principles of justice from behind a veil of ignorance. Finally, it should be noted that while the three principles I have adduced can be used to strengthen Rawls's theory, their interest is by no means limited to a Rawlsian framework. They are, I believe, significant principles which any adequate theory of rational choice would include.

March 1975

AMARTYA SEN

Justice: Means versus Freedoms

This article is concerned with the informational basis of justice. The informational basis of a judgment identifies the information on which the judgment is directly dependent and—no less important—asserts that the truth or falsehood of any other type of information cannot *directly* influence the correctness of the judgment.[1] The informational basis of judgments of justice thus determines the factual territory over which considerations of justice would *directly* apply. (The implications on other matters would be derivative.)

The analysis presented here derives a good part of its motivation and structure from Rawlsian theory of justice as fairness.[2] However, I argue

This is a part of a longer paper ("The Territory of Justice") which formed the text of my Marion O'Kellie McKay Lecture given at the University of Pittsburgh on September 16, 1988. My greatest debt is to John Rawls for his enormously helpful comments (even though I am critical of his theory of justice in this article). I have also profited a good deal from the suggestions of G. A. Cohen, Ronald Dworkin, Derek Parfit, Thomas Scanlon, and Kevin Sontheimer.

1. The diverse forms and varying roles of the informational basis of normative judgments have been discussed in my "Informational Bases of Alternative Welfare Approaches: Aggregation and Income Distribution," *Journal of Public Economics* 3 (1974): 387–403; "On Weights and Measures: Informational Constraints in Social Welfare Analysis," *Econometrica* 45 (1977): 1539–72; "Informational Analysis of Moral Principles," in *Rational Action*, ed. R. Harrison (Cambridge: Cambridge University Press, 1979), pp. 115–32; "Well-being, Agency and Freedom: The Dewey Lectures, 1984," *Journal of Philosophy* 82 (1985): 169–221; and "Information and Invariance in Normative Choice," in *Social Choice and Public Decision Making: Essays in Honor of Kenneth Arrow*, ed. W. P. Heller, R. M. Starr, and D. A. Starrett (Cambridge: Cambridge University Press, 1986), pp. 29–55.

2. J. Rawls, *A Theory of Justice* (Cambridge, Mass.: Harvard University Press, 1971); "Social Unity and Primary Goods," in *Utilitarianism and Beyond*, ed. A. Sen and B. Williams (Cambridge: Cambridge University Press, 1982), pp. 159–85; "Justice as Fairness: Political not Metaphysical," *Philosophy & Public Affairs* 14, no. 3 (Summer 1985): 223–51; "The Priority of Right and Ideas of the Good," *Philosophy & Public Affairs* 17, no. 4

that the interpersonal comparisons that must form a crucial part of the informational basis of justice cannot be provided by comparisons of holdings of *means* to freedom (such as "primary goods," "resources," or "incomes"). In particular, interpersonal variability in the conversion of primary goods into freedom to achieve introduces elements of arbitrariness into the Rawlsian accounting of the respective advantages enjoyed by different persons; this can be a source of unjustified inequality and unfairness.

This claim, which I had presented in a very elementary form in my Tanner Lecture at Stanford University in 1979,[3] has recently been disputed by Rawls. He has argued that my criticism of his theory presupposes the acceptance of some specific "comprehensive doctrine"—some unique view of the good—and thus goes against what he calls the "political conception" of justice.[4] I argue here that this claim is mistaken. More positively, I argue that a theory of justice based on fairness must be deeply and directly concerned with the *actual freedoms* enjoyed by different persons—persons with possibly divergent objectives—to lead different lives that they can have reason to value.

I. INFORMATION: PERSONAL AND COMBINATIONAL

The informational base of substantive theories that ground ethical judgments on the lives of persons can be roughly split into two types of intrinsically relevant information: (1) *focal personal features*, and (2) *combining characteristics*. To illustrate, for the standard utilitarian theory, the only intrinsically important focal personal features are *individual utilities*, and the only usable combining characteristic is *summation*, yielding the *total* of those utilities. "Welfarist" theories, of which utilitarianism is a particular example, retain the former part (utilities as the focal personal features), but can use other combining characteristics, for example, utility-based maximin (or lexicographic maximin), or summation of concave transforms of utilities (such as summation of the logarithms of utilities).

(Fall 1988): 251–76; "The Domain of the Political and Overlapping Consensus," mimeograph, 1988; "Political Constructivism and Public Justification," mimeograph, 1988; "Reply to Sen," mimeograph, 1988.

3. A. Sen, "Equality of What?" in *The Tanner Lectures on Human Values*, ed. S. McMurrin (Cambridge: Cambridge University Press, 1980), 1: 195–220.

4. Rawls, "The Priority of Right and Ideas of the Good"; "Reply to Sen."

Other examples of focal personal features are liberties and primary goods (Rawls), rights (Nozick), resources (Dworkin), commodity bundles (Foley, Varian), and various mixed spaces (Suzumura, Wriglesworth, Riley). Note that in some cases the personal features are broadly of the outcome type (for example, commodity bundles enjoyed), as they are in welfarist theories such as utilitarianism, whereas in other cases they relate to opportunities, defined in some way or other (for example, primary goods, rights, resources). The selection of personal features must be supplemented by the choice of a combining formula—for example, lexicographic priorities and maximin (Rawls), equality (Nozick, Dworkin, Foley), or various mixed rules (Varian, Suzumura, Wriglesworth, Riley).[5]

There is, obviously, much more to be said about each approach, including how each author sees the interpretational and justificatory issues (for example, the underlying foundational principles, the balance between teleological and deontological reasoning), and how the plural and heterogeneous characteristics of the respective features can be handled (for example, indexing of primary goods, fixing of the hierarchy of rights, evaluation of different resources, weighting of diverse utilities). But in these different approaches to ethics and justice we also see quite different types of informational selection, covering both personal and combining features.

II. Capability, Freedom, and Primary Goods

A person's achieved living can be seen as a combination of "functionings," or "doings and beings." Given n different types of functionings,[6] an "n-tuple" of functionings represents the focal features of a person's

---

5. Rawls, *A Theory of Justice*; R. Dworkin, "What Is Equality? Part 2: Equality of Resources," *Philosophy & Public Affairs* 10, no. 4 (Fall 1981): 283–345; R. Nozick, *Anarchy, State and Utopia* (New York: Basic Books, 1974); J. Wriglesworth, *Libertarian Conflicts in Social Choice* (Cambridge: Cambridge University Press, 1985): D. Foley, "Resource Allocation in the Public Sector," *Yale Economic Essays* 7 (1967): 45–98; J. Riley, *Liberal Utilitarianism* (Cambridge: Cambridge University Press, 1988); H. R. Varian, "Distributive Justice, Welfare Economics, and the Theory of Fairness," *Philosophy & Public Affairs* 4, no. 3 (Spring 1975): 223–47; K. Suzumura, *Rational Choice, Collective Decisions, and Social Welfare* (Cambridge: Cambridge University Press, 1983).

6. The same functioning at two different points in time can be formally treated as two different functionings if we are looking not at the achieved living at a particular point in time, but at the life profile of a person over time.

living, with each of its n components reflecting the extent of the achievement of a particular functioning.[7] A person's "capability" is represented by the set of n-tuples of functionings from which the person can choose any one n-tuple. The "capability set" thus stands for the actual freedom of choice a person has over alternative lives that he or she can lead.

On this view, individual claims are to be assessed not by the resources or primary goods the persons respectively hold, but by the freedoms they actually enjoy to choose between different ways of living that they can have reason to value. It is this actual freedom that is represented by the person's "capability" to achieve various alternative combinations of functionings, or doings and beings.[8]

How do primary goods relate to capabilities? Rawls explains that primary goods are "things that citizens need as free and equal persons," and "claims to these goods are counted as appropriate claims."[9] Primary goods are "things that every rational man is presumed to want," and include "income and wealth," "the basic liberties," "freedom of movement and choice of occupation," "powers and prerogatives of offices and positions of responsibility," and "the social bases of self-respect."[10] Since primary goods are diverse, some "index" of the holding of primary goods must serve as the comprehensive basis of interpersonal comparison for the Rawlsian assessment of justice. Primary goods can be seen as general-purpose *resources* that are useful for the pursuit of different ideas of the good that different individuals may have. The coverage of "re-

7. An n-tuple is made up by picking one element from each of n sets. The sets need not be numerically metricized (e.g., a set of alternative nutritional achievements may consist of "being well-nourished," "being calorie deficient but otherwise well-nourished," "being deficient in both calories and protein," etc.). Thus, thinking in terms of an n-tuple does not restrict the forms of description in any particular way. In the special case in which the elements of *each* set are measured in terms of real numbers, an n-tuple would be an n-vector, and the analysis would then be confined to the more commonly used—but also more restrictive—format of a vector space.

8. Capability reflects freedom to lead different types of lives. Lives can be defined broadly or narrowly. Furthermore, we also have objectives and values concerning things *other than* the types of lives we can lead, and our ability to achieve them is also a matter of our freedom, broadly defined. I shall not pursue these broader problems here, but their inclusion would not change the arguments presented in this article. On the distinctions between different notions of positive freedom (especially between "well-being freedom" and "agency freedom"), see my "Well-being, Agency and Freedom."

9. Rawls, "The Priority of Right and Ideas of the Good," p. 257.

10. See Rawls, *A Theory of Justice*, pp. 60–65; "Social Unity and Primary Goods," p. 162; and "The Priority of Right and Ideas of the Good," pp. 256–57.

sources" can be extended to include other *means*; Ronald Dworkin has taken his system of ethical accounting in that direction.[11] Though there are important differences between Rawls's and Dworkin's approaches, both focus on resources in making interpersonal comparisons, and both seek to answer the question "Equality of what?" in terms of *means* rather than what people can obtain *from* the means.[12]

Given the presumption of versatility of these primary goods or resources (as Rawls puts it, different "comprehensive conceptions of the good ... require for their advancement roughly the same primary goods"),[13] they are, in fact, meant to be general-purpose *means to freedom*, that is, they influence inter alia the set of alternative lives from which a person can choose. Indeed, that connection with freedom is one of the most attractive aspects of seeing the focal personal features as the holdings of primary goods, given their assumed versatility.

But if we are interested in freedom, is it adequate to concentrate on the *means* to freedom, rather than on the *extent* of the freedom that a person actually has? Since the conversion of these primary goods and resources into freedom to select a particular life and to achieve may vary from person to person, equality in holdings of primary goods or resources can go hand in hand with serious inequalities in actual freedoms enjoyed by different persons.

In the capability-based assessment of justice, individual claims are not to be assessed in terms of the resources or primary goods the persons respectively hold, but in terms of the freedoms they actually enjoy to choose between different ways of living that they can have reason to value. It is this actual freedom that is represented by the person's "ca-

---

11. Dworkin, "What Is Equality? Part 2: Equality of Resources." I have attempted to evaluate Dworkin's case for resource-based accounting in "Rights and Capabilities," in *Ethics and Objectivity*, ed. T. Honderich (London: Routledge, 1985), pp. 130–48, also published in my *Resources, Values and Development* (Cambridge, Mass.: Harvard University Press, 1984). See also G. A. Cohen, "Equality of What? On Welfare, Resources, and Capabilities," in *The Quality of Life*, ed. M. Nussbaum and A. Sen (Oxford: Clarendon Press, forthcoming), and his "On the Currency of Egalitarian Justice," *Ethics* 99 (1989): 906–44.

12. It must, however, be noted that Dworkin has also proposed enriching the perspective of "resources" by including *as if* insurance mechanisms against certain types of personal handicaps. To the extent that these insurance mechanisms even out differences in different people's ability to convert resources into capabilities, the equality of insurance-adjusted values of resources would be an indirect way of *approaching* the equality of capabilities. Much depends on the scope, coverage, and versatility of the *as if* insurance mechanisms.

13. Rawls, "The Priority of Right and Ideas of the Good," pp. 256–57.

pability" to achieve various alternative combinations of functionings, that is, doings and beings.

It is important to distinguish capability—representing freedom actually enjoyed—from both (1) primary goods (and other resources), and (2) actually chosen lives (and other realized results). To illustrate the first distinction, a person who has a disability can have more primary goods (in the form of liberties, income, wealth, and so on) but less capability (owing to the handicap). To take another example, this time from poverty studies, a person may have more income and more nutritional intake than another person, but less freedom to live a well-nourished existence because of a higher basal metabolic rate, greater vulnerability to parasitic diseases, larger body size, or pregnancy. Similarly, in dealing with poverty in the wealthier countries, we have to take note of the fact that many of those who are poor in terms of income and other primary goods also have characteristics—age, disability, disease-proneness, and so on—that make it more difficult for them to convert primary goods into basic capabilities, for example, the ability to move about, to lead a healthy life, and to take part in the life of the community. Neither primary goods nor resources, more broadly defined, can represent the capability a person actually enjoys.

In the context of inequality between women and men, the variable conversion rates of primary goods into capabilities can be quite crucial. Biological as well as social factors (related to pregnancy, neonatal care, conventional household roles, and so on) can place a woman at a disadvantage even when she has exactly the same bundle of primary goods as a man. The issue of gender cannot be properly addressed if advantage and disadvantage are seen merely in terms of holdings of primary goods, rather than the actual freedoms to lead different types of lives that women and men respectively enjoy.[14]

To illustrate the second distinction, a person may have the same capability as another person, but nevertheless choose a different bundle of functionings in line with his or her particular goals. Furthermore, two persons with the same actual capabilities and even the same goals may end up with different outcomes because of differences in strategies that they follow in exercising their freedoms.[15]

14. On this see my "Gender and Cooperative Conflict," WIDER discussion paper, 1985, in *Persistent Inequalities*, ed. I. Tinker (New York: Oxford University Press, 1989).
15. For arguments in favor of concentrating on achieved living, as opposed to capabili-

It is important to see the distinction both (1) between freedom and the means to freedom, and (2) between freedom and achievement. Rawls's belief that my case for comparing capabilities, as opposed to holdings of primary goods, must be based on choosing a specific "comprehensive" view of the good[16] ignores inter alia the significance that is attached to the distinction between freedom and achievement—specifically, between capabilities and functionings—in the capability approach.

III. FREEDOM AND COMPREHENSIVE VIEWS

In responding to my critique, Rawls summarizes his interpretation of my objection thus: "The idea of primary goods must be mistaken. For they are not what, from within anyone's comprehensive doctrine, can be taken as ultimately important: they are not, in general, anyone's idea of the basic values of human life. Therefore, to focus on primary goods, one may object, is to work for the most part in the wrong space—in the space of institutional features and material things and not in the space of basic moral values."[17] Rawls then responds to his interpretation of my objection as follows: "In reply, an index of primary goods is not intended as an approximation to what is ultimately important as specified by any particular comprehensive doctrine with its account of moral values."[18] Rawls sees the need to avoid commitment to a particular comprehensive view as crucial to the conception of justice as fairness. "The main restric-

---

ties, in answering the question "Equality of what?" see G. A. Cohen, "Equality of What? On Welfare, Resources, and Capabilities."

16. Rawls, "The Priority of Right and Ideas of the Good," pp. 258–59.

17. Ibid., pp. 256–59.

18. Ibid., p. 259. Rawls also has a rather different line of answering my criticism in his "Reply to Sen." He argues that his full theory of justice has more "flexibility" than I recognize, and that some of the interpersonal variations I am concerned with can be taken note of at later stages, such as "legislative" and "judicial" ones. It is not altogether easy to be sure what overall procedures and allocational principles would in fact be satisfied by such a complex stagewise structure, but if it is indeed the case that all the relevant interpersonal variations will be effectively dealt with at some stage or other, then that would certainly reduce the force of the criticism. Some of the issues raised by interpersonal variations in the conversion of primary goods into capabilities would then end up receiving attention after all. However, even in terms of this stagewise analysis, the different capabilities to influence legislation and political decisions may call for attention to be paid to this problem at earlier stages as well (e.g., in dealing with the disadvantage of the physically disabled, the undernourished, or the ill in influencing political decisions, even when they have the same bundle of primary goods as the nondisadvantaged).

tion would seem to be this: the ideas included must be political ideas. That is, they must belong to a reasonable political conception of justice so that we may assume (1) that they are, or can be, shared by citizens regarded as free and equal; and (2) that they do not presuppose any particular fully (or partially) comprehensive doctrine.[19]

I have discussed elsewhere whether this "political conception," with the insistence on avoiding any comprehensive view, may limit the scope and range of a theory of justice too severely.[20] But I shall not go into that question now. My main concern here is with scrutinizing the adequacy of primary goods specifically for Rawls's approach of justice as fairness, including his insistence on avoiding the use of any particular "comprehensive doctrine."

The first problem with Rawls's reply lies in his misinterpretation of the nature of my criticism. Capability reflects a person's *freedom* to choose between alternative lives (functioning combinations), and its value need not be derived from one particular "comprehensive doctrine" demanding one specific way of living. As discussed in Section II, it is important to distinguish between freedom (of which capability is a representation) and achievement, and the evaluation of capability need not be based on one exclusive comprehensive doctrine that orders the achievements, including the life-styles and the functioning n-tuples.

The second problem, related to the first, concerns Rawls's claim that primary goods are "not intended as an approximation to what is ultimately important as specified by any *particular comprehensive doctrine*" (emphasis added). The lack of correspondence between primary goods and achievements lies not only there, but also in the fact that, given variable conversion rates of primary goods into achievements, a disadvantaged person may get less from primary goods than others *no matter what comprehensive doctrine* he or she holds. To illustrate the point, consider two persons, 1 and 2, with 2 disadvantaged in some respect (for example, by a physical disability, mental handicap, disease vulnerability, or high basal metabolic rate[21]). Furthermore, 1 and 2 do *not* have the

19. Rawls, "The Priority of Right and Ideas of the Good," p. 253.

20. In "The Territory of Justice," secs. 4 and 5. Also discussed in my *Inequality and Freedom* (Oxford: Clarendon Press, forthcoming).

21. In wealthier communities a higher basal metabolic rate may well be an advantage in enabling one to eat more without getting fat, but in conditions of poverty it can increase one's requirements for food and therefore income (a primary good) to achieve the same level of nutritional functioning.

same objectives or the same conceptions of the good. 1 values A more
than B, while 2 values B more than A. Each values 2A more than A, and
2B more than B. The orderings of the two (representing the relevant
parts of their respective "comprehensive doctrines") are as follows:

Person 1	*Person 2*
2A	2B
2B	2A
A	B
B	A

With the given set of primary goods, person 1 can achieve 2A or 2B, as
well as—though there may be no great merit in this—A or B. On the
other hand, given 2's disadvantage, with the very same primary goods 2
can achieve only A or B. Thus, 1's capability set is (2A, 2B, A, B),
whereas 2's set is (A, B).

Person 1 proceeds to achieve 2A, while 2 settles for B. The problem is
not just that 2 is at a disadvantage in terms of one *particular* comprehensive doctrine (his or her own, or that of person 1), but that 2 has a
worse deal than 1 *no matter which* comprehensive doctrine is considered. Equality of primary goods has given 2 less *freedom to achieve* and
not just less *achievement* with respect to some *one* comprehensive doctrine.

If the comparisons were made not in terms of primary goods but in
terms of capabilities, 2's worse deal would be obvious. Person 2's capability set—(A, B)—is a proper subset of the capability set of 1, namely,
(2A, 2B, A, B), shorn of the best elements, no matter which comprehensive doctrine is considered. Capability represents freedom, whereas primary goods tell us only about the means to freedom, with an interpersonally variable relation between the means and the actual freedom to
achieve. Rawls is right to think that my objection did relate to primary
goods being *means* only, but that problem is not disposed of by saying
that they are "not intended as an approximation to what is ultimately
important as specified by any particular comprehensive doctrine."[22]

22. Dominance in the space of capabilities does not require agreement on any comprehensive doctrine, since one set can be a subset of another (as in the example given). Furthermore, even when the capability sets are not subsets of each other, for agreement to
exist on their ranking, we do not need the acceptance of any one comprehensive doctrine.
Partial rankings of capabilities can be based on superiority in terms of *each* of the relevant

IV. Plural Diversities and Justice

There are in fact two sources of variation in the relation between a person's *means* (such as primary goods or resources) and *ends*. One possibility is *inter-end* variation—different conceptions of the good that different people may have. The other is *interindividual* variation in the relation between resources (such as primary goods) and the freedom to pursue ends. Rawls shows great sensitivity to the first variation, and is keen on preserving respect for this diversity (rightly so, in line with his pluralistic political conception). Rawls does assume that the same primary goods serve all the different ends, and, presumably for the sake of fairness, it must not be the case that some people's ends are so minutely—even though positively—served by the primary goods (compared with the ends of others) that the first group may have a legitimate complaint about judging individual deals in terms of primary goods. This is a question of some importance, but I will not pursue it further here.[23]

My concern is with the second—*interindividual*—variation in the relation between resources and freedoms. A person's actual freedom to pursue his or her ends depends on both (1) what ends he or she has, and (2) what power he or she has to convert primary goods into the achievement of ends. The problem of converting goods into the achievement of ends, with which I am primarily concerned here, can be serious *even with* given ends, but it is *not* the case that it can be serious *only with* given ends. The reach and relevance of the second problem is in no way reduced by the existence of the first.

To conclude, we *are* diverse, but we are diverse in *different* ways. One variation relates to the differences that exist among our ends and objectives. The ethical and political implications of this diversity we now un-

---

comprehensive doctrines. On these and related matters see my *Choice, Welfare and Measurement* (Cambridge, Mass.: MIT Press, 1982), and *Commodities and Capabilities* (Amsterdam: North-Holland, 1985). See also I. Levi, *Hard Choices* (Cambridge: Cambridge University Press, 1986).

23. In fact, Rawls's comprehensive assertion that "there exists no other space of values to which the index of primary goods is to approximate" ("The Priority of Right and Ideas of the Good," p. 259) would seem to overlook the nature of this particular problem. If every possible list of primary goods (and every way of doing an index) makes some people's ends very well served and others terribly minutely so, then the important feature of "neutrality" is lost, and the entire line of reasoning of "justice as fairness" is significantly undermined. Thus, some strong requirements *are* imposed on the relation between primary goods and the space of other values. I shall not discuss this issue further in this article.

derstand much better than before as a result of Rawls's powerful analysis of justice as fairness. But there is another important diversity—variations in our ability to convert resources into actual freedoms. Variations related to sex, age, genetic endowments, and many other features give us unequal powers to build freedom in our lives even when we have the same bundle of primary goods.[24]

If the freedoms that persons enjoy constitute a major territory of justice, then primary goods provide an inadequate informational basis for the evaluation of what is just and what is not. We have to examine the capabilities that we can actually enjoy. The practical implications of the difference—political as well as ethical—can be enormous.

24. I have discussed some of the empirical issues involved in the variable conversion of primary goods (and resources) into capabilities (and freedoms) in "Indian Women: Well-being and Survival" (jointly with J. Kynch), *Cambridge Journal of Economics* 7 (1983): 363–80; *Resources, Values and Development*; *Commodities and Capabilities*; "Gender and Cooperative Conflict"; and *Hunger and Public Action* (jointly with Jean Drèze) (Oxford: Clarendon Press, 1989).

JUSTICE AND NATURAL ENDOWMENT:
TOWARD A CRITIQUE OF
RAWLS' IDEOLOGICAL FRAMEWORK

1

The reconciliation of morality with rationality is the central problem of modern moral philosophy. It is easy to achieve this reconciliation by fiat, to select a conception of rationality and a conception of morality so that the two fit. What is of greater interest and value is to attempt this reconciliation beginning with our intuitive conceptions of rationality and morality. *A Theory of Justice* claims to achieve this, for that part of morality which constitutes the realm of justice.

Rawls' theory of justice

> generalizes and carries to a higher level of abstraction the familiar theory of the social contract ... [11] ... on the contract view the theory of justice is part of the theory of rational choice [47]. ... the guiding idea is that the principles of justice for the basic structure of society are the object of the original agreement. They are the principles that free and rational persons concerned to further their own interests would accept in an initial position of equality as defining the fundamental terms of their association [11].

Thus the connection between rationality and justice is to be established in terms of an act of choice in an initial position of equality. In addition to an account of rationality and justice, then, the theory must provide an account of what Rawls usually refers to as the "initial situation [121]." The hypothesis, which makes the theory a genuine *theory*, is that an account can be given of these factors which both matches our considered judg-

---

Note: Throughout this issue, page numbers of Rawls' *A Theory of Justice* are shown in brackets [ ].

ments about them, and relates them so that the conception of justice would be embodied in the principles chosen by rational men in the initial situation.

Rawls explicitly recognizes the importance of this hypothesis with respect both to justice and to the initial situation. He suggests that

> It seems natural to think of the concept of justice as distinct from the various conceptions of justice and as being specified by the role which these different sets of principles, these different conceptions, have in common [5].

The theory must then provide that

> account of a person's sense of justice . . . which matches his judgments in reflective equilibrium. . . . this state is one reached after a person has weighed various proposed conceptions and he has either revised his judgments to accord with one of then or held fast to his initial convictions (and the corresponding conception) [48].

Furthermore

> There are . . . many possible interpretations of the initial situation. . . . But . . . there is one interpretation of the initial situation which best expresses the conditions that are widely thought reasonable to impose on the choice of principles yet which, at the same time, leads to a conception that characterizes our considered judgments in reflective equilibrium. This most favored, or standard, interpretation I shall refer to as the original position [121].

And so the theory of

> justice as fairness is the hypothesis that the principles which would be chosen in the original position are identical with those that match our considered judgments and so these principles describe our sense of justice [48].

But Rawls' account of rationality is significantly different from his account of justice and of the initial situation. He does not suggest that he is concerned with a particular conception of rationality, among the various possible conceptions which one might entertain, but rather with the concept itself.

> The concept of rationality invoked here . . . is the standard one familiar in social theory. Thus in the usual way, a rational person is thought to have a coherent set of preferences between the options open to him. He ranks these options according to how well they further his purposes; he follows the plan which will satisfy more of his desires rather than less, and which has the greater chance of being successfully executed [143].

Rawls makes, explicitly, one special assumption,

> that a rational individual does not suffer from envy. He is not ready to accept a loss for himself if only others have less as well [143].

This is part of the standard view, if "loss" is understood in relation to the purposes or desires of the agent. A better formulation of the special assumption is that there are certain *primary goods*, and

> the persons in the original position . . . prefer more rather than less primary goods [93].

No one's purposes are served by accepting less primary goods for himself, if only others have less as well.

The concept of rationality familiar in social theory identifies rationality with the maximization of individual utility. Rawls, then, accepts this identification, subject to the special assumption that there is a class of goods such that an increase in these goods always represents an increase in utility. This account of rationality is not advanced as a particular conception, competing with others as an adequate formualtion of our concept of rational man, but as expressing that concept itself. Hence the view, common in mediaeval thought, that the role of reason is to acquaint man with the divine law for human conduct must be not only mistaken, but *conceptually* mistaken.

An *ideology* may be characterized, in part, by the identification of a particular conception of rationality with the concept itself. Hence Rawls' assumption of that conception of reason that is prevalent in, and indeed fundamental to, our society both characterizes his own *ideological framework*, and identifies it, in one essential respect, with what I shall neutrally term the *liberal individualist* framework. In the present argument, then, I shall suggest a basis for a critique of that framework.

The argument has the following structure. In section 2, I shall introduce the central features of Rawls' conception of justice, and his account of the initial situation. In section 3, I shall show how the maximizing conception of rationality, in conjunction with the conception of the original position, seems to lead to the difference principle which characterizes Rawls' conception of justice. However, in sections 4 and 5, I shall show that a consideration of man's natural endowment, in relation first to the absence of society and then to man's social potential, requires revisions in the difference principle. In section 6, I shall examine the effect of these revisions on the type of society instituted by the adoption of the principles of justice, showing that contrary to Rawls' view, this proves to be civil or private society. Finally, in section 7, I shall mention an alternative conception of society and its relation to man's natural endowment, as the starting point for a critique of the maximizing conception of practical rationality.[1]

2

Rawls formulates the general conception of justice which is derived from his theory in this way:

> All social primary goods—liberty and opportunity, income and wealth, and the bases of self-respect—are to be distributed equally unless an unequal distribution of any or all of these goods is to the advantage of the least favored [303].

This general conception is used to derive a special conception which Rawls takes to be applicable to our actual circumstances. Among the primary goods, "fundamental rights and liberties" are distinguished from "economic and social benefits" [63].

The former are to be equally available to all; the latter are to be distributed in accordance with what Rawls terms the *difference principle*. In the most general form in which Rawls presents this principle—a form more general than that in which he employs it, yet less restrictive in its assumptions about actual conditions —the principle states that

> in a basic structure with n relevant representatives, first maximize the welfare of the worst-off representative man; second, for equal welfare of the worst-off representative, maximize the welfare of the second worst-off representative man, and so on until the last case which is, for equal welfare of all the preceding n-1 representatives, maximize the welfare of the best-off representative man. We may think of this as the lexical difference principle [83].

The difference principle, which I shall use in this most general, lexical form, distinguishes what Rawls calls democratic equality from liberal equality. Both liberal and democratic equality nullify "the influence of social contingencies," but the liberal conception

> still permits the distribution of wealth and income to be determined by the natural distribution of abilities and talents. Within the limits allowed by the background arrangements, distributive shares are decided by the outcome of the natural lottery; and this outcome is arbitrary from a moral perspective. There is no more reason to permit the distribution of income and wealth to be settled by the distribution of natural assets than by historical and social fortune [73—4].

The democratic conception, based on the difference principle, does not permit wealth and income to be determined by natural talents. Hence Rawls'

> conception of justice ... nullifies the accidents of natural endowment ... leaving aside those aspects of the social world that seem arbitrary from a moral point of view [15].

To anticipate, the particular aim of my argument is to show that this *nullificatory* feature of Rawls' conception of justice is incompatible with its *contractual* basis. I shall argue that if we accept the contractual framework, required by Rawls' maximizing conception of rationality, we are led to a conception of justice more closely resembling the liberal conception which Rawls would reject. Insofar as this liberal conception fails to satisfy our considered judgments and hence our sense of justice, rationality and morality are not reconciled.

The contractual basis of Rawls' thought requires, as we have seen, a specification of the initial situation in which the principles of justice are to be chosen. The favored specification is referred to as the original position. In the original position each person is assumed to be rational, and so is assumed to seek to maximize his well-being, subject to the constraint that he is free from envy. Each is subject, and knows he is subject, to what Rawls terms "the circumstances of justice," which

> may be described as the normal conditions under which human cooperation is both possible and necessary. ... Hume's account of them is especially perspicuous. ... For simplicity I often stress the condition of moderate scarcity (among the objective circumstances), and that of mutual disinterest or individuals taking no interest in one another's interests (among the subjective circumstances). Thus, one can say, in brief, that the circumstances of justice obtain whenever mutually disinterested persons put forward conflicting claims to the division of social advantages under conditions of moderate scarcity [126—8].

The persons in the original situation have a good deal of general knowledge about their situation, but they have no particular knowledge. They are to choose under a "veil of ignorance" which ensures that

> no one knows his place in society, his class position or social status; nor does he know his fortune in the distribution of natural assets and abilities, his intelligence and strength, and the like. Nor, again, does anyone know his conception of the good, the particulars of his rational plan of life, or even the special features of his psychology such as his aversion to risk or liability to optimism or pessimism [137].

There is more that is unknown about the nature and circumstances of the particular society. But what is essential to my
argument may be summarized from the passage quoted: *no one
knows who he is*. And since no one knows who he is, or in what
circumstances he will be, each man is everyman—or no-man.
Thus

> it is clear that since the differences among the parties are
> unknown to them, and everyone is equally rational and
> similarly situated, each is convinced by the same arguments.
> Therefore, we can view the choice in the original position
> from the standpoint of one person selected at random. If
> anyone after due reflection prefers a conception of justice to
> another, then they all do, and a unanimous agreement can be
> reached [139].

This sufficiently specifies the original position. The next task
is to show why rational persons in this position are supposed to
choose Rawls' conception of justice, and more specifically, the
lexical difference principle.

3

In examining the derivation of the difference principle as the
object of choice by rational persons subject to the circumstances of justice in the original position, I shall not trace
Rawls' own argument. An analysis of that argument would
require an essay in itself, and would, I believe, reveal certain
weaknesses which my own account is intended to avoid. Thus I
depart from Rawls, not to weaken the statement of his case so
that it will prove more amenable to criticism, but to present the
lexical difference principle in the most favorable light possible.
    In the derivation, it is essential to focus on two different
standpoints. First, of course, is the standpoint of of the reasoner in the original position, choosing "behind a veil of ignorance"
[12]. But second, there is the standpoint of the reasoner after
the principle is chosen, the resulting society is instituted, and
the veil of ignorance if lifted. I want to insist that a principle
establishing the terms of association must be rational, not only

prospectively, but also retrospectively. By this I mean, not that the choice made in ignorance be the choice one would make, if one could, when one is aware of the actual circumstances governing the outcome, but that awareness of the outcome should not lead one to judge the original choice irrational, when one in imagination reimposes the constraints under which it was made. The choice must be rationally acceptable, in this sense, to each representative person after the veil of ignorance is lifted. This requirement is, it seems to me, implicit in Rawls' insistence "that the original position be interpreted so that one can at any time adopt its perspective [139]."

Consider first the method of rational choice for a person who knows who he is. Such a person would choose those principles which would maximize his expected benefits. He would attach, to each possible set of principles, an expected future, which would be the probability-weighted average of the possible futures which might result from adoption of the principles. Then to each expected future he would assign a value, or utility, indicating its expected benefits to him. He would then choose those principles which maximized this value.

But in the original position no one knows who he is, so it is everyman's reasoning that we must attempt to formulate. If everyman were to reason in a manner similar to a particular person, then he would attach, to each possible set of principles, a set of expected futures—one member of the set representing the expected future of each possible representative person, each person who he might turn out to be. To each such expected future he would assign a value, representing its expected benefits to the person in question. To each set of expected futures he would then assign an expected value, representing the probability-weighted average of the values of its members (the probabilities here corresponding to the likelihood of being each of the possible persons). This last expected value is then what he would maximize by his choice of principles. And thus he would choose the principle of average utilitarianism, and not the difference principle.

Rawls discusses average utilitarianism at some length (section 28), but without presenting objections to it that are, in my view, fully convincing. The best argument against it, and in favor of the difference principle, seems to me to arise from a consideration of the situation of the person who finds himself to be least advantaged, when the veil of ignorance is lifted. Unless all are equal, there must be some representative person who finds both that no one is worse off than he is, and that his utility is less than the probability-weighted average which he expected. How is he to convince himself that his choice of principles was rational?

Insofar as his misfortune depends on the actual circumstances, this poses no real problem. He had reason to expect the circumstances to be otherwise, more favorable to his well-being. He can envisage himself under those other circumstances, enjoying greater well-being. This expected alternative makes his actual sacrifice of well-being acceptable to him; the outcome is unlucky, no more. He recognizes that, given the information available to him, the choice that he made was best.

But insofar as his misfortune depends on who he is, the situation in which he now finds himself is a quite different one. For even if the supposition that he had reason to expect to be another, more favored, person is intelligible, yet he can not now envisage *himself* as that other person, enjoying greater well-being. He can of course envisage himself in the circumstances of another person, but this is not the alternative he expected, for *ex hypothesi* his well-being, and thus his circumstances, are to depend on who he is. He can also envisage some other person enjoying greater well-being, and this indeed is the relevant expected alternative, but it does not now make his sacrifice of well-being acceptable to him. Now that he knows who he is, he does not suppose that the choice which he made was best for him. He realizes instead that his ignorance of who he was rendered him unable to make a best choice for himself.

This argument is, as I have said, not to be found in Rawls. But he does suggest some part of it [173–5], especially in his insistence that

> the expectation finally arrived at in the reasoning for the average principle seems spurious . . .: it is not, as expectations should be, founded on one system of aims . . . [175].

If everyman chooses those principles which lead to the maximization of average expected utility, he does not *thereby* choose those principles which maximize the expected utility of any of the representative persons who he may turn out to be. It is not, of course, possible for him to choose principles which would maximize the expected utility of all of these persons, for the outcome which would maximize one representative person's expected utility does not in general coincide with the outcome which would maximize some other person's expected utility. What alternative then is open to everyman?

Everyman must choose principles in such a way that when the veil of ignorance is lifted, each representative person will consider that he would rationally so have chosen. Given the assumed connection between rationality and maximization of benefit, one condition which everyman's choice of principles must satisfy is that the outcome determined by the principles be such that no representative person could expect to receive greater benefits, without some other person expecting to receive lesser benefits. For if someone finds that he could have expected to do better, at no expected cost to anyone else, then he will not consider that he has chosen rationally. Optimality in the Pareto sense, or efficiency, as Rawls prefers to term it, is thus a condition on everyman's choice.

But there are usually many Pareto-optimal outcomes, and so, many principles which would satisfy this condition. A second condition on everyman's choice is then required, and arises from the initial equality of each person. Everyman may not choose princples which favor the well-being of one person over another, if his choice is to be acceptable to each representative person. Although the persons are free from envy, and hence do not value the benefits they receive by comparing them with those received by others, the rational acceptability of a principle assigning a particular person a given set of expected benefits will depend on the relationship of that set to the sets of benefits assigned to other persons. A person will not consider everyman's choice rationally acceptable, if the principles chosen afford him expected benefits less than those expected by some other person, except insofar as the inequality could not be rectified by increasing his own benefits, but *only* by reducing the benefits of the more favored person.

The least advantaged person will therefore consider the choice of principles rational, only if there are no alternative principles which could afford him greater benefits, while he remains the least advantaged person, and no way in which he could cease to be the least advantaged person, without someone else becoming at least as disadvantaged as he now is. Everyman, then, must choose principles such that the least advantaged representative person does as well as possible. The position of the second least advantaged may then be considered, and so on; thus it is evident that everyman must choose the lexical difference principle, to determine the procedure by which benefits are to be distributed among the members of society. Or in other words, everyman must select those principles whose adoption institutes a society in which optimal benefits are produced, and distributed equally, if equal distribution is optimal, and if not, distributed so that the least-favored representative person does as well as possible, and compatibly with this so that the second least-favored person does as well as possible, and so on. Thus it seems that Rawls' claim to derive his conception of justice, involving the difference principle, from the maximizing conception of rationality and the original position of ignorance is upheld. But in the next two sections I shall argue that Rawls does not characterize satisfactorily the way in which the lexical difference principle is to be applied to the distribution of benefits, and that a more satisfactory account puts the principle in a very different light.

4

The lexical difference principle is to regulate the distribution of those primary social goods which are classified as economic and social benefits. Some of these goods are the creation of society. But others, in particular economic benefits, must be available in some measure under any circumstances. Hence we may ask, how are these goods to be distributed in the absence of agreement on a principle of distribution? What if there is no social contract?

To ask this is to ask about the "No Agreement Point" [147]. Rawls distinguishes two views of this point, which he terms "general egoism" and "the state of nature." He supposes that the original position itself corresponds to the state of nature [v. 12] but holds that general egoism is the outcome of no agreement. Unfortunately, he does not discuss general egoism in terms of the behavior of rational persons. However, I shall assume that by general egoism is meant that condition in which each man seeks directly to secure as much as possible for himself. The distribution of primary social goods, insofar as they exist apart from agreement and society as instituted by agreement, is the result of egoistic activity on the part of each person.

This distribution can not be expected to be equal. The persons who make up society differ in their natural endowment, and differences in natural endowment will affect differentially men's ability to secure economic goods for themselves in the condition of general egoism. Hence the "no agreement point" will provide a different level of well-being for different persons, albeit a low level for everyone.

Behind the veil of ignorance, no man knows his natural abilities and talents, and hence no man knows what he would obtain in the absence of agreement. Yet each knows that he has certain natural abilities and talents, and that men differ in this endowment, so that in the absence of agreement men would secure different levels of well-being. It is therefore possible for everyman to take account of the "no agreement point" in his reasoning, even though no particular man knows how it will affect him.

The rationale for agreement is provided by the circumstances of justice. Men "view society as a cooperative venture for mutual advantage [520]." Through cooperation they are able to produce more of the primary goods which each wants. I shall term those primary goods produced through cooperation, the *social surplus*; it is that portion of the total quantity of primary social goods which would not be produced without cooperation. The content of the agreement men make must ensure the production and provide for the distribution of this social surplus.

We may distinguish three limiting ways in which the social surplus might be distributed:

First, the distribution may redress the natural imbalance of primary goods which each would receive as a consequence of his natural talents and abilities, in the condition of general egoism. The total quantity of primary goods would then be distributed to maximize the minimum share, in accordance with the lexical difference principle.

Second, the distribution may ignore the natural imbalance of primary goods, and maximize the minimum share of the social surplus. The lexical difference principle would still regulate distribution, but it would be applied, not to the total quantity of primary social goods, but only to the quantity produced as a result of social cooperation.

Third, the distribution may be proportionate to the shares of primary social goods which each would secure for himself under general egoism.

The third of these possibilities constitutes what seems to me the most plausible interpretation of natural aristocracy, although it is an interpretation differing from Rawls' [v. 74]. On this view society ought to benefit each man in accordance with his natural talents and abilities, where these assets are estimated by the success of each man in providing for himself in the absence of society. Rather than nullify the accidents of natural endowment, this mode of distribution takes these accidents to be the basis of social desert.

The first possibility is the opposite of the third; instead of taking natural endowment as the basis of desert, it regards natural endowment as undeserved. Thus it requires that natural inequalities be redressed, insofar as this can be achieved by an optimal outcome. This is indeed the mode of distribution favored by Rawls:

> . . . we may observe that the difference principle gives some weight to the considerations singled out by the principle of redress. This is the principle that undeserved inequalities call for redress; and since inequalities of birth and natural endowment are undeserved, these inequalities are to be somehow compensated for. . . . Now the principle of redress has not to my knowledge been proposed as the sole criterion of justice, . . . But whatever other principles we hold, the claims of redress are to be taken into account. It is thought to represent one of the elements in our conception of justice. . . . Thus although the difference principle is not the same as that of redress, it does achieve some of the intent of the latter principle. . . . We see then that the difference principle represents, in effect, an agreement to regard the distribution of natural talents as a common asset and to share in the benefits of this distribution whatever it turns out to be [100–1].

But it is surely mistaken to hold that natural inequalities are undeserved. They are not deserved, they do not accord with desert, but equally they are not undeserved, they are not

217

contrary to desert. In distributing the social surplus, natural inequalities, as shown by the differential abilities of men to secure benefits for themselves in the position of no agreement, should be ignored.

Redress, or nullification of the accidents of natural endowment, is not a constituent of any principle to which rational persons concerned to further their own interests would agree, to regulate the distribution of the fruits of their cooperation. If each person is to agree freely, on equal terms, to cooperate with his fellows, then each will expect an equal share of the benefits which are to be achieved as a result of cooperation. When the veil of ignorance is lifted, and each is aware, both of what primary social goods he could have expected under general egoism, and what goods he can expect as a result of the society instituted by agreement, then each will want as many *additional* goods as possible to accrue to himself. A man will not consider his agreement rational, if his share of these additional goods is less than that of some other person, unless (for no man is envious) greater equality could be achieved only by reducing the share of that other person, and not by increasing his own. Thus the man who receives the smallest share of the social surplus will consider the agreement rationally acceptable, only if it is not possible for the least-favored person to receive a larger share. The principle agreed to must then require the maximization of the minimum share of the social surplus, and compatibly with this, the maximization of the second minimum share, and so on; it must be the lexical difference principle applied strictly to the social surplus, without regard to the inequalities in the distribution of those benefits attainable in the absence of agreement.

An individual utility-maximizer will not consider it rational to accept a lower level of well-being in society simply to maximize average benefit; this is one of the crucial objections to average utilitarianism. But equally, such a person will not consider it rational to accept a smaller share of the benefits of cooperation—the social surplus—simply to increase overall equality of benefit. The conception of rationality which Rawls accepts without question, leads men to agreement on principles of cooperation which maximize the *social* minimum.

5

Among the conceptions of justice criticized by Rawls is the view

> that equal justice means that society is to make the same
> proportionate contribution to each person's realizing the best
> life which he is capable of [510].

Rawls considers this conception, which he finds in the writings
of Frankena and Findlay [510n.], objectionable, not only because of practical difficulties in applying the standard, but

> A more important difficulty is that the greater abilities of
> some may give them a stronger claim on social resources
> irrespective of compensating advantages to others. One must
> assume that variations in natural assets will affect what is
> necessary to provide equal proportionate assistance to those
> with different plans of life. But in addition to violating the
> principle of mutural advantage, this conception of equality
> means that the strength of men's claims is directly influenced
> by the distribution of natural abilities, and therefore by
> contingencies that are arbitrary from a moral point of view
> [510–1].

If we suppose that our sense of justice is characterized by
those principles which would be agreed to by rational utility-
maximizers, then we must agree that violation of the principle
of mutual advantage is unacceptable. Indeed, mutural advantage
provides one of the arguments behind the insistence that the
lexical difference principle must be applied to the social surplus;
if it were applied to the total sum of primary goods it would be
in principle possible for some person well-favored under general
egoism to receive no benefit from society. But mutual advantage is not violated if the difference principle is applied, not to
the absolute quantity of primary social goods which each representative person is to receive, but rather to the proportionate
contribution made by these goods to each person's well-being.
The question is how to measure a person's share of primary
social goods. Should the principle of distribution maximize the

minimum *quantity* of these goods, or should it maximize the minimum *extent* to which any person's best life is realized?

Differences in natural endowment will affect not only the level of benefits men can provide for themselves in the absence of agreement, but also the possible levels of benefits which can be provided through cooperation. Let us then attempt to develop a measure of the potential social effects of differences in natural endowment.

Consider, abstractly, all possible arrangements for producing and distributing a social surplus. Negative distributions are not permitted; under each arrangement, each person must expect benefits at least equal to those he would expect in the absence of agreement. Hence a weak requirement of mutual advantage will be satisfied. Now we may suppose that different arrangements will affect both the total size of the surplus produced, and the share of the surplus which each representative person receives. We may restrict our attention to those arrangements which are pareto-optimal, or efficient; each representative person will have his well-being maximized by some optimal arrangement.

Differences in natural talents and abilities will manifest themselves as differences in the maximum levels of well-being which different persons can attain. If we compare the well-being which accrues to the naturally intelligent, strong, and enterprising, under that arrangement maximally beneficial to such persons, with the well-being which accrues to the naturally dull, weak, and lazy, under that arrangement maximally beneficial to them, we shall find the former to be greater. Indeed, we may find that the naturally gifted do better than the naturally deprived, even under those arrangement which maximize benefits to the deprived, for it may well be that in order to maximize the absolute quantity of social goods accruing to the deprived, the gifted, who are primarily responsible for producing the social surplus, must be rewarded with an even greater quantity of these goods.

I shall term the maximum well-being which each representative person can expect, under that optimal social arrangment most favourable to him, his *social potential*. Social potential is then a measure of the potential social effects of differences in natural endowment. Behind the veil of ignorance, no man knows what his social potential is, but each knows that he has a social potential, and that social potential differs from person to person. Hence everyman may take social potential into account in his reasoning.

We may distinguish three limiting ways in which social potential may be considered in distributing the social surplus:

First, social potential may be ignored, so that the social surplus is distributed directly in accordance with the lexical difference principle. Rawls' interpretation of the difference principle would differ from this only in distributing all primary social goods, and not only the social surplus.

Second, the social surplus may be distributed to maximize the minimum degree to which any person's social potential is fulfilled; thus the lexical difference principle would apply to the proportionate contribution of primary social goods to well-being.

Third, social potential may be taken as the criterion of desert, so that the social surplus may be distributed to maximize the satisfaction of the person with greatest social potential, and so on.

The third of these possibilities again seems to provide a form of aristocracy, perhaps "social aristocracy" to distinguish it from the natural aristocracy mentioned in the previous section. Natural talents and abilities are taken as indicative of merit, and so rewarded. This view runs counter to our intuitive conception of justice, and also would not be accepted by rational persons in an initial condition of equality.

But such persons would consider the first possibility to be equally unsatisfactory, because it tends to nullify the effects of natural abilities, treating them as undeserved. We are, it must be remembered, considering what principles of association will be adopted by free and rational persons concerned to further their own interests. Each person will expect to receive as much benefit from society as any other person, except where such equality could be achieved only by a reduction in the other's benefits. But how will each measure the benefit he receives? The natural measure, I suggest, is provided by social potential. If one person achieves almost the best life of which he is capable, and another receives social goods which permit him but a small fraction of his potential best life, then the first will be judged to benefit more, whatever the actual quantity of primary social goods which each receives.

Consider once again the situation when the veil of ignorance is lifted. Under Rawls' interpretation of the difference principle, natural endowments are to be taken as a common asset, so that the ratio of benefit received to talent employed and effort expended will decrease, as talent and effort increase. Hence the naturally gifted man will find his talents and efforts directed primarily to the advantage of the naturally deprived. But he will see no reason why he should not benefit from his own capacities to the same extent as anyone else. He will consider any other arrangement unfavorably discriminatory in relation to his natural endowment. Thus he will not consider it rational to agree to principles which require him to accept a lesser proportionate benefit, simply to increase overall equality of absolute benefit.

I conclude, then, that men who are rational in the sense assumed by Rawls, and who find themselves subject to the circumstances of justice in a position of original equality, will agree to a system of social cooperation regulated by a difference principle which specifies that each is to receive such benefits as he would expect apart from agreement, and in addition, each is to receive that share of the social surplus of primary goods which ensures that the lowest level of realization of social potential is maximized, and, for equal lowest levels, that the second lowest level of realization of social potential is maximized, and so on. The object of rational agreement is the lexical difference principle applied to the distribution of the social surplus proportionate to social potential. I shall henceforth refer to this as the *proportionate difference principle*.

6

The proportionate difference principle gives rise to a very different type of society from that envisaged by Rawls. Rawls supposes "that a society is well-ordered when it is not only designed to advance the good of its members but when it is also effectively regulated by a public conception of justice [4–5]." Rawls argues that the principles chosen in the original position give rise to a well-ordered society, for these principles are both accepted by all the members of the society as the basis of their conduct and embodied in the institutions of the society. Thus he is able to say that "justice as fairness is framed to accord with this idea of society [454]." The amendments which I have

made in the difference principle do not affect this characterization. The proportionate difference principle, as the object of
rational agreement in the original position, can equally give rise
to a well-ordered society, in which the good of its members is
secured through the optimal production of benefits, and justice
is served in the distribution of these benefits to maximize the
minimum level of fulfillment. The public conception of justice
is different from that advocated by Rawls, but there is no
reason to suppose that it will be less effective in regulating the
activities of individuals, and the structure of the society's institutions.

But Rawls further supposes that

> the principles of justice are related to human sociability. The
> main idea is simply that a well-ordered society (correspond-
> ing to justice as fairness) is itself a form of social union.
> Indeed, it is a social union of social unions. Both characteris-
> tic features are present: the successful carrying out of just
> institutions is the shared final end of all the members of
> society, and these institutional forms are prized as good in
> themselves [527].

Rawls is thus able to distinguish the type of society instituted
through the choice of principles embodying the conception of
justice as fairness from what he terms "private society."

> Its chief features are first that the persons comprising it . . .
> have their own private ends which are either competing or
> independent, but not in any case complimentary. And sec-
> ond, institutions are not thought to have any value in them-
> selves . . . . Thus each person assesses social arrangements
> solely as a means to his private aims. . . . everyone prefers
> the most efficient scheme that gives him the largest share of
> assets [521].

As he goes on to point out: "The theory of competitive markets
is a paradigm description of this type of society [521–2]."

Private society, or civil society as (Rawls notes) Hegel terms
it, is of course the form of society depicted in the classical
contract theories of Hobbes and Locke. But Rawls wants to
disassociate his use of the contractual model from its historical

connection with this type of society. Kant, not Hobbes, is after all Rawls' paradigm. Thus he says:

It is sometimes contended that the contract doctrine entails that private society is the ideal, at least when the division of advantages satisfies a suitable standard of reciprocity. But this is not so, as the notion of a well-ordered society shows [522].

This argument is, however, fallacious. It is not the conception of a well-ordered society, but of a society based on justice as fairness, which is to be distinguished from the notion of private society. Of course a well-ordered society need not be a private society, but as I shall show presently, a private society may be well-ordered. Rawls' argument, then, must be that the contract doctrine does not entail private society because in a suitably defined state of nature, the product of the contract is a society regulated by the conception of justice as fairness. But the argument of the preceding sections of this paper has shown that the social contract does not lead to the conception of justice expressed in Rawls' difference principle, but rather to the conception expressed in the proportionate difference principle. We must therefore ask whether a society based on this principle is a social union, or rather a private society.

The answer is clear. It is precisely a competitive market society, the paradigm of private society, which is characterized by the proportionate difference principle. For the competitive market is the mechanism by which an optimal social surplus is produced and distributed in accordance with the contribution which each person makes. The one restriction which the proportionate difference principle imposes is that each person's initial position in the market must reflect only his natural endowment, and not such factors as inherited wealth. But this is only to say that the principle carries individualism to its extreme. It breaks down the inheritance relationship which is maintained in existing market societies but which in fact contradicts the individualist suppositions which constitute the rationale of these societies.

If it be agreed that the proportionate difference principle is in fact the object of agreement by free and rational persons in an initial position of equality, then the contract doctrine, properly interpreted, does require private society. Furthermore, since the proportionate difference principle leads to a well-ordered society, the contract doctrine requires a well-ordered private society. Not all forms of private society need be well-ordered; a market society in which the initial position of each person depends largely on his inheritance need not satisfy a public conception of justice. And of course not all well-ordered societies are private. But social union, or any other well-ordered non-private society, can not be derived from an agreement among rational persons in the circumstances of justice.

At this point one might entertain an objection to this argument. A defender of Rawls, who nevertheless accepted the derivation of the proportionate difference principle from Rawls' premises, might then insist that the appropriate conclusion to be drawn from the derivation is that Rawls' account of the initial situation must be amended. The proportionate difference principle is derived by supposing that in the initial situation everyone knows that there are differences in natural endowment, although no one knows his own endowment. To yield Rawls' conclusion, and so to make social union compatible with the contract doctrine, the initial situation should be redescribed to make such knowledge unavailable.

But would such an amended account of the initial situation be satisfactory? The original position must be such that the choice made in it by rational men will continue to be rationally acceptable to them when the veil of ignorance is lifted. It is surely evident that such men, concerned to further their own interests, will not consider a set of social institutions acceptable if these institutions do not give appropriate recognition to differences in natural endowment. Viewing society as the means for producing and distributing an optimal social surplus, rational men will only accept principles of distribution if they restrict their scope to the surplus, and apportion it in accordance with the contribution each makes to its production.

Hence it is not Rawls' account of the initial situation, but his account of rationality which prevents the derivation of his conception of justice. The proportionate difference principle is the necessary result of the maximizing conception of rationality, and is the basis of private society, of a strongly individualist form of competitive market society. The instrumental conception of rationality which Rawls assumes leads to an instrumental conception of human society, a conception which Rawls wishes to reject. Rawls' ideological framework leads to the liberal individualist conception of justice and of society, not to democratic equality and the conception of social union.

7

The proportionate difference principle expresses that conception of justice which is required by the maximizing conception of rationality fundamental to our society. If rationality and morality are to be reconciled within our own ideological and social framework, then this is the form which the reconciliation must take, insofar as the realm of justice is concerned. It is not the reconciliation which Rawls proposes, but that in itself is no argument against it. If affording each person those benefits which maximize the minimum level of fulfillment leads to conclusions which match our judgments in reflective equilibrium, then we have an adequate alternative to Rawls' theory of justice.

Now I have not argued, and in this paper I do not propose to argue, either for or against the adequacy of the revised conception of justice embodied in the proportionate difference principle. But suppose we find it inadequate. Suppose we find that justice as fairness fits our reflective judgments better than this alternative. Yet justice as fairness is incompatible with the maximizing conception of rationality. What positions are open to us?

There are, I believe, but three. The first is to maintain the conception of justice as fairness while admitting it to be, not independent of rationality, but actually incompatible with it—irrational. This option is perhaps heroic, but absurd. The second is to revise one's conception of justice, and so of morality, to conform to the maximizing conception of rationality. One abandons the attempt to achieve reflective equilibrium, and simply accepts those judgments about justice required by the proportionate difference principle, however much they depart from one's intuitions. This is the only possible response within the ideological framework assumed by Rawls, and by other proponents of the economic and social theories familiar in our society. The third response is to recognize that the maximizing account of rationality is not, as Rawls describes it, the concept of rationality, but only a conception, and to seek to bring one's conception of rationality into reflective equilibrium with one's conception of morality. But this alternative involves transcending the conceptual horizons of our society. In questioning what not only social theory but also social practice takes to be the concept of rationality, it questions our everyday awareness of ourselves as men-in-society.

That everyday awareness involves conceiving the individual, with his natural endowment, as being essentially apart from society, however dependent he may be on society for his actual existence and well-being. It involves conceiving society instrumentally, as private society, as a means to the satisfaction of non-socially characterized individuals. It involves the supposition that human activity is to be understood primarily in terms of the attainment of individual well-being. And practical rationality then is conceived, and must be conceived, as the activity of determining what to do, in order to maximize individual benefits. In short, the status assigned to the individual and his natural endowment, the conception of society, and the conception of rationality, are all linked into a single, unified account of what it is to be human, based on the liberal individualist ideological framework.

Perhaps the most evident weak point in this account is the separation of man's natural endowment from the structure of society—a separation which plays such a crucial role in the derivation of the proportionate difference principle. We need not deny that there are some extra-social differences among persons, based on genetic structure, but we may suppose these of much lesser importance in characterizing an individual than socially-determined differences. Instead of thinking of an individual's abilities and talents as a natural endowment brought to society, we may think of it as largely a social creation. The individual is then conceived, not as a being essentially apart from society, but rather as the product of society. And society is conceived, not primarily as an instrument for increasing the well-being of individuals, but rather as the framework within which human beings, with their characteristic differences in mental, physical, and emotional qualities, are created. Human activity is then to be understood primarily as the activity of creating human beings—not, of course, merely by physical reproduction but by the social development of human individuality. The ultimate form of this activity is self-determination, the shaping of oneself through the shaping of society. And practical rationality may then be conceived, not as the activity of maximizing individual benefits, but as the activity of conscious self-determination.

There are of course other ways of conceiving practical rationality. My concern is not to propose a particular alternative to Rawls' view, but rather to suggest that the question of our conception of rationality must be put on the agenda of moral philosophy. Rawls' argument, by its welcome rigour in comparison with the arguments of most moral philosophers, enables us to see that the attempt to reconcile morality with rationality leads to a critique of practical rationality. And such a critique can not stop short of an examination of the ideological framework within which we find our conceptions of man and society, reason and morality.

NOTE

1. The position which I develop here as a corrective to Rawls' views may be found, in a positive formulation based on game-theoretic concepts, in my paper, "Rational Cooperation," *Nous* 8 (1974), 53–65.

David Gauthier
Department of Philosophy
University of Toronto

MAXIMIN, UNCERTAINTY, AND THE
LEISURE TRADE-OFF

R. A. MUSGRAVE

The magnificent edifice erected in Rawls's *A Theory of Justice* has been of great interest to economists, partly because a major wing of the structure is assigned to economic issues, but mostly because an economic way of thinking enters into much of its grand design. The economist can feel pleased to see the use of his tools thus extended, but I wonder whether this penetration has not been carried too far. What is sauce for the goose may not be sauce for the gander. The following, therefore, is an economist's view drawn (without union card) from the philosopher's perspective.[1]

ROLE OF UNCERTAINTY

Next only to the primacy of liberty, the difference principle lays the foundation for Rawls's system of justice. Interpreted in terms of maximin, its application as a rule of optimal distribution has caught the fancy of economists in exploring its implications for redistribution policy.[2] The underlying propositions — i.e., (1) that decisions in the original state should be made in ignorance of a person's future position and (2) that choices are determined by risk preference — leave the economist in familiar territory. Given his aversion to interpersonal utility comparison and fascination with risk, a view of the social contract as optimization under uncertainty offers an appealing approach to the design of a social welfare function.[3] My question is how such emphasis on risk fits into a philosopher's theory of justice.

1. I have greatly benefited from several discussions with John Rawls, but errors of interpretation or reasoning remain mine.
2. I am aware that Rawls means the application of the maximin principle to be more general than to the distribution of goods only. The present note, however, is limited to this aspect, without claiming that its reasoning would apply to other objects of choice, e.g., choice of religion. For economic applications of the model see E. S. Phelps, "Taxation of Wage Income for Economic Justice," this *Journal*, LXXXVII (Aug. 1973), 331-55; and Robert C. Cooter and Elhanan Helpman, "Optimal Income Taxation for Transfer Payments Under Different Social Welfare Criteria," this *Journal*, LXXXVIII (Nov. 1974), 656-70.
3. For what appears to be the first formulation of this proposition see J. D. Harsanyi, "Cardinal Utility in Welfare Economics and Theory of Risk

To separate out the role of various conditions in arriving at maximin, we make three sets of distinctions, including (a) whether or not the risk aversion of individuals in the original state is in fact total; (b) whether or not they know their earnings capacities; and (c) whether or not they may use such knowledge as they possess. In each case individuals participating in the decision process will vote their self-interest in determining what the state of distribution shall be.[4] The various possibilities and outcomes may then be tabulated as shown in the following table.

Risk aversion		Earnings capacities		
		Unknown	Known and unequal	
			Act as if unknown	Act accordingly
Infinite		(1)	(4)	
Less than infinite {	Act accordingly	(2)	(5)	(7)
	Act as if total	(3)	(6)	

Case (1) supposes that differential capacities are unknown and that risk aversion is infinite. The Rawlsian rule of maximin is then arrived at by utility maximization under uncertainty. This outcome is found to be just because it meets moral axioms such as equal worth of individuals and self-esteem and because it translates the accidental fortunes of unequal earnings capacities into a social asset. But given the assumptions of ignorance and infinite risk aversion, this solution is arrived at without any tension between self-interest narrowly defined and justice. It becomes the outcome of natural harmony. Though still a beautiful thought, this seems hardly the foundation of a contemporary theory of justice, applicable to a world that is above all characterized by conflict.

Now it might be argued that such tension need not prevail in the original position. It might "precede" this position, with the

---

Taking," *Journal of Political Economy*, LXI (Oct. 1953), 434–35. See also Harsanyi, "Cardinal Welfare, Individualistic Ethics, and Interpersonal Comparisons of Utility," *Journal of Political Economy*, LXIII (Aug. 1955), 309–21. A similar formulation was used by William Vickrey, "Utility, Strategy, and Social Decision Rules," this *Journal*, LXXIV (Nov. 1960), 507–535.

4. The implicit assumption throughout is that differential abilities will be translated into corresponding income differentials by application of some factor pricing rule, e.g., compensation in line with marginal productivity.

acceptance of equal worth made a precondition for participation;[5] or, it might "follow," when the individual comes to be confronted with the choice between obeying or circumventing the constitution as laid down in that position. Either solution, it seems to me, unduly narrows and sterilizes the original position process. The former simply moves the essential problem to an earlier stage. The latter, which is more in Rawls's spirit, seems to rest on too sharp a distinction between constitution making and its application. While it makes sense, as a matter of economy, to avoid reconstructing the social order every time that a trivial decision is made and hence to render such decisions in a constitutional framework, constitutions can be amended, and the process of constitution making (as indeed the original position) becomes a more or less continuing process.

All this was based on the assumption that risk aversion is indeed infinite. This, however, is unlikely. Even though the stakes are great, people may well wish to trade a reduction in the assured floor against the provision of larger gains. But if risk aversion is less than infinite, the outcome will not be maximin. A lesser degree of equality will result (case (2)), depending on the spread of risk preferences and on bargaining skills. The outcome will thereby lose its appeal of conforming to the broader axioms of justice that Rawls requires. To derive the maximin result under such conditions, it might be argued that individuals in the original state should act as if their risk aversion was infinite. The result (case (3)) will then be the same as under (1), and our previous concern regarding absence of tension no longer applies. This construction, however, would be rather forced. Since there is no intrinsic good in infinite risk aversion, the requirement to act as if it applied would be sanctioned only by the result of maximin. It would be simpler therefore, to require directly that maximin be accepted in the initial position, based on the axioms of equal worth and self-esteem from which it derives its sanction. In this case the procedure of optimizing under uncertainty becomes redundant, and the solution (case (8)) falls outside the preceding matrix.

Leaving the shape of risk preference, we now turn to the veil of ignorance. So far we have assumed that this veil does in fact apply, i.e., that people in the original position do not know their capacities and future potential. But this is an unlikely assumption, especially if we think of the state of nature not as an initial historical event,

5. For the former interpretation see Ronald Dworkin, "The Original Position," *University of Chicago Law Review*, XL (Spring 1973), 537.

but (as Rawls would have us) as a Gedankenexperiment to be made by people who already occupy a real-world position. If instead we postulate that differential earnings capacities are in fact known, we are left with two possibilities. One is to permit self-interested action (case (7)), leading to a result that depends on differentials in earnings capacity and on bargaining skills. Again, varying degrees of inequality might emerge, which may or may not conform with the maxims of a good society and which may or may not carry a moral sanction.[6]

Another possibility would be to adopt the axiom that people in the original state should act "as if" their earnings capacities were unknown to them. As distinct from a requirement to act as if risk aversion was infinite (case (3)), this requirement has a meaningful axiomatic foundation. To overlook one's earnings capacity is to act without self-interest. Provided that risk aversion is in fact infinite (case (4)), maximin is arrived at and in a more meaningful fashion than in case (1), since the element of tension is introduced by acceptance of the veil of ignorance. Note, however, that the maximin solution works only if risk aversion is in fact infinite. Since this is a forced assumption, we are pushed to case (5), where maximin does not follow or to case (6), which is open to the objections raised previously against case (3).

We are thus left with the conclusion that the veil of ignorance hypothesis — though appealing if accepted while abilities are known — is not enough to carry the day. Maximin follows only if combined with an "as if" acceptance of infinite risk aversion. Since this is an artificial formulation, we again conclude that maximin (and its acceptance in the original state) should be deduced directly from the more general axioms (such as equal worth, self-esteem, stability, and harmony) already contained in Rawls's system, rather than be derived from a model of optimizing under uncertainty. The uncertainty model, if such an exercise is to be retained, then changes its nature. Maximin becomes the predetermined variable in the system, and the role of the model is merely to find the pattern of risk preference under which maximin (or some other justice norm) would follow from optimization under uncertainty. In short, the veil of ignorance hypothesis is attractive as a device for securing a disinterested view of the good society, but the formulation of justice as a problem of optimizing behavior under uncer-

---

6. Edgeworth (*Papers Relating to Political Economy*; London: Macmillan, 1925, Vol. II) surmises that such bargaining would lead to a modification of the utilitarian (greatest happiness) solution such as to "conduce the greatest sum-total welfare of both parties, subject to the condition that neither should lose by the contract" (p. 102).

tainty, while fun and games for the economist, does not solve the essential issue.

Can the Maximin Principle Serve as a Basis for Morality? A Critique of John Rawls's Theory

JOHN C. HARSANYI

*University of California, Berkeley**

1. Introduction

John Rawls's *A Theory of Justice*[1] is an important book. It is an attempt to develop a viable alternative to *utilitarianism*, which up to now in its various forms was virtually the only ethical theory proposing a reasonably clear, systematic, and purportedly rational concept of morality. I shall argue that Rawls's attempt to suggest a viable alternative to utilitarianism does not succeed. Nevertheless, beyond any doubt, his book is a significant contribution to the ongoing debate on the nature of rational morality.

Rawls distinguishes two major traditions of systematic theory in post medieval moral philosophy. One is the *utilitarian* tradition, represented by Hume, Adam Smith, Bentham, John Stuart Mill, Sidgwick, Edgeworth, and many others, including a number of contemporary philosophers and social scientists. The other is the *contractarian* (social-contract) tradition of Locke, Rousseau, and Kant. The latter has never been developed as systematically as the utilitarian tradition, and, clearly, one of Rawls's objectives is to remedy this situation. He regards his own theory as a generalization of the classical contractarian position, and as its restatement at a higher level of abstraction (p. 11).

Rawls argues that the "first virtue" of social institutions (i.e., the most fundamental moral requirement they ought to satisfy) is *justice* (or *fairness*). Suppose that all members of a society—or, more precisely, all "heads of families" (p. 128; *pace* Women's Lib!)—have to agree on the general principles that are to govern the institutions of their society. All of them are supposed to be rational individuals caring only about their own personal interests (and those of their own descendants). But, in order to ensure that they would reach a fair-minded agreement (p. 12), Rawls assumes that they would have to negotiate with each other under what he calls the *veil of ignorance*, i.e., without knowing their own social and economic positions, their own special interests in the society, or even their own personal talents and abilities (or their lack of them). This hypothetical situation in which all participants would have to agree on the most basic institutional arrangements of their society while under this veil of ignorance, is called by Rawls the *original position*. In his theory, this purely hypothetical—and rather abstractly defined—original position replaces the historical or semi-historical "social contract" of earlier contractarian philosophers. He considers the institutions of a given society to be *just* if they are organized according to the principles that presumably would have been agreed upon by rational individuals in the original position (p. 17).

What decision rule would rational individuals use in the original position in deciding whether a given set of institutions was or was not acceptable to them? In the terminology of modern decision theory, the initial position would be a situation of *uncertainty* because, by assumption, the participants would be uncertain about what their personal circumstances would be under any particular institutional framework to be agreed upon.

There are two schools of thought about the decision rule to be used by a rational person under uncertainty. One proposes the *maximin principle*, or some generalization or modification of this principle, as the appropriate decision rule.[2] From the mid-'forties (when the problem first attracted wider attention) to the mid-'fifties this was the prevailing opinion. But then came a growing realization that the maximin principle and all its relatives lead to serious paradoxes because they often suggest wholly unacceptable practical decisions.[3] The other—Bayesian—school of thought, which is now dominant, proposes *expected-utility maximization* as decision rule under uncertainty.[4]

In my opinion, the concept of the original posi-

* This paper has been supported by Grant GS-3222 of the National Science Foundation, through the Center for Research in Management Science, University of California, Berkeley.
[1] Cambridge, Mass.: Harvard University Press, 1971.

[2] See Abraham Wald, *Statistical Decision Functions* (New York: John Wiley & Sons, 1950); Leonid Hurwicz, "Optimality Criteria for Decision Making Under Ignorance," *Cowles Commission Discussion Paper*, Statistics #370 (1951, mimeographed); and Leonard J. Savage, "The Theory of Statistical Decision," *Journal of the American Statistical Association*, 46 (March, 1951), 55–67.
[3] See Roy Radner and Jacob Marschak, "Note on Some Proposed Decision Criteria," in R. M. Thrall, C. H. Coombs, and R. L. Davis, eds., *Decision Processes* (New York: John Wiley & Sons, 1954), pp. 61–68.
[4] See, e.g., Leonard J. Savage, *The Foundations of Statistics* (New York: John Wiley & Sons, 1954).

tion is a potentially very powerful analytical tool for clarifying the concept of justice and other aspects of morality. In actual fact, this concept played an essential role in my own analysis of moral value judgements,[5] prior to its first use by Rawls in 1957[6] (though I did not use the term "original position"). But the usefulness of this concept crucially depends on its being combined with a satisfactory decision rule. Unfortunately, Rawls chooses the maximin principle as decision rule for the participants in the original position. By the very nature of the maximin principle, this choice cannot fail to have highly paradoxical implications.

2. The Maximin Principle and its Paradoxes

Suppose you live in New York City and are offered two jobs at the same time. One is a tedious and badly paid job in New York City itself, while the other is a very interesting and well paid job in Chicago. But the catch is that, if you wanted the Chicago job, you would have to take a plane from New York to Chicago (e.g., because this job would have to be taken up the very next day). Therefore there would be a very small but positive probability that you might be killed in a plane accident. Thus, the situation can be represented by the following double-entry table:

reasons other than a plane accident can be taken to be zero.) In contrast, if you choose the Chicago job then the worst possible outcome will be that you may die in a plane accident. Thus, the worst possible outcome in the first case would be much better than the worst possible outcome in the second case. Consequently, if you want to follow the maximin principle then you must choose the New York job. Indeed, you must not choose the Chicago job *under any condition*—however unlikely you might think a plane accident would be, and however strong your preference might be for the excellent Chicago job.

Clearly, this is a highly irrational conclusion. Surely, if you assign a low enough probability to a plane accident, and if you have a strong enough preference for the Chicago job, then by all means you should take your chances and choose the Chicago job. This is exactly what Bayesian theory would suggest you should do.

If you took the maximin principle seriously then you could not ever cross a street (after all, you might be hit by a car); you could never drive over a bridge (after all, it might collapse); you could never get married (after all, it might end in a disaster), etc. If anybody really acted this way he would soon end up in a mental institution.

Conceptually, the basic trouble with the maxi-

	If the N.Y.–Chicago plane has an accident	If the N.Y.–Chicago plane has no accident
If you choose the N.Y. job	You will have a poor job, but will stay alive	You will have a poor job, but will stay alive
If you choose the Chicago job	You will die	You will have an excellent job and will stay alive

The maximin principle says that you must evaluate every policy available to you in terms of the *worst possibility* that can occur to you if you follow that particular policy. Therefore, you have to analyze the situation as follows. If you choose the New York job then the worst (and, indeed, the only) possible outcome will be that you will have a poor job but you will stay alive. (I am assuming that your chances of dying in the near future for

---

[5] See John C. Harsanyi, "Cardinal Utility in Welfare Economics and in the Theory of Risk-Taking," *Journal of Political Economy*, 61 (October, 1953), 434–435; and "Cardinal Welfare, Individualistic Ethics, and Interpersonal Comparisons of Utility," *Journal of Political Economy*, 63 (August, 1955), 309–321.
[6] John Rawls, "Justice as Fairness," *Journal of Philosophy*, 54 (October, 1957), 653–662; and "Justice as Fairness," *Philosophical Review*, 67 (April, 1958), 164–194. The 1957 paper is a shorter version of the 1958 paper with the same title.

min principle is that it violates an important continuity requirement: It is extremely irrational to make your behavior wholly dependent on some highly unlikely unfavorable contingencies *regardless of how little probability you are willing to assign to them.*

Of course, Rawls is right when he argues that in *some* situations the maximin principle will lead to reasonable decisions (pp. 154–156). But closer inspection will show that this will happen only in those situations where the maximin principle is essentially *equivalent* to the expected-utility maximization principle (in the sense that the policies suggested by the former will yield expected-utility levels as high, or almost as high, as the policies suggested by the latter would yield). Yet, the point is that in cases where the two principles suggest policies very dissimilar in their consequences so that they are far from being equivalent, it is always the expected-utility maximization principle that is found on closer inspection to suggest reasonable policies, and it as always the maximin principle that is found to suggest unreasonable ones.

3. The Maximin Principle in the Original Position

In the last section I have argued that the maximin principle would often lead to highly irrational decisions in everyday life. This is already a sufficient reason for rejecting it as a decision rule appropriate for the original position. This is so because the whole point about the concept of the original position is to imagine a number of individuals ignorant of their personal circumstances and then to assume that under these conditions of ignorance they would act in a *rational manner*, i.e., in accordance with some decision rule which consistently leads to reasonable decisions under ignorance and uncertainty. But, as we have seen, the maximin principle is most definitely *not* a decision rule of this kind.

Yet, after considering the performance of the maximin principle in everyday life, I now propose to consider explicitly the more specific question of how well this principle would perform in the original position itself. In particular, do we obtain a satisfactory concept of justice if we imagine that the criteria of justice are chosen by people in the original position in accordance with the maximin principle?

As Rawls points out, use of the maximin principle in the original position would lead to a concept of justice based on what he calls the *difference principle*, which evaluates every possible institutional arrangement in terms of the interests of the *least advantaged* (i.e., the poorest, or otherwise worst-off) individual (pp. 75–78). This is so because in the original position nobody is assumed to know what his own personal situation would be under any specific institutional arrangement. Therefore, he must consider the possibility that he might end up as the worst-off individual in the society. Indeed, according to the maximin principle, he has to evaluate any particular institutional framework *as if* he were *sure* that this was exactly what would happen to him. Thus, he must evaluate any possible institutional framework by identifying with the interests of the worst-off individual in the society.[7]

Now, I propose to show that the difference

[7] In cases where a more specific principle is necessary, Rawls favors the *lexicographical* difference principle: In comparing two possible societies, first compare them from the point of view of the *worst-off* individual. If they turn out to be equally good from his point of view, then compare them from the point of view of the *second-worst-off* individual. If this still does not break the tie, then compare them from the point of view of the *third-worst-off* individual, etc.

principle often has wholly unacceptable moral implications. As a first example, consider a society consisting of one doctor and two patients, both of them critically ill with pneumonia. Their only chance to recover is to be treated by an antibiotic, but the amount available suffices only to treat one of the two patients. Of these two patients, individual A is a basically healthy person, apart from his present attack of pneumonia. On the other hand, individual B is a terminal cancer victim but, even so, the antibiotic could prolong his life by several months. Which patient should be given the antibiotic? According to the difference principle, it should be given to the cancer victim, who is obviously the less fortunate of the two patients.

In contrast, utilitarian ethics—as well as ordinary common sense—would make the opposite suggestion. The antibiotic should be given to A because it would do "much more good" by bringing him back to normal health than it would do by slightly prolonging the life of a hopelessly sick individual.

As a second example, consider a society consisting of two individuals. Both of them have their material needs properly taken care of, but society still has a surplus of resources left over. This surplus can be used either to provide education in higher mathematics for individual A, who has a truly exceptional mathematical ability, and has an all-consuming interest in receiving instruction in higher mathematics. *Or*, it could be used to provide remedial training for individual B, who is a severely retarded person. Such training could achieve only trivial improvements in B's condition (e.g., he could perhaps learn how to tie his shoelaces); but presumably it would give him some minor satisfaction. Finally, suppose it is not possible to divide up the surplus resources between the two individuals.

Again, the difference principle would require that these resources should be spent on B's remedial training, since he is the less fortunate of the two individuals. In contrast, both utilitarian theory and common sense would suggest that they should be spent on A's education, where they would accomplish "much more good," and would create a much deeper and much more intensive human satisfaction.[8]

Even more disturbing is the fact that the difference principle would require us to give *absolute* priority to the interests of the worst-off individual, *no matter what*, even under the most extreme conditions. Even if his interest were affected only in a very minor way, and all other individuals in society had opposite interests of the greatest impor-

[8] This argument of course presupposes the possibility of interpersonal utility comparisons, at least in a rough and ready sense. I shall discuss the possibility of such comparisons in Section 8 on page 600.

tance, his interests would always override anybody else's. For example, let us assume that society would consist of a large number of individuals, of whom one would be seriously retarded. Suppose that some extremely expensive treatment were to become available, which could very slightly improve the retarded individual's condition, but at such high costs that this treatment could be financed only if some of the most brilliant individuals were deprived of all higher education. The difference principle would require that the retarded individual should all the same receive this very expensive treatment at any event—*no matter how many* people would have to be denied a higher education, and *no matter how strongly* they would desire to obtain one (and no matter how great the satisfaction they would derive from it).

Rawls is fully aware that the difference principle has implications of this type. But he feels these are morally desirable implications because in his view they follow from Kant's principle that people should "treat one another not as means only but as ends in themselves" (p. 179). If society were to give priority to A's interests over B's on the utilitarian grounds that by satisfying A's interests "more good" or "more utility" or "more human satisfaction" would be produced (e.g., because A could derive a greater benefit from medical treatment, or from education, or from whatever else), this would amount to "treating B as means only, and not as end in himself."

To my own mind, this is a very artificial and very forced interpretation of the Kantian principle under discussion. The natural meaning of the phrase "treating B as means only, and not as end in himself" is that it refers to using B's *person*, i.e., his mental or physical faculties or his body itself, as *means* in the service of other individuals' interests, without proper concern for B's own interests. One would have to stretch the meaning of this phrase quite a bit even in order to include an unauthorized use of B's material *property* (as distinguished from his person) in the service of other individuals.

This, however, is still not the case we are talking about. We are talking about B's merely being *denied* the use of certain resources over which he has no prior property rights, and this is done on the ground that other individuals have "greater need" for these resources, i.e., can derive greater utility from them (and let us assume, as may very well be the case, that almost all impartial observers would agree that this was so). But there is no question at all of using B's person or property for the benefit of other individuals. Therefore, it is very hard to understand how the situation could be described as "treating B as a means only, and not as end in himself."

In any case, even if we did accept such an unduly broad interpretation of the Kantian principle, the argument would certainly cut both ways—and indeed, it would go much more against the difference principle than in favor of it. For suppose we accept the argument that it would be a violation of the Kantian principle if we gave priority to a very important need of A over a relatively unimportant need of B, because it would amount to treating B as a mere means. Then, surely, the opposite policy of giving absolute priority to B's *unimportant* need will be an even stronger violation of the Kantian principle and will amount *a fortiori* to treating A now as a mere means rather than as an end.

4. Do Counterexamples Matter?

Most of my criticism of Rawls's theory up to now has been based on counterexamples. How much weight do arguments based on counterexamples have? Rawls himself seems to have considerable reservations about such arguments. He writes (p. 52): "Objections by way of counterexamples are to be made with care, since these may tell us only what we know already, namely that our theory is wrong somewhere. The important thing is to find out how often and how far it is wrong. All theories are presumably mistaken in places. The real question at any given time is which of the views already proposed is the best approximation overall."

To be sure, counterexamples to some minor details of an ethical theory may not prove very much. They may prove no more than that the theory needs correction in some minor points, and this fact may have no important implications for the basic principles of the theory. But it is a very different matter when the counterexamples are directed precisely against the most fundamental principles of the theory, as are the maximin principle and the difference principle for Rawls's theory. In this case, if the counterexamples are valid, it can only mean that the theory is *fundamentally* wrong.

Admittedly, all my counterexamples refer to rather special situations. It is quite possible that, in *most* everyday situations posing no special problems, Rawls's theory would yield quite reasonable practical conclusions. Indeed, it is my impression that in most situations the practical implications of Rawls's theory would not be very different from those of utilitarian theories. But of course, if we want to *compare* Rawls's theory with utilitarian theories in order to see which of the two yields more reasonable practical conclusions, we have to concentrate on those cases where they yield significantly different conclusions.

Clearly, as far as Rawls's theory often has implications similar to those of utilitarian theories,

I must agree with his point that counterexamples do not prove that his theory does not have at least *approximate* validity in most cases. But my understanding is that Rawls claims more than approximate validity *in this sense* for his theory. Though he does not claim that his theory is absolutely correct in every detail, he does explicitly claim that at the very least the basic principles of his theory yield more satisfactory results than the basic principles of utilitarian theories do. Yet, in my opinion, my counterexamples rather conclusively show that the very opposite is the case.

5. An Alternative Model of Moral Value Judgments

All difficulties outlined in Section 3 can be avoided if we assume that the decision rule used in the original position would not be the maximin principle but would rather be the expected-utility maximization principle of Bayesian theory.

In the two papers already quoted,[9] I have proposed the following model. If an individual expresses his preference between two alternative institutional arrangements, he will often base his preference largely or wholly on his personal interests (and perhaps on the interests of his family, his friends, his occupational group, his social class, etc.). For instance, he may say: "I know that under capitalism I am a wealthy capitalist, whereas under socialism I would be at best a minor government official. Therefore, I prefer capitalism." This no doubt would be a very natural judgment of personal preference from his own point of view. But it certainly would not be what we would call a *moral* value judgment by him about the relative merits of capitalism and socialism.

In contrast, most of us will admit that he would be making a moral value judgment if he chose between the two social systems *without knowing* what his personal position would be under either system. More specifically, let us assume that society consists of n individuals, and that the individual under consideration would choose between the two alternative social systems on the assumption that under either system he would have the same probability, $1/n$, of taking the place of the best-off individual, or the second-best-off individual, or the third-best-off individual, etc., up to the worst-off individual. This I shall call the *equiprobability assumption*. Moreover, let us assume that in choosing between the two social systems he would use the principle of expected-utility maximization as his decision rule. (This is my own version of the concept of the "original position.")

It is easy to verify that under these assumptions

[9] Harsanyi, "Cardinal Utility . . . ," and Harsanyi, "Cardinal Welfare. . . ."

our individual would always choose that social system which, in his opinion, would yield the higher *average utility level* to the individual members of the society. More generally, he would evaluate every possible social arrangement (every possible social system, institutional framework, social practice, etc.) in terms of the average utility level likely to result from it. This criterion of evaluation will be called the *principle of average utility*.

Of course, in real life, when people express a preference for one social arrangement over another, they will often have a fairly clear idea of what their own personal position would be under both. Nevertheless, we can say that they are expressing a *moral value judgment*, or that they are expressing a *moral preference* for one of these social arrangements, if they make a serious effort to *disregard* this piece of information, and make their choice *as if* they thought they would have the same probability of taking the place of any particular individual in the society.

Thus, under this model, each individual will have two different sets of preferences: he will have a set of *personal preferences*, which may give a particularly high weight to his personal interests (and to those of his close associates); and he will have a set of *moral preferences*, based on a serious attempt to give the same weight to the interests of every member of the society, in accordance with the principle of average utility.

While Rawls's approach yields a moral theory in the contractarian tradition, my own model yields a moral theory based on the principle of average utility and, therefore, clearly belonging to the utilitarian tradition.

6. Rawls's Objection to Using Probabilities in the "Original Position"

Rawls discusses my model primarily in Chapters 27 and 28 of his book. One of his critical comments is directed against my use of probabilities in the original position, in the form of the equiprobability assumption. He does not object to the equiprobability assumption as such *if* probabilities are to be used at all. He accepts Laplace's principle of indifference in the limited sense that in a situation of complete ignorance, *if* we want to use probabilities at all, *then* it is reasonable to assign equal probabilities to all possibilities (p. 169).[10] What he objects to is the very use of probabilities in the original position, and

[10] My equiprobability assumption obviously can be regarded as an application of the principle of indifference. But it also has another possible interpretation. It may be regarded as an expression of the purely *moral* principle that, in making basic moral value judgments, we must give the same *a priori* weight to the interests of all members of the society.

in all those cases where these probabilities are not based on empirical evidence. That is, he objects to using *subjective* probabilities or even *logical* probabilities,[11] in the absence of *empirical* probabilities estimated on the basis of empirical facts. (He does not insist, however, that these empirical probabilities should be estimated on the basis of observed statistical frequencies. He is willing to accept more indirect empirical evidence.)

The need and justification for using subjective probabilities have been extensively discussed by Bayesian decision theorists.[12] But Rawls makes no attempt to refute their arguments. Here I shall make only two points.

(a) The only alternative to using subjective probabilities, as required by Bayesian theory, would be to use a decision rule chosen from the maximin-principle family; and, as I have argued (in Section 2), all these decision rules are known to lead to highly irrational decisions in important cases.

(b) Bayesian decision theory shows by rigorous mathematical arguments that any decision maker whose behavior is consistent with a few—very compelling—rationality postulates simply *cannot help* acting *as if* he used subjective probabilities. (More precisely, he cannot help acting *as if* he tried to maximize his expected utility, computed on the basis of some set of subjective probabilities.) I shall quote only two of these rationality postulates: (1) "If you prefer A to B, and prefer B to C, then consistency requires that you should also prefer A to C"; (2) "You are better off if you are offered a *more valuable* prize with a given probability, than if you are offered a *less valuable* prize with the same probability." The other rationality postulates of Bayesian theory are somewhat more technical, but are equally compelling.

To illustrate that a rational decision maker simply *cannot help* using subjective probabilities, at least implicitly, suppose I offered you a choice between two alternative bets and said: "*Either*, I shall pay you $100 if candidate X *wins* the next election, and shall pay you nothing if he does not. *Or* I shall pay you $100 if he does *not* win, and pay you nothing if he does. Which of the two bets do you choose?"

First of all, it would be clearly irrational for you to refuse both bets, because *some* chance of obtaining $100 is surely better than no chance at all—since you can get this chance for free. So, if you are rational, you will choose one of the two bets. Now, if you choose the first bet then I can

infer that (at least implicitly) you are assigning a subjective probability of 1/2 or *higher* to Mr. X's winning the next election. On the other hand, if you choose the second bet then I can infer that (at least implicitly) you are assigning a subjective probability of 1/2 or *lower* to Mr. X's winning the election. Thus, whichever way your choice goes, it will amount to choosing a subjective probability for Mr. X's winning the election—either a probability in the range [1/2, 1], or one in the range [0, 1/2].

By the same token, if a decision maker follows the maximin principle, he is not really avoiding a choice of subjective probabilities, at least implicitly. Of course, he may not think explicitly in terms of probabilities at all. But, whether he likes it or not, his behavior will really amount to assigning probability one (or nearly one) to the worst possibility in any given case. He may very well regard the task of choosing subjective probabilities as a rather burdensome responsibility: but he has no way of escaping this responsibility. For instance, if his reliance on the maximin principle results in a foolish decision because it amounts to grossly overestimating the probability of the worst possibility, then he cannot escape the consequences of this foolish decision. (He certainly cannot escape the consequences by saying that he has never explicitly assigned any numerical probability to the worst possibility at all; and that in actual fact he acted in this foolish way only because he wanted to avoid any explicit choice of numerical probabilities.)

Rawls also argues that a given individual's actions in the original position will be easier to justify to other people, including his own descendants, if these actions are based on the maximin principle, than if they are based on the equiprobability assumption (p. 169). But it seems to me that the exact opposite is the case.

As we have seen (cf. Footnote 10), the equiprobability assumption can be justified by the principle of indifference, and also by the moral principle of assigning the same *a priori* weight to every individual's interests. On the other hand, using the maximin principle in the original position is equivalent to assigning unity or near-unity probability to the possibility that one may end up as the worst-off individual in society; and, as far as I can see, there cannot be any rational justification whatever for assigning such an extremely high probability to this possibility.

Rawls's argument becomes much more convincing if it is turned around. If the original position were an historical fact, then any person, other than the worst-off individual in society, would have a legitimate complaint against his ancestor if the latter in the original position voted for an institutional arrangement giving undue priority to

---

[11] Following Carnap, by logical probabilities I mean subjective probabilities completely determined by symmetry considerations (if appropriate symmetry postulates are added to the standard rationality postulates of Bayesian theory).

[12] See footnote 4.

the interests of the worst-off individual. (For instance, to take the examples discussed in Section 3, he would have a legitimate complaint if his ancestor's vote in the original position now had the effect of depriving him of some life-saving drug, or of a much-desired higher education, etc.)

7. Do von Neumann-Morgenstern Utility Functions have any Place in Ethics?

In my model, every person making a moral value judgment will evaluate any institutional arrangement in terms of the average utility level it yields for the individual members of the society, i.e., in terms of the arithmetic mean of these individuals' von Neumann-Morgenstern ($=$vNM) utility functions.[13] This means that, under my theory, people's vNM utility functions enter into the very definition of justice and other moral values. Rawls objects to this aspect of my theory on the ground that vNM utility functions basically express people's attitudes toward risk-taking, i.e., towards gambling—and these attitudes have no moral significance. Therefore, Rawls argues, vNM utility functions should not enter into our definitions of moral values (pp. 172 and 323).

This objection is based on a misinterpretation of vNM utility functions, which is unfortunately fairly widespread in the literature. To be sure, the vNM utility function of any given individual is estimated from his choice behavior under risk and uncertainty. But this does not mean that his vNM utility function is *merely* an indication of his attitudes toward risk taking. Rather, as its name shows, it is a utility function, and more specifically, it is what economists call a cardinal utility function. This means that the primary task of a vNM utility function is *not* to express any individual's attitudes toward risk taking; rather, it is to indicate how much utility, i.e., how much subjective *importance*, he assigns to various goals.

For example, suppose we find that a given individual is willing to gamble at very unfavorable odds—say, he is willing to pay $5 for a lottery ticket giving him a 1/1000 chance of winning $1000. This allows us the inference that his vNM utility function assigns (at least) 1000 times as much utility to $1000 as it assigns to $5. Thus, the theory of vNM utility functions suggests the following explanation for this individual's willingness to gamble at unfavorable odds: he is acting this way because he is attaching unusually *high* importance to getting $1000, and is attaching unusually *low* importance to losing $5. More generally, people are willing to gamble at unfavorable odds, if they feel they would need a large sum of

money *very badly* (but do not care too much about losing a small sum of money).

Consequently, vNM utility functions have a completely legitimate place in ethics because they express the subjective importance people attach to their various needs and interests. For example, I cannot see anything wrong with a concept of justice which assigns high priority to providing university education for a given individual partly on the ground that he attaches very high *utility* to receiving such an education (i.e., wants to receive one very badly)—as shown by the fact that he would be prepared to face very considerable personal and financial *risks*, if he had to, in order to obtain a university education.

8. Do Interpersonal Utility Comparisons Make Sense?

Rawls objects to the use of interpersonal utility comparisons in defining justice (p. 173). In contrast, my own model makes essential use of such comparisons in the sense that it requires any person making a basic moral value judgment to try to visualize what it would be like to be in the shoes of any other member of the society. That is, he must try to estimate what utility level he would enjoy if he himself were placed in the *objective* physical, economic, and social conditions of any other individual—and if at the same time he also suddenly acquired this individual's *subjective* attitudes, taste, and preferences, i.e., suddenly acquired his utility function.

Admittedly, the idea of evaluating another individual's personal circumstances in terms of *his* utility function, and not in terms of our own, is a difficult concept. But it is a concept we cannot avoid in any reasonable theory of morality. Clearly, if I want to judge the fairness of a social policy providing a diet very rich in fish for a given group of individuals (e.g., for students living in a certain dormitory), I obviously must make my judgment in terms of these individuals' liking or disliking for fish, and not in terms of my own.

As I tried to show in my 1955 paper,[14] the ultimate logical basis for interpersonal utility comparisons, interpreted in this way, lies in the postulate that the *preferences and utility functions of all human individuals* are *governed by the same basic psychological laws*. My utility function may be very different from yours. But, since both of our utility functions are governed by the very same basic psychological laws, if I had your personal characteristics—and, in particular, if I had your biological inheritance and had your life history behind me—then presumably I would now have a utility function exactly like yours.[15] This means

---

[13] As defined by John von Neumann and Oskar Morgenstern, *Theory of Games and Economic Behavior*, 2nd ed. (Princeton, N.J.: Princeton University Press, 1947), pp. 15–31.

[14] Harsanyi, "Cardinal Welfare. . . ."

[15] This statement would admittedly require appropriate qualifications if the psychological laws governing

that any *inter*personal comparison I may try to make between your present utility level and my own, reduces to an *intra*-personal utility comparison between the utility level *I* myself *do* now enjoy, and the utility level *I* myself *would* enjoy under certain hypothetical conditions, namely if I were placed in your physical, economic, and social position, and also had my own biological and biographical background replaced by yours.

This means that interpersonal utility comparisons have a completely specific theoretical meaning, in the sense that, "under ideal conditions," i.e., if we had full knowledge of the psychological laws governing people's preferences and their utility functions, and also had sufficient information about other people's personal characteristics, then we could make perfectly error-free interpersonal utility comparisons. Of course, in actual fact, our knowledge of psychological laws and of other people's personal characteristics is very limited, and, therefore, interpersonal utility comparisons are often subject to considerable error—but, of course, so are many other judgments we have to make before we can reach practical decisions, whether these are moral decisions or purely pragmatic ones. Nevertheless, in many *specific* cases, we may have enough background information to be quite confident in our judgments of interpersonal utility comparison—and this confidence is often justified by the fact that in many of these cases there is a reasonable agreement between the conclusions reached by different competent observers when they try to make such comparisons.

In any case, we all make, and cannot help making, interpersonal utility comparisons all the time. We have to decide again and again which particular member of our family, or which particular friend of ours, etc., has a more urgent need for our time or our money, or could derive greater satisfaction from a present, and so on. Likewise, as voters or public officials, we have to decide again and again which particular social group would derive the greatest benefit from government help, etc. To my mind, it makes no sense to deny the legitimacy of a mental operation we all perform every day, and for which a completely satisfactory logical analysis can be provided.[16]

Rawls expresses considerable doubts about the validity of interpersonal utility comparisons (pp. 90 and 321–324). But he makes no attempt to refute my theory of such comparisons, stated in my 1955 article (and briefly summarized above). Instead, he concentrates his criticism on two highly artificial procedures suggested in the literature for making interpersonal utility comparisons (pp. 321–323). One is based on equating the smallest noticeable utility differences of different people. The other is based on equating all individuals' highest possible utility levels, and then again equating their lowest possible utility levels. Of course, he has no trouble showing that, in order to use either procedure in moral philosophy, we would have to introduce some highly arbitrary and implausible moral postulates. But none of these criticisms applies to my own theory of interpersonal utility comparisons.

This completes my discussion of Rawls's objections to my own version of utilitarian theory. I shall now discuss some objections of his to utilitarian theories in general.

9. Utilitarianism and Supererogatory Actions

Commonsense morality distinguishes between morally good actions we have a duty to perform, and morally good actions which go beyond the call of duty (supererogatory actions). But, as Rawls points out (p. 117), classical utilitarianism cannot accommodate this distinction because it claims that our duty is always to perform the actions likely to produce the *greatest* good for society. This would mean that, even if we were constantly engaged in the most heroic acts of altruistic self-sacrifice, we would merely do our duty, and no human action could ever be correctly described as supererogatory. I agree with Rawls that it is a serious shortcoming of classical utilitarianism that it cannot admit the existence of supererogatory actions, and draws the line between morally permissible and impermissible conduct at an absurdly high level of moral perfection.

This shortcoming, however, can be easily remedied without going beyond the principles of utilitarianism. The mistake of the classical utilitarians was to overlook the fact that people attach considerable utility to *freedom* from unduly burdensome moral obligations. It may be true (though this is by no means a foregone conclusion) that society will reach a higher level of economic prosperity and cultural excellence if its moral code requires all people all the time to act in the most public-spirited manner, and to set themselves the highest possible standards in their economic and cultural activities. But most people will prefer a society with a more relaxed moral code, and will feel that such a society will achieve a higher level of average utility—even if adoption of such a moral code should lead to some losses in economic and cultural accomplishments (so long as these losses remain within tolerable limits). This means that utilitarianism, if correctly inter-

---

people's utility functions were found to be probabilistic, rather than deterministic. But this would not affect the basic validity of my analysis, though it would necessitate its restatement in a more complicated form.

[16] For a more detailed discussion of the epistemological problems connected with interpersonal utility comparisons, see my 1955 paper cited in footnote 5.

preted, will yield a moral code with a standard of acceptable conduct very much below the level of highest moral perfection, leaving plenty of scope for supererogatory actions exceeding this minimum standard.

10. Vagueness Versus Simplemindedness in Moral Philosophy

As Rawls correctly states (p. 320), the utilitarian concept of morality inevitably shows some degree of vagueness or indeterminacy because of its dependence on—more or less uncertain—interpersonal utility comparisons. Other authors have pointed out another source of indeterminacy, no less important, in the dependence of utilitarian morality on uncertain predictions about the short-run and long-run consequences of alternative social policies and institutional arrangements. As a result, two equally well-intentioned and well-informed, and equally intelligent utilitarians may very well disagree in many specific situations about what is socially useful or socially harmful and, therefore, also about what is right or wrong, and just or unjust, etc.

Rawls's own theory, of course, cannot completely escape such ambiguities either, but it is certainly much less affected by them than utilitarian theories are. First of all, Rawls's basic postulate, the difference principle, is much less dependent on interpersonal utility comparisons than the basic utilitarian principles (for example, the principle of average utility) are; therefore, it yields more specific practical conclusions than the latter do in many cases. In addition, Rawls supplements the difference principle by second-order rules, which are supposed to rank the major values of human life according to their relative moral importance. Thus, for example, according to Rawls, people's basic liberties should always be given absolute priority over their economic and social interests, etc. Clearly, if we are willing to accept such rigid second-order rules of priority, then they will often go a long way toward deciding our moral uncertainties in a fairly unambiguous manner.

Yet, I very much doubt that this is really an advantage. It seems to me that the uncertainties of utilitarian morality merely reflect the great complexity and the unavoidable dilemmas of real-life moral situations. Simple minded rigid mechanical rules cannot possibly do justice to the complexity of moral problems; and they cannot resolve our moral dilemmas satisfactorily, because they cannot help choosing the wrong horn of the dilemma in many important cases.

For example, there are good reasons to believe that in an underdeveloped country in many cases economic growth cannot be set in motion without concentrating a good deal of power in the hands of the government and perhaps even without *some* curtailment of civil liberties (though this does not mean that there is any need or justification for a complete suppression of civil liberties as practiced by the arbitrary dictatorial governments now existing in many of these countries).

Who is the moral philosopher to lay down the law for these countries and tell them that no amount of economic and social development, however large, can ever justify any curtailment of civil liberties, however small? Should we not rather say, with the utilitarian philosophers, that judgments about any particular policy must always depend on the balance of the advantages and disadvantages it is likely to yield, and that the main task of the moral philosopher is to ensure that people will not overlook any major advantage or disadvantage in reaching a decision?

11. Saving as a Moral Duty to Future Generations

What proportion of national income ought to be saved as a matter of moral duty (as a matter of justice) to future generations? As Rawls rightly argues (p. 286), utilitarianism (at least as it is usually interpreted) gives an unsatisfactory answer to this question, in that it seems to require unreasonably high savings. The mathematical problem of computing the morally optimal amount of savings under utilitarian criteria was solved by Keynes's friend, the brilliant economist-philosopher Frank P. Ramsey, in 1928.[17] Of course, the numerical answer depends on the utility functions used. But Ramsey showed that, if we use reasonable-looking utility functions, then the utilitarian model may easily yield optimal savings amounting to much more than one half of national income, which is clearly an unacceptable conclusion.

How well does Rawls's own theory deal with this problem? It is easy to verify that the difference principle would suggest *zero* net savings from one generation to another. This is so because, even without any net savings, as a result of mere technological progress, future generations will be much better off than the present generation is, anyhow (provided the population explosion can be brought under control). Therefore, any positive net saving would be inconsistent with the difference principle since it would amount to a transfer of economic resources from a much poorer generation to much richer generations. Thus, while utilitarian theory seems to require unduly high savings, Rawls's difference principle would certainly require unduly low (viz., zero) savings. Rawls is aware that the difference principle would have this undesirable implication (p. 291).

[17] Frank P. Ramsey, "A Mathematical Theory of Saving," *Economic Journal*, 38 (December, 1928), 543–559.

Nevertheless, surprisingly enough, he seems to imply that his theory handles the saving problem much *better* than utilitarian theory does (pp. 297–298). The truth is that he can avoid the zero-savings conclusion only by giving up the difference principle altogether in dealing with the saving problem, and by replacing it with a completely *ad hoc* motivational assumption. (Whereas in all other respects he makes the participants of the original position complete egoists, in this one respect, viz., in relation to future generations, he endows them with considerable altruism.) Of course, by introducing *ad hoc* assumptions of its own, utilitarianism could just as easily avoid the unwelcome logical necessity of enjoining excessive savings.

In actual fact, in order to obtain a reasonable solution for the problem of optimal savings in terms of utilitarian principles, we have no need for *ad hoc* assumptions. All we have to do is to take a second look at Ramsey's utility functions. The utility functions he postulates seem to be reasonable enough if they are meant to measure the utility that a given individual in the present generation would derive from higher income levels (on the assumption that other people's incomes would remain more or less unchanged). But they greatly overstate the extra utility that future generations are likely to derive from higher incomes as a result of substantially increased saving and investment by the present generation. There are at least three reasons for this:

(1) The *risk effect:* there is always a considerable risk that future changes in technology and in social customs will drastically reduce the benefit that future generations would derive from investments undertaken by the present generations. (For instance, the United States and some European countries invested very large amounts of money in building canals just before the railway age. These huge investments almost completely lost their usefulness very soon thereafter as a result of railway construction.)

(2) The *relative-income effect:* a rise in a given person's income, when other people's incomes remain largely the same, will tend to increase his social status. But if his income rises as a result of a general increase in society's income then of course this effect will be lost. Therefore, in the former case the rise in his income will produce a much greater increase in his utility than it will do in the latter case.

(3) The *inherited-wealth effect:* inherited wealth often has a very powerful influence on human motivation. Some of this influence may be beneficial. (People born into very rich families develop highly idealistic and altruistic attitudes, and may take a strong interest in social causes or in political, philanthropic, and cultural activities.)

But some of this influence may be highly detrimental for a person's chances of leading a happy and socially useful life. (People born into very rich families often lack all interest in serious work, including altruistic or intellectual work; and they may be offered so many opportunities to amuse themselves that they may lose all ability to enjoy the normal pleasures of human life.) It is not unreasonable to assume that if society as a whole inherits very high levels of material abundance, so that there is very little pressure on the average man to earn a living by serious work, then the negative effects are likely to predominate. (We can already see some indications of this in our own society.) Therefore, the net benefit that future generations are likely to derive from increased saving and investment by the present generation may be much smaller than at first one might think.

Thus, if the likely utility of much higher incomes to future generations is reassessed in a more realistic manner then utilitarian theory will yield much lower levels of optimal savings, and in fact will furnish a completely satisfactory solution for this problem, without any need for *ad hoc* assumptions.

12. The Stability of a Just Society

Rawls raises a very interesting problem, so far largely neglected by moral and political philosophers. Suppose there is a society with a strong sense of justice among its citizens, and with completely (or almost completely) just institutions. Would such a society be stable? He strongly argues that the answer is in the affirmative (pp. 490–504). He also suggests that a society based on his own conception of justice would be more stable than one based on a utilitarian conception (p. 498).

The just society he describes in this connection, however, is not merely an improved version of the best societies now existing; rather, it is unlike any society known to political scientists or historians or other competent observers. It is a society where citizens and legislators are never motivated by their own selfish interests or (in the case of the legislators) by the selfish interests of their constituents, but rather are always motivated by their strong sense of justice. As such, this society is almost the opposite of the society pictured in Anthony Downs's *An Economic Theory of Democracy*.[18]

Of course, Rawls is quite right in rejecting Downs's motivational assumptions as a fully realistic picture of human motivation. It is certainly not true that ordinary citizens never care about

[18] Anthony Downs, *An Economic Theory of Democracy* (New York: Harper and Brothers, 1957).

anything but their narrow economic (and perhaps other) self-interest, or that politicians never care about anything but their chances for election or reelection. Indeed, it is quite clear that under *some* conditions many rich people will strongly support legislation benefiting the poor but greatly increasing their own taxes (though it is much less clear under what conditions this will or will not happen). Again, we have all seen elected officials follow their own moral and political convictions and make highly unpopular decisions, greatly endangering their prospects for reelection (and sometimes we wished they did not, while at other times we were glad they did). Indeed, it is quite obvious that Downs does not claim that his oversimplified motivational assumptions are literally true; all he claims is that our political system operates most of the time *as if* these motivational assumptions *were* correct.

Nevertheless, the fact that Downs's motivational assumptions come so close to being true, should make us stop to think before accepting Rawls's theory of stability. Should we not take this fact as an indication that the very high levels of public-spirited motivation that Rawls assumes for his just society, would be intrinsically *unstable?* Indeed, our historical experience seems to show that whole societies can achieve such motivational states only for rather short periods (e.g., during revolutions or some very popular wars). The same experience also shows that these highly idealistic— and often highly fanatical and intolerant—motivational states of a society are far from being an unmixed blessing.

It seems to me that any healthy society needs a proper balance between egoistic and altruistic motivation. Without political leaders fighting for altruistic objectives, or without private citizens giving them political support, present-day democratic societies would not have achieved even that, no doubt imperfect, level of social justice and of good government they currently enjoy.

On the other hand, political movements based largely or wholly on well-understood self-interest are an equally essential component of any political system. Citizens pressing for their sectional economic interests may be very biased judges of the public interest, but at least they are well-informed judges in most cases. In contrast, citizens pursuing highly altruistic objectives might often fight for causes about which they know very little, or about which they have strikingly onesided information. Steelworkers pressing for their own economic interests will at least know what they are talking about. But faraway benevolent millionaires fighting for the steelworkers' interests might have very mistaken ideas about what these steelworkers really want or need. A society where everybody neglects his own interests, and

is busily looking after everybody else's interests, probably would not be a very stable society—and certainly would not be a very happy one.

Accordingly, it seems to me that a just society with a reasonable prospect for social stability would *not* be a society where ordinary citizens and legislators would be primarily motivated by their sense of justice. Rather, it would be a society where most people would be motivated by the normal mixture of egoistic and altruistic interests. Of course, it would have to be a society where people have a strong sense of justice—but this does not mean that a pursuit of justice would have to be their main and continual preoccupation. It only means that they would have to show enough respect for justice so as to stop pressing their own egoistic—and altruistic—objectives *beyond* the point where they would violate the just legal and moral rights of other people; and so as to fight for restoring these rights if they have been violated by injustices of the past.

13. Conclusion

To conclude, in spite of my numerous disagreements with Rawls's theory, I strongly recommend his book to all readers interested in moral and political philosophy. He raises many interesting and, to my mind, highly important problems, even though some of us may question the solutions he proposes. The author's serious concern for truth and justice is evident on every page of the book. He makes a real effort to look at both (or all) sides of every difficult or controversial problem, and to reach a fair and balanced conclusion. Where he touches on problems of topical interest, he does not hesitate for a moment to express unpopular views, for example, by pointing out the possible destabilizing effects that very widespread civil disobedience might have on democratic institutions (p. 374). In the political climate of Harvard in the late 'sixties or early 'seventies it must have required no little moral courage to express such an opinion.

We live in an age where our moral attitudes are rapidly changing, and so are many of our social institutions, with end results very hard to predict; where traditional world views are more and more replaced by a world view based on science and depriving man of his privileged position in nature; where the fast progress of technology poses very difficult moral dilemmas and is likely to pose incomparably more difficult ones in the not-too-distant future (e.g., when it may become feasible to double the present human life span, opening up new dimensions for the problem of overpopulation; or when it may become possible to undertake large-scale genetic and reproductional engineering; or when robots and computers truly competitive with humans may become available, and so on). In an age like this, any investigation into the criteria of rational choice between alternative moral codes is of much more than merely theoretical significance.

Therefore, there is no question whatever in my mind that Rawls poses problems of the greatest importance. But this is precisely the reason why I feel it is important to *resist* the solutions he proposes for these problems. We should resist any moral code which would force us to discriminate against the legitimate needs and interests of many individuals merely because they happen to be rich, or at least not to be desperately poor; or because they are exceptionally gifted, or at least are not mentally retarded; or because they are healthy, or at least are not incurably sick, etc. We should resist such a moral code, because an alternative moral code, the utilitarian one, is readily available to us; and the latter permits us to give equal *a priori* weight to every person's legitimate interests, and to judge the relative importance of any given need of a particular person in each case by its merits, as assessed by commonsense criteria —rather than forcing us to judge them according to rigid, artificial, and often highly discriminatory rules of priority.

Postscript

This paper was written in May 1973. In the meantime, John Rawls has tried to answer some of my criticisms in a paper entitled "Some Reasons for the Maximin Criterion."[19] His defense to the counterexamples I have put forward against using the maximin principle as a moral principle (in Section 3 of the preceding paper) is that "the maximin criterion is not meant to apply to small-scale situations, say, to how a doctor should treat his patients or a university its students. . . . Maximin is a macro not a micro principle" (p. 142). Regretfully, I must say that this is a singularly inept defense.

First of all, though my counterexamples do refer to small-scale situations, it is very easy to adapt them to large-scale situations since they have intrinsically nothing to do with scale, whether small or large. For example, instead of asking whether a doctor should use a life-saving drug in short supply for treating patient A or patient B, we can ask whether, in allocating scarce medical manpower and other resources, society should give priority to those patients who could best benefit from medical treatment, or should rather give priority to the most hopelessly sick patients—a policy problem surely affecting several hundred thousand individuals in any major country at any given time. Or, again, instead of asking

whether scarce educational resources should be used for the benefit of individual A or individual B, we can ask whether, in allocating educational expenditures, society should give priority in certain cases to several hundred thousand highly gifted students, who could presumably benefit most, or to several hundred thousand seriously retarded individuals, who could derive only minor benefits from additional education, etc. I am really astonished that a distinguished philosopher like Rawls should have overlooked the simple fact that the counterexamples I have adduced (and the many more counterexamples one could easily adduce) have nothing whatever to do with scale at all.

In fact, it would be *a priori* rather surprising if, at the most fundamental level, the basic principles of morality should take different forms for large-scale and for small-scale situations. Does Rawls seriously think that there is a certain number x, such that a situation involving *more* than x people will come under moral principles basically different from a situation involving *fewer* than x people?

In any case, what moral considerations will determine this curious boundary number x itself? More fundamentally, what are the basic logical reasons that should make large-scale and small-scale situations essentially different from a moral point of view? I cannot see how anybody can propose the strange doctrine that scale is a fundamental variable in moral philosophy, without giving credible answers to these questions at the same time.

I have argued that in *most* situations Rawls's theory will have much the same policy implications as utilitarian theory does, but that there are *some* important situations where this is not the case. Moreover, I have tried to show that, in those situations where the two theories do have quite dissimilar policy implications, Rawls's theory consistently yields morally highly *unacceptable* policy conclusions whereas utilitarian theory consistently yields morally fully *acceptable* ones (Sections 3 and 4 of the preceding paper).

Arrow has expressed a similar view.[20] After saying that in the real world the maximin principle and the utilitarian principle would have very similar practical consequences, he adds: " . . . the maximin principle would lead to unacceptable consequences if the world were such that they [these consequences] really differed." My only disagreement with Arrow is that I think the world is in fact so constituted that these two principles *do* have very different practical consequences in some important cases. (In effect, in some parts of

[19] John Rawls, "Some Reasons for the Maximin Criterion," *American Economic Review*, 64, Papers & Proc. (May, 1974), 141–146.

[20] Kenneth J. Arrow, "Some Ordinalist-Utilitarian Notes on Rawls's Theory of Justice," *The Journal of Philosophy*, 70 (May 10, 1973), 255.

his paper, Arrow himself seems to admit that much—pp. 251–252.) But we do agree on the main point, viz., on the conditional statement that, *if* such differences exist, they all speak very strongly against the maximin principle.

In my opinion, if this criticism is valid, then it completely disqualifies Rawls's theory as a serious competitor to utilitarian theory. (Why should anybody choose a theory that often does much worse, and never does any better, than utilitarian theory does?) For this reason, I find it rather unfortunate that Rawls's paper does not even try to answer this criticism at all.

To be sure, the maximin principle does have its valuable uses, and we must be grateful to Rawls for calling our attention to it. Even if it cannot serve as a *basic* principle of moral *theory*, it can be used as a principle of approximate validity in practical *applications*, such as the theory of optimal income distribution or of optimal taxation. In such applications, its relative independence of detailed interpersonal utility comparisons, and of the actual mathematical form of people's von Neumann-Morgenstern utility functions for money, is an important advantage, and can be fruitfully exploited in economic studies.[21]

Of course, from the point of view of a utilitarian observer, the results of a study of, e.g., optimal income tax rates, based on the maximin principle, will have only approximate validity. For example, if the study finds that, owing to the disincentive effect of very high marginal tax rates, the marginal income tax for the highest income group should be (say) 50 per cent, then a utilitarian observer

[21] Arrow, p. 259.

can infer that this tax rate should certainly be *no more* than 50 per cent. Indeed, he can infer that, if the study had been based on the average utility principle instead of the maximin principle, then the marginal tax rate at the top would have come out presumably *a little lower* than 50 per cent, though perhaps not very much lower. (Sensitivity analysis may even enable us to estimate the actual percentage points by which studies based on the maximin principle are likely to overestimate the optimal tax rates for various income groups.)

It is regrettable that Rawls has ever made the untenable claim that he is proposing a moral *theory* superior to utilitarian theory. This claim can only obscure the practical merits of the maximin principle as an easily applicable postulate of approximate validity. These practical merits of course do not in any way provide a reason for abandoning utilitarian moral philosophy. (Basic philosophical principles must be exactly right, and not merely approximately right.) But they do provide a reason, even for a utilitarian moral philosopher, to use the maximin principle as an admissible approximation in many cases. Had Rawls only made this more modest, but much more realistic, claim for the maximin principle, few people would have contradicted him.

One thing that all of us must have learned in the last fifty years is that we must never commit ourselves seriously to moral principles or political ideologies that are bound to lead to morally utterly *wrong* policies from time to time—however great the advantages of these principles or ideologies may be in terms of administrative convenience, ease of application, and readier understandability.

Indian Philosophical Quarterly, Vol. XIII, No. 2, April-June 1986

IN DEFENCE OF THE USE OF MAXIMIN PRINCIPLE OF CHOICE UNDER UNCERTAINTY IN RAWL'S ORIGINAL POSITION *

The principles chosen by the agents of construction in the original position to assign basic rights and duties and to determine the division of social benefits are the principles of justice according to Rawls. The parties in the original position are conceived as not knowing certain particular facts. Rawls assumes that the agents in the original position will make their choice by following the maximin principle of choice under uncertainty. The assumption of Rawls has been criticized severely by Harsanyi. His contention is that 'the maximin principle is not a rational principle of choice under uncertainty. According to him the only rational principle of choice under uncertainty is the principle of maximization of expected utility.' In this essay it has been shown that given the kind of ignorance the parties in the original position suffer from, it is not possible for them to follow the principle of maximization of expected utility. Rather, it is rational for them to follow the maximin principle of choice under uncertainty.

I

To appreciate fully what should be the principle of choice under uncertainty for the parties in the original position, we have to know what the parties in the original position do not know. "First of all, no one knows his place in society, his class position or social status; nor does he know his fortune in the distribution of natural assets and abilities,

---

* An earlier draft of the paper was read in the 'All India Seminar on Utilitarianism and Its Ethics and Marx's Concept of man', held at the Department of Philosophy, Jadavpur University, March 21, 22, 23, 1984.

his intellgence and strength, and the like. Nor, again does anyone know his conception of the good, the particulars of his rational plan of life, or even the special features of his psychology such as his aversion to risk or liability to optimism or pessimism....... parties do not know the particular circumstances of his own society. That is they do not know its economic or political situation, or the level of civilization and culture it has been able to achieve. The persons in the original position have no information as to which generation they belong."[1] The veil of ignorance is quite a thick one.

The outcome of the decision to adopt principles made under such ignorance will depend on which circumstances the person finds himself in when the veil of ignorance is lifted, i.e., the parties are facing a decision problem under uncertainty.

II

According to Rawls the parties in the original position will use the maximin principle of choice under uncertainty.[2] "The maximin rule tells us to rank alternatives by their worst possible outcomes. We are to adopt the alternative the worst outcome of which is superior to the worst outcome of others".[3]

Rawls is aware that "the maximin rule is not, in general, a suitable guide for choice under uncertainty."[4] But he thinks "it is attractive in situations marked by certain special features".[5] He claims that there are three chief features of the situation that give plausibility to this rule. First, the situation is one in which a knowledge of likelihoods is impossible or at best extremely insecure. "In this case it is unreasonable not to be skeptical of probabilistic calculations unless there is no other way out particularly if the decision is a fundamental one that needs to be justified to others".[6] Secondly "the person choosing has a conception of good such that he cares very little, if anything, for what he might gain above the minimum stipend that he can, in fact, be sure of by following the maximin rule".[7] Lastly "the rejected alternatives have outcomes that one can hardly accept".[8] Original position has been so defined that all these three features are present. The veil of ignorance leaves no basis for determining likelihoods. Secondly ' the minimum assured by the two principles in lexical order (which is the maximin solution) is not one that the parties wish to jeopardise for the sake of greater economic and social advantage".[9] Lastly "other conceptions of justice may lead to institutions that the parties would find intolerable".[10]

III

Harsanyi severely criticizes the use of maximin principle of choice under uncertainty in the original position. He undermines the rationality of the use of maximin principle for choice under uncertainty by showing that it leads to very paradoxical implications for the choice under uncertainty that we face in day to day life. "If you took the maximin principle seriously then you could not ever cross a street (after all, you might be hit by a car), you could never drive over a bridge (after all, it might collapse), you could never get married (after all, it might end in a disaster), etc. If anybody really acted this way he would soon end up in a mental institution".[11] As we have already noted this point is conceded by Rawls. What Harsanyi needs to show is that it is irrational to use the maximin principle in the original position. The use of the maximin principle in the original position would lead to the adoption of the difference principle, the principle which evaluates every possible institutional arrangement in terms of the interests of the least advantaged individual: Out of any two alternative institutional arrangements in society, that institutional arrangement is preferable in which the least advantaged individual enjoys a higher welfare level than the welfare level of the least advantaged individual of the other institutional arrangement. Harsanyi argues "that the difference principle often has wholly unacceptable moral implications".[12] He gives many examples. A typical example is that of a society consisting of one doctor and two patients both of them critically ill. Medicine available suffices only to treat one of the two patients. One of these two patients is a basically healthy person apart from his present illness, the other individual is a terminal cancer victim but even so the medicine could prolong his life by several months. Which patient should be given the medicine? According to the difference principle it should be given to the cancer victim, who is obviously the less fortunate of the two patients.[13] But Harsanyi claims, "In contrast, utilitarian ethics — as well as ordinary common sense would make the opposite suggestion".[14] The medicine should be given to the healthy person bcause, "it would do 'much more good' by bringing him back to normal health than it would do by slightly prolonging the life of a hopelessly sick individual".[15]

Rawl's reply to the various counter examples of Harsanyi against using the maximin principle in the original position is that "the maximin criterion is not meant to apply to small-scale situations, say, to how a doctor should treat his patients or a University its students...... Maximin is a macro not a micro principle".[16] Harsanyi's rejoinder to this reply was, "Regretfully, I must say that this is a singularly inept defense,........ I cannot see how anybody can propose the strange doctrine that scale is a fundamental variable in moral philosophy......".[17] Rawls appears to have conceded the force of Harsanyi's counter examples for in as late as 1980 he stipulated it as a condition of a well-ordered society that "no one suffers from unusual needs that are especially difficult to fulfil for example, unusual and costly medical requirements". And he maintained "it is sensible to lay aside certain difficult complications. If we can work out a theory that covers the fundamental case, we can try to extend it to other cases later".[18]

But it appears to me that Harsanyi's counter examples do not help in proving the point for which they are intended. Harsanyi's claim appears to be plausible only because he has failed to incorporate a few vital features of society stipulated by Rawls. Firstly "a well-ordered society is conceived as on-going society.....Its members view their common polity as extending backwards and forward in time over generations and they strive to reproduce themselves, and their cultural and social life in perpetuity, practically speaking; that is they would envisage any final date at which they were to wind up their affairs as inadmissible and foreign to their conception of their association".[19] Secondly a well-ordered society is conceived as "a system of co-operation designed to advance the good of those taking part in it".[20] And lastly, "a well-ordered society does not have a manna economy, nor are its economic arrangements a zero-sum game in which none can gain unless others lose".[21] Once we accept these stipulations, the recommendation of utilitarianism as against that of difference principle does not appear to be intuitively acceptable. For it would amount to systematic deprivation of the unfortunate. It would amount to violation of the Kantian precept 'treat one another not as means only but as an end in themselves'. But Harsanyi thinks that the cancer victim is "merely being denied the use of certain resources over which he has no prior property rights, and this is done on the ground that other individuals have 'greater need' for the resources i.e., can derive greater utility from them.....".[22] Therefore the recommendation of the utilitarianism does not amount to violation of the precept. But this claim of Harsanyi is indefensible once we acknowledge that the medicine is produced by the co-operation of all as required by the stipulations mentioned above. Under such circumstances denying the cancer victim the use of medicine will not amount to "merely denying him the use of certain resources over which he has no prior property rights". To this argument Harsanyi may reply as in fact he does, that "the opposite policy of giving absolute priority to cancer victim's unimportant need will be an even stronger violation of the Kantian principle and will amount a fortiori to treating the healthy person now as a mere means rather than as an end".[23] But this contention is wrong. For this policy has the approval of both in the original position. The healthy person cannot complain now after the veil of ignorance has been lifted. The circle of the argument is now complete. We are back to from where we had started. Will or will not the parties in the original position accept the maximin principle for choice under uncertainty?

Other examples given by Harsanyi also fail to undermine the rationality of the use of the maximin principle in original position.

IV

According to Harsanyi the proper principle of choice under uncertainty is the principle of maximization of expected utility which should have been attributed to parties in the original position. He claims that any decision maker whose behaviour is consistent with a few-very compelling rationality postulates simply cannot help acting as if he used subjective probabilities and he cannot help acting as if he tried to maximize his expected utility, computed on the basis of some set of subjective probabilities.[24] A few of these rationality postulate are: (1) "If you prefer A to B, and prefer B to C, then consistency requires that you should also prefer A to C". (2) "You are better off if you are offered a more valuable prize with a given probability, then if you are offered a *less valuable* prize with the same probability"[25] (the sure thing principle). (3) You should be indifferent between two risky lotteries if these yield you the same prizes with the same probabilities — even if these two lotteries use quite different physical processes to generate these possibilities (the principle of probabilistic equivalence)[26]. "The other rationality postulates of

Bayesian theory... are equally compelling" according to Harsanyi.[27] His claim is that parties in the original position should follow these postulates of Bayesian theory. Any decision which violates any of these Bayesian postulates will be an irrational decision.

One cannot reject the principle of maximization of expected utility for choice under uncertainty without rejecting the set of Bayesian postulates of rationality i.e., without rejecting at least one of these postulates.

So the question is: should we characterize the rational behaviour of the parties in the original position as described by Rawls by this set of postulates?

But before we take up this question let us have a look at the alternative model of moral value judgements as given by Harsanyi. According to him a person "would be making a moral value judgement if he chooses between the two social systems *without knowing* what his personal position would be under either system".[28] If the society consists of indviduals then the individual would choose between the two alternative social systems on the assumption that under either system he would have the same probability $\dfrac{1}{n}$, of taking the place of any one of the n individuals.[29] Since in choosing between two social systems he would use the principle of expected-utility maximization as his decision rule, he "would always choose that social system which, in his opinion, would yield the higher average utility level to the individual members of the society".[30] Ths is Harsanyi's version of the concept of the original position.

It may be noted that the ignorance condition as envisaged by Rawls is different from the ignorance condition stipulated by Harsanyi. The only information denied by Harsanyi to an individual in the original position is "what his personal position would be under either system". Rawls would call it a 'thin veil of ignorance'. According to Rawls 'thin veil of ignorance' is imposed "to prevent the parties from reasoning according to the principle: to persons according to their threat-advantage".[31] "The veil of ignorance is thin, because no more knowledge is excluded than is necessary to secure this result, the parties still know the general configuration of society, its political structure and economic organization and so on".[32]

Rawls calls his own version of veil of ignorance a 'thick veil of ignorance' which we described before. Rawls denies much of the information to the parties which is allowed to be known to the parties by Harsanyi. The reason as given by Rawls for the exclusion of so much information from the parties in the original position is that the parties are not to be influenced by any particular information that is not part of their representation as free and equal moral persons with a determinate (but unknown) conception of the good, unless this information is necessary for a rational agreement to be reached".[33]

With this clarification and distinction in mind let us come back to our question; should we characterize the rational behaviour of the parties in the original position as described by Rawls by Bayesian rationality postulates? My question is not whether 'the thin' or 'the quick' veil of ignorance should be imposed on parties in the original position. Also, I am not questioning the validity of the Bayesian rationality postulates for the parties in Harsanyi's 'thin veil of ignorance' version of the original position. Rather I am asking: given that Rawlsian 'thick veil of ignorance' has been imposed on the parties in the original position should these agents follow the Bayesian rationality principles? My answer is in the negative.

Under the ignorance condition stipulated by Rawls and the type of decision they have to make, the ascription of the last of the three Bayesian postulates given above, i.e., the principle of probabilistic equivalence to the parties is not meaningful. This principle assumes the comparability of the two different events in regard to their objective probability. The ignorance condition is so designed by Rawls that there is no possibility of the knowledge of objectve probabilities of various circumstances that prevail. "The parties have no basis for determining the probable nature of their society, or their place in it". So there is no meaning in the original position to say regarding parties "that they should be indifferent between two risky lotteries if these yield him the same prizes with the same probabilities — even if the two lotteries use quite different processes to generate these possibilities". Rather we have to say that two lotteries which use different physical processes to generate possibilities are non-comparable for the parties in the original position. This, in technical language of the decision theory, means that the parties in the original position will find acts with different domains non-comparable.

The sure thing principle is also unacceptable for the parties in the original position. The original position is designed to be fair to all individuals. But as Diamond has shown the sure thing principle may go against fairness.[34] The example that Diamond considers is the following. Let U_A and U_B stand respectively for welfare levels of individuals A and B, and let L^1 and L^2 be two lotteries with a fifty-fifty probability of two social alternatives specified thus:

	Prize 1	Prize II
Lottery L^1	$U_A = 1$, $U_B = 0$	$U_A = 0$, $U_B = 1$
Lottery L^2	$U_A = 1$, $U_B = 0$	$U_A = 0$, $U_B = 0$

It seems reasonable to be indifferent between the second prize of L^1 and that of L^2 because they seem very much the same except for the substitution of name tags A and B. But the first prize of both the lotteries is the same, so that the sure thing principle would make us indifferent between L^1 and L^2. But lottery L^2 seems so unfair to individual B while lottery L^1 gives B a fair stake. Hence, the sure thing principle goes against the fairness of the original position.

Harsanyi finds Diamond's argument unconvincing. He constructs some hypothetical situations to undermine the persuasiveness of Diamond's argument. In one example he considers two societies A and B such that A has extreme inequality, without any social mobility, and B is exactly like A except that "by old custom, all bodies born in B during any given calendar month are randomly distributed by government officials among all families who had a body denying that period, so that everybody born in that month will have the same chance of ending up in any given family". Asks Harsanyi, "should we now say that society B would be morally less objectionable than society A, because in B all individuals would have a 'fair chance' of ending up in a rich family and, therefore, in a privileged social and economic position? By assumption, B is a society with an income distribution just as unfair as A is. In both societies, any individual's social and economic position has nothing to do with personal merit, but rather is completely a matter of 'luck'. In A it depends wholly on the accident of birth — on the 'great lottery of life' which decides who is born into what particular family. In contrast, in B it depends wholly on a government conducted lottery. Why should we assign higher moral dignity to a lottery organized by government bureaucrats than we assign to the 'great lottery of life' which chooses a family for each of us without the benefit of government intervention? Why should a bureaucratic lottery be regarded as being a 'fairer' allocative mechanism than the great biological lottery produced by nature?"[35]

Harsanyi is guilty of confusing two points of view: that of parents and that of babies. Looked at from the point of view of parents both A and B are equally unjust. Since their children in both the alternatives are going to suffer the hereditary social and economic inequalities. The only difference is that in A they retain their biological off-springs, while in B their children are assigned to them by the lottery, whom they accept as their children by custom. Looked at from the point of view of children, there is a difference between society A and B. In society A some suffer because of birth while in B they have a fair chance with others to end up in rich families. Harsanyi of course will remain unconvinced by this argument. For he will reply "Indeed, suppose we would obtain reliable information to the effect that the families are born into are always choosen literally by huge heavenly lottery. Can anybody seriously assert that this metaphysical information would make the slightest difference to our moral condemnation of hereditary social and economic inequalities?"[36] Reply to this is that Harsanyi is taking only post lottery distribution into account. But what is relevant is the pre-lottery evaluation of the two social situations. In one the inequalities are predetermined while in the other every body has equal chance to end up in rich and poor family. Post lottery distribution may turn out to be identical in both the societies yet the society with lottery is better morally than society without lottery.

Probably the argument will be clearer by taking the second example of Harsanyi against Diamond's argument. In this example government has a choice between two policies. In the first policy protective tariff will be removed benefiting everybody except the workers and employers of the protected industry, which would suffer moderate economic losses. In the second policy the same distribution of gains and losses is envisaged, but the losses and gains are distributed by government conducted lottery. Now asks Harsanyi, "would it make any sense to assert that the second-policy would be morally preferable to the first". His answer is in the negative. For, "under the first policy, the loosers would be the members of one particular industry, who presumably have entered this industry by family association or by other accidents of personal life history. Thus, being a member of the loser group would be just as much a matter of personal 'bad luck as would be under the second policy where the losers would be selected literally by a lottery."[37] Even though Harsanyi finds this convincing, this goes against the moral sensibility of many of us. Many people die in industrial accidents. Suppose it is established (may be by astrologers) that a certain number of persons will die by industrial accidents in a calendar year and if as many persons are sacrificed to propriate God no one will die any more by industrial accidents. Now we have two options to continue to live under risk or sacrifice the established number of persons from a certain industry. If we accept the type of reasoning accepted by Harsanyi then we should be indifferent between both the options after all, end result is the same in both cases and the death of persons of the particular industry is as much personal bad luck as the death due to actual industrial accident. But this is surely wrong. The second option is morally pernicious.

According to Rawls the parties in the original position must enter into agreement only if they can honour it even should the worst possibility prove to be the case. That is they must take into account the strains of commitment. Now the sure thing principle goes against this requirement. Consider the following modification of the above mentioned example:

	Prize 1	Prize 2
L^1	$U_A = 10, \quad U_B = 0$	$U_A = 0, \quad U_B = 10$
L^2	$U_A = 4, \quad U_B = 4$	$U_A = 4, \quad U_B = 4$

According to the sure thing principle lottery L^1 is to be preferred to L^2 since the expected utility allocation $U_A = 5$ $U_B = 5$ given L_1 is better than the expected utility allocation $U_A = 4$ $U_B = 4$ given by L_2. But if strains of commitment is taken into account then the lottery L^2 is better than L^1. Hence the sure thing principle is not acceptable in the original position.

The expected utility maximisation principle looks attractive because of the implicit assumption that by consistent application of this principle on each occasion of choice under uncertainty the agent is not likely to lose on the long run as the chances are not expected to be against him systematically. Principle of maximisation of expected utility is therefore attractive where the decision is one of the many so that losses due to one decision is likely to be made good in another decision. Since the quality of entire life is at stake, and there is going to be no second time, the parties in the original position cannot accept the principle of maximisation of expected utility as their guide.

The point of the controversy is that according to Harsanyi there is no such, thing as 'non-probabilizable uncertainty', while Rawls' claim is that the uncertainty in his version of the original position is an instance of 'non-probabilizable uncertainty'. Can we find a plausible set of postulates to characterize the rational choice of parties in the original position which rules out the ascription of subjective probabilities to events? Such a set of postulates is now available. Miche'le Cohen and Jean Yves Jaffray's set of axioms[38] of rational behaviour under complete ignorance should be used to characterize the rational choice of parties under uncertainty in the original position. The intuitive idea behind their axioms is that when all information on the events is denied then the decision makers' rational behaviour should show a certain "symmetry" with respect to events.[39] The intuitive ideas captured by some of the axioms are as follows:

(a) A refinement of the description of an uncertain event can always be made[40] (b) Two comparable acts must have the same domain[41] (c) the sub-division or the grouping together of states of nature should have no influence on preferences[42] (d) the identities of the states of nature on which two given acts yield, respectively, such and such outcomes 'should have no effect on a decision maker's pre-

I.P.Q.   5

ferences between those acts.[43] The intuitive ideas behind the other axioms are also equally plausible.

It has been proved that if acts give different outcomes depending on which event takes place then the rational preference under complete ignorance which satisfies Cohen and Jaffray's axioms are not compatible with the ascribing of personal probabilities to the events.[44] But the rational decision criteria under complete ignorance as defined by their axioms make up an extensive family but one which excludes all criteria based on the ascribing of probabilities to events.[45]

Now we face the problem of justifying the selection of maximin criteria of rational decision for using in the original position, from this family of rational decision criteria.

If we assume that in the original position the alternatives available for choice are such that the least outcome of each is different from the least outcome of every other alternative then under this assumption it is an easy matter to check that the maximin principle of choice under uncertainty satisfies all the six axioms of rational behaviour under complete ignorance.[46] This list of alternatives for choice presented to the parties in the original position by Rawls is such that this assumption is readily acceptable. Rawls himself seems to make this assumption when he claims, to justify the use of maximin principle of decision, that "the rejected alternatives have outcomes that one can hardly accept."[47] This contention together with his claim that "the person choosing has a conception of the good such that he cares very little, if anything, for what he might gain above the minimum stipend that he can, in fact, be sure of by following the maximin rule"[48] justifies the selection of maximin rule from the set of criteria allowed by the axioms of rational choice under complete ignorance given by Cohen & Jaffray.

But these two features of the original position have been questioned by Fiskin. According to him these two features together constitute the assumption of a threshold for an agent in the original position, there is some share — "what he can, in fact, be sure, of by following the maximum rule" — such that, on the one hand "he cares very little if anything" for what he might gain above it and such that that on the other hand he would regard anything less as a share "that one can hardly accept".[49] The threshold for each person depends on the rational plan of life that he has. "Now once it is granted that the definition of rational plans would require extreme disparities between the thresholds determined by different plans......then it becomes evident that the proposed maximin choice procedure would require that the highest threshold determined by any plan must set the standard for everyone. For if there is no way of dismissing some plans as unlikely, and if an allocation which falls short of the threshold is by definition, disastrous then that possibility (whose probability is beyond further evaluation behind the veil of ignorance) must be avoided at all costs......"[50] Now says Fiskin "the highest threshold of satiation which is required by *any* rational plan admissible according to the stated criteria must prove to be a level so high that it could be met for everyone only under condition which fall outside of what Rawls defines as the "circumstances of justice".[51] Hence concludes Fiskin, "the threshold level corresponding to the second and third "features" is unsupported by the premises available and by the doctrine of rational plans, in particular. In fact.... were such a threshold to be defined it would by definition not be applicable to the problem of justice."[52]

Fiskin's objections do not seem to hold good against Rawls. The parties in the original position are not required to take into account each and every rational plan of life as assumed by Fiskin, for the plan of life should not merely be rational but must be consistent with justice too. Be it noted that the ideal person is presumed to have two highest order interests i.e., to exercise effective sense of justice and to exercise his capacity to understand his conception of good. Hence the plan of life should not merely be rational as required by the later interest but should be consistent with the sense of justice too as required by the first highest order interest. But consistency, with the sense of justice, of a rational plan of life cannot be judged without first deciding what the principles of justice are. Hence no appeal to any specific rational plan of life be made without first deciding justice of it. Hence granting of highest threshold as required by any rational plan of life will be required only after that rational plan of life is shown to be consistent with justice, the principles of which are yet to be decided. Fiskin may reply that if this argument is accepted then Rawls himself also cannot appeal to the rational plan of life for deriving desire for primary goods in the original position without first showing the consistency of these with the principles of justice. But this reply is wrong for primary goods are for all purposes means for executing any rational plan of life and hence any just rational plan of life. But the highest threshold required by any rational plan of life need not be (and in fact it will not be) the highest threshold required by any just rational plan of life.

The justice and also the rationality of a plan of life depends on whether it is in accordance with the just distributive share of a person. Just distributive share of a person does not depend on any specific rational plan of life (say which requires the highest threshold). Fiskin may reply that this argument in fact is against Rawls as he himself requires the distributive share to depend on threshold for rational plan of life and since persons are ignorant about their specific rational plans they will strive to secure the highest threshold required by any rational plan of life (may be with qualification that it be just). But Fiskin is wrong in assuming that the last two of the three features which justify the use of maximin principle of choice under uncertainty in original position define a threshold. For what Rawls says is that the alternatives have some outcomes, which persons can hardly accept. He does not imply that any outcome less than what is guaranteed by the maximin principle is unacceptable. Fiskin may reply that what is more important for defining threshold is according to Rawls the persons in the original position care very little for what they may get above the minimum assured by the maximin principle. But what is the meaning of the claim referred to by Fiskin? Rawls himself explains in respect of a person in the original position "it is not worthwhile for him to take a chance for the sake of a further advantage, especially when it may turn out that he loses much that is important to him".[53] A person cares very little for further advantage not because it is a satiation point in respect to his rational plan of life as assumed by Fiskin but because he does not desire to take any risk of losing the minimum guaranteed by the maximin principle, for the sake of greater advantage. Hence contrary to what Fiskin says, the two features of the original position do not define a threshold. But it may be argued that this construction of Rawls' second feature is irrational as it implies that the parties in the original position have infinite risk aversion. But Rawls argues that it is reasonable for a person to have a high degree of aversion to risk in the original position since by taking risk it may turn out that he loses much that is important to him as the quality of an entire life is at stake. But this contention of Rawls, says Arrous, "raises some questions about the meaning of the utilities and does not do justice to the fact that, at least in Vickrey and Harsanyi, the utilities are already measured as to reflect risk aversion."[54] Rawls rejects expected utility maximisation principle of choice under uncertainty not merely on the ground of difficulties with the idea of inter-personal comparison of cardinal utilities but primarily because of non-probablizable nature of the original position as shown above.

Department of Philosophy,   **BINOD KUMAR AGARWALA**
Lucknow University,
LUCKNOW.

NOTES

1. John Rawls, *A Theory of Justice* (Oxford University Press, 1971), p. 137.

2. It is generally maintained that Rawls attributed the maximin principle of choice under uncertainty to the parties in the original position and this interpretation of Rawls's view has been accepted in this essay. But Rawls merely stated, "There is an analogy between the two principles and the maximin rule for choice under uncertainty". (*Ibid.*, p. 152). It is not clear how seriously he thought his two principles to be the maximin solution of the decision problem in the original position. In one of his latter writings he emphasized "that the maximin equity criterion and the so-called maximin rule for choice under uncertainty are two very different things," and he formulated "the reasons for the equity criterion so that they are completely independent from this rule". John Rawls, "Some Reasons for the Maximin Criterion", *The American Economic Review*, vol. 64, Papers and Proc. (May, 1974) 141-146, esp. 141.

3. Rawls, *A Theory of Justice*, p. 152.

4. *Ibid.*, p. 153.

5. *Ibid.*, p. 153.

6. *Ibid.*, p. 154.

7. *Ibid.*, p. 154.

8. *Ibid.*, p. 154.

9. *Ibid.*, p. 156. The clause in the brackets added by the present author.

10. *Ibid.*, p. 156.

11. John C. Harsanyi, "Can the Maximin Principle serve as a basis for Morality? A critique of John Rawls's Theory, *"The American Political Science Review*, Vol. 69, (1975).

12. *Ibid.*, p. 596.

13. In any real society the difference principle will have the implication that the medicine be given to the basically healthy person because otherwise the welfare level of the hopelessly sick individual will be even worse for he will be deprived of the help and care of the healthy person etc.

14. *Ibid.*, p. 596.

15. *Ibid.*, p. 596.

16. Rawls, "Some Reasons for the Maximin Criterion", p. 142.

17. Harsanyi, p. 605.

18. John Rawls, "Kantian Constructivism in Moral Theory: The Dowey Lectures 1980", *The Journal of Philosophy*, Vol. LXXVII, No. 9, (September, 1980), 575-572, p. 546.

19. *Ibid.*, p. 536.

20. Rawls, *A Theory of Justice*, p. 4.

21. Rawls, "Kantian Constructivism", p. 536.

22. Harsanyi, "Can the Maximin Principle serve as a Basis for Morality?" p. 597.

23. *Ibid.*, p. 597.

24. *Ibid.*, p. 599.

25. *Ibid.*, p. 599.

26. John C. Harsanyi, "Bayesian Decision Theory and Utilitarian Ethics", *The American Economic Review*, Vol. 68, Paper and Proc. (May, 1978), p. 224.

27. Harsanyi, "Can the Maximin Principle serve as a Basis for Morality?" p. 599.

28. *Ibid.*, p. 598.

29. *Ibid.*, p. 598.

30. *Ibid.*, p. 598.

31. Rawls, "Kantian Constructivism", p. 549.

32. *Ibid.*, 549.

33. *Ibid.*, 549.

34. Diamond, 'Cardinal Welfare, Individualistic Ethics and Interpersonal Comparisons of Utility', *Journal of Political Economy* 75 (October 1967).

35. Harsanyi, John C., "Nonlinear Social Welfare Functions", *Theory and Decision*, Vol. 6 (1975), p. 317.

36. *Ibid.*, p. 317.

37. *Ibid.*, p. 318.

38. Michele Cohen and Jean Yves Jaffray, "Rational Behaviour Under Complete Ignorance", *Econometrica*, Vol. 48, No. 5 (July, 1980), 1281-1299, esp. pp. 1281-1286.

39. *Ibid.*, p. 1284.

40. *Ibid.*, p. 1282.

41. *Ibid.*, p. 1283.

42. *Ibid.*, p. 1283.

43. *Ibid.*, pp. 1284-85.

44. *Ibid.*, pp. 1287-1288.

45. *Ibid.*, pp. 1296.

46. Cohen and Jaffray give an example (Example 4) of the rational decision criterion under complete ignorance which satisfy a'l their axioms. This rational criterion reduces to the maximin criterion under our special assumption. *Ibid.*, p. 1295.

47. Rawls, *A Theory of Justice*, p. 154.

48. *Ibid.*, p. 154.

49. Fiskin, James, "Justice and Rationality: Some objections to the Central Argument in Rawls' Theory", *The American Political Science Review*, Vol. LXI, No. 2 (June, 1975), p. 618.

50. *Ibid.*, p. 619.

51. *Ibid.*, p. 620.

52. *Ibid.*

53. *A Theory of Justice*, p. 154.

54. Arrous, K. J. "Some Ordinalist-Utilitarian Notes on Rawls' Theory of Justice", *The Journal of Philosophy*, Vol. LXX, No. 9 (May 10, 1973), p. 251.

Democratic Equality*

Joshua Cohen

"GUIDANCE WHERE GUIDANCE IS NEEDED"

In this article I examine John Rawls's maximin criterion of distributive equity.[1] According to maximin, social and economic inequalities are just only if they work to the maximum benefit of those in the least advantaged social position.[2] I think that maximin is a reasonable distributive principle, find much that Rawls says in support of it plausible, but believe that that support has not been well understood.[3] So I will present an interpretation, extension, and defense of the arguments for maximin proposed in *A Theory of Justice* (hereafter *TJ*) and in Rawls's more recent papers.[4]

There are three main themes in the article. First, and most important, I emphasize that maximin is a part of a "democratic conception" of equality (pp. 75–83). It is a natural consequence of the idea that we should seek to address distributive controversy by "extending" to that controversy the democratic ideal of a political association based on the mutual respect of free and equal citizens.[5] I will come back to this first theme after introducing the second and third.

* I would like to thank Larry Blum, Paul Horwich, Michael Sandel, and especially Norman Daniels for discussions of some of the issues in this article, and the editors of this journal for comments on an earlier draft. I also wish to thank John Rawls, with whom I have had the good fortune of discussing *A Theory of Justice* over the past fifteen years.

1. Most references to *A Theory of Justice* (hereafter *TJ*) are contained in the body of the article (Cambridge, Mass.: Harvard University Press, 1971).

2. Throughout I use the term "maximin" rather than "the difference principle."

3. I will not pursue several points on which I disagree with Rawls, including the best interpretation of the ideal of democracy and the implications of that ideal for economic order. See Joshua Cohen and Joel Rogers, *On Democracy: Toward a Transformation of American Society* (Harmondsworth: Penguin, 1983), chaps. 3, 6; and Joshua Cohen, "Deliberation and Democratic Legitimacy," in *The Good Polity*, ed. A. Hamlin and P. Pettit (Oxford: Blackwell, in press), and "The Economic Basis of Deliberative Democracy," *Social Philosophy and Policy* (in press).

4. Among the many limitations of my discussion are that I do not address problems that arise when "chain-connection" fails, and I say virtually nothing about the problems of characterizing the minimum position or of addressing conflicts among those who are in it.

5. *TJ*, p. 319, John Rawls, "Some Reasons for the Maximin Criterion," *American Economic Review, Papers and Proceedings* 64 (1974): 141–46, esp. 144–45, and "Reply to Alexander and Musgrave," *Quarterly Journal of Economics* 88 (1974): 633–55, esp. 648.

Ethics 99 (July 1989): 727–751

Second, to present the case for maximin, I will compare Rawls's two principles of justice with three "mixed conceptions" of justice. Like Rawls's conception, each of the mixed views requires equal basic liberties and fair equality of opportunity. But they reject maximin in favor of: (M1) maximizing average utility; (M2) ensuring that no one is below a poverty line, and, subject to that constraint, maximizing average utility; (M3) ensuring that no one is below a poverty line, and subject to that constraint, maximizing average utility discounted by a factor reflecting the degree of income concentration (e.g., the Gini coefficient).[6] To argue the case for maximin, then, I will want to show how considerations of self-respect and stability that provide support for the two principles in preference to utilitarianism (pp. 177–83) also carry over to providing reasons for the two principles in preference to the mixed conceptions.[7]

Third, I will present the case for maximin from the point of view of the original position. I will not, however, rely on the maximin rule of choice under ignorance but will emphasize instead that the parties in the original position aim to ensure that their social positions are "acceptable" (see pp. 734–35 below). This account of the original position clarifies and strengthens the arguments for maximin, but it also makes the original position less essential to their statement than one might have thought, an issue that I will come back to at the end.

To return now to the first theme, Rawls holds that a reasonable conception of justice should aim to "accommodate our firmest convictions and . . . provide guidance where guidance is needed" (p. 20). Justice as fairness accommodates convictions concerning religious toleration, rights of political participation, and racial and sexual discrimination by including an equal right to basic liberties, requiring that positions of social and economic advantage be open to all citizens, and affirming that these advantages must operate for the common benefit. To provide guidance, it includes a conception of democratic equality mandating fair equality of opportunity and maximin. Maximin in particular provides needed guidance because it addresses "the correct distribution of wealth and authority," an area in which "we have much less assurance" about what is right than we do on issues of basic liberties, and so "may be looking for a way to remove our doubts" (p. 20).

This lack of "assurance" is fueled in part by the conjunction of two conditions. The first is the intuitive power of certain ideals associated with "the tradition of democratic thought," in particular the fundamental

6. For discussion of this comparison, see *TJ*, sec. 49, "Some Reasons for the Maximin Criterion," pp. 141–46, "Reply to Alexander and Musgrave," pp. 646–53. On the motivations for the alternative distributive norms, see below, p. 730.

7. Since the problem is to select a conception of justice that includes a principle regulating the distribution of wealth and authority, and not simply to choose a principle of distribution, such phrases as "reasons for maximin" are shorthand for "reasons for including maximin along with the requirements of equal basic liberties and fair equality of opportunity."

ideal that, as citizens, we are free and equal, however much our social class, our talents, our aspirations, or our fortune may distinguish us and that our institutions should respect our freedom and equality.[8] The second is the fact of inequality. Born into different social positions, we have different expectations about the resources we are likely to have over the course of our lives (p. 96). In view of the importance of democratic ideals, it is not surprising that the legitimate extent of these inequalities is controversial. Maximin, when it is understood as addressed to this controversy, has a clear intuitive rationale: If the well-being of the least advantaged is maximized, the least advantaged have no reason to complain. And if the least advantaged have no reason to complain, then how, consistent with accepting the equality of citizens, could anyone have good reason to complain?

So justice as fairness aims both to accommodate and to guide. But as my sketch of the intuitive rationale for maximin indicates, the idea is not simply to supplement principles that accommodate with independent principles that guide. Instead the aim is to guide judgment about the distribution of resources by "extend[ing] the range of some existing consensus" (p. 582), in particular by showing that ideals that are ingredient in the democratic tradition, and that are (imperfectly) embodied in modern democracies, provide a *unified rationale* for principles requiring equal liberties, fair equality of opportunity, and maximin. The argument from the original position presents that rationale. Modeling the fundamental ideal of respect for citizens as free and equal, the original position provides (so the argument goes) a justification for the basic liberties associated with citizenship in a democratic state *and* for maximin, thus giving force to the claim that maximin provides a natural extension of democratic ideals.

Whatever its intuitive basis, however, maximin has been the target of three main lines of criticism:[9] that it is an *implausible* principle whose implications are at odds with firm intuitions about just distributions; that choice in the original position is *irrelevant* to justification, and so irrelevant

---

8. The quote is from John Rawls, "Justice as Fairness: Political not Metaphysical," *Philosophy and Public Affairs* 14 (1985): 223–51, quote on 233. In general, see Rawls, "Kantian Constructivism in Moral Theory: The Dewey Lectures 1980," *Journal of Philosophy* 72 (1980): 515–72, esp. 517–19, "Justice as Fairness," pp. 233–34, 240–44, and "The Idea of an Overlapping Consensus," *Oxford Journal of Legal Studies* 7 (1987): 1–25, esp. 2.

9. The criticisms are stated in a particularly instructive way in Kenneth Arrow, "Some Ordinalist-Utilitarian Notes on Rawls' Theory of Justice," *Journal of Philosophy* 70 (1973): 245–63; Brian Barry, *The Liberal Theory of Justice* (Oxford: Oxford University Press, 1973); Ronald Dworkin, "The Original Position," *University of Chicago Law Review* 40 (1973): 500–533; David Gauthier, *Morals by Agreement* (Oxford: Oxford University Press, 1986), esp. pp. 245–54; John Harsanyi, "Can the Maximin Principle Serve as a Basis for Morality? A Critique of John Rawls' Theory," *American Political Science Review* 69 (1975): 594–606; Thomas Nagel, "Rawls on Justice," *Philosophical Review* 83 (1973): 220–34; Robert Nozick, *Anarchy, State and Utopia* (New York: Basic, 1974), chap. 7; Michael Sandel, *Liberalism and the Limits of Justice* (Cambridge: Cambridge University Press, 1982).

to the justification of maximin in particular; and that maximin would
not be the principle of choice in the original position. I will be focusing
on the third criticism. While limits of space prevent me from discussing
the implausibility objection in any detail, I do want to sketch one element
of it in order to help to motivate the later argument.[10]

Critics of maximin who find some of its implications implausible
commonly blame those implications on its "informational poverty" and
rigidity.[11] Maximin is impoverished in that it focuses the evaluation of
distributions exclusively on the size of their minima, discarding information
about, for example, central tendencies and dispersions. It is rigid in that
it replaces nuanced judgments about the sufficiency of the minimum (as
reflected in, e.g., debates about the location of the poverty line) with the
rule that the minimum be maximized.[12] The force of these concerns can
be addressed by comparing justice as fairness with the mixed conceptions
M1–M3, since their distributive components are sensitive to facts that
maximin neglects: M1 considers the mean; M2 considers the minimum
and the mean; and M3 considers the minimum, the mean, and the
dispersion.[13] Furthermore, M2 and M3 avoid the rigidity of maximin by
rejecting maximization in favor of the less definite requirement of an
adequate minimum, namely, a poverty line.[14]

But why pursue this comparison via the original position? Why not
simply consider whether these norms, or other more complicated principles,
conform to our distributive intuitions and precepts? The reason is that
all distributive principles can be expected to conflict with some intuitions
and precepts. That is why we need guidance in the first place. The
controversy surrounding distribution, and the fact that richness and flexibility may be disadvantages in fundamental distributive norms (see below,
p. 745), make it hopeless to pursue that guidance by more thoroughly
canvassing our intuitions, or by developing richer and more flexible

10. I do think, however, that many of the cases in which maximin is alleged to have
strikingly counterintuitive implications can be addressed by keeping in mind that maximin
assumes the operation of the first principle and fair equality of opportunity and is to be
applied to the rules of the socioeconomic game and not to particular distributions.

11. I do not discuss Amartya Sen's variant of the informational poverty objection,
which emphasizes the problems of focusing on resources rather than human well-being
(see his "Equality of What?" in his *Choice, Welfare, and Measurement* [Cambridge, Mass.:
MIT Press, 1982], chap. 16).

12. For discussion of the American debates on the location of the poverty line, see
James T. Patterson, *America's Struggle against Poverty, 1900–1985* (Cambridge, Mass.: Harvard
University Press, 1986), esp. chap. 5.

13. For variety, I will sometimes use the term "justice as fairness" as a substitute for
"the two principles."

14. One can also give additional weight to lower positions by specifying a social welfare
function with a parameter that discounts individual utilities as those utilities increase. I
will not pursue this idea here since the problem of the arbitrariness in fixing the parameter
parallels some of the problems with M2 and M3. For discussion, see Rawls, "Reply to
Alexander and Musgrave," pp. 643–46; and Anthony B. Atkinson and Joseph E. Stiglitz,
Lectures on Public Economics (New York: McGraw-Hill, 1980), pp. 339–40.

distributive norms in the hope of producing equilibrium between them and a more comprehensive range of distributive intuitions or precepts.

What the implausibility objection really does is to underscore again the importance of the theoretical strategy of looking to more settled ideas outside the sphere of distribution in order to guide judgment within it, of "look[ing] for possible bases of agreement where none seem to exist" (p. 582). This is the aim of an account of democratic equality that addresses the distribution of resources by asking, Which distributive principles would be chosen by free and equal citizens seeking to choose a full conception of justice that includes principles for liberties and opportunities as well? This strategy for pursuing distributive guidance differs from the approach to questions of distribution that is adopted by Nozick and Gauthier, for example, who do not explain how their views of rights and rational bargaining might account for convictions about the liberty of expression, political liberties, or rights to equal protection of the laws, and that is pursued in the many other approaches to issues of the distribution of resources that do not explicitly incorporate that problem into a wider framework of normative and institutional argument that also accommodates fundamental convictions.[15] An important claim in the argument for maximin, then, is that when we do constrain our evaluation of distributional norms by embedding it in a more comprehensive argument for principles of justice that must also "accommodate our firmest convictions," we will see the reasonable motivations for maximin's (superficially implausible) guidance and its austere informational basis.

ORIGINAL POSITION AND SOCIAL EQUILIBRIUM

In this section I will clarify the *strategy* of the argument for maximin. I begin by sketching the structure of Rawls's argument for the two principles over average utility.[16] Then I discuss the extension of that structure to the argument for justice as fairness over the mixed conceptions, emphasizing the importance in that argument of the social ideal of a well-ordered society.

The Argument in TJ

A central aim of *TJ* is to defend the two principles in preference to utilitarianism (p. 150). The virtues of maximin are relevant to that defense, but they play only a supporting role in the arguments, which turn principally on the uncertain implications of utilitarianism for basic liberties. So the case for maximin itself is not clear. Still, by sketching the argument for the two principles over average utility we will be in a better position to understand the case for the two principles over the mixed conceptions:

15. See, e.g., Nozick; Gauthier.
16. See Steven Strasnick, "Review of Robert Paul Wolff's *Understanding Rawls: A Reconstruction and Critique of 'A Theory of Justice,'* " *Journal of Philosophy*, vol. 76 (1979), sec. 5.

Argument A: Two principles and average utility

A1. Each party in the original position must seek to ensure that his or her position is satisfactory (or adequate).

A2. The two principles of justice ensure a "satisfactory minimum" (p. 156; also, p. 175).

A3. Because the two principles ensure a satisfactory minimum, they also ensure satisfactory positions above the minimum.[17]

A4. Average utility does not ensure a satisfactory minimum and may in fact impose "hardship" on some that will be "intolerable" (p. 175).

A5. The gains above the minimum guaranteed by choosing the two principles that might result from choosing average utility (assuming one lands in a position above the minimum) are highly uncertain as to likelihood and magnitude.

A6. Given A1–A5, it is rational to choose the two principles over average utility.[18]

Two points about Argument A are important here. First, the choice of average utility threatens "intolerable" conditions (A4) principally because it provides uncertain support for basic liberties (p. 156). But the liberties and fair equality are protected under the mixed conceptions, and M2 and M3 also put a floor under income and wealth. In considering the choice between the two principles and the mixed conceptions, then, we must drop the claim about intolerable hardships, thus making the arguments less straightforward.

Second, Argument A appeals to the idea that the positions under the two principles, and in particular the minimum position, are satisfactory. Later I will present an interpretation of the relevant notion of "satisfactory." Here I want only to enter a point that will be relevant to that interpretation, namely, that much of *TJ* aims to defend the thesis about satisfactory positions. For example, virtually all of part 3, including the arguments about self-respect and stability, is intended to show that the two principles provide a satisfactory minimum (A2), and thus support the choice of

17. I make this point explicit in order to address concerns stated by Nozick, p. 192; and Gauthier, p. 247.

18. Argument A follows Rawls's claim that the original position exhibits to a high degree the conditions that make the maximin rule of choice suitable—conditions of extreme ignorance, involving grave risks, in which "the person choosing has a conception of the good such that he cares very little if anything, for what he might gain above the minimum stipend that he can, in fact, be sure of by following the maximin rule" (*TJ*, p. 154). A5 corresponds to the extreme ignorance condition, A4 to the grave risks condition, and A1–A3 to the "cares very little" condition. Note that the "cares very little" passage is not offered as a characterization of the parties in the original position but as a statement of one of the conditions that make the maximin choice rational. What needs to be shown is that an analogous situation obtains in the original position. If A1–A3 obtain, then there is such an analogy. While the parties represent individuals who do care about getting more than the minimum (they prefer more primary goods to less), they must act to ensure that positions are acceptable. Since getting to an acceptable position is much more important than getting past that position, the analogy obtains.

justice as fairness over average utility. There is no formal derivation of the principles that proceeds independently from these "informal" arguments,[19] but only the relatively straightforward point (A6) that if the informal arguments are right, then it is rational to make the conservative choice. So when I present a case for maximin in terms of self-respect and stability, I mean to be providing a case parallel to the argument for the two principles over average utility.

The Argument with the Mixed Conceptions

I will begin the discussion of the reasons favoring the two principles of justice over M1–M3 by sketching an argument modeled on Argument A:

> Argument B: Two principles and mixed conceptions
> B1. Each party in the original position must seek to ensure that his or her position, whatever it is, is satisfactory (or adequate).
> B2. The two principles of justice ensure a satisfactory minimum.
> B3. Because the two principles ensure a satisfactory minimum, they also ensure satisfactory positions above the minimum.
> B4. M1–M3 do not ensure a satisfactory minimum.
> B5. The gains above the minimum guaranteed by the two principles that might result from choosing a mixed conception (assuming one lands in a position above the minimum) are highly uncertain as to likelihood and magnitude.
> B6. Given B1–B5, it is rational to choose the two principles over the mixed conceptions.

Argument B differs from A in part because it drops the claim about "intolerable" outcomes (compare A4 and B4). To see whether the balance of reasons still supports justice as fairness, we need a better grip on B1–B4. So first I will discuss the notion of a satisfactory position. Then I will show how B1 falls into place. Finally, in the next section, I will present arguments for maximin which aim to provide support for B2–B4, in light of B5.

There are two ways to interpret the notion of an adequate minimum. The first, which I will call the "natural threshold interpretation" (hereafter NTI), holds that there is a threshold level of primary goods such that any human being with a rational life plan attaches infinite value to attaining that level, and a finite value (if any value at all) to getting over it.[20] So a conception of justice ensures a satisfactory minimum if and only if it ensures that everyone gets over the natural threshold. One virtue of NTI is that, by defining a satisfactory position as a position over the threshold, it explains why the parties in the original position are concerned to ensure

---

19. As is suggested by, among many others, T. M. Scanlon, "Contractualism and Utilitarianism," in *Utilitarianism and Beyond*, ed. A. Sen and B. Williams (Cambridge: Cambridge University Press, 1982), pp. 125–27.

20. Brian Barry was, I think, the first interpreter to endorse NTI. Many followed him. See Barry, p. 97.

satisfactory positions (B1). In addition, it shows the special importance of an adequate minimum (B2), since if any positions are below the threshold the minimum position will be. And finally it explains why the adequacy of the minimum implies the adequacy of all positions (B3), since a minimum above the threshold implies that all positions are over it.

But if NTI is right, then Rawls's argument is transparently wrong.[21] First, it is implausible that rationality and human nature do combine to yield a definite threshold that is uniform across people and circumstances. Second, the existence of a threshold does not support the two principles but requires only that everyone ought to get to the threshold before anyone goes over it. Beyond the threshold, the requirements of equity would remain indeterminate. Third, given that the threshold is assigned infinite utility, any of M1–M3 would do equally well in ensuring the threshold, since average utility will always increase more by pulling people to the threshold than by pushing people over it. The transparency of these difficulties suggests (correctly, I think) that NTI is misguided. But rather than arguing that case, I will propose an alternative account of the adequate minimum that does not assume a natural threshold.

I will call this alternative the "social equilibrium interpretation" (SEI).[22] The SEI begins from the fact that the parties in the original position are choosing principles for a well-ordered society with a number of distinct social positions. A conception of justice provides a satisfactory minimum, then, just in case those who occupy the minimum social position in a society regulated by the conception can reasonably expect to find that position acceptable. To explicate the notion of an acceptable social position, I need to say something about the idea of a well-ordered society.

Justice as fairness, as Rawls has emphasized, is addressed to a "modern democratic society" and seeks principles suited to a well-ordered society.[23] These two points are connected in that the notion of a well-ordered society is meant to capture certain aspects of the fundamental democratic ideal of a system of social cooperation among citizens who recognize each other as free and equal and who share an understanding of fair terms of association. Focusing, then, on the notion of a well-ordered society, two features of it play an important role in interpreting the notion of an acceptable position. First, the members of a well-ordered society share a conception of justice, and it is common knowledge that the basic institutions of the society conform to that conception. Recognizing the role

---

21. On the difficulties noted in this paragraph, see ibid., chap. 9.

22. In thinking about SEI I have benefited from Scanlon's "Contractualism," esp. pp. 119–28; and from Edward F. McLennen, "Justice and the Problem of Stability," *Philosophy and Public Affairs* 18 (1989): 3–30.

23. On addressing a "democratic society," see *TJ*, p. viii, "Some Reasons for the Maximin Criterion," p. 142, "Kantian Constructivism in Moral Theory," p. 518, "Justice as Fairness," sec. 2, "The Idea of an Overlapping Consensus," secs. 1–2. On the notion of a well-ordered society, see *TJ*, p. 4, sec. 69, "Reply to Alexander and Musgrave," sec. 1, "Kantian Constructivism in Moral Theory," pp. 535–40.

of the institutions in shaping their powers, opportunities, and aspirations, they affirm the legitimacy of those institutions and accept the effects on their powers, opportunities, and aspirations as reasonable. Second, each member has a conception of the good which he or she takes to be worth pursuing. Using that conception as a point of departure, each would arrive at the conclusion that it is rational to have the shared conception of justice, given that others have it as well; they would conclude that justice and goodness are "congruent" (p. 456).

In a well-ordered society, then, each person recognizes the justice of the society and on the basis of that recognition willingly complies with the terms of association and recognizes that their conception of justice is rational and on the basis of that recognition willingly endorses the conception of justice that leads them to comply. The question, then, is, Are there principles suited to such a society? Are there principles such that (1) if institutions satisfy the principles, and are known by members to satisfy them, then over time new members would come to understand the principles, to develop an allegiance to them, and to accept the institutions as just because of their conformity to the principles; and (2) each would develop a conception of the good which is worth pursuing and which is congruent with his or her sense of justice? If principles meet these two conditions, then a social order that satisfies them is supported by both moral and prudential reasons, and each position in the order is an acceptable position.

The SEI interprets the notion of a satisfactory position in Argument B in terms of this conception of an acceptable social position in a well-ordered society. Thus a position is satisfactory just in case a person in that position can be expected to acquire a sense of justice which affirms the legitimacy of the system of positions and a conception of the good which they take to be worth pursuing and which supports their sense of justice. Rawls emphasizes that the parties in the original position concentrate on the acceptability of the minimum position (B2). But this concentration is explained by the fact that the minimum position is most likely to be a problem. More fundamentally, they aim to ensure that their position is acceptable, whatever it is. And so in my discussion of the choice of principles, I will consider acceptability at positions above the minimum as well as acceptability at the minimum (B3). But before coming to that discussion, I need to consider one final preliminary issue.

Having identified a satisfactory position with an acceptable social position, I need to explain why the parties in the original position conservatively focus on the *acceptability* of positions (B1). The simple answer is that the original position is set up to force them to be conservative, whatever their natural predilections in matters of risk-taking (p. 172). But this simple answer gives rise to two further questions.

First, *why* set up the original position to force a conservative choice? The answer lies in the ethical idea that underlies the design of the original position. The point of the original position is to find principles for a well-ordered society, and the ideal of universal acceptability is one of the features that defines such a society. A variant of the initial situation in which the parties did not seek to ensure the acceptability of their position would be flawed. Put otherwise, the conservativism reflects the fact that the original position is designed to choose principles for a society on the assumption that it is well-ordered, and not to evaluate the ethical ideal of a well-ordered society itself.

Second, *how* is the original position set up to ensure that the parties focus on acceptability? The requirement that the parties are to *make an agreement* that is *final* requires that they come to terms that they expect to be able to keep; "no one is permitted to agree to a principle if they have reason to doubt that they will be able to honor the consequences of its consistent application."[24] So they look for arrangements that are acceptable, since the combination of moral and prudential reasons that make up acceptability should minimize noncompliance, resistance, and efforts at renegotiation. In this way the motivation for the contractual requirement in the original position "lies in its correspondence with the features of a well-ordered society," in particular with the condition of general acceptability.[25] Furthermore, the veil of ignorance prevents knowledge about the likelihood of being in an unacceptable position, if there are any unacceptable positions. And this means that no one can agree to a principle if there is reason to doubt that anyone, in any position, will be able to "honor the consequences of its consistent application." By choosing principles that are generally acceptable, the parties do their best to meet this requirement.

ARGUMENTS

I now come to the choice between the two principles and the mixed conceptions. Following the structure of Argument B, we need to show that: B2, the minimum position under the two principles is acceptable; B3, the other positions are acceptable given that the minimum is; and B4, the minimum under the alternatives may be unacceptable. Using this structure to organize the presentation, I will present the case for maximin by showing how the considerations of self-respect and stability that Rawls uses to defend justice as fairness against utilitarianism also provide reasons for preferring it to the mixed conceptions, thus substantiating the claim that maximin is a natural extension of democratic ideas.

Self-respect

The argument from self-respect is animated by three principal ideas. First, since self-respect is a fundamental good, whose presence is almost certainly required for acceptability (p. 440), the parties must ensure

24. "Reply to Alexander and Musgrave," p. 652; see also, *TJ*, pp. 175, 183.
25. "Reply to Alexander and Musgrave," p. 651.

conditions favorable to their self-respect. So important support for maximin would be provided if it were shown that the two principles support self-respect at the minimum position (B2) as well as above the minimum (B3), while the mixed conceptions may not support self-respect at the minimum (B4). The rationality of ensuring self-respect is reinforced by B5, that is, by the ignorance surrounding the magnitude of the gains that one may forgo in seeking to ensure self-respect.

While self-respect is not itself subject to public distribution, the second animating idea is that certain supporting conditions or "social bases" of self-respect are. Among those conditions are both the resources (including liberties and opportunities, as well as wealth) that enable us to develop and to pursue our aspirations with self-confidence and the recognition by others (who are themselves respected) of our worth.[26] I will call these the "resource" and "recognitional" bases of self-respect.

A third point aims to give content and plausibility to the idea that self-respect has social foundations by distinguishing two types of social foundation. I will call the first the "associational conditions" for self-respect, the conditions that bear more or less directly on "what we do in everyday life" (p. 441). Self-respect typically requires activity in association with others, including friends, or co-workers, or intimates, or those with whom we share political, intellectual, or spiritual ideals. Such association contributes to both the resource and recognitional foundations of self-respect. But when the basic framework of social and political institutions is unfavorable, these associational conditions may be absent or may fail to have their desired effects. For example, political obstacles may formally restrict the formation of associations; the distribution of wealth may effectively prevent some citizens from advancing their aims; some associations that are formally permitted may nevertheless be subject to public condemnation; and, in the absence of bases of mutual respect that extend across different associations and communities, comparisons across those separate groups may put citizens at odds and weaken the support for self-respect that those associations and communities would otherwise provide. To secure the foundations of self-respect, then, it is important that the framework of institutions and associated forms of public argument—what I will call the "framework conditions" of self-respect—support and foster the associational conditions.[27]

The parties in the original position must, therefore, assess the effects of different principles on both the resource and recognitional foundations of self-respect, taking into account both associational and framework conditions. Thus, they support the liberties of conscience, association, and expression in part because these liberties help to establish a framework

26. On the importance of recognition to the sense of self, see G. W. F. Hegel, *The Phenomenology of Spirit*, trans. A. V. Miller (Oxford: Oxford University Press, 1977), pp. 111–19.

27. On the associational conditions, see *TJ*, pp. 441–42; on the framework conditions, see *TJ*, pp. 178–80; on their combined operation, see *TJ*, pp. 234, 442.

that enables citizens to form and to sustain the associations that support their self-respect.[28] They are concerned about their level of resources because they want to be able to use their liberties to pursue their aims with self-confidence.[29] Further, they reject perfectionist principles in favor of "democracy in judging each other's aims" (pp. 442, 527), in part because perfectionist norms would likely run counter to the values pursued in at least some associations and thereby undermine the experience of respect in those associations. They embrace the notion of a *right* to liberties because the public understanding that liberties are a matter of right provides a clear affirmation of the worth of each that extends across the plurality of associations, thus enhancing the experience of respect within them. And they require a fair value for political liberty in part because of the public recognition that comes from political equality.[30]

Thus far justice as fairness and M1–M3 are in agreement. But they part company over the proper distribution of resources. To make a case for maximin, one needs to show how the considerations of self-respect that support the points of agreement (the right to basic liberties, the fair value of political liberty, the rejection of perfectionism, and some acceptable level of resources) can be extended to provide support for maximin. More specifically, we need to show that maximin assures the foundations of self-respect at the minimum position, that it will ensure those foundations above the minimum as well, and that M1–M3 will not assure the foundations of self-respect at the minimum position. Let's take up these points in turn.

Consider first the adequacy of justice as fairness in supporting self-respect at the minimum position. Maximin only permits inequalities that contribute to lifetime expectations at the least well-off position. Smaller inequalities would reduce expectations, as would greater inequalities. Let's assume that the value of liberties to a person depends on the level of resources available to the person. (While this seems implausible for the case of the political liberties, their worth is ensured by a proviso in the first principle requiring the fair value of political liberty.)[31] So the minimum value of the liberties under maximin is greater than the minimum value under the alternative principles.[32] Self-respect depends, in turn,

28. See *TJ*, pp. 536, 543–46, "The Basic Liberties and Their Priority," in John Rawls et al., *Tanner Lectures on Human Values*, vol. 3 (Salt Lake City: University of Utah Press, 1982), pp. 32–34.

29. While *TJ*, pp. 543–46, ties self-respect exclusively to the basic liberties, elsewhere maximin is said to contribute to the foundations for self-respect (see *TJ*, pp. 179, 180, 499, 536, "Some Reasons for the Maximin Criterion," p. 145, "The Basic Liberties and Their Priority," pp. 32, 34).

30. On self-respect and the fair value of political liberties, see *TJ*, p. 234, "The Basic Liberties and Their Priority," p. 32.

31. *TJ*, pp. 224–27, 277–78, "The Basic Liberties and Their Priority," pp. 42–45, 72–79.

32. See *TJ*, pp. 204–5, and the more qualified formulation in "The Basic Liberties and Their Priority," pp. 40–41. Norman Daniels criticizes this account of the value of liberties in his "Equal Liberty and Unequal Worth of Liberty," in *Reading Rawls*, ed. N.

on the value of the liberties, since a greater value enables a more confident pursuit of one's aims. Justice as fairness, then, builds strong resource support for self-respect at the minimum position into the framework of association.

Furthermore, this guarantee of the maximal worth of the liberties is part of a *public understanding* about the nature and limits of legitimate inequalities. That understanding identifies an acceptable minimum position as a maximized minimum, and so represents a commitment to ensure advantages irrespective of the particulars of social position, natural endowment, and good fortune that distinguish the free and equal members of a well-ordered society. To forgo possible advantages because the changes in public rules required to provide them would also reduce expectations at the minimum is to express respect for those at the minimum and fully to affirm their worth. Given the importance of self-respect, it is rational to build such public recognition of worth into the framework of association by choosing maximin, thereby supporting the recognitional bases of respect in more particular associations.

So the choice of maximin strengthens the foundations of self-respect. While the primary support for self-respect may be provided by the associational conditions, the principles of justice and the institutions that satisfy them strengthen the effects of the associations in terms of resources, by ensuring that the minimum level is as large as possible, and in terms of recognition, by providing a framework of public rules and terms of public argument that support a sense of self-worth (pp. 234, 442–43).

I now consider a complication in this argument.[33] Maximin is formulated in terms of the expectations at the minimum *position*, not in terms of the expectations of the *occupants* of that position (p. 64). Suppose that some farmers are in the minimum position in a maximin system with no agricultural price supports. Introducing price supports might move the farmers out of the minimum, while reducing the minimum expectation by increasing food prices. When this move is rejected as a violation of maximin, farmers cannot be told that their well-being is fully affirmed under maximin because they would be less well-off under an alternative principle. The argument instead must be that respect for the farmers is expressed by maximizing the expectation at their position.

Daniels (New York: Basic, 1975), pp. 253–81. He holds that the value of a liberty to a person is a function of that person's relative position in the distribution of resources (p. 271). In arguing for this thesis he considers only the case of political liberty, where the argument is strongest because the nature of politics makes the value of the liberties competitive. The requirement of a fair value for the political liberties reflects this fact (see "The Basic Liberties and Their Priority," secs. 7, 12). But extended to liberties more generally, Daniels's point does not seem right, because the use of other liberties is not, as a general matter, competitive.

33. After writing the first draft of this article, I read an essay by Brian Barry, "In Defense of the Difference Principle" (paper presented at American Political Science Association annual meeting, Washington, D.C., August 1985), which makes the points in this paragraph. I would like to thank John Rawls for bringing Barry's paper to my attention.

But this seems plausible, since it shows no disrespect for the farmers to refuse to improve their condition when such improvement would make another group worse off than the farmers were when they were at the minimum. Or at least this argument has force on condition that the farmers do not embrace the idea that there is something especially inappropriate about *farmers* being in the minimum position. And they are committed to rejecting this if they accept the idea that citizens are equals, regardless of social position or aspirations. This is an important qualification, which I will return to below.

We come now to the adequacy of maximin for self-respect at positions above the minimum. Nozick states the problem this way: "No doubt, the difference principle presents terms on the basis of which those less well-endowed would be willing to cooperate. (What *better* terms could they propose for themselves?) But is this a fair agreement on the basis of which those *worse* endowed could expect the willing cooperation of others?"[34] Applied to the foundations of self-respect, Nozick's question may appear purely rhetorical. Those in the minimum position have the social bases of self-respect secured in part *by the fact that they are doing as well as they are.* So how could maximin threaten the self-respect of those who are doing *even better?*

One answer is that those who are better off might focus their attention on the transfers and other forms of government activity required by maximin and find the foundations of their self-respect weakened by the fact that those highly visible forms of state action are explicitly keyed to the benefits of those in other positions. But this is a very weak reason. While the activities of the "transfer branch" (pp. 276–77) are not themselves aimed at the benefit of those above the minimum, the social arrangement as a whole is more advantageous to their position than it is to the minimum position. While they are not as well off as they would like to be, the problem, as Nozick's remark indicates, is not to ensure that all citizens are as well off as they would like to be but to find a fair basis for willing cooperation. Furthermore, since maximin imposes no absolute ceiling on the magnitude of the top position, the further success of those who are better off is never treated as worthless. This, too, affirms the foundations of self-respect above the minimum.

But these responses are not satisfactory as they stand because they skirt around the most important difficulty. In particular, they assume that equality is the proper baseline or benchmark for judging advantages. Given that premise, it follows that positions above the minimum are more advantaged *by social cooperation* than those at the minimum. Although those above the minimum prefer still greater advantages, they will not take the fact that their position could be higher under M1, for example, as a threat to their self-respect under maximin. They accept that if the

34. Nozick, p. 192.

foundations of self-respect are secure at the minimum position, then they are secure above the minimum.

But why should agents behind the veil of ignorance suppose that they will construe an equal distribution as a reasonable benchmark, if they should occupy a position above the minimum? They might affirm the ethical relevance of conceptions of the good and natural assets. And if they did, then it would be natural for them to hold that the relevant baseline is a state of nature in which people accumulate property in pursuit of their aspirations and on the basis of their natural assets.[35] But with that baseline, a comparison of positions in the distribution of resources in society provides inconclusive evidence about the relative benefits that flow *from social cooperation*. To accept the state of nature baseline is to reject the claim that advantages *in* society derive *from* social cooperation. Those who are better off might hold that maximin forces absolute concessions on them, or at least that their benefits relative to the relevant baseline are not as great as are the relative benefits for those at the minimum. Even though they are better off, the social order as a whole fails to affirm their worth as fully as the worth of those at the minimum. Concerned to secure their self-respect, they have reason to reject maximin in favor of, for example, maximax, or Gauthier's minimax relative concession, or a principle requiring Pareto improvements over the state of nature.

Of course if they did select one of these alternatives, they might find themselves in a pretty grim minimum. So the conclusion to draw may not be that some alternative to maximin is the principle of choice. Instead it might be that there is no way to secure self-respect at every position and that there does not exist a social equilibrium for a well-ordered society.

In responding to this objection, we need to keep in mind that M1–M3 as well as justice as fairness include requirements of equal basic liberties, the fair value of political liberty, and fair equality of opportunity. The parties have already agreed to these principles, having seen their rationale, and now are considering distributive norms for a society regulated by them. But then they must assume that whatever more particular position they hold, they are committed to accepting the understanding that the members are basically equal and, in particular, to accepting that social class, natural endowments, and conceptions of the good are all ethical contingencies that provide no reasons for differential treatment. If they do not accept that view, then it is not clear why they would accept the equal right to liberties of conscience, of expression, and of participation, the fair value of political liberty, and fair equality of opportunity. But if

---

35. See, e.g., ibid.; Gauthier; and James Buchanan, *The Limits of Liberty: Between Anarchy and Leviathan* (Chicago: University of Chicago Press, 1975). For a critical appraisal of such accounts of the social contract, cf. Jean-Jacques Rousseau's *Discourse on Inequality*, trans. Victor Gourevitch (New York: Harper & Row, 1986), p. 183, with his *On the Social Contract*, trans. Judith R. Masters (New York: St. Martin's, 1978), bk. 1, chap. 6, pars. 6–7.

they do accept it, then it is reasonable for them to regard equality as the benchmark for determining advantages. For to advance an alternative would be to assume that some people, or some aims, or some talents, or some contributions, are more important than others. But given a benchmark of equality, securing the social foundations of self-respect at the minimum position does secure them above the minimum. So the background assumption of equality provides a rationale for focusing on the bottom position and for supposing that secure foundations of self-respect at the minimum implies secure foundations above the minimum.

Suppose instead that they were to take the position that natural assets and conceptions of the good are relevant. To give content to this view, they imagine a state of nature in which individuals, guided by their aspirations, use their assets to accumulate resources. And they seek to assess the value of social cooperation to individuals by reference to this baseline. Putting to the side the problems of thinking of current aspirations and abilities as the aspirations and abilities people would have in a state of nature, it seems implausible that this line of thought would lead to any of M1–M3. In fact, it appears to provide a rationale for rejecting the requirements of fair equality of opportunity as well as the principle of equal political liberty. For once it is agreed that the baseline is a state of nature with differential holdings of property, then a rational social contract only requires improvements with respect to the inequalities of that preinstitutional situation. And such improvements might be secured through a system of constitutional government with inherited differences in real opportunities or in which political rights correspond to property ownership, or sex, or race.[36] So M1–M3 seem to be unstable alternatives to maximin. And at least some theories that reject maximin seem also to provide reasons for rejecting the equality of basic liberties and fair equality of opportunity as well, thus promising distributional guidance without accommodating more fundamental convictions.

We now come to the sufficiency of the minimum under the mixed conceptions (B4). Consider first M1. M1 provides weaker assurance of the social bases of self-respect than maximin does. While the adherents of M1 accept the equality of basic liberties and the need for a fair value of political liberty, they reject the idea of maximizing the minimum value of the liberties. Because the resource minimum may be lower, those who are in the minimum position may end up less able to pursue their aims than the occupants of the minimum position under maximin. And this lower value of the liberties weakens the resource support for self-respect, though the extent of that weakening is uncertain.

Furthermore, in view of the recognitional bases of self-respect, it is important to consider the justification of the magnitude of the minimum, and not simply its level. And under M1, no one can say, "The inequalities cannot go farther than this because of the losses to those in my position."

36. For discussion, see Joshua Cohen, "Structure, Choice, and Legitimacy: Locke's Theory of the State," *Philosophy and Public Affairs* 15 (1986): 301–24.

Because of publicity, each knows that *no* loss either of resources or of utility at their position ever provides a sufficient reason for rejecting a policy. A policy of loose labor markets, for example, with its predictable distributional implications, might then be supported *because* the combination of utility gains above the minimum and utility losses at the minimum produces an increase in average utility. And this is a weaker guarantee of the recognitional bases of respect than is available with maximin.

The support for self-respect also is weaker under M2 and M3 than under maximin, even though both include a minimum requirement. Thus, suppose that distributional institutions satisfy maximin and that I am in the minimum position. Still, my situation is adequate from the point of view of self-respect. As the economy grows, suppose that there is an announced shift to M2 or M3 under a transition rule that initially fixes the minimum at a level equal to the minimum expectation under maximin. Thereafter, however, the minimum will not be maximized. But since it never falls below what we assume to be an adequate level, how could the new minimum fail to be adequate?

This line of thought has considerable force on NTI. If everyone was above the threshold under maximin, M2 or M3 would by stipulation maintain people above that threshold. But the threshold notion is not a suitable understanding of the foundations of self-respect. It is public knowledge under M2 and M3 that the rules of the economic game do not work over time to maximize the minimum. So if I am in the minimum position, then I know that I could do better if those who are better off were prepared to forgo some of their advantages. And I know that this loss of advantage to me is not just for a stretch of time but covers the course of my entire life. Others know this, and know that I know it, and so on. Still they accept the advantages. This is a manifestly weaker affirmation of worth than is provided by maximin. How much weaker depends on where exactly the minimum is fixed under M2 or M3. A political determination of the adequate minimum might match its principled maximization under maximin. If the parties are counting on this, they might just as well choose the more rigid maximin principle. But since this matching seems unlikely, the maximizing specification has advantages over M2 and M3.

In sum, maximin provides stronger support for self-respect than M1–M3. Self-respect might be widespread under the alternatives to maximin; even at the minimum the associational conditions may be sufficient, especially with the support from the fair value of political liberty and fair equality of opportunity. But the background institutional support is less firm. In view of the importance of self-respect, justice as fairness is preferable.

Stability

We come now to the second argument, which parallels and extends Rawls's account of the stability of the two principles relative to utilitarianism (pp. 177–78, 496–504). The core of Rawls's argument is that a society is *stably just* only if there exists a social mechanism that preserves just conditions (should they obtain); that the most plausible mechanism is a shared sense of justice, and in particular a shared sense of justice that is rational for each citizen to affirm on reflection (pp. 454–58); and that a sense of justice organized around the two principles could more plausibly play this role than the average utility principle.

Why, however, would the parties, who are assumed not to be moved by considerations of justice at all, be so concerned with the stability of the conception that they choose? The earlier discussion of the ethical ideal of a well-ordered society provides the basis for an answer. What *makes* a conception of justice stable is that a society that conforms to it meets the two conditions I discussed earlier in the account of the acceptability of positions in a well-ordered society: Assuming a society that conforms to the conception of justice, the members of the society *acquire* the conception to which institutions conform; and that sense of justice is congruent with their good. So what underlies the concern with stability in the original position is the concern with acceptability. Assuming this latter concern, then, and following the structure of Argument B, the parties need to consider acquisition and congruence for maximin at the minimum position (B2) and for positions above the minimum (B3), and then the suitability of the mixed conceptions from the minimum standpoint (B4).

The problem of *acquisition* is to find principles such that individuals who are brought up in a well-ordered society regulated by those principles can be expected to acquire them in the normal course of their maturation. Acquisition has both cognitive and motivational aspects (pp. 485, 494–95). I will start with the cognitive.

The principles of justice must be learned, their content and implications understood. So it is important to choose principles that are "perspicuous to reason" (p. 499). Since each person occupies the position of equal citizen, this issue, I will assume, can be addressed without special reference to more particular positions. The main issue, then, is the relative ease with which different principles and their implications can be understood. So consider a society whose institutions are regulated by the two principles. The institutions conform to those principles, and conform to them in part because the members seek to preserve that conformity. In this society, the principles, as well as the conceptions of the person and social association that animate them, are learned in part as a consequence of the fact that they are expressed in certain obvious features of public institutions— for example, equality before the law, political liberties, public support for education, and tax and transfer policies aimed at ensuring that inequalities benefit the least advantaged. Acting within those institutions, citizens learn about their obligations and legitimate expectations, and about the features of individuals that are relevant to public argument.[37]

37. On the idea that citizens acquire norms by participating in institutions that conform to them, see Rousseau, *On the Social Contract*, bk. 3, chaps. 12–15; and G. W. F. Hegel, *The Philosophy of Right*, trans. T. M. Knox (Oxford: Oxford University Press, 1952).

Furthermore, the principles are acquired as a consequence of their role in providing the terms of public argument and justification among equal citizens (pp. 472–73).

Considered from the point of view of these processes of acquisition, maximin has the advantage of *relative* ease of understanding. Compared to other principles maximin is relatively simple, the information on which it depends is relatively accessible, and its rigidity makes its implications relatively definite. Relative clarity and ease of understanding should help to smooth the way to acquisition and to support a common understanding of the principles despite the differences in the circumstances in which they are learned.

These points about relative ease of understanding are weakest against M1 because it is simpler than M2 or M3. But M1–M3 all require relatively inaccessible utility information and cardinal interpersonal comparisons of utility (pp. 320–24). M2 and M3 (even if they are reformulated in terms of resources instead of utility) are also more complex than maximin, and both are less determinate (rigid) in their specification of the minimum. In short, the informational poverty of maximin, and the limits that its rigidity places on the role of political judgment in defining an acceptable minimum, have a point once when we take into account the importance of perspicuousness to reason. Since these advantages are shared by maximax, they are certainly not decisive. But we are looking to see how the "balance of reasons" (p. 183) comes out, and not to find a single decisive reason.

A natural objection is that questions about the implications of distributional principles are not well understood, and so this appeal to relative ease of understanding is spurious. Applying maximin requires, for example, a definition of the least well-off group and judgments about the kind of transfer scheme best suited to maximizing those expectations and the level of government at which it should be implemented. So even with public agreement about maximin, considerable public disagreement would likely remain. This objection correctly highlights that principles of justice can never eliminate the need for judgment. But it does not undermine the point that I am urging here, which concerns the *relative* simplicity, accessibility of information, and determinateness of maximin. Like all principles, maximin leaves considerable room for disagreements about its proper interpretation. But leaving room for disagreement is consistent with providing greater focus and guidance for public debate on distributional issues. And that is the only issue here.

This brings me to the motivational issue. Acquisition requires that citizens develop a disposition to judge and to act with the guidance of the principles, and the feelings (guilt, indignation) that are appropriate to them. Rawls emphasizes, plausibly I think, that reciprocity plays a central role in the formation of moral motivations: when others display a concern for our good, we develop a disposition to respond in kind (pp. 485, 494–95). What, then, are the implications of this psychological thesis for the assessment of principles?

I will begin by considering whether maximin contributes to acquisition at the minimum (B2). Thus suppose that citizens in the minimum position do learn the principles and recognize the commitment to their good reflected in those principles. As we saw in the discussion of self-respect, justice as fairness expresses that commitment by requiring both that inequalities work to the maximum advantage of the least well-off and that public argument proceed in terms of that advantage. Understanding this, those at the minimum position recognize that they (and those to whom they have attachments) benefit from the fact that others act on maximin. The tendency to reciprocate then leads those at the minimum position to develop a sense of justice whose content is given in part by maximin. For having such a sense of justice is tantamount to having a commitment to the good of each of those others who acts for their good. So when other citizens act from maximin they display a concern for my good and the good of those to whom I am attached. Responding in kind, I develop a concern for their good, and express this concern in part through an allegiance to the principles, including maximin.

The force of this point about motivation formation is supported by features of maximin that I mentioned in the discussion of the cognitive side of acquisition. Since maximin relies on more accessible information, it reduces temptations to manipulation and thus helps to establish trust. And by rigidly requiring that the minimum be maximized, and not simply that it be "suitable" or "decent," it provides added assurance of the willingness to reciprocate on the part of those in the minimum position.

In all of these respects, M1–M3 are less satisfactory (B4). The bonds of trust, for example, are weakened by the reliance on more manipulable information. But more important, assuming the importance of reciprocity to acquisition, the mixed conceptions are less likely to be acquired than maximin. Those conceptions may require sacrifices at the minimum for the benefit of positions above the minimum. In the case of M1, the absence of a minimum requirement makes this clear enough. With M2 and M3, there is a minimum requirement, but it is weaker. And this makes acquisition at the minimum less likely since affirming the distributive norms would be tantamount to affirming the good of those who do not fully respect one's good.

It may be objected that this appeal to the sacrifices imposed at the minimum by M1–M3 is indefensible. I propose to elaborate on the objection and to respond to it by considering the problem of acquisition at positions above the minimum (B3). The objection arises in response to the suggestion that the alternatives to maximin are weaker triggers to reciprocity because of the "sacrifices" they impose at the minimum. In response, it may be said that maximin is equally weak because of the sacrifices it imposes above the minimum. Positions above the minimum could (virtually) always be improved by the departures from the maximin point required by M1–M3. If sacrifices lead to problems of acquisition at the minimum under M1–M3, then there ought also to be obstacles to acquisition at positions above the minimum under maximin. Put otherwise, the argument about acquisition at the minimum may suggest that the only way to trigger reciprocity at *any* position is to maximize the expectation at that position. But then the acceptability of the minimum position under maximin will conflict with the acceptability of other positions, thus undermining B3.

This difficulty cannot be answered by reference to the intrinsic characteristics of reciprocity. It is a commonplace of social psychology that reciprocity is a universal norm. But it is equally commonplace that the content of reciprocity depends on shifting understandings of which values are "equivalent."[38] For example, when capitalists pay more than market-clearing wages, workers often respond by increasing the intensity of their labor. Akerlof has proposed that this response reflects workers' background understanding of the compensation that they can reasonably expect, namely, market clearing wages.[39] So when capitalists pay above market-clearing wages, workers respond with the "gift" of additional effort. If, by contrast, workers took themselves to be entitled to the higher wage, there would be no such gift exchange. Similarly, consider those whose understanding of entitlements assumes as a background the distribution of natural assets and the accumulations of wealth that would result from that distribution in a notional state of nature. They are unlikely to hold the view that treatment in accordance with maximin displays a concern for their good that ought to be reciprocated with a concern for the good of others as expressed in maximin. Instead, they can be expected to construe such "concern" as the moral equivalent of armed robbery.

In addressing this issue, we come back again to points that I discussed in connection with self-respect at positions above the minimum (pp. 741–42 above). Agreement has already been reached on equal liberties and fair equality of opportunity. Everyone sees the rationale for those principles; the problem is to choose distributive norms for a society that is regulated by them and that embodies the conception of equality expressed in them. But the fact that the parties accept one another as equals supports the view that equality is the benchmark. And if it is, then they must reject the view that maximin imposes sacrifices above the minimum, since those above the minimum are already doing better relative to the relevant benchmark than others whose position is supposed to be acceptable. So given the background democratic understanding that equality is the benchmark, considerations of reciprocity do support acquisition of maximin at the minimum and at positions above the minimum.

<hr/>

38. For both commonplaces, see Roger Brown, *Social Psychology*, 2d ed. (New York: Free Press, 1986), chap. 2, esp. pp. 48–53, 60–63. Rawls's view is stronger than the near consensus position which concerns the regularity of behavioral reciprocity and not the role of reciprocity in the formation of new motives, which is Rawls's concern in *TJ*.

39. George Akerlof, "Labor Contracts as Partial Gift Exchange," *Quarterly Journal of Economics* 87 (1982): 543–69.

We come now to *congruence.* The problem of congruence arises once we assume that the members of the society have acquired a sense of justice defined by the basic norms that govern their society. The issue that remains is whether it is rational for them to have that sense of justice, given its content and its role in regulating judgment, action, and feeling. More specifically, we need to consider the rational response by a member of a well-ordered society to the fact that other members have a sense of justice (p. 568). If it is rational to respond by embracing the sense of justice that one has acquired, then the principles meet the test of congruence, thus contributing to the argument for them.

My discussion of congruence will be limited in two important ways. First, I will not consider the overall likelihood of congruence, but only whether the choice of the two principles rather than M1–M3 strengthens the case for congruence. So I put to the side issues about congruence that raise difficulties for all the conceptions that I have been examining—for example, the potential conflicts between conscientious convictions and the principles of justice. Second, I will concentrate exclusively on a case for congruence that draws on the "Aristotelian principle" and the idea of a just society as a "social union of social unions" (p. 571).[40] Rawls argues that, in virtue of the Aristotelian principle, membership in a just society is a "great good" (p. 571). But he does not discuss the role of maximin in making it such a good.[41] That will be my focus here. I will begin with three background remarks about this argument for congruence.

First, on each of the conceptions of justice that we have considered, a just society provides a framework that encourages the expression of a wide range of human powers. The liberties and fair equality of opportunity formally enable individuals and associations to deploy their powers in pursuit of a plurality of aspirations. The rejection of perfectionism and the embrace of a pluralism of ideas of the good encourages variety in the forms of human expression. And each of the distributive principles provides some support to the pursuit of those diverse aims.

Second, a natural consequence of this first point is that citizens who share a sense of justice share the aim of coordinating their activities in ways that encourage the expression of human powers; they endorse the ideal of securing a framework of conditions in which a plurality of human goods can flourish. Sharing in that aim, they identify with (do not experience alienation from) the aspirations and activities of others who pursue aims and develop powers that they cannot pursue and develop themselves.

Third, there is a pair of psychological ideas. The first is the Aristotelian principle, according to which the enjoyment of our own activities is a function of (among other things) the complexity of those activities (p. 426). The second, the "companion effect" of the Aristotelian principle,

40. See also "The Basic Liberties and Their Priority," pp. 34–38.
41. Maximin does not play an explicit role in any of the arguments for congruence in *TJ*, sec. 86.

states that we enjoy the self-realizing activities of others (pp. 426, 428), at least when we are able to develop and to express our own powers as well (p. 523).

These three points together provide some support for congruence on M1–M3 as well as justice as fairness. Thus, to have a sense of justice is to have the aim of coordinating action in ways that provide favorable conditions for the expression of a wide range of human powers in pursuit of a plurality of aims. Bringing such coordination out of this diversity of forms of human expression is an activity of great complexity (p. 528). So if the enjoyment of one's own activities depends in part on their complexity, then there is some reason for embracing the common aim by affirming the sense of justice. For it is in virtue of that affirmation that one's own actions are guided by the aim of maintaining the scheme, and being so guided contributes to their complexity.

Further, having a sense of justice, we take an interest in the interests and activities of others; we respect them as free and equal citizens and have among our aims the provision of circumstances which enable them to develop and to realize their powers. This aim strengthens the companion effect, since the affirmation of justice makes their activities, in a way, our own. By contrast, persons who act in ways that undercut their sense of justice may lose the enjoyment that comes from taking the complex activity of coordinating on fair terms as their own and from identifying with the diverse aspirations of others and the achievements that follow on those aspirations.

While these considerations provide some grounds for congruence, they do not turn on the presence of maximin. To see whether maximin strengthens the case for congruence, let's begin with its contribution at the minimum position. I will consider both the relative benefits of affirming the sense of justice, and the costs of doing so.

On the side of benefits, embracing maximin involves a stronger attachment to the interests of others than does M1–M3, for reasons that I suggested in the discussions of reciprocity and the social foundations of self-respect. M1, for example, rests on a willingness to improve one's own situation even if the result is a worsening of the situation of others who are less well-off to begin with. Neither the minimum requirement included in M2 and M3 nor the constraint on dispersion in M3 changes the fact that maximin embodies a more complete affirmation of the interests of others. So maximin provides a firmer basis for the operations of the Aristotelian principle and the companion effect than the mixed conceptions. The stronger attachments reflected in maximin reduce alienation and dispose us "to appreciate the perfections of others" (p. 523). The limited respect expressed in the other principles correspondingly limits the appreciation.

In addition, the respect expressed in maximin and the resources ensured by it help to ensure that the least well-off are in a position to develop and to express their powers. So they are not offered the proposal that they find their (vicarious) enjoyment in advancing the aims of others. This aids in the operation of the companion effect, according to which our enjoyment of the activities of others is fostered by our own self-realization.

On the side of costs, there is no additional cost at the least advantaged position in affirming the sense of justice when maximin is added than there is when it is not part of the scheme. So there are added benefits, and no additional costs, and this implies that the contribution to congruence at the minimum by maximin is greater than the contribution by M1–M3.

What about those at higher positions? Why is it rational for them to find the enjoyments that come from a sense of justice preferable to the additional advantages they might derive from fewer constraints on the use of their current advantages to pursue their aspirations? Here again we should focus on the relative judgment: Is congruence more plausible under the two principles or under a mixed conception? In this case, there seems to be no clear advantage for maximin. The benefits of affirming it are greater for the same reasons that I mentioned in connection with the benefits at the minimum position. But the costs are greater as well, since the advantages at positions above the minimum under M1–M3 are almost certain to be greater than under maximin and are likely to be greatest under M1. So the case for congruence above the minimum might be greater with M1 than with maximin, though the balance of benefits and costs would presumably vary with circumstances. However, the fact that the costs are greater, and the case for congruence correspondingly weaker than one might have hoped, is not deeply troubling. None of the alternatives has a stronger overall case for congruence, and the costs are not so high as to make it impossible to live a decent life while affirming the principles of justice. That is not true at the minimum position, and so it is not true at higher positions either—at least if the parties accept the democratic idea that standards of decency are not fixed by class background.

CONCLUSIONS

On balance, then, the considerations I have discussed support maximin and give it a natural place in the ideal of democratic association. To conclude, I want to consider two related objections to my general interpretation of arguments from the original position.

In presenting the case for maximin, I have focused on the notion of a well-ordered society in which all positions are acceptable. But this may obscure the role of the original position in the argument. Why consider the choice of principles from behind a veil of ignorance? Why not simply consider the conditions that are required for an arrangement to be acceptable at each position? Answering the former question requires an answer to the latter, since the parties in the original position must consider the acceptability of positions. But once we have an answer to the latter, the initial choice seems to be an "unnecessary shuffle" (p. 32). We want to know what would be chosen in the original position *because* we want to know which arrangements (if any) are acceptable from each point of view. We can answer this question without proceeding through an initial choice situation. So isn't the original position pointless?

I do not think so. Proceeding via the original position focuses attention on the question, Which principles (if any) are acceptable from each position? It helps to bring out the ethical interest of this question and to get a clearer picture of how to answer it. We answer by attributing certain basic interests to citizens and by considering what people with those interests would rationally choose. Asking what would be chosen from behind the veil of ignorance brings focus and clarity by depriving people of the information that is irrelevant to the problem of acceptability and by providing a unified point of view from which that problem can be addressed. The original position is not *essential* to the argument for principles, since we can address the question of acceptability without introducing it at all. Still, this does not represent a serious objection to it. The original position is a device for solving a problem. Like most devices, it is not essential. Like other good devices, it is helpful. Like other good intellectual devices, it helps by clarifying.

But this response to the first objection suggests a second difficulty: treating the original position as a device for clarifying the problem of finding a social equilibrium for a well-ordered society may appear to deprive choice in the original position of its ethical interest. For it might be thought to reduce the problem of justice to an issue of social stability and, in particular, to the issue of what conditions might people be brought to accept. But this criticism misses the point of the SEI. The SEI does not identify the problem of justice with the problem of social stability but with the problem of finding the conditions required for stability *in a well-ordered society.* Whatever ethical interest the generic problem of stability might have, the more specific issue of the stability of a well-ordered society does have ethical interest. Or at least it has as much interest as the questions, What principles of justice are appropriate for a democratic society of free and equal citizens?

291

An Empirical Test of Rawls's Theory of Justice: A Second Approach, in Korea and the United States

Doug Bond
Harvard University

Jong-Chul Park
Korea Institute of Social Studies

The authors conduct an experimental/empirical test of Rawls's theory of justice with subjects from Korea and the United States. The subjects begin from Rawls's "original position." Then, from behind this study's experimental "veil of ignorance," they simulate Rawls's "derivation" of principles of distributive justice, both individually and collectively. The authors explore and attempt to explain the cross-cultural differences. The design of this study borrows from earlier (1987) tests conducted by Frohlich, Oppenheimer, and Eavey who found no support for Rawls. But significant differences in this study's approach make this an independent test. The authors find partial empirical support for Rawls's difference principle among the Korean subjects only and suggest that his assumptions and reasoning need to be refined to better account for concerns and considerations beyond levels of income and the balancing of individual monetary interests.

KEYWORDS: *cross-cultural; distributive justice; Korea; original position; Rawls; simulation; veil of ignorance*

John Rawls's (1971) theory of justice has received enormous attention from scholars in a wide range of disciplines. It also has provoked unprecedented interest from the popular media. The response, both academic and popular, has included criticism. But generally this has been constructive in nature. Indeed, even Rawls's harshest critics acknowledge that a "thorough

AUTHORS' NOTE: The authors are indebted to Professors Norm Frohlich and Joe Oppenheimer for generously sharing materials and ideas from their experiments. Thanks also are due to the editor and several anonymous reviewers who provided constructive suggestions on earlier versions.

SIMULATION & GAMING, Vol. 22 No. 4, December 1991 443-462

critique [is] not only justifiable but essential" (Schaefer 1979, p. 6). Thus the task of reading, examining and understanding Rawls has mushroomed into a broad, spirited debate.[1]

One of the central issues in this ongoing debate concerns the relationship between political philosophy and the social sciences. In particular, the substantive (liberal) assumptions guiding Rawls's approach have been questioned. These assumptions constrain the formulation of Rawls's "original position" and, in turn, his derivation of social principles. In reference to different, but no less plausible, assumptions, Fisk suggests that "the existence of the associated alternative conceptions of human nature undercuts the title to neutrality of the liberal conception. It appears that Rawls's working conception of human nature does not supply the principles of justice he derives from the original position with moral weight outside the context of liberal democracy" (Fisk 1975, p. 57).

One such context is found in the tradition of hierarchical stratification and communal values that permeates Korean society.[2] It was this context that stimulated our inquiry into Rawls's claims that the assumptions underlying his "original position" are "widely accepted, weak, innocuous and trivial" (1971, p. 18). For example, it seemed to us that many Koreans could not easily conceive of themselves as being "mutually disinterested" (1971, p. 13). Interpersonal relations in Korea coalesce around small group communities such as clans, families, schools, and regional-based collectivities. And although this interconnected complex of communities does not comprise a single national hierarchy, Korean society remains communal and hierarchical in both structure and dynamics.

Thus two fundamentally different conceptions of human nature are evident: one embodied in (Rawls's) liberal democracy and the other rooted in the traditional Korean hierarchical society[3] based on communal (as opposed to individualistic) values.[4] We examine the extent to which these alternative conceptions have an influence on the derivation of principles of distributive justice in a laboratory setting.

Our Approach

We suspect that Rawls's conditions and presumptions are not all "natural and plausible" in the Korean context. But Rawls's judgments about human nature are not absolute. Indeed, he describes the process of derivation as working from both ends to arrive at a "reflective equilibrium" (1971, p. 20). One way to refine the equilibrium is to have subjects with different backgrounds, but operating from Rawls's original position behind an experimental veil of ignorance, choose or derive principles of justice. If these principles diverge from Rawls's, a modification or refinement of Rawls's conditions and/or principles would be suggested.[5] On the other hand, empirical support for his assumptions and/or principles would be evident if confirmed by both Koreans and Westerners from behind a veil of ignorance.

Frohlich, Oppenheimer, and Eavey (1987a, 1987b) have conducted a series of laboratory tests to empirically evaluate one aspect of Rawls's theory, the choice of a principle of income distribution. Their subjects were from the United States and Canada. More recently, Lissowski, Tyszka, and Okrasa (1988) have replicated the experiments with Polish students. These earlier experiments yielded almost no support for Rawls's difference principle in favor of a mixed principle that takes into account not only the position of the worst-off individual but also the potential expected gain for the rest of society.

We too establish experimentally an "original position" and a "veil of ignorance" to derive principles of distributive justice. Our subjects are drawn from different (Korean and Western) contexts. We compare their preferred principles with Rawls's "derivations" in an attempt to test this central variable in Rawls's theory.

The present design, however, is sufficiently different from the earlier experiments to be characterized as an independent test. The basic departure is twofold: We standardize means in the illustrative examples and we present the examples on a continuum. We modified the design in an effort to facilitate comparison of the resultant structures of the various income redistribution principles. These structures of economic relations represent overall or basic *patterns* of income distribution rather than absolute levels or amounts of income.

Our modification in experimental design yields a *static* test of Rawls where the overall size of the "pie" to be divided is held constant. It is important to note that this design has a conservative bias with respect to Rawls's derivation. In a situation where one's future placement in a society is unknown, a fixed mean design favors principles that impose caps on high incomes (unlike Rawls) because such measures necessarily benefit those with incomes below the mean. In particular, a fixed mean design allows one to minimize worse case risk by choosing to cap high incomes.

Our approach is empirical/experimental. We borrow from (but, again, do not replicate) the previous laboratory experiments developed by Frohlich et al. for, as they have argued, Rawls's principles "would only be compelling, as an ethical argument, if — as the ideal were approximated empirically — the behavior of individuals came to approximate that predicted in the ideal" (1987a, p. 7).

To be sure, the present test of Rawls's hypothetical derivation of principles of distributive justice is imperfect and incomplete. But our focus on basic structures and, especially, our conservative bias push our approximation toward, rather than away from, the ideal. Our design takes on importance because it shows the boundary conditions for the earlier experiments. And as even more rigorous tests are developed and replicated, we should be able to further specify the conditions under which Rawls's derivations might be supported.

Rawls's Theory of Distributive Justice

Rawls suggests certain patterns of distribution are more just than others. He develops an "expository device" to identify the conditions, constraints, and principles of the fairest distribution of income. Rawls begins with an original position: "the appropriate initial status quo which assures that the fundamental agreements reached in it are fair." (1971, p. 17). Rawls argues for his "most favored" interpretation by working from "widely accepted but weak premises to more specific conclusions," and specifies four conditions (Rawls, 1971, pp. 18-19):

1. no one should be advantaged or disadvantaged by natural fortune or social circumstances in the choice of principles;
2. it should be impossible to tailor principles to the circumstances of one's own case;
3. particular inclinations and aspirations, and persons' conceptions of their good do not affect the principles adopted;
4. the parties in the original position . . . all have the same rights in the procedure for choosing principles; each can make proposals, submit reasons for their acceptance, and so on.

He also describes a "veil of ignorance" to be used together with these conditions to "nullify the effects of specific contingencies which put men at odds and tempt them to exploit social and natural circumstances." Most simply, this veil is a set of assumptions guiding his subsequent derivation of principles. The assumptions include that "no one knows his place in society, his class position or social status; nor does he know his fortune in the distribution of natural assets and abilities, his intelligence, strength, and the like" (1971, pp. 136-137).

Finally, Rawls derives the following two principles of justice from the original position (Rawls, 1971, p. 60):

First: each person is to have an equal right to the most extensive basic liberty compatible with a similar liberty for others.
Second: Social and economic inequalities are to be arranged so that they are both (a) reasonably expected to be to everyone's advantage, and (b) attached to positions and offices open to all.

Our Test of Rawls's Theory

Our laboratory test of Rawls's expository device focuses on patterns of distribution (what Rawls calls the basic structures of society) which support the range of alternative principles of distributive justice. Departing from the earlier experiments, we array these alternative patterns or structures on a *continuum of redistribution systems* from no redistribution (i.e., no taxation) to "absolute" redistribution (equalizing all incomes). Each of the patterns is associated with a principle of distributive justice.

Our subjects, working in groups of four to six people, chose collectively a preferred principle of distributive justice (i.e., a pattern of income distribution). The subjects also chose individually their personal preferences (by ranking) at four different times throughout the experiment.

Both the individual and collective choices were made in an experimental original position. At the time of their choice, the subjects did not know the economic class into which they were to be randomly assigned. They also did not know the extent of their ability to perform three tasks. The tasks involved answering 10 to 15 true-false and fill-in type questions. The tasks were designed to create a wide range of scores that were subsequently used to calculate payoffs. Most questions required a general knowledge (e.g., name the author of *1984*), some were almost trivial in nature (e.g., identify the 48th state of the United States), and still others were more technical (e.g., what is the chemical formula for benzene?).[6]

Thus, three variables — choice, luck, and skill — operated jointly, much as they do in Rawls's expository device, to approximate a veil of ignorance.

The subjects were paid for their participation in the experiment. Total remuneration ranged from a low of some $10 to a high of some $50 per subject. The high variance in payoffs provoked much discussion, and clearly impressed our subjects (as related by the subjects during the postexperiment debriefing) with the magnitude of the hypothetical, "real life" implications of the experiment.

Research Questions

Our initial thoughts on the likely outcome of experimental derivations of principles in Korea and the United States were somewhat ambivalent concerning possible cross-cultural differences. We thought the strong communal bonds in Korean society might sway preferences toward structures of redistribution that tie high and low earners in (hierarchical) intricate patterns of obligation and privilege. Rawls's difference principle, in which the least advantaged receive the greatest benefit, consistent with promoting benefits to the society as a whole, seemed to us to be compatible with this line of argument, although out of context with Rawls's original formulation. Likewise, we thought that individuals in the West, operating behind an effective "veil of ignorance," also might choose Rawls's principle. But here we surmised their rationale would be based more on the maximization of (unknowable) individual interests that were coincident with benefits to the society at large. Our primary interest, therefore, was on exploring and explaining any differences between cultures and in light of Rawls's derivation. Toward this end we articulated several questions.

1. About the group preferences (decisions):
    What is the nature of the group decisions, that is, are they agreed by consensus, (paired) majority vote, or are the groups unable to reach a collective decision? What are the preferred principles of justice? What differences, if any, are evident between Korean and Western group preferences?
2. About the individual preferences (rankings):
    What are the preferred principles of justice? What differences, if any, are evident between Korean and Western individual preferences? What experimental effects might account for the preferences? What other (social-psychological) factors may have affected these preferences?
3. About the stated and/or apparent rationale for the preferences:
    What concerns were expressed during the group discussions? What comments were expressed by individual subjects?

Subjects

Five of the 26 Korean subjects were graduate students and 21 were undergraduate students. They ranged in age from 19 to 30; the mean age was just over 22 years. Ten of the Korean subjects were female, 16 were male. Both parents of all Korean subjects were born in Korea, as were the subjects themselves.

Fifteen of the 24 non-Korean subjects were graduate students, 4 were undergraduate students and 10 were not enrolled in a degree program, but worked in research/clerical capacities on campus. They ranged in age from 21 to 29, averaging just over 24 years-old. Six of these subjects were female, 18 were male. The heritage of these non-Korean subjects was diverse: their parents' birthplaces included Australia, France, Iran, The Netherlands, Norway, the Soviet Union, Syria, the United Kingdom, and the United States. The subjects' birthplaces were similarly heterogenous. But none had lived anywhere in East Asia prior to their current sojourn. The commonality among these non-Koreans was their North American-Western European upbringing. All were raised and associated themselves with Western — as opposed to Eastern — values. Thus we refer to them as the "Western" subjects.

Experimental Procedures

We ran the experiment five times in September and October, 1988 at five large universities in Korea. Three of the universities are located in Seoul, one in Inchon, and one in Kangwon Province. Each group was composed of 5 (Korean) students. All of these sessions were conducted entirely in Korean. In addition, we ran the experiment once in Seoul in August (in English) with another group of students, one of whom was Korean. The lone Korean in this mixed group was a resident assistant who lived with the Westerners in an international dormitory. He was fluent in English, comfortable with the "Western" group, and was clearly atypical in his exposure to Western culture. The total number of Korean subjects was 26. The other Korean subjects were recruited with announcements made in regular (Korean) political science classes.

We ran the experiment four times in the United States (in English) from November, 1988 to January, 1989. One of these groups had 4 subjects, one had 6, and the other two had 5 each. The total number of non-Korean subjects was 24 (this includes the four from the mixed group run in Seoul). The non-Korean subjects were recruited from among foreign students at an international school in Seoul (for the one mixed group), and with announcements posted at Harvard University.

The experiment was conducted in four parts and lasted about 2.5 hours. The purpose of Part 1 was to develop a common understanding among the subjects of the terminology, purpose and procedures. In Part 2 we sought to impress on the individual subjects the elements of luck, skill, and their choice of a principle as they effected their remuneration for the experiment, thereby simulating the veil of ignorance. The group discussion and choice of a principle were conducted during Part 3. Here each subject's remuneration depended in part on the group (as opposed to individual) choice of a principle. Part 4 served as a "debriefing" period in which the subjects discussed their experience and completed a short attitude and background information questionnaire.

The specific activities included the following:

Part 1: introduction to the principles; *initial ranking* of principles; discussion of the principles; comprehension tests; correction and calculation of payoffs; review of principles and procedures; and *base ranking* of the principles. For the comprehension tests, the payoff was $0.50 for each correct answer on the first try. The maximum (possible and actual) payoff was $7.50; the minimum actual payoff on the first try was $5.00. For those few who had to take the test again (only the incorrect test items), $0.25 was paid for each correct answer.

Part 2: Task 1 (choice of principle, completion of task, and drawing of income class); correction and calculation of payoffs; Task 2 (another choice of principle, completion of task, and drawing of income class); correction and calculation of payoffs; review of principles and procedures; and *pretest ranking*. For Tasks 1 and 2 the payoff was determined by first locating the column (see Table 1) of the individually chosen principle, then the row of the randomly drawn income class, and multiplying this figure by the task skill score as expressed in a percentage (the range was 0% to 100% for Task 1 and 0% to 120% for Task 2). Note the experimental "interclass mobility" offered by the skill score range extending above 100%. The actual skill score range was 20% to 100% on Task 1 and 0% to 100% on Task 2.

Part 3: group discussion; closure of discussion — by consensus; group decision first by consensus, or if none, then by paired majority vote, or if none, imposed (at random); Task 3 (completion of task and drawing of income class); correction and calculation of payoffs; and *posttest ranking*. For Task 3, the payoff was determined as above except the group rather than individual choice was used to locate the column, and the random drawing was modified so that each group member would draw a different income class; the payoffs for the group-defined principles were calculated separately with values between columns 4 and 5. The actual range of skill scores on Task 3 was 0% to 120%, out of a possible 150%.

Part 4: completion of background questionnaire; debriefing; calculation of total remuneration; and payments.

Table 1 details the U.S. dollar payoffs for the Western subjects. The Korean subjects' payoffs were in Korean won and ranged from about 3 to 30 thousand won.

TABLE 1:   Payoff Calculations (in U.S. Dollars)

Income Class	Principles				
	MAXAVE	FLRSUP	MAXFLR	RNGCST	EQLINC
High	22.79	22.26	20.65	19.22	11.33
Middle high	15.27	14.92	13.83	13.68	11.33
Middle	10.40	10.16	9.43	9.88	11.33
Middle low	7.08	6.86	9.07	9.07	11.33
Low	4.20	6.86	9.07	9.07	11.33

Principles of Distributive Justice

Our MAXAVE (maximize average) principle represents the preredistribution, actual income pattern of urban Korea in 1986. The FLRSUP (floor support) principle subsidizes low income earners to a level of 60% of the average income. The HGHFLR (high floor) principle represents Rawls's "derived" difference principle, and has a subsidy level of 80%. Both the FLRSUP and HGHFLR principles are funded with a flat tax in our illustrative examples, the former at 2.3% and the latter at 9.4%. As we move along the continuum toward more equal patterns of income distribution, a progressive tax is needed to compress the income pattern. Our RNGCST (range constraint) principle uses a progressive tax of 16% on the high earners (the top 10 percentile group) and subsidizes low earners to 80% of the average income. Those in the 30th to 70th percentile groups (the middle class) are taxed at 5% under the range constraint principle, and those between the 70th and 90th (the middle high class), at 10%. Finally, our EQLINC (equal incomes) principle completes the range of alternatives with an equal income distribution.

GRPALT6 and GRPALT7 (group alternatives 6 and 7) are group-defined principles. Both are variants of the range constraint principle: GRPALT6 has a progressive tax of 25%, 12%, and 4% for high, middle-high, and middle classes respectively; GRPALT7 has rates of 25%, 5%, and 1% for the same classes. The main difference between them lies in the floor; GRPALT6 subsidizes all incomes up to 80% of the group average; GRPALT7 stipulates subsidies up to only 70% of the average.

TABLE 2:   Group Choices of Principles of Justice

	Principles							
Number	MAXAVE	FLRSUP	HGHFLR	RNGCST	EQLINC	GRPALT6	GRPALT7	Totals
Combined	0	2	1	4 (6)	1	NA	NA	10
Korean	0	1m	1m	3c	0	NA	NA	5
Western	0	1m	0	1m (3)	1c	2m	0	5

NOTE: "m" identifies a paired majority vote, "c" a consensus decision; numbers in parentheses indicate frequencies when the group defined alternatives (6 and 7) are included in the count for the range constraint principle, of which they are variants; the General Association CMH statistic (1.800, $df = 3$, $p > 0.61$) reveals no significant difference between the Korean and Western groups in their choices of preferred principles.

Group Preference (Decisions)

Table 2 presents the group decisions in aggregate and by culture (Korean or Western), along with a notation on the nature of the decision.

We find no significant differences between our Korean and Western subjects in their group choices of principles of justice. When we consider the group-defined alternatives as variants of our range constraint illustration, both Korean and Western groups converge on the range constraint principle. But a cross-cultural difference is evident in the way in which the group choices were made. All of the Korean groups that chose the range constraint principle were unanimous in their decisions.[7] But all of the Western groups that chose the range constraint principle (or a variant) required a (paired majority) vote to break the resistance to capping high incomes.

Individual Preferences (Rankings)

Table 3 presents the posttest mean rankings for all subjects combined and for the separate cultures. Note these rankings were done after the group decision. If the individual subjects disagreed with the group decision, they were told to base their rankings on their own feelings rather than on the group decision.

Because our principles already are arrayed on a continuum, we assign numerical values to indicate choices along this continuum: MAXAVE = 1, FLRSUP = 2, HGHFLR = 3, RNGCST = 4, EQLINC = 5. Values approaching 1.0 indicate less taxation or redistribution of income. Values approaching 5.0

TABLE 3:   Posttest Individual Mean Rankings

Ranking of Mean Value	Subjects					
	Korean		Combined		Western	
First	RNGCST	1.73	RNGCST	1.82	RNGCST	1.92
Second	HGHFLR	1.92	HGHFLR	2.46[a]	HGHFLR	3.04
Third	FLRSUP	2.50	FLRSUP	2.88[b]	FLRSUP	3.29
Fourth	MAXAVE	4.35	EQLINC	3.98[c]	EQLINC	3.46
Fifth	EQLINC	4.46	MAXAVE	4.40	MAXAVE	4.46

NOTE: Superscripts a, b, and c indicate significant differences between Korean and Western subjects as follows:
a. $t = -4.55$, $p < .01$; b. $t = 2.32$, $p < .05$; and c. ($t = 2.59$, $p < .05$. For the 10 Western subjects who had ranked 6 or 7 principles instead of 5, rankings less than 5th place on all principles except the range constraint were assigned a value of 5; and for these same 10 subjects, their highest (toward 1st place) ranking among the three range constraint variants (RNGCST, GRPALT6, and GRPALT7) was used to facilitate comparison between the Korean and other Western subjects who ranked only the 5 principles.

indicate more redistribution of income by taxing higher incomes to provide more for those with lower incomes.

For example, at one extreme, a value of 1.0 represents no redistribution of income. All keep what they earn. No subsidies are mandated for low earners. Values between 1.0 and 2.0 represent provision only for a "safety net" or minimum income to be guaranteed by the chosen principle of distributive justice. But values around 4.0 and above represent principles of redistribution that tend to equalize all incomes as the value increases. And at the other extreme, a value of 5.0 indicates a "complete" redistribution of income to render all incomes equal.

We find agreement between Western and Korean individual subjects on the preference for the RNGCST principle (or one of its variants) and on the rejection of the MAXAVE principle. But marked differences are evident as well. Note especially the break between the first and second mean rankings for the Western subjects, but between the second and third for the Koreans; similarly, the Western mean rankings reveal a break between the fourth and fifth places, whereas a break occurs between the third and fourth places for the Koreans.

Experimental Effects

To determine the extent to which our experimental process might have influenced the choice of principles prior to the group discussion, we exam-

303

ined the differences between the subjects' initial- and base-test rankings. Recall the base ranking was done after the comprehension tests but before the skill exercises (Tasks 1 and 2) designed to impress on the subjects the monetary implications of their choices, and before the group discussion and final task (3). No significant differences were found between the initial- and base-test rankings of the principles for either the Korean or Western subjects. We also looked for changes in ranking that appeared after the base ranking but before the group discussion, that is, during the skill exercises. Again, no significant differences were found between the base- and pretest for either the Korean or Western subjects.

Social-Psychological Factors Affecting Preferences

Rawls argues that worst-case risk aversion is an important ground for the selection of his two principles (1971, pp. 176-177). We followed Frohlich et al. in asking the subjects how much they would pay for and sell a lottery ticket to tap into the notion of risk aversion. We created two variables from the data: RISK and PROFIT. RISK is computed by dividing the amount a subject was willing to pay for a ticket by its probable or mathematically expected return. PROFIT is computed by dividing the amount for which a subject was willing to sell his/her ticket (less its cost) by the probable return. Values above one suggest a willingness/desire to take more risks/profit. Values below one suggest the opposite.

We asked also about the subjects' degree of financial independence as indicated by the source of funds for their college education. This variable, SELFSUP, is expressed as a percentage, and includes individual savings, personal loans, and earned scholarships.

AGE was another variable. It should be self explanatory. SCHLYEAR represents the subjects' year in school from 1 (freshman) to 4 (senior) for undergraduates, 6 for MA students and 8 for students enrolled in a Ph.D. program.

Finally, the subjects were asked to agree or disagree with a series of statements about relevant issues. The scale was 1 (*strongly disagree*) to 5 (*strongly agree*). The statements are listed below along with their variable names:

EQUALITY: Relative equality of wealth is a good thing.
GVNTGUAR: Governments should ensure that all people have a relatively decent
    level of living.

GVNTSUP: Governments ought to support people who are disadvantaged by unavoidable natural events.

INDEFORT: The greatest accomplishments in history were individual effort.

INFERIOR: In every country there are groups of people who are naturally inferior.

SURVIVAL: For some people to succeed, others must fail.

Table 4 presents the significant bivariate correlations between preferences for each of the five principles and the social-psychological variables listed above.

The universal rejection of MAXAVE and preference for RNGCST are apparent in that no significant bivariate correlations[8] were evident on the MAXAVE and RNGCST principles at the aggregate level of analysis. This held true also for separate analyses by culture, by gender, and by culture and gender, with one exception.[9] Also a uniformity in the Korean preferences is evidenced by the lack of (within-culture) significant correlations except for the interesting negative correlation between GVNTGUAR and a preference for the EQLINC principle. It seems that the Korean subjects who want the government to guarantee a decent level of living, do not want a high floor that would tend to equalize incomes.

With respect to the FLRSUP principle, the Korean subjects held fast to a hierarchical view of society, considering some people to be naturally inferior significantly more than the Western subjects (means = 3.35 and 2.33, respectively).[10] The Koreans also were more willing to take economic risks (means = 0.86 and 0.39, respectively). Multiple (stepwise) regression analyses revealed GVNTSUP and INFERIOR to be significant predictors of a preference for the FLRSUP principle.[11]

Both SCHLYEAR and AGE were negatively correlated with the choice of the HGHFLR (Rawls's) principle. The older the subject and the more advanced in education, the less he or she chose this principle. But when analyzed separately by culture, the Koreans had no significant correlations and the Westerners had only one — on the SELFSUP variable. Those Westerners who made it on their own resented the high guaranteed minimum income, but this sentiment was not shared by the Koreans. SELFSUP and SCHLYEAR were predictors of a preference for the HGHFLR principle in the multiple regression.[12]

As expected, the variable EQUALITY was positively correlated with the principle of equal incomes at the aggregate level of analysis. But separate analyses reveal two additional variables, GVNTGUAR and SCHLYEAR, to be correlated as well. GVNTGUAR is significant with both Korean and Western subjects but, as noted above, in opposite directions. Finally, the

TABLE 4:   Significant (Bivariate) Correlations Between Individual Preferences and Selected Variables

Preferred Principle	Variables (by Subjects)								
	Korean	r^a	p	Combined	r^a	p	Western	r^a	p
MAXAVE	none significant			none significant			none significant		
FLRSUP	none significant			INFERIOR^c	.46	.01	INFERIOR	0.59	0.01
				GVNTSUP	−.37	.01	GVNTSUP	−0.51	0.05
				RISK^d	.30	.05	RISK	0.57	0.01
							GVNTGUAR	−0.51	0.05
							EQUALITY	−0.53	0.01
HGHFLR	none significant			SCHLYEAR^e	−0.49	0.01			
				SELFSUP^f	−0.49	0.01	SELFSUP	−0.43	0.05
				AGE^g	−0.31	0.05			
				SURVIVAL	0.31	0.05			
RNGCST^b	none significant			none significant			none significant		
EQLINC	GVNTGUAR	−0.54	0.01	EQUALITY	0.29	0.05	EQUALITY	0.61	0.01
							GVNTGUAR	0.50	0.05
							SCHLYEAR	−0.44	0.05

a. These are Pearson product-moment correlations. The sign has been reversed so that high (toward 1st place) rankings are associated with high (agreement) scores on the variables.
b. The transformation procedure described in the note to Table 3 was employed here.
Superscripts c, d, e, f, and g indicate significant differences between Korean and Western subjects as follows:
c. $t = 2.25, p < .05$; d. $t = 2.69, p < .05$; e. $t = -5.34, p < .01$; f. $t = -2.60, p < .05$; and g. $t = -2.88, p < .01$.

Western subjects' SCHLYEAR was negatively correlated with a preference for the EQLINC principle.

Subjects' Rationale

During the group and postexperiment discussions the Korean subjects expressed a concern more with preventing abuse at high levels than with eliminating those high levels. The Korean subjects' rejection of MAXAVE is consistent with this concern. They also expressed a concern for a high guaranteed minimum income, as revealed in their second place ranking of the HGHFLR principle. Indeed, the mean rank for this principle (1.92) was very close to their first place ranking of the RNGCST principle (1.73), and far above the third place mean of 2.50. We interpret this to be a dual preference for a high floor (Rawls's principle) and a constraint on the range.

The major arguments advanced during the group discussions by the Korean subjects centered around whether the advantaged should be limited in their individual pursuits, thus the split preference between the flat tax (HGHFLR) and progressive tax (RNGCST) principles. There seemed to be more agreement around the idea that the disadvantaged should receive a relatively high, dignified (as opposed to a subsistence or minimum) level of support, reflecting the hierarchically organized community's responsibility to its lowest members. Both the HGHFLR and RNGCST principles offer a higher level of support than the FLRSUP principle. But for some, the unchecked (flat tax) high incomes of the floor support and high floor principles was argued to be leaving the door open to abuses by those at the top. Many of the contemporary abuses were cited during the group discussions. Indeed a consensus was reached on the range constraint principle in three of the Korean groups. Even the individual rankings, done privately, were influenced by this public fervor. Hierarchical social structures do undermine social integrity when the community trust is broken with overt corruption.

Interestingly, little concern was expressed for a higher floor because of its income-equalizing effect. In fact the equal-income principle was universally rejected by the Korean subjects. In contrast, the group and postexperiment discussions with Western subjects seemed to focus on the balance between the individual and social equality. A cap on high incomes was desired insofar as it could be applied fairly, realistically, reasonably, and toward the goal of social equality. Our RNGCST illustration, with a maximum tax rate of 16% seem to be well within the bounds of reason. Indeed, two of the groups raised this rate to 25% (GRPALT6). But one of the (Western) groups, comprised of four unrelated members of a single household, chose to affirm equality over individual interests in their (unanimous) group decision. They articulated an "imperative to transform society."

The opposing goal of free-market individualism (tempered with a social "safety net") seemed to be equally compelling as a goal to most Western subjects. Invariably, the range constraint and its variants were presented as a reasonable, albeit reluctant compromise. No consensus was achieved by the Western groups that chose a range constraint principle.

Conclusions

Recall our hypotheses concerning Rawls's derivation of a most favored principle of distributive justice. We suspected that even modern Korean society would manifest traditional influences that tended to accept hierarchically organized social structures in which individualistic attitudes were discouraged in favor of "proper" relationships within and among a complex of small-group communities. We surmised that the sense of unity within these communities generally overrides most economic differences.

Methodologically, the absence of significant differences in group choices between our Korean and Western subjects is notable. This convergence suggests that the group choices are not a function of group background or culture, and hence the present empirical/experimental approach to testing for justice is implementable. Rawls's theoretical idea of an "original position" from which principles of justice may be derived is supported as well.

But our empirical results diverge from earlier experiments. Much of this difference is attributable to the significant difference in design (noted above) between this and earlier studies. Both the present static and the previous dynamic comparisons approximate very imperfectly the theoretical conditions and assumptions stipulated in Rawls's theory. But to the extent the complementary laboratory settings approximate theoretical parameters, we expect to see some convergence of theory and data.

Indeed our Korean subjects' dual preference shows some convergence with Rawls's theory, and this finding lends support to this theoretical derivation. But, we suggest, the explanation is not to be found in Rawls's assumptions and rationale.

The goal of social equality seems to be elusive in Korean culture, the recent populism notwithstanding. The strong sense of community, bound with intricate roles and obligations, serves as a substitute. This legacy of Korea's traditional values is still influential as evidenced by our Korean subjects' universal concern for a high minimum income (provided by both HGHFLR and RNGCST) even as they lacked consensus on the need for a cap or compression of the range of incomes (provided only by RNGCST).

In contrast, the concerns voiced by our Western subjects are more congruent with Rawls's theoretical development. Most cite equality as a key issue, even if only as a goal or ideal. But without exception a reluctance was expressed (during the postexperiment debriefings) about having to choose between individual and collective interests. This reluctance was underscored by the high degree of tension evident during the individual and highly variable payoffs at the end of the experiment, especially among those in the group that chose the equal income principle.

The tension for our Korean subjects seemed to lie in an inconsistency between public (i.e., group decisions) and private (i.e., individual rankings) sentiments. This suggests other considerations were deemed important, particularly those concerning small-group alliances. Within these alliances, the rules of hierarchical deference and protocol were strictly followed during the public (group) discussions. But their private (individual) rankings revealed a complex range of concerns anchored by the desire for a high floor minimum income as opposed to an equal income approach to dealing with the poor.

In this respect, our Korean subjects focused less on relative income levels among individuals and the balancing of individual versus group monetary interests than on their respective groups. At least in traditional Korean culture, individuals are separate entities with their own interests only within the context of their roles in particular identity or reference groups. These interdependent groups taken together comprise the larger community. The roles carry with them a host of complex obligations to other individuals, groups, and to the community as a whole. When these obligations are not fulfilled, the individual's primary identity groups are weakened. This in turn undermines the power and influence of these groups within the larger community. Thus the sense of distributive justice for our Korean subjects is bound to the integrity of the collectivities in which their identities are expressed.

We offer these cross-cultural results and interpretation as an independent empirical/experimental appraisal of Rawls's theory of distributive justice. We suggest the primacy of the individual in his assumptions needs to be reconsidered and refined. And we encourage further use of this empirical/experimental approach as a way to inform normative theory.

Appendix: Illustration of Principles

Each of the columns in the illustration below represents one principle of distributive justice with its associated pattern of distribution. Each pattern has five different levels of income. The first column represents an actual pretax or preredistribution pattern where the ratio of the floor to the average income is about 40% (6,307/16,996). We chose the 60% (10,290/16,996) and 80% (13,610/16,996) figures for the FLRSUP and the HGHFLR principles because these figures lie at equal intervals between the relatively unequal (actual) distribution and an equal distribution. But remember, the absolute income and tax levels are not as important as the relative levels within each principle that constitute its pattern of distribution.

Principles Reflecting Five Patterns of Distribution

Income Class	MAXAVE	FLRSUP	HGHFLR	RNGCST	EQIN
High (top 10%)	34,191	33,394	30,971	28,830	16,996
Middle high (next 20%)	22,905	22,373	20,747	20,515	16,996
Middle (middle 40%)	15,602	15,237	14,141	14,825	16,996
Middle low (next 20%)	10,622	10,290	13,610	13,610	16,996
Low (bottom 10%)	6,307	10,290	13,610	13,610	16,996
Average (x)	16,996	16,996	16,996	16,996	16,996
Top (high)	34,191	33,394	30,971	29,046	16,996
Floor (low)	6,307	10,290	13,610	13,610	16,996
	(40% of x)	(60% of x)	(80% of x)	(80% of x)	(100% of x)
Range	27,884	23,104	17,361	15,220	0
Tax type	none	flat	flat	progressive	progressive
Tax rate	0%	2.3%	9.4%	0% to 16%	0% to 50%

Notes

1. A selcted bibliography of works on Rawls appearing through the mid-1980s is included in Martin (1985); important, early, book-length studies include Barry (1973), Nozick (1974), Daniels (1975), Wolf (1977), and Blocker and Smith (1980).

2. Of course there are many other contexts as well. And although the traditional Korean context does not happen to be the particular conception discussed by Fisk, traditional values will continue to influence modern Korean society for generations to come. See Mitchell (1986, pp. 15-33) for a discussion of the dynamics of this process.

3. Pyong-Choon Hahm notes, "Koreans in the past have been more impressed by differences among men than by their sameness. . . . They thought therefore that the subordination of inferior men to superior men was unavoidable" (1967, p. 35).

4. Gregory Henderson suggests a "major determinant of the Korean cultural persona" is the public impingement on individual and personal behavior and thought: "What one has for central power is far from love, it is not even respect, nor is it by any means always fear nor even apprehension. It is a kind of chronic consciousness often heightening to a preoccupation with a force with which one has almost constantly to cope" (1987, p. 3). See Henderson (1968) for a more complete discussion of the phenomenon.

5. Both this suggestion and its obverse assume that our experimental conditions fairly approximate Rawls's hypothetical conditions. In any case, our position here represents less an advocacy for or against Rawls's principles than a contribution to the experiemental/empirical approach to the study of justice as discussed by Soltan (1982) and Frohlich and Oppenheimer (1989).

6. These questions are all from the English test. Appropriate "equivalents" were used for the Korean version.

7. But some private dissent against the group decisions was evident: six subjects (of 15 in the three Korean groups that chose the range constraint principle) did not rank it first in the posttest.

8. We also ran multiple (stepwise) regression analyses, regressing each of the five principles onto all of the social-psychological variables, which revealed nonsignificant results for both MAXAVE and RNGCST.

9. The exception was for self-supporting Korean males who preferred ($r = 0.60, p < .05$) the MAXAVE principle.

10. Although the Korean and Western males reveal no significant difference on this variable, the Western females have no variance on their strong disagreement (mean = 1.0) with the notion of inferior people, whereas Korean females had a mean of 3.2, above the midpoint on the scale ($t = 4.49, p < .01$).

11. The significant ($p < .01$) regression equation is

$$FLRSUP = -0.25 - 0.72 \text{ GVNTSUP} + 0.28 \text{ INFERIOR} + error$$

(R square = 0.27). The signs have been reversed as described in note a to Table 4.

12. The significant ($p < .01$) regression equation is

$$HGHFLR = -1.32 - 0.01 \text{ SELFSUP} - 0.17 \text{ SCHLYEAR} + error$$

(R square = 0.34). Again, the signs have been reversed.

References

Barry, B. (1973). *A liberal theory of justice*. Oxford: Clarendon.

Blocker, H. G., & Smith, E. M. (1980). *John Rawls' theory of social justice: An introduction*. Athens: Ohio University Press.

Daniels, N. (Ed.). (1975). *Reading Rawls: Critical studies on Rawls'* A theory of justice. Oxford: Basil Blackwell.

Fisk, M. (1975). History and Reason in Rawls' Moral Theory. In N. Daniels (Ed.), *Reading Rawls: Critical studies on Rawls'* A theory of justice. Oxford: Basil Blackwell.

Frohlich, N., & Oppenheimer, J.A. (1989). *Principles of distributive justice: An empirical approach*. Unpublished manuscript.

Frohlich, N., Oppenheimer, J. A., & Eavey, C. L. (1987a). Laboratory results on Rawls' distributive justice. *British Journal of Political Science, 17*, 1-21.

Frohlich, N., Oppenheimer, J. A., & Eavey, C. L. (1987b). Choices of principles of distributive justice in experimental groups. *American Journal of Political Science, 31*, 606-636.

Hahm, P. (1967). *The Korean political tradition and the law.* Seoul: Seoul Computer Press.

Henderson, G. (1968). *Korea: The politics of the vortex.* Cambridge, MA: Harvard University Press.

Henderson, G. (1987). Grappling with the Korean persona. In R. A. Morse (Ed.), *Wild asters: Exploration in Korean thought, culture, and society.* New York: University Press of America.

Lissowski, G., Tyszka, T., & Okrasa, W. (1988). *Principles of distributive justice: Preferences of Polish and American students.* Unpublished manuscript.

Martin R., (1985). *Rawls and rights.* Lawrence: University of Kansas Press.

Mitchell, T. (1986). Generational change and Confucianism. *Transactions of the Royal Asiatic Society, Korea Branch* (Vol. 61).

Nozick, R. (1974). *Anarchy, state and utopia.* New York: Basic Books.

Rawls, J. (1971). *A theory of justice.* Cambridge: Harvard University Press.

Schaefer, D. (1979). *Justice or tyranny? A critique of John Rawls's theory of justice.* Port Washington, NY: Kennikat Press.

Soltan, K. E. (1982). Empirical studies of distributive justice. *Ethics, 92*, 673-691.

Wolff, R. P. (1977). *Understanding Rawls: A reconstruction and critique of* A Theory of Justice. Princeton: Princeton University Press.

Doug Bond is Research Associate at the Program on Nonviolent Sanctions, Harvard University, where he is developing a framework for the systematic assessment of nonviolent direct action.

Jong-Chul Park is Research Fellow at the Korea Institute of Social Studies, and has published several articles on the political economy of South Korea and Southeast Asian politics.

ADDRESSES: DB, Program on Nonviolent Sanctions, Center for International Affairs, Harvard University, 1737 Cambridge Street, Cambridge, MA 02138, USA. JCP, Korea Institute of Social Sciences, Kang-dong P.O. Box 200, Seoul, 134-600, Republic of Korea.

Acknowledgments

Pogge, Thomas. "A Brief Sketch of Rawls's Life," 1–15. Previously unpublished. Printed with the permission of Thomas Pogge.

Gutmann, Amy. "The Central Role of Rawls's Theory," *Dissent* 36 (1989): 338–42. Reprinted with the permission of the Foundation for the Study of Independent Social Ideas, Inc.

Mardiros, Anthony M. "A Circular Procedure in Ethics," *Philosophical Review* 61 (1952): 223–25.

Margolis, Joseph. "Rule-Utilitarianism," *Australasian Journal of Philosophy* 43 (1965): 220–25. Reprinted with the permission of the Australasian Association of Philosophy.

McCloskey, H.J. "'Two Concepts of Rules' — A Note," *Philosophical Quarterly* 22 (1972): 344–48. Reprinted with the permission of Basil Blackwell Ltd.

Care, Norman S. "Contractualism and Moral Criticism," *Review of Metaphysics* 23 (1969): 85–101. Reprinted with the permission of Catholic University of America.

Scanlon, T.M. "Rawls' Theory of Justice." In *Reading Rawls: Critical Studies on Rawls A Theory of Justice*, edited by Norman Daniels (New York: Basic Books, 1975): 169–205. Reprinted with the permission of HarperCollins Publishers.

Bedau, Hugo Adam. "Social Justice and Social Institutions," *Midwest Studies in Philosophy* 3 (1978): 159–75. Reprinted with the permission of the University of Minnesota Press. Copyright 1978.

Hampton, Jean. "Contracts and Choices: Does Rawls Have a Social Contract Theory?" *Journal of Philosophy* 77 (1980): 315–38. Reprinted with the permission of the Journal of Philosophy, Inc., Columbia University.

Ricoeur, Paul. "On John Rawls' *A Theory of Justice*: Is a Pure Procedural Theory of Justice Possible?" *International Social Science Journal* 42 (1990): 553–64. Reprinted with the permission of Blackwell Publishers Ltd.

Arrow, Kenneth J. "Some Ordinalist-Utilitarian Notes on Rawls's *Theory of Justice*," *Journal of Philosophy* 70 (1973): 245–63. Reprinted with the permission of the Journal of Philosophy, Inc., Columbia University, and the author.

Schwartz, Adina. "Moral Neutrality and Primary Goods," *Ethics* 83 (1973): 294–307. Reprinted with the permission of the University of Chicago Press.